International Criminal Justice Series

Volume 10

Series Information

The *International Criminal Justice Series* aims to create a platform for publications in the whole field of international criminal justice. It, therefore, deals with issues relating, among others, to:

- the work of international criminal courts and tribunals;
- transitional justice approaches in different countries;
- international anti-corruption and anti-money laundering initiatives;
- the history of international criminal law.

The series concentrates on themes pertinent to developing countries. It is peer-reviewed and seeks to publish high-quality works emanating from excellent scholars, in particular from African countries.

Editorial Office

Prof. Dr. Gerhard Werle
Humboldt-Universität zu Berlin
Faculty of Law
Unter den Linden 6,
10099 Berlin, Germany
gerhard.werle@rewi.hu-berlin.de
moritz.vormbaum@rewi.hu-berlin.de

More information about this series at http://www.springer.com/series/13470

Gerhard Werle · Moritz Vormbaum
Editors

The African Criminal Court

A Commentary on the Malabo Protocol

ASSER PRESS

Springer

Editors
Gerhard Werle
Faculty of Law
Humboldt-Universität zu Berlin
Berlin
Germany

Moritz Vormbaum
Faculty of Law
Humboldt-Universität zu Berlin
Berlin
Germany

ISSN 2352-6718 ISSN 2352-6726 (electronic)
International Criminal Justice Series
ISBN 978-94-6265-149-4 ISBN 978-94-6265-150-0 (eBook)
DOI 10.1007/978-94-6265-150-0

Library of Congress Control Number: 2016950894

Published by T.M.C. ASSER PRESS, The Hague, The Netherlands www.asserpress.nl
Produced and distributed for T.M.C. ASSER PRESS by Springer-Verlag Berlin Heidelberg

Printed on acid-free paper

This Springer imprint is published by Springer Nature
The registered company is Springer Science+Business Media B.V.
The registered company address is: Van Godewijckstraat 30, 3311 GX Dordrecht, The Netherlands

Acknowledgements

This book is based on a meeting of experts that convened in July 2015 at Humboldt-Universität zu Berlin to discuss the issues surrounding the African Union's Protocol aimed at vesting the African Court of Justice and Human and Peoples' Rights with criminal jurisdiction. The meeting was organized by the South African-German Centre for Transnational Criminal Justice, which is run cooperatively by the Law Faculties of the University of the Western Cape and Humboldt-Universität zu Berlin. The editors would like to express their gratitude to the German Academic Exchange Service (DAAD) and the German Federal Foreign Office for generously funding the centre in the framework of the "African Excellence" initiative.

We would also like to express our thanks to Hanna Takeuchi and Rebecca van Es, who proofread the chapters, to Marshet Tadesse Tessema, who helped select the materials in the appendix to the book, and to Anna-Julia Egger and Nella Sayatz for formatting the chapters.

While editing this book, South Africa and Burundi notified the Secretary General of the United Nations of their intention to withdraw from the Statute of the International Criminal Court. Other African states have expressed an intention to do similarly. It remains to be seen which impact this will have on the work of the International Criminal Court in Africa. It is clear, however, that alternative approaches to prosecute crimes under international law in Africa, including the creation of an "African Criminal Court", will become increasingly important.

Berlin, November 2016

Gerhard Werle
Moritz Vormbaum

Acknowledgements

Contents

Part III General Principles and Rules of Procedure in the Annex to the Malabo Protocol

Editors and Contributors

About the Editors

Gerhard Werle is Professor of German and International Criminal Law, Criminal Procedure and Modern Legal History at Humboldt-Universität zu Berlin and Director at the South African-German Centre for Transnational Criminal Justice. In addition, he is Extraordinary Professor at the University of the Western Cape and Honorary Professor at North-West University of Political Science and Law (Xi'an, China).

Moritz Vormbaum obtained his doctoral degree in criminal law from the University of Münster (Germany) and his postdoctoral degree from Humboldt-Universität zu Berlin. He is Senior Researcher at Humboldt-Universität, as well as a coordinator and lecturer at the South African-German Centre for Transnational Criminal Justice. Currently, he is Adjunct Professor at Universität Hamburg.

Contributors

Ademola Abass is a special adviser to the Governor, Office of Overseas Affairs and Investment, in Lagos State, Nigeria. Previously he was, among others, a research fellow and the Head of the Peace and Security Programme at the United Nations University Institute on Comparative Regional Integration Studies (UNU-CRIS), Brugge (Belgium).

Kai Ambos is Professor of Criminal Law, Criminal Procedure, Comparative Law and International Criminal Law at Georg-August-Universität Göttingen, where he is also the Director of the Research Centre for Latin-American Criminal Law and Criminal Procedure. He also serves as a Judge of the District Court of Göttingen.

Lovell D Fernandez is Professor of Criminal Law at the University of the Western Cape and Director at the South African-German Centre for Transnational Criminal Justice. Before joining UWC Law Faculty, he lectured at the University of Witwatersrand, University of Cape Town and the University of Namibia.

Martin Heger is Professor for Criminal Law, Criminal Procedure, European Criminal Law and Modern Legal History at Humboldt-Universität zu Berlin, where he is also the Director of the student exchange program "Network East-West".

Florian Jeßberger is Professor of Criminal Law, Criminal Procedure, International Criminal Law and Modern Legal History at Universität Hamburg. Amongst others, he serves as the Director of the Institute of Criminal Justice Studies and Vice Dean of the Faculty of Law and is a Co-Editor of the Journal of International Criminal Justice.

Gerhard Kemp is Professor of International Criminal Law, Criminal Law and Criminal Procedure at Stellenbosch University, South Africa. Among others, he serves on the editorial board of the African Yearbook on International Humanitarian Law.

Selemani Kinyunyu is an advocate in the High Court of Tanzania and has worked for the Pan African Lawyers Union, where he assisted in drafting the Protocol to vest the African Court with criminal jurisdiction. He currently serves as coordinator of the African Governance Architecture Programme of the African Court on Human and Peoples' Rights.

Chantal Meloni is Associate Professor of Criminal Law at the University of Milan. She has worked as a legal assistant at the International Criminal Court and serves as a Legal Adviser for the International Crimes and Accountability Program at the European Center for Constitutional and Human Rights.

Fatuma Mninde-Silungwe is a national legal expert in the UN Development Programme's Elections Project. Previously she worked as a prosecutor in Malawi. Currently she is working on her doctoral thesis on regionalization of international criminal justice in Africa.

Volker Nerlich is Legal Adviser at the International Criminal Court, currently seconded to the Extraordinary Chambers in the Courts of Cambodia, and Honorary Professor at Humboldt-Universität zu Berlin. Prior to his post at the International Criminal Court, he was an associate expert in the United Nations Office on Drugs and Crime.

Dire Tladi is Professor of International Law at the University of Pretoria and an Extraordinary Professor at the University of Stellenbosch and a member of the UN International Law Commission. Previously, he served as the Principal State Law Adviser for International Law for the South African Department of International Relations and Cooperation.

Harmen van der Wilt is Professor of International Criminal Law at the University of Amsterdam and a Judge ad litem in the Extradition Chamber of the District Court in Amsterdam. In addition, he has been a member of the Research Council of the EU (F7)-project on the European Arrest Warrant.

Abbreviations

AC	Appeals Chamber
AU	African Union
AUCPCC	African Union Convention on Preventing and Combating Corruption
DRC	Democratic Republic of Congo
EAC	East African Community
EC	European Commission
ECOWAS	Economic Community of West African States
ed(s)	editor(s)
edn	edition
e.g.	for example (*exempli gratia*)
EJIL	European Journal of International Law
et al.	and others (*et alii*)
et seq.	and the following (*et sequens; et sequentes*)
EU	European Union
FATF	Financial Action Task Force
GA	General Assembly
i.e.	that is (*id est*)
ibid.	in the same place (*ibidem*)
ICC	International Criminal Court
ICJ	International Court of Justice
ICTR	International Criminal Tribunal for Rwanda
ICTY	International Criminal Tribunal for the former Yugoslavia
JICJ	Journal of International Criminal Justice
marg. number(s)	marginal number(s)
n., nn.	footnote(s) (*nota, notae*)
NGO	Non-Governmental Organization
no(s).	number(s)
OAU	Organization of African Unity
OTP	Office of the Prosecutor (at the International Criminal Court)

p, pp	page(s)
para(s)	paragraph(s)
PTC	Pre-Trial Chamber
Res.	Resolution
SADC	Southern African Development Community
SCSL	Special Court for Sierra Leone
SERAP	Socio-Economic Rights and Accountability Project
TC	Trial Chamber
UN	United Nations
UNCAC	United Nations Convention against Corruption
UN Doc.	Documents of the United Nations
UNTOC	United Nations Convention against Transnational Organized Crime
UNTS	United Nations Treaty Series
USAID	United States Agency for International Development
USD	United States Dollars
v	against (*versus*)
VCLT	Vienna Convention on the Law of Treaties of 1969

Part I
Introduction

Chapter 1
Creating an African Criminal Court

Gerhard Werle and Moritz Vormbaum

At its Twelfth Ordinary Session in February 2009 in Addis Ababa, Ethiopia, the Assembly of the African Union requested the Commission of the African Union

> in consultation with the African Commission on Human and Peoples' Rights, and the African Court on Human and Peoples' Rights, to examine the implications of the Court being empowered to try international crimes such as genocide, crimes against humanity and war crimes.

Since then, the African Union has repeatedly adopted resolutions to establish an international, or more precisely, an inter-African criminal jurisdiction. Finally, in June 2014, the African Union, at its Summit meeting in Malabo, Equatorial Guinea, adopted a protocol (the "Malabo Protocol") which included in its Annex an amendment to the Statute of the African Court of Justice and Human and Peoples' Rights. The Court is a merger of the African Court of Justice and the African Court on Human and Peoples' Rights. Its merger protocol currently awaits ratification. According to the Statute, as amended by the Annex to the Malabo Protocol, the Court will have three Sections, namely, "a General Affairs Section, a Human and Peoples' Rights Section and an International Criminal Law Section" (see Article 16 of the Annex to the Malabo Protocol). Even though the ratification of the Malabo Protocol and its Annex may be a protracted process with some important questions still to be resolved, the establishment of, simply speaking, an "African Criminal Court" is becoming an increasingly concrete possibility, particularly because South Africa and Burundi have given notice of their withdrawal from the International Criminal Court and other states might follow suit.

Whereas the resolutions of the African Union to empower the African Court of Justice and Human and Peoples' Rights with criminal jurisdiction initially

G. Werle · M. Vormbaum (✉)
South African-German Centre for Transnational Criminal Justice,
Humboldt-Universität zu Berlin, Berlin, Germany
e-mail: moritz.vormbaum@rewi.hu-berlin.de

G. Werle
e-mail: gerhard.werle@rewi.hu-berlin.de

G. Werle and M. Vormbaum (eds.), *The African Criminal Court*, International Criminal Justice Series 10, DOI 10.1007/978-94-6265-150-0_1

attracted scant public attention, the situation has now changed. It seems, however, that the current debate—as Dire Tladi notes in his chapter in this book—is less about a thorough legal analysis and more about either broadly supporting or opposing the efforts to create an "African Criminal Court". To its supporters, the envisaged Court has the potential of contributing to the development of international criminal law and could, eventually, become even a useful complement to the International Criminal Court. To critics, it is no more than a political ploy by the African Union to weaken the International Criminal Court, which, for the last couple of years, has been the target of its pointed attacks.

This book focuses on the legal analysis of the Malabo Protocol and its Annex. The starting point of this analysis is that a regional court with jurisdiction over international crimes would be a novel phenomenon in the landscape of international courts and tribunals. Until now, so-called hybrid courts for special situations have been established in different countries. Noteworthy, given the subject of this book, are the Extraordinary African Chambers in the Courts of Senegal that convicted Hissène Habré in 2016 for systematic crimes committed in Chad. The UN-ad hoc Tribunals have also exercised jurisdiction in specific regions, in particular, the Yugoslavian Tribunal for the Balkan region. What has not taken place is the regionalization of international criminal law in the sense of developing a body of international criminal law that is particularly suitable for a specific region. Such regionalization of international criminal law could consist in extending the catalogue of crimes over which a regional court could have jurisdiction, while retaining the four core crimes under international law. And this is exactly what is provided for in the Annex to the Malabo Protocol.

We do not consider such regionalization a retrogressive step. In the field of human rights law, regionalization has taken place through the adoption of human rights treaties in Europe, America and Africa. This has not watered down the core content of universally accepted human rights; on the contrary, human rights have been undoubtedly strengthened through the work of regional human rights courts. A similar development is conceivable in the field of international criminal law. The Annex to the Malabo Protocol does not in any way question the validity of the international core crimes. What the protocol does do, however, is to add crimes of specific relevance in the African context. Here, the best example is the crime of unconstitutional change of government. Outside of Africa, unconstitutional changes of governments have become a rare phenomenon, even in regions such as South America where such changes occurred commonly only a few decades ago. In Africa, by contrast, violent coups, or leaders who remain in office unconstitutionally are a common phenomenon, with countries like Burkina Faso and Burundi being the most recent cases in point. Such unconstitutional coups threaten, in the worst case, to destabilize whole states and even regions without the possibility of the culprits being prosecuted before national courts. It, therefore, made sense that already in 2007 the African Charter on Democracy, Election and Governance declared such conduct to be an international crime, punishable by a court of the African Union. The Annex to the Malabo Protocol follows up on this attempt.

If then, the creation of an African Criminal Court is not to be rejected from the outset, and indeed could enrich the international criminal justice landscape, a closer analysis of the protocol's contents does nevertheless raise concerns. As the contributors to this book show, some provisions clearly need improvement. The protocol fails, for example, to regulate its relationship with the International Criminal Court. Moreover, the immunity for heads of state and heads of government, as well as for high-ranking officials, is a feature which could constitute the Achilles heel of the future Court.

However, whatever its present flaws, the Statute of the African Court of Justice and Human and Peoples' Rights, as amended by the Annex to the Malabo Protocol, will not be changed or amended. This means that the Malabo Protocol, should it, together with its Annex, receive the necessary number of ratifications, will become operational as it stands now. It is, therefore, crucial to clarify the contents of the future Statute of the African Court of Justice and Human and Peoples' Rights as far as the provisions on international criminal law are concerned. For this purpose, this book includes contributions by international experts in the field of international criminal law who comprehensively analyze the central provisions of the Annex to the Malabo Protocol.

The book begins with a chapter by Ademola Abass that gives an overview on the historical and political background of the establishment of a regional criminal court for Africa. Abass stresses that the idea of creating such a court did not originate, as one may think, with the deterioration of the relations between the African Union and the International Criminal Court over the Al Bashir-case. Instead, he refers to examples such as the proposed court to deal with the crime of apartheid in the 1970s, and he also points to the obligation of the African Union to create a competent court to prosecute the crime of unconstitutional change of government, as reflected in the African Charter on Democracy, Election and Governance of 2007. Abass rejects the argument that empowering the African Court of Justice and Human and Peoples' Rights with criminal jurisdiction is incompatible with the Rome Statute. In his view "an inquiry into the legality of the proposed international criminal jurisdiction in Africa with reference to the Rome Statute is fallacious, fundamentally mistaken and unscrupulous". The Rome Statute, he argues, is no *primus inter pares* and therefore cannot possibly forbid its Member States from creating another criminal court at the regional level. Yet, the author sees a number of serious challenges which the Court would face in practice. Besides some procedural issues which, according to Abass, result from the combination of civil and criminal jurisdiction, he stresses that it is unclear how the Court could be financed. The author points to the fact that the cost of a single trial for crimes under international law—the Charles Taylor trial, for example, cost more than USD 50 million—could easily outstrip the entire annual budget of the African Court of Justice and Human and Peoples' Rights.

Kai Ambos analyzes the definitions of the core crimes under international law in the Annex to the Malabo Protocol by comparing them with those in the ICC Statute. His analysis shows that the crimes in both legal instruments overlap considerably. Yet, Ambos also identifies some striking differences. As regards genocide, for example, the drafters added "acts of rape or any other form of sexual violence" as a genocidal act. In the provision of crimes against humanity, further criminal acts were added, too. In addition, according to the Annex to the Malabo Protocol, not only an "attack" but also an "enterprise" (which is not defined in the Annex to the Malabo Protocol) against a civilian population satisfies the chapeau-requirements. The provision on war crimes is likewise, according to the author, considerably wider than that in the ICC Statute, as it criminalizes, among other things, the use of nuclear weapons and "conscripting or enlisting children under the age of eighteen years" (instead of fifteen years as in the ICC Statute). As regards the crime of aggression, the Annex to the Malabo Protocol, according to Ambos, is more comprehensive in different ways, for example, explicitly covering acts of "non-State actors" and "any foreign entity". Ambos regards these changes, for the most part, as problematic. At the same time he regrets that the drafters of the Malabo Protocol took over provisions of the ICC Statute which have been criticized for good reasons. For example, the "civilian population" element is, in his words, an "infamous transplant from international humanitarian law". In this regard, Ambos sees a missed opportunity for Africa to come up with a better statute than the ICC's.

A crime which has attracted considerable attention, especially since it has until now been unknown in the sphere of international criminal law, is the crime of unconstitutional change of government. In their chapter, Gerhard Kemp and Selemani Kinyunyu shed light on the drafting process of this crime. According to the authors, the origins of the crime go back to the late 1990s, when a political solution was sought to tackle the problem of the numerous coup d'états and attempted coups d'états in Africa at the Pan-African level. In 2007, a provision on unconstitutional change of government appeared in Article 23 of the African Charter on Democracy, Elections and Governance, which also included sanctions against perpetrators to be tried "before a competent court of the African Union". This provision also represents the core of Article 28E(1) of the Malabo Protocol (Annex). After evaluating the elements of the crime thoroughly, the authors conclude that the provision could have been drafted better, yet insist that the creation of such a provision is a step in the right direction for tackling an urgent problem in Africa.

Apart from the core crimes under international law and the crime of unconstitutional change of government, the Annex to the Malabo Protocol includes a number of other crimes. Florian Jeßberger rightly stresses that these transnational crimes must be distinguished clearly from the crimes under international law within the jurisdiction of the Court, such as genocide or war crimes. In his chapter he deals with piracy, mercenarism and terrorism, crimes of specific relevance to Africa. He explores the origins of these crimes in international treaties and analyzes the elements of each crime. Jeßberger's analysis shows that the Court will be the first international tribunal ever provided with jurisdiction over these and other transnational crimes. He concludes his chapter with the recommendation not to repudiate rashly the ambitious project of regionalizing the enforcement of international and transnational criminal law.

The stability of states or of unions of states can be affected not only by armed conflict and human rights atrocities. It is also weakened by large-scale economic crimes that have the potential of undermining the financial system of such states. It is, therefore, of great interest that the Annex to the Malabo Protocol includes the crimes of corruption and money laundering. In his chapter, Lovell Fernandez examines the feasibility of including these crimes within the jurisdiction of the African Court of Justice and Human and Peoples' Rights. He focuses on specific aspects of the two crimes, particularly their relationship to other economic crimes. In Fernandez's view, the immunity granted to heads of state or government raises questions about the legitimacy of the African Court of Justice and Human and Peoples' Rights, particularly in regard to crimes such as corruption and money laundering. He argues that definitional and jurisdictional issues will pose major challenges to successful prosecution as will the fact that practical issues, related to the ability of Member States to co-operate in criminal investigations, appear to have been overlooked in adding these two crimes to the catalogue of international crimes.

Fatuma Mninde-Silungwe deals with two other transnational crimes which the African Court of Justice and Human and Peoples' Rights will be competent to deal with, namely trafficking in drugs and trafficking in persons. The author discusses the history of these two crimes which can be traced back, partly, to the UN Convention against Illicit Traffic in Narcotic Drugs and Psychotropic Substances and to the Palermo Convention. In both these international instruments, the acts in question were not explicitly criminalized. The author regards this as a critical shortcoming, insisting that the "approach [...] should not be to simply copy the definition under a convention, but to reformulate it and give it the constitutive elements of a crime". Mninde-Silungwe analyzes the wording of the provisions in the Annex to the Malabo Protocol and considers its significance for the administration of international criminal justice in Africa. In her conclusion, Mninde-Silungwe points out that the criminalization at the regional level is not an end in itself, given that recent research has shown that trafficking in persons takes place more *within* states than across state borders. Mninde-Silungwe, therefore, argues that the strengthening of domestic laws in African states should become a priority.

While the States Parties to the ICC Statute could not agree on extending the crimes contained in the ICC Statute to include crimes against the natural environment, the Annex to the Malabo protocol does so by incorporating the crimes of trafficking in hazardous wastes and illicit exploitation of natural resources. In his chapter, Martin Heger points to the fact that pollution committed on a vast scale has long been a problem for Africa as European states have often used Africa as their "trash bin". Heger gives an overview of the international instruments that regulate the trafficking in hazardous wastes and the illicit exploitation of natural resources. He shows that, so far, the task of *criminalizing* serious acts of pollution has been left to the domestic legislator. In contrast, the Annex to the Malabo Protocol directly criminalizes trafficking in hazardous wastes and the illicit exploitation of natural resources, a contribution to the development of international law that Heger welcomes in principle. However, the crimes in the Annex to the Malabo

Protocol have some problematic features, insofar as they constitute, in Heger's view, a too far-reaching criminalization.

The Annex to the Malabo Protocol contains several comprehensive provisions on modes of responsibility. Article 28N, for example, covers the following modes: "inciting", "instigating", "organizing", "directing", "facilitating", "financing", "counseling", "participating as principle, co-principle, agent or accomplice", "aiding and abetting", "acting as an accessory before or after the act", "participating in a collaboration or conspiracy" and "attempting to commit a crime". In addition, the Protocol includes corporate criminal liability. In her chapter, Chantal Meloni offers an in-depth analysis of these provisions. Although Meloni is critical of the fact that, among other things, some of the provisions are not couched in sufficiently clear language and are overly broad in scope, she also mentions some positive features. Her view is that the criminal responsibility of corporations, in particular, represents "a progressive and positive development for international criminal law and could perhaps serve as an inspiration for future amendments of the ICC Statute". It will be the duty of the judges of the African Court of Justice and Human and Peoples' Rights to interpret the complex and not always coherent provisions of the Malabo Protocol's Annex in the future.

In his comprehensive chapter Volker Nerlich defines the parameters of the criminal jurisdiction of the African Court of Justice and Human and Peoples' Rights. According to his evaluation, while the provisions on jurisdiction have been largely modelled along the ICC Statute, they are considerably broader. In contrast to the International Criminal Court, the African Court of Justice and Human and Peoples' Rights will be vested also with the authority to exercise jurisdiction on the basis of the passive personality principle and the protective principle. While, according to Nerlich, this is an acceptable decision, he identifies a number of loopholes. Most notably he points to Article 46E*bis*(3) of the Malabo Protocol (Annex) which contains a provision that is "curiously incomplete" as it provides as follows: "If the acceptance of a State which is not a Party to this Statute is required under para 2, that State may, by declaration lodged with the Registrar, accept the exercise … [sic!—end of sentence]". According to Nerlich, the provision has no meaningful content in its current form and he makes reference to Article 12 of the ICC Statute in order to identify what was intended by the drafters. Nerlich concludes that the provisions on jurisdiction do "provide for a workable regime regarding the scope of and exercise of jurisdiction". However, he argues that additional procedural rules are likely to be needed to make the African Court of Justice and Human and Peoples' Rights' jurisdictional regime in criminal matters fully functional in practice.

A crucial practical question in connection with the future criminal jurisdiction of the African Court of Justice and Human and Peoples' Rights is its relationship with the International Criminal Court. Harmen van der Wilt analyzes this issue in his chapter by scrutinizing the provision on complementarity in the Annex to the Malabo Protocol. He sees certain dangers, namely, that African states may "outsource" the prosecution of crimes committed on their territory, perpetuating the strained relationship between the African Union and the International Criminal

Court. However, he also identifies possibilities on how the courts could work together effectively by sharing their work and by assisting each other: The competence of the African Court of Justice and Human and Peoples' Rights to prosecute transnational crimes creates the possibility for the Court to focus on these crimes, while the International Criminal Court could act as the main international court to prosecute the core crimes under international law.

In the concluding chapter Dire Tladi deals with probably the most contentious provision of the Annex to the Malabo Protocol—the exclusion of immunities for sitting heads of state and other government officials, as provided for in Article 46A*bis*. In the author's view, the debate about this provision combines political and legal arguments, which has caused confusion and has led to a "hero-villain" perception, with the International Criminal Court cast either as "hero" and the African Union as the "villain" or vice versa. From a legal point of view, as Tladi argues, customary international law is silent about immunities for sitting heads of state before international criminal courts and tribunals. Whether it is advisable to include a provision on the exclusion of immunity with a view to combating impunity in Africa, or rather to exclude it to protect state sovereignty, may be debatable, according to Tladi. However, what in his view needs to be stressed is that the creation of the provision on immunity in the Annex to the Malabo Protocol does not in any way affect the jurisdiction by the International Criminal Court over these persons.

The appendix of the book contains a collection of relevant documents. Included among the latter are the Malabo Protocol and its Annex, together with a list of the crimes in the Annex to the Malabo Protocol which are juxtaposed with the provisions of various international treaties after which the crimes were modelled. Included in the appendix, too, are the protocol which merges the African Court of Justice and the African Court on Human and Peoples' Rights ("Maputo Protocol"), the protocol of the African Court of Justice, and the protocol on the establishment of the African Court on Human and Peoples' Rights. The appendix contains, in addition, a collection of the Decisions by the African Union on the establishment of an "African Criminal Court".

Chapter 2
Historical and Political Background to the Malabo Protocol

Ademola Abass

Abstract In June 2014 the Assembly of the African Union adopted the Malabo Protocol which in its Annex includes amendments to the Statute of the African Court of Justice and Human and Peoples' Rights empowering the Court with international criminal jurisdiction. This chapter gives an overview of the historical and political background to the Malabo Protocol and discusses the rationales behind conferring on an African regional court international criminal jurisdiction. It also addresses certain constraints that, from the point of view of the author, will prevent the Court from effectively prosecuting international crimes in Africa, even if the protocol ever enters into force.

Keywords Africa · African Union · International Criminal Court · African Court of Justice and Human and Peoples' Rights · Unconstitutional change of government

Contents

This chapter is an updated version of an article that first appeared as Abass (2013) European Journal of International Law 24:933–946.
All internet sources in this chapter were last visited on 30 June 2016.

A. Abass (✉)
Office of Overseas Affairs and Investment, Lagos State, Nigeria
e-mail: Ade111@hotmail.com

G. Werle and M. Vormbaum (eds.), *The African Criminal Court*, International Criminal Justice Series 10, DOI 10.1007/978-94-6265-150-0_2

2.1 Introduction

At its 18th ordinary session in January 2012, the Assembly of Heads of State and Government of the African Union (hereafter the AU Assembly), requested the African Union Commission "to place the Progress Report of the Commission on the implementation of Assembly Decision on the ICC on the agenda of the forthcoming Meeting of Ministers of Justice and Attorneys General for additional input".[1] In a 2009 text referred to herein as the "Assembly Decision", the AU Assembly requested that the African Union, "in consultation with the African Commission on Human and Peoples' Rights, and the African Court on Human and Peoples' Rights [...] examine the implications of the Court being empowered to try international crimes such as genocide, crimes against humanity and war crimes, and report thereon to the Assembly in 2010".[2]

The resultant draft protocol, which amended the Protocol on the Statute of the Court by extending its jurisdiction to cover international crimes,[3] was endorsed by the African Ministers of Justice and Attorneys General on Legal Matters in May 2012.[4] However, contrary to common expectations, the July 2012 AU Assembly did not adopt the new Protocol. Instead, it requested the Commission in collaboration with the African Court of Human and Peoples' Rights, to "prepare a study on the financial and structural implications resulting from the expansion of the jurisdiction of the African Court" and urged the Union to adopt a definition of the crime of unconstitutional change of government. The Commission was to submit its report for consideration by the policy organs at the January 2013 Summit.[5]

An experts' meeting, which was convened by the African Union Commission on 19 and 20 December 2012 in Arusha, Tanzania, to consider the Assembly's requests, decided that there was no need to amend sub articles 1 and 2 of Article 28E of the Draft Protocol,[6] which embodies the crime of unconstitutional change of government. Regarding the financial and structural implications, the group

[1] Assembly/AU/Dec. 397 (XVIII) (2012).

[2] Assembly/AU/Dec. 213 (XII) (2012).

[3] EX.CL/731 (XXI)a; (2013).

[4] Min/Legal/ACJHR-PAP/3(II) Rev. 1.5.

[5] Decision on the Protocol on Amendments to the Protocol on the Statute of the African Court on Human and Peoples' Rights, Assembly of the African Union, 19th Ordinary Session, Assembly/AU/Dec. 427 (XIX) (2012).

[6] AfCHPR/LEGAL/Doc. 3, at 4.

adopted an arguably simplistic and over-optimistic approach, concluding that "the only additional expenses envisaged will be in the expanded structure and operation of the African Court on Human and Peoples' Rights".[7]

The January 2013 AU Assembly would seem to have accepted the experts' meeting's verdict on the crime of unconstitutional change of government, that is if one were to take its non-revisiting the issue as indicative of its position, although it clearly did not share the group's finding on the financial and structural implications of the expansion. Consequently, the Assembly requested the African Union Commission to prepare a report on that subject. Interestingly, the Assembly also requested the Commission, acting in conjunction with the AU Peace and Security Council, to "conduct a more thorough reflection [...] on the issue of popular uprising in all its dimensions, and on the appropriate mechanism capable of deciding the legitimacy of such an uprising."[8] The Commission was required to submit its report on these requests to the May 2013 Assembly. Contrary to the expectation of many, in its twenty-fifth ordinary session, the AU's Assembly of Heads of State and Government adopted the Protocol in Malabo, Equatorial Guinea on 27 June 2014.

It is uncertain whether the Protocol will get the fifteen ratifications of AU Members States that it needs to enter into force,[9] but the prospect of the African regional court adjudicating on international crimes portends some troubling times for the International Criminal Court, but more so for international criminal justice in Africa. On the one hand, the International Criminal Court will suffer a major dent to its vital referral mechanism—self-referral by African ICC States Parties, aside from losing "ad hoc referral" by African non-States Parties to the Rome Statute. The impact of this double loss is significant if one recalls that of all the situations currently pending before the International Criminal Court, three were self-referred (Uganda, Democratic Republic of Congo, and the Central African Republic) and one involved the voluntary (ad hoc) acceptance of ICC jurisdiction (Côte d'Ivoire).[10] On the other hand, an operational but ineffective international criminal jurisdiction—a highly likely scenario in light of the discussion below—raises myriad questions about what to do with African *genocidaires* and culpable heads of state and other governmental officials.

---

[7] Ibid., at 5.

[8] EX.CL/Dec. 766 (XXII), at 1 Doc. PRC/Rpt (XXV). Although this remit did not form part of the issues the 2012 Summit referred to the Commission, it would appear that the January 2013 Assembly took this issue on board given the extensive attention the Dec. 2012 AU Experts' Meeting in Arusha gave the issue.

[9] Thus far eight countries have signed the Protocol, namely: Benin, Congo, Kenya, Ghana, Guinea-Bissau, Mauritania, Sierra Leon, Sao Tome and Principe, AU, http://au.int/en/sites/default/files/treaties/7804-sl-protocol_on_amendments_to_the_protocol_on_the_statute_of_the_african_court_of_justice_and_human_rights_19.pdf. See also Amnesty International, Malabo Protocol, Legal and Institutional Implications of the Merged and Expanded African Court, 2016.

[10] The Prosecutor v. Laurent Gbagbo, Case No. ICC-02/11-01/11; see also Bamba 2003.

In addition to a number of practical challenges confronting the ratification of the Annex to the Malabo Protocol, which will not be discussed here, the instrument itself contains several flawed provisions that the AU experts' meeting in Arusha did not deal with, that will severely curtail the ability of the African Court of Justice and Human and Peoples' Rights to prosecute international crimes, should the Court's criminal jurisdiction become operative. First, the combination of civil and criminal jurisdictions through the General Affairs Section, the Human and Peoples' Rights Section, and the International Criminal Section, in a single court is not only almost unprecedented in international judicial practice, but is also fraught with myriad substantive and procedural problems that the Court, under the current proposal, will be unable to handle.[11] Furthermore, the provision of the new protocol on the complementarity principle[12] raises many perplexing questions.

The second section of this chapter discusses the grounds for proposing international criminal jurisdiction for an African regional court. The pervasive, but arguably erroneous assumption is that Africa began prospecting for international criminal jurisdiction *after* and as a *consequence* of the fall-out over the Al Bashir arrest warrant. As I will show in this section, this is inaccurate. This section also argues that creating an African Court with international criminal jurisdiction is, in fact, an obligation that the African Union must fulfil partly because its legal regimes require it and partly because not doing so will result in an absurd situation whereby its treaties codify or create crimes none of which its court can prosecute. The third section of this chapter responds to the argument that the prosecution of international crimes by an African regional court is incompatible with the Rome Statute. The fourth section discusses some of the most fundamental legal constraints on the projected effectiveness of the African Court of Justice and Human and Peoples' Rights.

The chapter concludes that whereas there is a clear and compelling case to be made for the conferment of international criminal jurisdiction on the African regional court, the added value of that court is extremely doubtful. This doubt does not arise from any *ipso facto* undesirability of such a court, but from the low probability that African leaders will ever allow the court to discharge the *ultima ratio* of international criminal justice—ending impunity for heinous international crimes—and not turn the Court into a torment chamber for opposition parties and dissident activists.

---

[11] The only known instance of combined jurisdiction by an international tribunal, though in particular circumstances, is the Caribbean Court of Justice. Article 4 of the Agreement establishing the Court provides that "subject to para 2, an appeal shall lie to the Court with the special leave of the Court from any decision of the Court of Appeal of a Contracting Party in any civil or criminal matter": available at: www.caribbeancourtofjustice.org/wp-content/uploads/2011/09/ccj_agreement.pdf. But see Viljoen 2012, arguing that the African Union's proposition in this regard is unprecedented.

[12] Article 46 of the Malabo Protocol (Annex). See on this provision the chapter by van der Wilt in this book.

2.2 The Grounds for Establishing International Criminal Prosecution in Africa

There are at least three fundamental bases to support the prosecution of international crimes by an African regional court. These are: (1) a historical necessity for such a court to prosecute crimes which are committed in Africa but which are of no prosecutorial interest to the rest of the world; (2) a treaty obligation to prosecute international crimes in Africa; and (3) the existence of crimes peculiar to Africa but over which global international criminal tribunals, such as the International Criminal Court, have no jurisdiction.

2.2.1 Historical Necessity for Prosecuting International Crimes in Africa

For most commentators, Africa's quest for its regional court to prosecute international crimes was politically motivated and began as a consequence of the fallout between the African Union and the International Criminal Court over Al Bashir's arrest warrant.[13] While there is no denying that the Al Bashir affair exacerbated Africa's desire to prosecute international crimes, it is misleading to conclude that this episode lies at the foundation of Africa's quest for international criminal jurisdiction.

Africa first expressed a desire to prosecute international crimes in the 1970s during the discussion on the African Charter on Human and Peoples' Rights.[14] Although the Committee of Experts responsible for drafting the Charter rejected the proposal to include a court with international criminal jurisdiction in its provisions, recalling the reasons for the proposal and its rejection will allow for a better understanding of the historical pedigree.

In the introduction to the first draft document in the *travaux préparatoires* to the African Charter on Human and Peoples' Rights, the Charter author, M'Baye, argued the prematurity of establishing an African judicial institution with criminal jurisdiction as part of the Human Rights Charter system, especially,[15] since the

[13] See, for instance, Murungu 2011, p. 1073. According to Murungu, "the origin of an African idea or priority to prosecute international crimes in Africa had begun in 2006". As for Deya 2012, p. 24 "[t]he first body to suggest that due consideration should be given to an additional international criminal jurisdiction for the African Court was the group of (African) Experts, who were commissioned by the African Union (AU) in 2007–2008 to advise it on the 'merger' of the African Court of Human and Peoples' Rights with the African Court of Justice". While Murungu clearly erred in thinking that 2006 was the first attempt ever for Africans to contemplate the idea of international prosecution, Deya limited his dateline to only when the idea was first suggested in the context of the proposed African Court.

[14] See M'Baye 2002, p. 65.

[15] Ibid.; see also Viljoen 2004, pp. 4–5.

International Convention on the Suppression and Punishment of the crime of apartheid[16] already provided for "an international *penal* court" and the United Nations was then considering establishing "an international court to repress crime against mankind".[17]

Thus the proposal to prosecute international crimes in 1970s Africa was primordially motivated by the crime of apartheid in South Africa, which the UN General Assembly had in 1966 labelled a crime against humanity,[18] a determination affirmed by the Security Council in 1984.[19] From 1948 until 1990 apartheid existed as an international crime, but there was no international criminal court that could prosecute it. The international penal court that African states had hoped would be established to prosecute the crime—on the basis of which they forewent providing for such a court in the African Charter of Human Rights—did not materialize.[20] Nor did the special penal court contemplated by the United Nations in the 1980s to try apartheid offences ever materialize. Instead, "it was left to States to enact legislation to enable them to prosecute apartheid criminals on the basis of a form of universal jurisdiction."[21] The impact this "dupe", so to speak, had on Africans was significant, but it underscored the fact that not every crime committed in Africa would be of prosecutorial interest to the rest of humanity.

2.2.2 *The Establishment of International Criminal Prosecution in Africa as a Legal Obligation*

A distinct legal basis for prosecuting international crimes in Africa derives from the obligation incurred by the African Union under its Constitutive Act (AU Act) and other treaties to prosecute crimes prescribed in those treaties.

Article 4(h) of the AU Act provides for "the right of the Union to intervene in a Member State pursuant to a decision of the Assembly in respect of grave circumstances, namely: war crimes, genocide and crimes against humanity as well as a *serious threat to legitimate order to restore peace and stability to the Member State* of the Union upon the recommendation of the Peace and Security Council." These crimes are, with the exception of "threat to legitimate order" (which is a

[16] 28 UN GAOR Supp. (No. 30), at 75, UN Doc. A/9030 (1974), 1015 UNTS 243, entered into force 18 July 1976.

[17] "Rapporteur's Report of the Ministerial Meeting in Banjul, The Gambia, Organization of African Unity", at para 13, OUA Doc. CAB/LEG/67/Draft. Rapt. Rpt (II) Rev. 4, reprinted in Heyns (ed.) 2002, p. 95 (emphasis added).

[18] UN GA Res 2202 A (XXI), 16 Dec. 1966.

[19] UN Doc. S/RES/556 (1984) adopted 23 Oct. 1984.

[20] Article V of the Apartheid Convention.

[21] See Dugard 2008. See also Article V of the Apartheid Convention.

new crime added to the provision by virtue of an amendment in 2003), the same crimes over which the International Criminal Court has jurisdiction.

The proscription of the foregoing international crimes by the AU Act necessarily implies the obligation to take measures to redress violations. It cannot be the case that with its Constitutive Act the African Union legislates on crimes it does not intend its own court to prosecute. The question to ask is, in the absence of the International Criminal Court or any other comparable judicial institution, what would happen in the event of crimes itemized in Article 4(h) of the AU Act? Should we hope that the national courts of concerned African states would prosecute such crimes even when committed by senior officials of their own governments, or should we expect courts of other African states to prosecute such high-profile culprits from fellow African nations on the basis of the much-maligned universal jurisdiction principle?

An instructive case on this point is the trial of Hissène Habré, the former president of Chad.[22] Belgium issued an arrest warrant against Habré, who was at that time in asylum in Senegal.[23] Senegal refused to extradite the culprit to Belgium,[24] and with the blessing of the African Union chose to prosecute Habré instead before the Extraordinary African Chambers.[25] The Chambers convicted Habre for crimes against humanity, torture and war crimes, and sentenced him to life imprisonment in May 2016.[26] Although Senegal and Chad were found to possess jurisdiction to try Habré,[27] Senegal refused to yield Habré to Chad based on the claim that, as a former Head of State, Habré enjoyed absolute immunity for crimes he committed while he was in office, a position most African countries indeed subscribe to.[28]

While I am not questioning the African Union's resolve to prosecute Habré in Africa, the fact is that with Senegal not prosecuting him and not giving him up to Chad either, the only remaining option was for the organization to turn to its own courts. The Committee of Eminent African Jurists[29] set up by the African Union specifically to advice on all ramifications of the Habré case reported[30] that neither

[22] See AU Committee of Eminent African Jurists 2006.

[23] See Human Rights Watch 2005.

[24] Ibid.

[25] See Assembly/AU/Dec. 127 (VII) (Doc. Assembly/AU/3/VII).

[26] See Amnesty International 2016.

[27] See AU Committee of Eminent African Jurists 2006, para 22 et seq.

[28] But see Decisions of the Committee Against Torture Under Article 22 of the Convention Against Torture, and Other Cruel, Inhuman or Degrading Treatment, Committee Against Torture, 36th Session, Communication No. 181/2001 (2001), where the Committee condemned Senegal for refusing to extradite *Habré* to Belgium and held that the country had violated Articles 5(2) and 7 of the Torture Convention to which Senegal is a party.

[29] Decision on the Hissène Habré Case and the African Union, Assembly of the African Union, 6th Ordinary Session, Assembly/AU/Dec. 103 (VI) (2006).

[30] See AU Committee of Eminent African Jurists 2006.

of the AU's two courts could prosecute the fugitive. The Committee made other specific recommendations pertaining to the Habré issue,[31] but, with an eye on similar cases that might arise in the future, it also suggested:

> the possibility *of conferring criminal jurisdiction on the African Court of Justice* [to confer criminal competence that can be adopted by states within a reasonable time-frame] to make the respect for human rights at national, regional and continental levels a fundamental tenet of African governance.[32]

What this case shows is that neither national courts of putative African criminals, especially government officials, nor the courts of other African states can be trusted to dispense justice under those circumstances.

2.2.3 The Obligation to Prosecute Crimes Peculiar to African States

Aside from the general obligation to prosecute all crimes proscribed by its treaties, the African Union incurs a distinct obligation to prosecute crimes which are *peculiar* to Africa but over which the International Criminal Court has no jurisdiction. The non-inclusion of such crimes in the jurisdiction of the Court could be attributable either to a perception among a great majority of ICC States Parties that such acts do not constitute international crimes *at all*, or to a perception that these international crimes are not "serious" enough for the purposes of the International Criminal Court.

There are a number of crimes peculiar to Africa, but one is particularly worth mentioning due to its importance. Unconstitutional changes of government are undoubtedly one of the most common sources of conflict in Africa, howsoever they are brought about.[33] The examples of Zimbabwe's Mugabe, Kenya's Kibaki and Ivory Coast's Gbagbo readily come to mind. The rampant menace of the unconstitutional takeover of government and its direct impact on the peace and stability of African countries drove the African Union to adopt the African Charter on Democracy, Election, and Governance in 2007.[34] The treaty entered into force in February 2012. Through Article 23 of the Charter the African Union lists and criminalizes the various acts constituting the crime of unconstitutional change of government,[35] in the hope of promoting a greater respect for the rule of law and inducing a concomitant reduction in the prevalence of armed conflicts.[36]

---

[31] Ibid., para 31.

[32] Ibid., para 34.

[33] On this crime see the chapter by Kemp and Kinyunyu in this book.

[34] Assembly/AU/Dec. 147 (VIII) (2007).

[35] See also Article 28(E)(1)(D) of the Malabo Protocol (Annex).

[36] See preamble to the Charter on Democracy, Election, and Governance.

The Rome Statute is limited to the most serious international crimes, which, although common to the whole of humanity, are often committed in the aftermath of the breakdown of law and order. Hence, one could say that while the International Criminal Court prosecutes crimes mostly committed *after* violence or disorder has already ensued in a state, by criminalizing unconstitutional changes of government the African Union aims to prevent the occurrence of such crimes *ab initio* through the proscription of acts that may precipitate violence and disorder in a state.

In order for the African regional court to prosecute the crime of unconstitutional change of government, it is not enough that the crime be legislated upon by the African Union treaty, but it is also important that the crime be regarded as a "serious" international crime. That is not to say that whenever a regional treaty proscribes a crime other than the classical ones there must always be a determination that the crime is an international crime before a regional court can adjudicate on it. There are several international crimes *par excellence*, such as piracy, over which an international criminal tribunal may not have jurisdiction. But when a regional treaty proscribes a crime—such as unconstitutional change of government—that is not universally recognized as an international crime, it is crucial first to consider the status of that crime under international law.

The trajectory of unconstitutional change of government from a crime previously dealt with within the confines of national law at the individual country level in Africa to an international crime that an African regional court can now prosecute involves a formidable pedigree and confirms the influence of state practice in the crystallization of customary norms into treaty obligations. The treatment of unconstitutional change of government is one of the few norms in Africa that gradually evolved through custom, culminating in its codification by the African Charter on Democracy, Election, and Governance.

The rejection of unconstitutional changes of government in Africa dates back to the time of the Organization of African Unity, which, after several pronouncements and a major decision in 1999 against the practice,[37] adopted the Lomé Declaration in 2000,[38] shortly followed by the 2001 New Partnership for Africa Development.[39] Within the New Partnership, African leaders adopted the Declaration on Democracy, Political, Economic and Corporate Governance, and affirmed democratic governance.[40] In 2002, the AU Assembly adopted the Declaration on the Principle Governing Democratic Elections in Africa.[41] In despair over the pervasiveness of the crime of unconstitutional change of government in Africa and in recognition of the ineffectiveness of responses by the

37 OAU Doc. AHG/Dec. 141 (XXXV) (1999); OAU Doc. AHG/Dec. 142 (XXXV). Both decisions condemned unconstitutional changes of government in Africa.

38 OAU Doc. AHG/Dec. 5 (XXXVI) (2000).

39 OAU Doc. AHG/Dec. 1 (XXXVII) (2001).

40 AU Doc. AHG/Dec. 235 (XXXVIII), Annex 1 (2002).

41 OAU Doc. AHG/Dec. 1 (XXXVIII) (2002).

Organization of African Unity and the African Union, the AU Assembly adopted the African Charter on Democracy, Election, and Governance on 30 January 2007. The status of unconstitutional change of government as an international crime was further confirmed by the entry into force of the treaty in February 2012.

Without conferring on its court jurisdiction to prosecute international crimes, the African Union will permanently face a rather absurd situation in which its Member States recognize the existence of a crime in their region—a crime that they regard as very serious, as their practice dating back at least two decades shows—but one that the Union's court cannot prosecute. Several AU Member States that are to date still afflicted by unconstitutional changes of government are States Parties to the Rome Statute that established the International Criminal Court, which has no jurisdiction over unconstitutional change of government. It is plausible to argue, therefore, that even if the African Union were to concede the prosecution of classical international crimes codified by Article 4(h) of the AU Act exclusively to the International Criminal Court, the likelihood that the Union will continue to seek jurisdictional competence for its Court over *other* serious crimes, like unconstitutional change of government, remains very high. Short of amending the Rome Statute to incorporate this crime, which affects many of its African States Parties but over which the International Criminal Court currently has no jurisdiction, it will be hard to argue against the need for the African Union to create a court that can prosecute such Africa-specific crimes.

The foregoing analysis does not presuppose that the African Court of Justice and Human and Peoples' Rights would, as a matter of fact, be able to adjudicate on unconstitutional change of government cases when, and if, the time comes. Although the AU Assembly's sensitivity to the unconstitutional change of government issue at its July 2012 summit was absent from its January 2013 summit, its charge that the Commission should look more deeply into the meaning of "popular uprisings" and who may determine the legitimacy of such is disconcerting. Should the Assembly possess the power to determine the legitimacy of popular uprisings, just as the AU Peace and Security Council has been proposed to exercise a similar authority in respect of unconstitutional change of government, then a government which violates the African Charter on Democracy, Election, and Governance, say, by not relinquishing power after losing an election may find itself maintained in office by the Assembly's determination that an uprising against it is illegitimate.

2.3 The Legality of African International Criminal Prosecution *Vis-à-Vis* the Rome Statute

The view has lately gained currency that there is no basis in the Rome Statute for allowing regional prosecution of international crimes, and that such jurisdiction as has been proposed for the African Court of Justice and Human and Peoples'

Rights is incompatible with the ICC Statute.[42] To those advocating this view, one may address three preliminary questions. First, why should a court created by a multilateral treaty require the approval of another multilateral treaty creating a similar court to justify its own existence? Secondly, under what rules of international law, based on treaty or general principles, do states ratify a treaty to the exclusion of all other treaties, even those governing the same subject as the pre-existing one? Thirdly, why should the African Union, being a non-signatory to the Rome Statute, seek the legality of its own court under that Statute?

Those who impugn the legality of the proposed international criminal jurisdiction for the African Court on the basis of "incompatibility with the Rome Statute" draw support partly from the opinion of the Committee of African Eminent Jurists on the Hissène Habré case, and partly from the complementarity principle of the Rome Statute.[43] After proposing the establishment of the African Court of Justice, the Committee said:

> this new body be granted jurisdiction to undertake criminal trials for crimes against humanity, war crimes and violations of Convention Against Torture [...] [and] that *there is room in the Rome Statute* for such a development and that it would not be a duplication of the work of the International Criminal Court.[44]

The need to justify the existence of the African international criminal jurisdiction with reference to the provisions of the Rome Statute has also been linked to the "principle of complementarity" in the Rome Statute. As argued, "the Rome Statute only envisaged national criminal jurisdiction and not regional or sub-regional criminal jurisdictions in so far as the question of complementarity is concerned".[45] Thus, "the Rome Statute does not expressly *allow or even imply that regional courts* such as the proposed Criminal Chambers be conferred with jurisdiction to try international crimes that are under the jurisdiction of the ICC."[46] In the light of this view, the commentator then asks, "Does the proposed Criminal Chamber have a legal basis under the ICC Statute?"[47]

For several reasons, an inquiry into the legality of the proposed international criminal jurisdiction in Africa *with reference* to the Rome Statute is fallacious, fundamentally mistaken and unscrupulous. No provision of the Statute forbids its States Parties from concluding other treaties, even if those were to establish courts of a similar nature to the International Criminal Court. The Rome Statute is not a *primus inter pares* among treaties and cannot fetter the competence of its States Parties to deploy their consent in international law. It is but a manifestation

[42] See, for instance, Murungu 2011, p. 1081.

[43] Ibid.

[44] Abraham 2015, p. 8.

[45] Murungu 2011, p. 1075.

[46] Emphasis added.

[47] Murungu 2011, p. 1081.

of uncritical appraisal now to regard the Rome Statute as the *fons et origo* of all international crimes and their international prosecution.

By way of comparison, despite the fact that Article 92 of the UN Charter designates the International Court of Justice, as the "principal judicial organ" of the organization, several regional dispute settlement mechanisms exercise jurisdiction similar to the one of the International Court of Justice. And before the creation of the International Criminal Court, the International Criminal Tribunals for the Former Yugoslavia and Rwanda prosecuted the same crimes that the International Criminal Court now does, even if those two had a more limited mandate. No one has argued that the creation of those two tribunals extinguished the right of other international tribunals to prosecute the same crimes, lest the International Criminal Court would be the poorer for it.

There are two well-known situations in international law in which the validity/legality of a subsequent treaty may be determined by reference to a pre-existing treaty. First, where the States Parties to a treaty decide to conclude another treaty which establishes obligations similar to those in the previous treaty, the only legal requirement they must satisfy is that their obligations under the later treaty do not *conflict* with obligations assumed under the previous treaty, especially if there is a specific provision in the pre-existing treaty to that effect. Hence, Article 103 of the UN Charter states:

> In the event of a conflict between the obligations of the Members of the United Nations under the present Charter and their obligations under any other international agreement, their obligations under the present Charter shall prevail.

There is no provision of the Rome Statute comparable to this Article.

Secondly, if a pre-existing treaty embodies a *jus cogens* obligation, then States Parties to that treaty are forbidden to conclude another treaty containing a provision that violates a peremptory norm. Thus, if Treaty A to which states X, Y, and Z are parties forbids the use of force (now widely regarded as a *jus cogens*), then whereas those states are not precluded from adopting another treaty that may govern the use of force, they may not adopt Treaty B *if one of its provisions violates the peremptory obligation* in Treaty A.

Article 53 of the Vienna Convention on the Law of Treaties provides that "[a] treaty is void if, at the time of its conclusion, it conflicts with a peremptory norm of general international law". It is noteworthy that this provision forbids only the creation of treaties that may breach a peremptory norm of international law already assumed under another treaty, but not the creation of a new treaty per se. In any case, there are no peremptory norms in the Rome Statute, and if one accepts some of the crimes under the Statute (e.g. genocide) as being subject to *jus cogens* rules, the creation of an African court to *prosecute* such crimes is confirmatory of, not conflictual with, such a peremptory norm in the Rome Statute.

Some argue that the complementarity principle of the Rome Statute "does not allow" regional courts and binds the International Criminal Court and its States Parties in an exclusive relationship.[48] The complementarity principle is the mecha-

[48] Ibid.

nism by which the Rome Statute orders a jurisdictional relationship between the Court and its States Parties so that the latter will always have the first go at a case unless where, according to Article 17 and preambular para 10 of the Statue, they are "unwilling" or "genuinely unable" to investigate or prosecute a case. This principle exists for the benefit of the International Criminal Court and its States Parties so that any obligation imposed or envisaged by that principle can exist only with respect to those states.

The African Union is an international organization with legal personality separate from those of its Member States.[49] The obligations assumed by any AU Member State under the ICC Statute, specifically with respect to the complementarity rule or other rules or principles, cannot apply to the Union under international law. Article 34 of the Vienna Convention on the Law of Treaties states that "[a] treaty does not create either obligations or rights for a third State without its consent". Thus, if there is an obligation imposed by the complementarity principle against the creation of an alternative international criminal jurisdiction—and there is no convincing reason to believe that such an obligation exists—a common sense application of the rules of international law dictates that the obligation can *only* apply to States Parties to that Statute.

The right of the African Union to establish whatever courts it deems fit, regardless of what other court may have jurisdiction over the same crimes, is unassailable in international law. International law is created by the consent of states, and it is almost unthinkable, except in the context of peremptory norms, that there would be firewalls against the reach of state consent. Consequently, one does not need to construct "a progressive interpretation of positive complementarity"[50] of the Rome Statute or any other fanciful jargon, for that matter, in order to argue for the right of the African Union to establish a court. One has to emphasize again that the African Union Member States have a different legal personality from the African Union, and that the two cannot be confused.

2.4 Some Challenges to the Court's Effectiveness

2.4.1 The Problem of Combined Civil and Criminal Jurisdiction

According to Article 16 of the Malabo Protocol (Annex) the African Court of Justice and Human and Peoples' Rights shall have a General Affairs Section, a Human and Peoples' Right Section, and an International Criminal Law Section.

49 See App. No. 001/2011, *Femi Falana v. African Union,* Judgment of 26 June 2012.

50 See Murungu 2011, p. 1081.

The first two sections embody the civil jurisdiction of the Court while the third embodies its criminal jurisdiction. Thus, the African Court of Justice and Human and Peoples' Rights combines civil and criminal jurisdictions. A full discussion of the huge practical and procedural complications attendant on combined jurisdiction is beyond the scope of this endeavour, but it is worthwhile to remark briefly on some matters arising.

Article 18(4) of the Malabo Protocol (Annex) provides that "[t]he Appellate Chamber may affirm, reverse the decision appealed against. The decision of the Appellate Chamber shall be final". It is unclear whether this provision refers to appeals arising from criminal matters only or appeals from other sections of the Court. This ambiguity is not helped by the fact that the only "Appellate Chamber" mentioned in the protocol is in relation to the International Criminal Law Section.[51] The implication is that a criminal Appellate Chamber will sit on appeals arising from civil cases. This arrangement clearly leaves much to be desired.

The Court will also have to grapple with the resource implications of its combined jurisdiction. The cost of prosecuting one international crime could well outstrip the annual budget of the African Court of Justice and Human and Peoples' Rights as a whole. The cost of prosecuting Liberian Charles Taylor stands at a whopping USD 50 million, while the annual budget of the Sierra Leonean justice sector is about USD 13 million.[52] The high cost of international criminal prosecutions derives mainly from the excruciating evidentiary processes associated with criminal prosecutions. Proving a case beyond reasonable doubt—the evidentiary standard of criminal prosecution—involves an investment of huge financial and time resources, comprehensive and expensive investigations, exhaustive examination of extensive materials, and, above all, the servicing of different levels of chambers within the Court itself. The International Criminal Law Section of the African Court of Justice and Human and Peoples' Rights, for instance, consists of the Office of the Prosecutor, a Pre-Trial and Trial Chambers, and an Appellate Chamber, all of these with their distinct staff.[53]

2.4.2 *The Complementarity Principle of the African Court of Justice and Human and Peoples' Rights*

Article 46 of the Malabo Protocol (Annex) provides for the complementarity principle.[54] This Article states that "the jurisdiction of the Court shall be complementary to that of the National Courts, and to the Courts of the Regional Economic Communities where specifically provided for by the Communities". Impliedly the

[51] See Article 16 of the Malabo Protocol (Annex).

[52] Hirsch 2012.

[53] Article 19*bis* of the Malabo Protocol (Annex).

[54] See on this issue the chapter by van der Wilt in this book.

African Court of Justice and Human and Peoples' Rights can accept a case, not only after the national court of an indicted person has proved "unwilling" or "unable" to prosecute, but also after a court of a Regional Economic Community has failed to prosecute that person. Thus, instead of the scheme of complementarity under the Rome Statue, which makes a case admissible once a national court has failed the twin criteria, admissibility of cases to the African Court of Justice and Human and Peoples' Rights requires the "double failure" of national courts and Regional Economic Communities' courts under the same twin standard.

For many reasons this provision is not only problematic but also ill-advised. First, most states in Africa belong to more than one Regional Economic Community. For instance, the majority of ECOWAS[55] Member States are also members of CENSAD,[56] and there is a great overlap between the membership of COMESA[57] and that of SADC.[58] Therefore, the question is which of the Regional Economic Communities' courts should be considered for the purposes of the complementarity principle where the national state of an accused person holds multiple memberships. Furthermore, whereas national courts are accessible to individuals some regional courts are not automatically accessible to individuals. For instance, the African Court of Human and Peoples' Rights can only admit a case directly from an individual if the respondent state has deposed to the Court's jurisdiction under Article 34(6) of the Protocol establishing the Court. It was principally on this basis that the Court declined jurisdiction in *Michelot Yogogombaye v. The Republic of Senegal*.[59] Also, community courts, by their very nature, do not deal with the criminal responsibility of individuals. The contentious jurisdiction of the ECOWAS Court of Justice, for instance, concerns only violations of human rights of ECOWAS citizens. How then can a court not accessible to individuals, or which cannot determine the criminal responsibility of individuals, be asked to make an initial determination of such a nature before their Member State's national court has recourse to the African Court of Justice and Human and Peoples' Rights?

A close reading of Article 46 of the Malabo Protocol (Annex) on complementarity also discloses another serious loophole relating to the requirement of "inability to prosecute". The formula adopted in the Rome Statute is that there must be

[55] The Economic Community of West African States was founded on 28 May 1975, with the signing of the Treaty of Lagos.

[56] The Community of Sahel-Saharan States, established on 4 February 1998 with its seat in Libya. See http://www.au.int/en/recs/censad.

[57] The Common Market for Eastern and Southern Africa was established in December 1994, with its head-quarters in Lusaka, Zambia. See http://www.comesa.int/overview-of-comesa/.

[58] The Southern African Development Community was established on 1 April 1980, and has its seat in Gaborone, Botswana. See www.sadc.int/.

[59] Judgment, Communication No. 001/2008 (African Court on Justice and Human Rights, 30 July 2010).

"genuine" inability to prosecute. The word "genuine" serves to prevent a trivialization of that criterion by states. However, the formula adopted by the draft protocol dispenses with "genuineness". The non-qualification of "inability to prosecute" dangerously lowers the evidentiary standard of "inability" and may seriously undermine that criterion. It implies that African states will easily avoid prosecuting their nationals and offload such cases on to the African Court of Justice and Human and Peoples' Rights, thereby unduly burdening the Court and making it a Court of first rather than last resort.

2.5 Conclusions

The decision of the African Union to confer on its Court international criminal jurisdiction is an unassailable exercise in sovereignty. However, it is uncertain whether the Protocol will ever get the necessary ratifications by the AU Member States. If it eventually does the challenge will be for the Court to be able to investigate and prosecute crimes relating to anyone regardless of their status. Whether the Court can perform this duty in respect of African heads of state and senior government officials, who cannot be expected to be brought before their national courts, either because of immunity or because they are shielded by the deployment of raw political force, remains to be seen.[60] It would have been unrealistic to expect Al Bashir or Gaddafi to have been prosecuted by their national courts. And if there is any serious lesson to be learned from the cat-and-mouse game of the Ugandan regime and the "Lord's Resistance Army" before the referral of the case to the International Criminal Court, it is precisely that domestic justice may not be suitable where potential culprits have as much or even more fire power than the state, or where the government is itself morally compromised.

The tension between the International Criminal Court and Africa[61] is regrettable but, to put it in context, it was a disaster waiting to happen. Had the International Criminal Court and the Africa Union not fallen out over the Al Bashir affair, they would probably still have done so over a different issue, if maybe with less acrimony. The International Criminal Court is a court designed to prosecute crimes that more frequently arise *after* a complete breakdown of law and order in a country. Genocide, crimes against humanity and war crimes are all crimes mostly committed *during* an ugly interface in human society—at the outbreak of violence. They are crimes rarely committed when the rule of law reigns. What the African Union urgently requires today is a court that can prosecute crimes the *occurrence* of which *may lead* to the breakdown of law and order if not prevented. One such crime is unconstitutional change of government.

---

[60] On this issue see the chapter by Tladi in this book.

[61] On this issue see Werle et al. (eds.) 2014.

In not countenancing such crimes as unconstitutional change of government, the international community ignores the pedigree of *particular* international law. Although the popularity of "regional custom" has waned considerably in modern times, its attraction has not diminished. It allows a few states existing in a given region, bound together perhaps by the same culture or other common attributes, to recognize certain practices amongst themselves as constituting international law. The International Court of Justice recognized this practice in the *Asylum case* between Peru and Colombia.[62] Although it rejected the Peruvian claim on evidential grounds, the Court never doubted that such a principle in fact existed—it only stressed that its existence must be rigorously proved by the state alleging it as manifesting the necessary *opinio juris*.[63]

Regardless of the fate of the protocol, the future of international criminal justice in Africa lies not in the duplicity of international judicial institutions but in the prosecutors of the International Criminal Court discharging their duties and responsibilities with candour and impartiality. The ICC Prosecutor cannot afford to deal with the ICC States Parties as though she is a headmaster prevailing over a pack of unruly pupils.

References

Abraham G (2015) Africa's Evolving Continental Court Structures: At the Crossroads? SAIIA Occasional Paper 209. http://www.saiia.org.za/occasional-papers/669-africa-s-evolving-continental-court-structures-at-the-crossroads/file

African Union Committee of Eminent African Jurists (2006) Report of the Committee of Eminent African Jurists on the Case of Hissene Habré. https://www.hrw.org/legacy/justice/habre/CEJA_Repor0506.pdf

Amnesty International (2016) Hissene Habre verdict: Landmark decision brings justice for tens of thousands of victims. https://www.amnesty.org/en/latest/news/2016/05/hissene-habre-verdict-landmark-decision-brings-justice-for-tens-of-thousands-of-victims

Bamba M (2003) Déclaration de Reconnaisance de la Compétence de la Cour Pénale Internationale. https://www.icc-cpi.int/NR/rdonlyres/CBE1F16B-5712-4452-87E7-4FDDE5DD70D9/279779/ICDE.pdf

Deya D (2012) Worth the wait: pushing for the African Court to exercise jurisdiction for international crimes. OpenSpace Int. Crim. Justice 2:22–26

Dugard J (2008) International Convention on the Suppression and Punishment of the Crime of Apartheid. In: Audiovisual library of international law. http://legal.un.org/avl/pdf/ha/cspca/cspca_e.pdf

Heyns C (ed) (2002) Human rights law in Africa. Kluwer, The Hague/London/New York

Hirsch A (2012) Charles Taylor is guilty—but what's the verdict on international justice? The Guardian. www.guardian.co.uk/commentisfree/libertycentral/2012/apr/26/charles-taylor-guilty-abetting-war-crimes

Human Rights Watch (2005) Ex-Chad dictator indicted in Belgium. www.hrw.org/news/2005/09/29/ex-chad-dictator-indicted-belgium-0

[62] *Asylum (Colombia v. Peru)* [1950] ICJ Rep 266.

[63] Ibid., at 277.

M'Baye K (2002) Introduction to the Draft African Charter on Human and Peoples' Rights, OAU Doc. CAB/ LEG/67/1, reprinted in Heyns C (ed) Human rights law in Africa

Murungu CB (2011) Towards a criminal chamber in the African Court of Justice and Human Rights. J. Int. Crim. Justice 9:1067–1088

Viljoen F (2004) A human rights court for Africa, and Africans. Brooklyn J. Int. Law 30:1–66

Viljoen F (2012) AU assembly should consider human rights implications before adopting the amending merged African Court Protocol, AfricLaw, 23 May 2012. http://africlaw.com/2012/05/23/au-assembly-should-consider-human-rights-implications-before-adopting-the-amending-merged-african-court-protocol

Werle G, Fernandez L, Vormbaum M (eds) (2014) Africa and the International Criminal Court. T.M.C. Asser Press, The Hague

Part II
The Crimes in the Annex to the Malabo Protocol

Chapter 3
Genocide (Article 28B), Crimes Against Humanity (Article 28C), War Crimes (Article 28D) and the Crime of Aggression (Article 28M)

Kai Ambos

Abstract The section on jurisdiction ("International Criminal Jurisdiction of the Court") in the Annex to the Malabo Protocol contains among the 14 (sic!) crimes or crime groups the four core crimes recognized by the Statute of the International Criminal Court (ICC Statute), i.e., genocide, crimes against humanity, war crimes and the crime of aggression. While these provisions are largely modeled upon those of the ICC Statute, they also extend the latter's scope, either by broadening the *chapeau* (in the case of crimes against humanity) or by adding new underlying acts (in the case of genocide, war crimes, and the crime of aggression). At the same time, the opportunity to improve upon certain flaws in the drafting of the crimes contained in the ICC Statute has been missed. The chapter takes a critical look at the changes *vis à vis* the crimes in the ICC Statute and highlights some of the opportunities for improvement which have been neglected.

Keywords Africa · African Union · International Criminal Court · genocide · crimes against humanity · war crimes · crime of aggression

All internet sources in this chapter were last visited on 30 June 2016.

K. Ambos (✉)
Criminal Law, Criminal Procedure, Comparative Law and International Criminal Law, Centro de Estudios de Derecho Penal Y Procesal Penal Latinoamericano (CEDPAL); Georg August Universität Göttingen (GAU), Göttingen, Germany; the District Court of Göttingen, Göttingen, Germany
e-mail: kambos@gwdg.de

G. Werle and M. Vormbaum (eds.), *The African Criminal Court*, International Criminal Justice Series 10, DOI 10.1007/978-94-6265-150-0_3

Contents

3.1 Extracts from the Malabo Protocol (Annex)

Article 28B Genocide

For the purposes of this Statute, 'genocide' means any of the following acts committed with intent to destroy, in whole or in part, a national, ethnical, racial or religious group, as such:

(a). Killing members of the group;
(b). Causing serious bodily or mental harm to members of the group;
(c). Deliberately inflicting on the group conditions of life calculated to bring about its physical destruction in whole or in part;
(d). Imposing measures intended to prevent births within the group;
(e). Forcibly transferring children of the group to another group;
(f). Acts of rape or any other form of sexual violence.

Article 28C Crimes against Humanity

1. For the purposes of this Statute, 'crime against humanity' means any of the following acts when committed as part of a widespread or systematic attack or enterprise directed against any civilian population, with knowledge of the attack or enterprise:

   (a). Murder;
   (b). Extermination;
   (c). Enslavement;
   (d). Deportation or forcible transfer of population;
   (e). Imprisonment or other severe deprivation of physical liberty in violation of fundamental rules of international law;
   (f). Torture, cruel, inhuman and degrading treatment or punishment;
   (g). Rape, sexual slavery, enforced prostitution, forced pregnancy, enforced sterilization, or any other form of sexual violence of comparable gravity;
   (h). Persecution against any identifiable group or collectivity on political, racial, national, ethnic, cultural, religious, gender or other grounds that are universally recognized as impermissible under international law;
   (i). Enforced disappearance of persons;
   (j). The crime of apartheid;

(k). Other inhumane acts of a similar character intentionally causing great suffering, or serious injury to body or mental or physical health.

2. For the purpose of para 1:

(a). 'Attack directed against any civilian population' means a course of conduct involving the multiple commission of acts referred to in para 1 against any civilian population, pursuant to or in furtherance of a State or organizational policy to commit such attack;
(b). 'Extermination' includes the intentional infliction of conditions of life, inter alia the deprivation of access to food and medicine, calculated to bring about the destruction of part of a population;
(c). 'Enslavement' means the exercise of any or all of the powers attaching to the right of ownership over a person and includes the exercise of such power in the course of trafficking in persons, in particular women and children;
(d). 'Deportation or forcible transfer of population' means forced displacement of the persons concerned by expulsion or other coercive acts from the area in which they are lawfully present, without grounds permitted under international law;
(e). 'Torture' means the intentional infliction of severe pain or suffering, whether physical or mental, upon a person in the custody or under the control of the accused; except that torture shall not include pain or suffering arising only from, inherent in or incidental to, lawful sanctions;
(f). 'Forced pregnancy' means the unlawful confinement of a woman forcibly made pregnant, with the intent of affecting the ethnic composition of any population or carrying out other grave violations of international law. This definition shall not in any way be interpreted as affecting national laws relating to pregnancy;
(g). 'Persecution' means the intentional and severe deprivation of fundamental rights contrary to international law by reason of the identity of the group or collectivity;
(h). 'The crime of apartheid' means inhumane acts of a character similar to those referred to in para 1, committed in the context of an institutionalized regime of systematic oppression and domination by one racial group over any other racial group or groups and committed with the intention of maintaining that regime;
(i). 'Enforced disappearance of persons' means the arrest, detention or abduction of persons by, or with the authorization, support or acquiescence of, a State or a political organization, followed by a refusal to acknowledge that deprivation of freedom or to give information on the fate or whereabouts of those persons, with the intention of removing them from the protection of the law for a prolonged period of time

Article 28D War Crimes
For the purposes of this Statute, 'war crimes' means any of the offences listed, in particular when committed as part of a plan or policy or as part of a large scale commission of such crimes.

(a). Grave breaches of the Geneva Conventions of 12 August 1949, namely, any of the following acts against persons or property protected under the provisions of the relevant Geneva Convention:

(i). Wilful killing;
(ii). Torture or inhuman treatment, including biological experiments;
(iii). Wilfully causing great suffering, or serious injury to body or health;
(iv). Extensive destruction and appropriation of property, not justified by military necessity and carried out unlawfully and wantonly;
(v). Compelling a prisoner of war or other protected person to serve in the forces of a hostile Power;
(vi). Wilfully depriving a prisoner of war or other protected person of the rights of fair and regular trial;
(vii). Unlawful deportation or transfer or unlawful confinement;
(viii). Taking of hostages.

(b). Grave breaches of the First Additional Protocol to the Geneva Conventions of 8 June 1977 and other serious violations of the laws and customs applicable in international armed conflict, within the established framework of international law, namely, any of the following acts:

(i). Intentionally directing attacks against the civilian population as such or against individual civilians not taking direct part in hostilities;
(ii). Intentionally directing attacks against civilian objects, that is, objects which are not military objectives;
(iii). Intentionally directing attacks against personnel, installations, material, units or vehicles involved in a humanitarian assistance or peacekeeping mission in accordance with the Charter of the United Nations, as long as they are entitled to the protection given to civilians or civilian objects under the international law of armed conflict;
(iv). Intentionally launching an attack in the knowledge that such attack will cause incidental loss of life or injury to civilians or damage to civilian objects or widespread, long-term and severe damage to the natural environment which would be clearly excessive in relation to the concrete and direct overall military advantage anticipated;
(v). Intentionally launching an attack against works or installations containing dangerous forces in the knowledge that such attack will cause excessive loss of life, injury to civilians or damage to civilian objects which will be excessive in relation to the concrete and direct overall military advantage anticipated;
(vi). Attacking or bombarding, by whatever means, towns, villages, dwellings or buildings which are undefended and which are not military objectives;

(vii). Killing or wounding a combatant who, having laid down his arms or having no longer means of defence, has surrendered at discretion;

(viii). Making improper use of a flag of truce, of the flag or of the military insignia and uniform of the enemy or of the United Nations, as well as of the distinctive emblems of the Geneva Conventions, resulting in death or serious personal injury;

(ix). The transfer, directly or indirectly, by the Occupying Power of parts of its own civilian population into the territory it occupies, or the deportation or transfer of all or parts of the population of the occupied territory within or outside this territory;

(x). Intentionally directing attacks against buildings dedicated to religion, education, art, science or charitable purposes, historic monuments, hospitals and places where the sick and wounded are collected, provided they are not military objectives;

(xi). Subjecting persons who are in the power of an adverse party to physical mutilation or to medical or scientific experiments of any kind which are neither justified by the medical, dental or hospital treatment of the person concerned nor carried out in his or her interest, and which cause death to or seriously endanger the health of such person or persons;

(xii). Killing or wounding treacherously individuals belonging to the hostile nation or army;

(xiii). Declaring that no quarter will be given;

(xiv). Destroying or seizing the enemy's property unless such destruction or seizure be imperatively demanded by the necessities of war;

(xv). Declaring abolished, suspended or inadmissible in a court of law the rights and actions of the nationals of the hostile party;

(xvi). Compelling the nationals of the hostile party to take part in the operations of war directed against their own State, even if they were in the belligerent's service before the commencement of the war;

(xvii). Pillaging a town or place, even when taken by assault;

(xviii). Employing poison or poisoned weapons;

(xix). Employing asphyxiating, poisonous or other gases, and all analogous liquids, materials or devices;

(xx). Employing bullets which expand or flatten easily in the human body, such as bullets with a hard envelope which does not entirely cover the core or is pierced with incisions;

(xxi). Employing weapons, projectiles and Materials and methods of warfare which are of a nature to cause superfluous injury or unnecessary suffering or which are inherently indiscriminate in violation of the international law of armed conflict

(xxii). Committing outrages upon personal dignity, in particular humiliating and degrading treatment;
(xxiii). Committing rape, sexual slavery, enforced prostitution, forced pregnancy, enforced sterilization, or any other form of sexual violence also constituting a grave breach of the Geneva Conventions;
(xxiv). Utilizing the presence of a civilian or other protected person to render certain points, areas or military forces immune from military operations;
(xxv). Intentionally directing attacks against buildings, material, medical units and transport, and personnel using the distinctive emblems of the Geneva Conventions in conformity with international law;
(xxvi). Intentionally using starvation of civilians as a method of warfare by depriving them of objects indispensable to their survival, including wilfully impeding relief supplies as provided for under the Geneva Conventions;
(xxvii). Conscripting or enlisting children under the age of eighteen years into the national armed forces or using them to participate actively in hostilities;
(xxviii). Unjustifiably delaying the repatriation of prisoners of war or civilians;
(xxix). Willfully committing practices of apartheid and other inhuman and degrading practices involving outrages upon personal dignity, based on racial discrimination;
(xxx). Making non-defended localities and demilitarised zones the object of attack;
(xxxi). Slavery and deportation to slave labour;
(xxxii). Collective punishments;
(xxxiii). Despoliation of the wounded, sick, shipwrecked or dead;

(c). In the case of an armed conflict not of an international character, serious violations of article 3 common to the four Geneva Conventions of 12 August 1949, namely, any of the following acts committed against persons taking no active part in the hostilities, including members of armed forces who have laid down their arms and those placed hors de combat by sickness, wounds, detention or any other cause:

(i). Violence to life and person, in particular murder of all kinds, mutilation, cruel treatment and torture;
(ii). Committing outrages upon personal dignity, in particular humiliating and degrading treatment;
(iii). Taking of hostages;
(iv). The passing of sentences and the carrying out of executions without previous judgment pronounced by a regularly constituted court, affording all judicial guarantees which are generally recognized as indispensable.

(d). Paragraph (c) applies to armed conflicts not of an international character and thus does not apply to situations of internal disturbances and tensions, such as riots, isolated and sporadic acts of violence or other acts of a similar nature.

(e). Other serious violations of the laws and customs applicable in armed conflicts not of an international character, within the established framework of international law, namely, any of the following acts:

- (i) Intentionally directing attacks against the civilian population as such or against individual civilians not taking direct part in hostilities;
- (ii) Intentionally directing attacks against buildings, material, medical units and transport, and personnel using the distinctive emblems of the Geneva Conventions in conformity with international law;
- (iii) Intentionally directing attacks against personnel, installations, material, units or vehicles involved in a humanitarian assistance or peacekeeping mission in accordance with the Charter of the United Nations, as long as they are entitled to the protection given to civilians or civilian objects under the international law of armed conflict;
- (iv) Intentionally directing attacks against buildings dedicated to religion, education, art, science or charitable purposes, historic monuments, hospitals and places where the sick and wounded are collected, provided they are not military objectives;
- (v) Pillaging a town or place, even when taken by assault;
- (vi) Committing rape, sexual slavery, enforced prostitution, forced pregnancy, enforced sterilization, and any other form of sexual violence also constituting a serious violation of article 3 common to the four Geneva Conventions;
- (vii) Conscripting or enlisting children under the age of eighteen years into armed forces or groups or using them to participate actively in hostilities;
- (viii) Ordering the displacement of the civilian population for reasons related to the conflict, unless the security of the civilians involved or imperative military reasons so demand;
- (ix) Killing or wounding treacherously a combatant adversary;
- (x) Declaring that no quarter will be given;
- (xi) Subjecting persons who are in the power of another party to the conflict to physical mutilation or to medical or scientific experiments of any kind which are neither justified by the medical, dental or hospital treatment of the person concerned nor carried out in his or her interest, and which cause death to or seriously endanger the health of such person or persons;

(xii) Destroying or seizing the property of an adversary unless such destruction or seizure be imperatively demanded by the necessities of the conflict;
(xiii) Employing poison or poisoned weapons;
(xiv) Employing asphyxiating, poisonous or other gases, and all analogous liquids, materials or devices;
(xv) Employing bullets which expand or flatten easily in the human body, such as bullets with a hard envelope which does not entirely cover the core or is pierced with incisions;
(xvi) Intentionally using starvation of civilians as a method of warfare by depriving them of objects indispensable to their survival, including wilfully impeding relief supplies;
(xvii) Utilizing the presence of a civilian or other protected person to render certain points, areas or military forces immune from military operations;
(xviii) Launching an indiscriminate attack resulting in death or injury to civilians, or an attack in the knowledge that it will cause excessive incidental civilian loss, injury or damage;
(xix) Making non-defended localities and demilitarised zones the object of attack;
(xx) Slavery;
(xxi) Collective punishments;
(xxii) Despoliation of the wounded, sick, shipwrecked or dead.

(f). Paragraph (e) applies to armed conflicts not of an international character and thus does not apply to situations of internal disturbances and tensions, such as riots, isolated and sporadic acts of violence or other acts of a similar nature. It applies to armed conflicts that take place in the territory of a State when there is protracted armed conflict between governmental authorities and organized armed groups or between such groups.
(g). Using nuclear weapons or other weapons of mass destruction.

Article 28M Crime of Aggression

A. For the purpose of this Statute, "Crime of Aggression" means the planning, preparation, initiation or execution, by a person in a position effectively to exercise control over or to direct the political or military action of a state or organization, whether connected to the state or not of an act of aggression which, by its character, gravity and scale, constitutes a manifest violation of the Charter of the United Nations or the Constitutive Act of the African Union and with regard to the territorial integrity and human security of the population of a State Party."
B. The following shall constitute acts of aggression, regardless of a declaration of war by a State, group of States, organizations of States, or non-State actor(s) or by any foreign entity:

(a). The use of armed forces against the sovereignty, territorial integrity and political independence of any state, or any other act inconsistent with the provisions of the Constitutive Act of the African Union and the Charter of the United Nations.
(b). The invasion or attack by armed forces against the territory of a State, or military occupation however temporary, resulting from such an invasion or attack, or any annexation by the use of force of the territory of a State or part thereof.
(c). The bombardment by the armed forces of a State against the territory of another State or the use of any weapons by a State against the territory of another State.
(d). The blockade of the ports, coasts or airspace of a State by the armed forces of another State.
(e). The attack by the armed forces of a State on the land, sea or air forces, or marine and fleets of another State.
(f). The use of the armed forces of one State which are within the territory of another State with the agreement of the receiving State, in contravention of the conditions provided for in the African Union Non Aggression and Common Defence Pact or any extension of their presence in such territory beyond the termination of the agreement.
(g). The action of a State in allowing its territory, which it has placed at the disposal of another State to be used by another State for perpetrating an act of aggression against a third State.
(h). The sending or materially supporting by or on behalf of a State of armed bands, groups, irregulars or mercenaries, which carry out acts of armed force against another State of such gravity as to amount to the acts listed above, or its substantial involvement therein.

3.2 Genocide (Article 28B)

The proposed crime of genocide differs from the ICC Statute only in one respect, namely as to a new subpara (f), which adds as a new group of genocidal acts—"acts of rape or any other form of sexual violence". At first sight, this would appear to be a welcome expansion given the sexual violence widespread particularly in African conflicts, but a closer look makes plain that this new subparagraph hardly offers any added value in terms of the traditional scope of the crime of genocide. In fact, sexual violence and, in particular, rape, is already covered by subparas (b) and (d). The Trial Chambers of both the International Criminal Tribunal for the former Yugoslavia (ICTY) and the International Criminal Tribunal for Rwanda (ICTR) have taken causing serious bodily or mental harm (subpara (b)) to include acts of sexual violence and, specifically, rape.[1] Measures "intended to prevent

[1] Ambos 2014, p. 11 with references in nn. 68–69.

births" (subpara (d)) usually include forced sterilization of the sexes, sexual mutilation, forced birth control, separation of the sexes, and prohibition of marriage.[2] In Akayesu, the International Criminal Tribunal for Rwanda referred by way of example to a "case where, during rape, a woman of the said group is deliberately impregnated by a man of another group, with the intent to have her give birth to a child who will consequently not belong to its mother's group."[3] The same Chamber held that "rape can be a measure intended to prevent births when the person raped refuses subsequently to procreate […]"[4]

Of course, the fact that a particular form of conduct is already, at least implicitly, covered by other provisions does not necessarily mean that this behavior should not be explicitly penalized. There may be good reasons for so doing, in particular the desire or need to stress the societal impact of the conduct in question by utilizing the expressive function of such an explicit criminalization.[5] Still, drafters should be aware of possible overlaps since difficulties in the subsequent practical application may otherwise arise. Unnecessary over- or multiple charging as well as delimitation problems for the prosecutorial and judicial authorities may result.

In any case, if the drafters really thought it necessary to expand the scope of the crime of genocide they could have added political groups to the (closed) list of groups in the *chapeau*. In so doing, they would have met a long-standing demand on the part of human rights advocates[6] and have put the crime in the Malabo Protocol (Annex) on an equal footing with some national legislatures (e.g. Colombia).[7]

3.3 Crimes Against Humanity (Article 28C)

The definition of crimes against humanity proposed in para 1 differs in three respects from that of Article 7 of the ICC Statute; the more concrete definitions of individual offences in para 2 are, by contrast, identical.

3.3.1 Instead of getting rid of the "civilian population" element, the infamous transplant from international humanitarian law (a relic of the war crimes origin of

---

[2] Ambos 2014, p. 14.

[3] Akayesu, No. ICTR-96-4-T, para 507.

[4] Ibid., para 508.

[5] On expressivism in International Criminal Law see Drumbl 2007, pp. 173 et seq. and, more recently, Werkmeister 2015, pp. 272 et seq.; with regard to positive general prevention see Ambos 2013, pp. 71–72.

[6] See on the respective discussion Schabas 2009, pp. 153–165.

[7] See Article 101 of the Criminal Code of Colombia ("El que con el propósito de destruir total o parcialmente un grupo nacional, étnico, racial, religioso o *político*, por razón de su pertenencia al mismo, ocasionare la muerte de sus miembros […]" [emphasis added]).

the definition of crimes against humanity),[8] the provision broadens the *chapeau* by adding the term "enterprise" directly after "attack". This certainly requires clarification and will generate controversy. First of all, while "attack" is defined in para 2(a), "enterprise" is not. In other words, the provision introduces a new term without defining it. Secondly, given the expansive definition of "attack" in case law—just recall the broad definition of the Akayesu Trial Chamber encompassing non-violent conduct, e.g. "imposing a system of apartheid […] or exerting pressure on the population to act in a particular manner […]"[9]—and the potential of this term to capture almost any kind of criminal undertaking,[10] one wonders whether introducing the term "enterprise" adds anything to the existing definition. Thirdly, if "enterprise" is meant to add anything, it would have to be understood even more extensively than "attack", for example—in line with the Joint Criminal Enterprise case law[11]—as any concerted or collective conduct directed against a civilian population.[12] Of course, such an interpretation may turn out to be overly broad. Indeed, an entirely different explanation for the addition of the term "enterprise" may follow from the criminal responsibility of legal persons provided for by Article 46C of the Malabo Protocol (Annex). Arguably, this shows that the drafters may, by the use of the term "enterprise" in the *chapeau* of Article 28C, have wished to clarify that legal persons, too, can commit crimes against humanity. The legal meaning of "enterprise"—as an "organization or venture, especially for business purposes"[13]—seems to confirm this hypothesis. Of course, whether this interpretation reflects the true intent of the drafters is unclear since there are no *travaux*. At any rate, Article 28C in its current form does not make legal persons possible agents of the crime but puts the term "enterprise" directly after attack, thereby making clear that it complements the context element of crimes against humanity captured by the widespread and systematic "attack".

3.3.2 As to the crime of torture, para 1(f) adds "cruel, inhuman and degrading treatment or punishment" without, however, defining the latter conduct.[14]

[8] See Ambos 2014, pp. 52, 55, 63 et seq.

[9] Akayesu, No. ICTR-96-4-T, para 581. See also Pre-Trial Chamber II, Situation in the Republic of Kenya, No. ICC-01/09-19, Decision Pursuant to Article 15 of the Rome Statute on the Authorization of an Investigation into the Situation in the Republic of Kenya, para 80 (31 March 2010): "a campaign or operation carried out against the civilian population", albeit not limited to a "military operation" (referring to para 3 of the Introduction to Article 7 in the Elements of Crimes, UN Doc. PCNICC/2000/1/Add.2).

[10] See Ambos 2014, pp. 58–59.

[11] See Ambos, in Triffterer/Ambos 2016, Article 25 marginal no. 9.

[12] See in this vein the definition in the Oxford Advanced Learner's Dictionary 2015, p. 512: "[A] large project, especially one that is difficult."

[13] Garner 2004, p. 572.

[14] See e.g. Article 7 of the International Covenant on Civil and Political Rights which distinguishes between the two.

Surprisingly, para 2(e) contains exactly the same definition as Article 7(2)(e) of the ICC Statute, i.e. only torture is defined. In fact, the difference between torture and the said treatment is one of degree. This point has been most clearly developed in the case law of the European Court of Human Rights, in which torture has come to be defined as an "aggravated and deliberate form of cruel, inhuman or degrading treatment or punishment."[15] The ensuing "humiliation or debasement [...] must attain a particular level and must in any event be other than that usual element of humiliation [...]."[16] As to an inhuman or degrading punishment, the Court held that "the suffering or humiliation involved must in any event go beyond that inevitable element of suffering or humiliation connected with a given form of legitimate punishment."[17] Overall, then, the Court regards the degree of severity of the particular punishment as decisive. Ill-treatment amounts to torture if it causes very serious and grave suffering. A treatment is inhuman if it entails severe psychological or physical suffering, creating in the victim feelings of fear and inferiority.[18]

3.3.3 As to the crime of persecution, para 1(h) adopts the definition of Article 7(1)(h) of the ICC Statute without, however, defining gender.[19] More importantly, para 1(h) also omits the connection requirement, i.e., the requirement that the persecutory conduct take place in "connection with any act referred to in this paragraph or any crime within the jurisdiction of the Court".[20] Thus, given the nature of persecution as a kind of umbrella crime that needs to be fleshed out by the underlying acts,[21] it is unclear how the persecutory conduct must be performed. Para 2(h) of Article 28C offers no further clarification either since here, again, the Malabo Protocol (Annex) adopts the International Criminal Court definition *verbatim*, i.e., without any reference to a concrete form of conduct.

3.4 War Crimes (Article 28D)

As in the ICC Statute, the war crimes provision contains the highest number of individual crimes. In fact, it even goes beyond the 53 crimes of Article 8 of the ICC Statute, adding 14 more and thus bringing the total to 67 crimes. We will return to the new crimes below and will analyze the provisions in order of

---

[15] European Court of Human Rights, Ireland v. the United Kingdom, 18 January 1978, Case No. 5310/71, para 167.

[16] European Court of Human Rights, Tyrer v. UK, Judgment 25 April 1978, Case No. 5856/72, para 30.

[17] European Court of Human Rights, Soering v. UK, Judgment 7 July 1989, Case No. 14038/88, para 100.

[18] See Grabenwarter 2014, Article 3 marginal no. 4.

[19] As defined in Article 7(3) of the ICC Statute.

[20] Article 7(1)(h) of the ICC Statute.

[21] For a further explanation of the persecution crime see Ambos 2014, pp. 104–108.

appearance, focusing on the differences or missed opportunities *vis à vis* Article 8 of the ICC Statute.

3.4.1 First of all, the *chapeau* is identical to that in Article 8 of the ICC Statute. Thus, the drafters missed the opportunity to delete the highly controversial limitation brought about by the phrase "in particular when committed as part of a plan or policy or as part of a large scale commission of such crimes." While the harm done by this invention of the Rome drafters has been reduced by its interpretation as a jurisdictional element,[22] it still remains an unnecessary limitation of the war crimes provision, and one not required by international (humanitarian) law.[23]

3.4.2 The explicit reference to the 1977 Additional Protocol I to the Geneva Conventions in Article 28D(b) of the Malabo Protocol (Annex) is redundant since Additional Protocol I belongs to the "established framework of international law" referred to in both Article 8(2)(b) of the ICC Statute and Article 28D(b) of the Malabo Protocol (Annex).

3.4.3 Subparagraph (v) of Article 28D(b) adds a new crime of international armed conflict: "Intentionally launching an *attack against works or installations containing dangerous forces* [emphasis added] in the knowledge that such attack will cause excessive loss of life, injury to civilians or damage to civilian objects which will be excessive in relation to the concrete and direct overall military advantage anticipated." This crime is based on Article 56 of the Additional Protocol I which prohibits attacks on "[W]orks or installations containing dangerous forces, namely dams, dykes and nuclear electrical generating stations […]", but the provision nonetheless poses certain difficulties. First of all, it is not possible simply to turn a primary international humanitarian law prohibition into a criminal provision without further ado. In the light of the consequences for possible suspects, the criminalization of such a prohibition calls for special justification. It is unclear whether such a justification existed in the minds of the drafters since there are no *travaux* that might inform us to that effect. Secondly, the Additional Protocol I prohibition is by no means absolute but rather allows for attacks on the works or installations in question if used for military purposes.[24] This is only reasonable. Take, for example, the case that a party to a conflict uses a dam for military purposes. An attack by the other party would then be justified by military necessity. By contrast, the Malabo Protocol's proposal implies that such attacks are absolutely prohibited and may, therefore, be criminalized. This does not reflect the state even of international humanitarian law, let alone that of international criminal law.

22 See Ambos 2014, pp. 118–119.

23 See Dörmann, in Triffterer/Ambos 2016, Article 8 marginal no. 55 ("practical guideline"); see also Tadić, No. ICTY-IT-94-1-T, Opinion and Judgment, 7 May 1997, para 573 and Delalic et al., No. ICTY-IT-96-21-T, Judgment, 16 November 1998, para 195.

24 See Article 56(2) of the Additional Protocol I according to which the protection "shall cease" if the respective installation is used "in regular, significant and direct support of military operations and if such attack is the only feasible way to terminate such support."

3.4.4 As to the *crime of employing weapons and methods of warfare* "which are of a nature to cause superfluous injury or unnecessary suffering or which are inherently indiscriminate in violation of the international law of armed conflict", para (b)(xxi) omits the "provided that" part of Article 8(2)(b)(xx) of the ICC Statute.[25] This means that the Malabo Protocol drafters assume that the employment of the weapons mentioned in this subparagraph is prohibited by international (humanitarian) law and may be criminalized notwithstanding their merely being listed in an annex. This seems a reasonable enough approach insofar as one may consider the employment of such weapons—in light of the certain longstanding prohibitions[26] and general principles of international humanitarian law, in particular the maxim of humanity[27]—to be prohibited by customary law[28] and serious enough to be criminalized. Also, arguably, the "provided that" part of Article 8(2)(b)(xx) of the ICC Statute was not added to limit the provision, but rather to make it easier to add further weapons since many states considered the original to be too narrow.[29] In any case, it seems preferable to have such a list for reasons of legal certainty.

3.4.5 Subparagraph (b)(xxvii) criminalizes "[c]onscripting or enlisting children under the age of eighteen years into the *national armed forces* [emphasis added] or

---

[25] This part reads: "provided that such weapons, projectiles and Materials and methods of warfare are the subject of a comprehensive prohibition and are included in an annex to this Statute, by an amendment in accordance with the relevant provisions set forth in articles 121 and 123."

[26] See Article 23(e) of the Annex to the Hague Convention IV ("In addition to the prohibitions provided by special Conventions, it is especially forbidden […] To employ arms, projectiles, or material calculated to cause unnecessary suffering.") and the Declaration of St. Petersburg of 1868 (stating that legitimate warfare "would be exceeded by the employment of arms which uselessly aggravate the sufferings of disabled men, or render their death inevitable" and that "the employment of such arms would, therefore, be contrary to the laws of humanity").

[27] See International Court of Justice, Advisory Opinion on the Legality of the Threat or Use of Nuclear Weapons, 1996, paras 74-87 (while not finding a specific rule regarding nuclear weapons, see also infra note 51, the Court refers to the principles and rules of international humanitarian law, especially the principles of humanity and distinction).

[28] See Customary International Humanitarian Law I 2005, rule 70, p. 237 ("The use of means and methods of warfare which are of a nature to cause superfluous injury or unnecessary suffering is prohibited.") and rule 71, p. 244 ("The use of weapons which are by nature indiscriminate is prohibited."). See also rule 73, p. 256 ("The use of biological weapons is prohibited.") and rule 74, p. 259 ("The use of chemical weapons is prohibited."). See also Cottier and Křivánek, in Triffterer and Ambos 2016, Article 8 marginal no. 566 (distinguishing between two approaches: "On the one hand, a general principle of humanitarian law prohibits the use of means of warfare that cause superfluous injury or unnecessary suffering or are inherently indiscriminate, leaving it to practice to specify what types of weapons and other means of warfare are thereby excluded. On the other hand, certain weapons are banned per se under specific treaties and customary international law.") and Dörmann, in Triffterer and Ambos 2016, Article 8 marginal no. 203 ("The ICJ in its advisory opinion on nuclear weapons has equated the use of indiscriminate weapons with a deliberate attack on civilians.").

[29] See Cottier and Křivánek, in Triffterer and Ambos 2016, Article 8 marginal no. 571; see also ibid., marginal no. 609 (arguing that the "provided that" part is superfluous, "since States Parties to the Rome Statute are free to add new crimes to the Rome Statute regardless of this specific provision.").

using them to participate actively in hostilities." Here, the drafters missed the opportunity to explicitly include non-state actors, especially militia groups, as the most important agents of this crime in practice. The parallel non-international armed conflict crime explicitly includes such "groups",[30] but is, of course, only applicable to a non-international armed conflict. Thus, in case of an international armed conflict, the conscription or enlisting of children by a non-state actor is not punishable. The Lubanga Pre-Trial Chamber has advanced a broad interpretation, arguing that the qualifier "national" does not entail that the armed forces needs must be "governmental".[31] Yet this is not convincing.[32] On the contrary, the term "national" was introduced precisely for the purpose of limiting the scope of the provision to official armed forces.[33] Also, in international humanitarian law, the term "armed forces" is reserved to the armed forces provided for in national legislation.[34] A broad interpretation to include non-state actors in the provision cannot be reconciled with the principle of legality, which calls for a strict interpretation and prohibits an extension of the offence definition by analogy.[35] Against this background, it would have been wiser for the Malabo Protocol drafters to explicitly include non-state actors ("groups") in the *actus reus* of the international armed conflict crime of enlisting children. As this has not been done, the African Court of Justice and Human and Peoples' Rights will face the same problem as the International Criminal Court with regard to the enlistment of child soldiers into militia groups, namely that a particular conflict has to be qualified as a non-international one in order to be able to apply the non-international armed conflict crime provision in Article 28D(e)(vii).

3.4.6 Article 28D adds a total of further 13 further war crimes in addition to para (b) subpara (v) already cited above. On the one hand, para (b) adds six further crimes of international armed conflict:

(xxviii). Unjustifiably delaying the repatriation of prisoners of war or civilians;
(xxix). Willfully committing practices of apartheid and other inhuman and degrading practices involving outrages upon personal dignity, based on racial discrimination.
(xxx). Making non-defended localities and demilitarised zones the object of attack;
(xxxi). Slavery and deportation to slave labour;
(xxxii). Collective punishments;
(xxxiii). Despoliation of the wounded, sick, shipwrecked or dead;

30 See in contrast Article 8 (2)(e)(vi) of the ICC Statute and here para (e)(vii).

31 Lubanga, No. ICC-01/04-01/06-803-tEN, para 277.

32 Ambos 2014, p. 179.

33 Von Hebel and Robinson 1999, p. 118.

34 See Junod 1987, marginal no. 4462. See also Akayesu, No. ICTR-96-4-T, para 625; Prosecutor v. Musema, No. ICTR-96-13-T, Trial Chamber Judgment, para 256 (27 January 2000).

35 See Article 22 of the ICC Statute and Ambos 2013, pp. 88–95.

On the other hand, para (e) adds seven further crimes of non-international armed conflict:

(xvi). Intentionally using starvation of civilians as a method of warfare by depriving them of objects indispensable to their survival, including willfully impeding relief supplies;

(xvii). Utilizing the presence of a civilian or other protected person to render certain points, areas or military forces immune from military operations;

(xviii). Launching an indiscriminate attack resulting in death or injury to incidental civilian loss, injury or damage;civilians, or an attack in the knowledge that it will cause excessive

(xix). Making non-defended localities and demilitarised zones the object of attack;

(xx). Slavery;

(xxi). Collective punishments;

(xxii). Despoliation of the wounded, sick, shipwrecked or dead.

If one examines the sources of international humanitarian law (the Hague and Geneva law) to identify the legal bases of these crimes, one finds that the six further crimes of *international* armed conflict introduced in para (b) are based on the Geneva Conventions I–IV, the Hague Conventions and the Additional Protocol I. More precisely, subpara (b)(xxviii) is based on Article 118 of the Geneva Convention III[36] and Article 85(4)(b) of the Additional Protocol I;[37] subparas (b)(xxix)[38] and (xxx)[39] likewise find a basis in international humanitarian law. With regard to subpara (b)(xxxi), the general maxim of the humane treatment of prisoners[40] and the rule of fair remuneration of their work[41] apply. Collective punish-

[36] The provision reads: "Prisoners of war shall be released and repatriated without delay after the cessation of active hostilities."

[37] The provision prohibits "unjustifiable delay in the repatriation of prisoners of war or civilians." See also Article 20 of the Annex to the Hague Convention IV.

[38] See Article 16 of the Geneva Convention III ("all prisoners of war shall be treated alike by the Detaining Power, without any adverse distinction based on race") and Article 85(4)(c) of the Additional Protocol I (prohibiting "practices of *apartheid* and other inhuman and degrading practices involving outrages upon personal dignity, based on racial discrimination"). See also Article 4 of the Annex to the Hague Convention IV (prisoners of war "must be humanely treated".).

[39] See Article 11 of the Geneva Convention IV ("In no circumstances may hospital and safety zones be the object of attack. They shall be protected and respected at all times by the Parties to the conflict."). See also Article 60(1) of the Additional Protocol I and Article 25 of the Annex to the Hague Convention IV.

[40] See Article 13 of the Geneva Convention III ("Prisoners of war must at all times be humanely treated."). See also Article 6 of the Annex to the Hague Convention IV (the tasks of the prisoners "shall not be excessive").

[41] See Article 62 of the Geneva Convention III (prisoners "shall be paid a fair working rate of pay by the detaining authorities direct").

ment in the sense of subpara (b)(xxxii) is prohibited by Article 87 of the Geneva Convention III.[42] Finally, subpara (b)(xxxiii) is covered by the property provision of Article 51 of the Geneva Convention II.[43]

The seven crimes of *non-international* armed conflict also rely on several primary provisions of international humanitarian law. Subparagraph (e)(xvi) is based on Article 14 of the Additional Protocol II.[44] Subparagraphs (e)(xvii)[45] and (xviii)[46] find a legal basis in the Geneva Conventions I, IV and the Additional Protocol II. The legal basis of subparas (e)(xix),[47] (xx),[48] (xxi)[49] and (xxii)[50] is identical to that of the prohibitions mentioned above with reference to international armed conflict.

Thus, in sum, all new crimes have a basis in primary provisions of international humanitarian law, but this does not automatically justify their criminalization. There must be an additional element of wrongfulness and gravity that makes

---

[42] The provision reads: "Collective penalties […] are prohibited." See also Article 75(2)(d) of the Additional Protocol I ("The following acts are and shall remain prohibited at any time and in any place whatsoever, whether committed by civilian or by military agents: […] collective punishments."). See also Article 50 of the Annex to the Hague Convention IV.

[43] It defines as a "grave breach" "extensive destruction and appropriation of property, not justified by military necessity and carried out unlawfully and wantonly". See also Article 21 of the Hague Convention IV ("obligations of belligerents with regard to the sick and wounded are governed by the Geneva Convention."), Article 46 and Article 47 of the Annex to the Hague Convention IV.

[44] The provision reads: "Starvation of civilians as a method of combat is prohibited." See also Article 23 of the Geneva Convention IV.

[45] See Article 28 of the Geneva Convention IV ("The presence of a protected person may not be used to render certain points or areas immune from military operations.") and Article 17 of the Additional Protocol II ("Civilians shall not be compelled to leave their own territory for reasons connected with the conflict."). See also Article 83 of the Geneva Convention IV.

[46] See Article 50 of the Geneva Convention I (prohibiting "willfully causing great suffering or serious injury to body or health, and extensive destruction and appropriation of property, not justified by military necessity and carried out unlawfully and wantonly."). Article 13(2) of the Additional Protocol II protects the "civilian population as such, as well as individual civilians" from attacks. See also Article 23 of the Hague Convention IV.

[47] See Article 11 of the Geneva Convention IV and Article 25 of the Hague Convention IV.

[48] See Article 4(2)(f) of the Additional Protocol II (prohibiting "at any time and in any place whatsoever: […] slavery and the slave trade in all their forms."). See also Article 13 of the Geneva Convention III, Article 62 of the Geneva Convention III, Article 49 of the Geneva Convention IV.

[49] See Article 4(2)(b) of the Additional Protocol II (prohibiting "at any time and in any place whatsoever: […] collective punishments."). See also Article 87 of the Geneva Convention III, Article 33 of the Geneva Convention IV, Article 50 of the Annex to the Hague Convention IV ("No general penalty, pecuniary or otherwise, shall be inflicted upon the population on account of the acts of individuals for which they cannot be regarded as jointly and severally responsible.").

[50] See Article 4(2)(g) of the Additional Protocol II (prohibiting "at any time and in any place whatsoever: […] pillage." See also Article 51 of the Geneva Convention II, Article 21, Article 46, Article 47 of the Annex to the Hague Convention IV.

criminalization necessary. It would have been up to the drafters to demonstrate that this is the case for each new crime proposed.

3.4.7 Paragraph (g) adds a new armed conflict crime with regard to the use of "nuclear weapons or other weapons of mass destruction". However, this blanket criminalization lacks the necessary differentiation called for in the International Court of Justice's advisory opinion on the matter. The Court held that neither customary nor conventional international law specifically authorizes or prohibits the threat or use of nuclear weapons.[51] It further held that such use would only be unlawful if it contravened Article 2(4) of the UN Charter and was not justified by self-defence under Article 51 of the UN Charter.[52] Ultimately, the Court left open whether such a threat or use "would be lawful or unlawful in an extreme circumstance of self-defense, in which the very survival of a State would be at stake."[53] Thus, to claim that the threat and, *a fortiori*, the use of nuclear weapons is unlawful and may even be criminalized requires much more than the laconic statement of para (g). Ultimately, the question is whether the use of these weapons contravenes the provisions in international humanitarian law mentioned above, which prohibit the employment of weapons that "cause superfluous injury or unnecessary suffering."[54] In any case, the fact that nuclear weapons have not been included in the annex referred to in Article 8(2)(b)(xx) of the ICC Statute[55] argues against their criminalization under existing law.

3.4.8 Article 28D omits Article 8(3) of the ICC Statute. This is a step to be welcomed since the reaffirmation of "the responsibility of a Government to maintain or re-establish law and order in the State or to defend the unity and territorial integrity of the State, by all legitimate means" (with regard to the non-international armed conflict crimes) can easily be used by authoritarian governments to justify a lack of respect for the prohibition under international humanitarian law and any subsequent criminalization under international criminal law.

3.4.9 Last but not least, it is worth pointing out on a general note that Article 28D opts for an almost complete merger of international and non-international armed conflict crimes. It thereby suggests the abolition of the traditional two-box approach in favor of one common category of armed conflict crimes and thus

---

51 See International Court of Justice, Advisory Opinion on the Legality of the Threat or Use of Nuclear Weapons, 1996, para 105 2(A) and (B) ("There is in neither customary nor conventional international law any specific authorization of the threat or use of nuclear weapons [...]. There is in neither customary nor conventional international law any comprehensive and universal prohibition of the threat or use of nuclear weapons as such.").

52 Ibid., 2(C) ("A threat or use of force by means of nuclear weapons that is contrary to Article 2, para 4, of the Charter of the United Nations and that fails to meet all the requirements of Article 51 is unlawful.").

53 Ibid., 2(E).

54 See Article 35(2) of the Additional Protocol I and Article 35(3) of the Additional Protocol I (regarding "widespread, long-term and severe damage to the natural environment"). See also supra note 26.

55 See already supra note 25.

follows the same approach as the German Code of International Criminal Law (*Völkerstrafgesetzbuch*).[56]

3.5 Crime of Aggression (Article 28M)

3.5.1 First of all, it is striking that this "crime of crimes" is located after all other crimes, including the transnational ones, at the end of the crimes Sect.

3.5.2 The *first paragraph* of the provision in which the "Crime of Aggression" is defined entails an unclear and controversial expansion of the *actus reus* instead of its much needed limitation. It reads as follows:

> A. For the purpose of this Statute, "Crime of Aggression" means the planning, preparation, initiation or execution, by a person in a position effectively to exercise control over or to direct the political or military action of a state or organization, whether connected to the state or not of an act of aggression which, by its character, gravity and scale, constitutes a manifest violation of the Charter of the United Nations or the Constitutive Act of the African Union and with regard to the territorial integrity and human security of the population of a State Party. [The underlined part is new in relation to Article 8*bis*(1) of the ICC Statute.]

Thus, on the one hand, this definition adopts Article 8*bis*(1) of the ICC Statute, including the controversial criminalization of mere preparatory acts ("planning, preparation"),[57] and it omits to introduce any limitation, especially at the subjective level by way of a special aggressive intent (*animus aggressionis*).[58] On the other hand, the definition extends the "manifest violation" element to violations of the "Constitutive Act of the African Union" and, more importantly, to violations of ("with regard to") "the territorial integrity and human security of the population of a State Party". Thus, a "manifest violation" of the UN Charter is not required. Rather, a violation—the wording "with regard to" is somewhat unclear– of "territorial integrity and human security" is deemed to suffice. This despite the considerable ambiguity of the latter term in particular.

3.5.3 The *second paragraph* defining the underlying "acts of aggression" differs in various respects from Article 8*bis*(2) of the ICC Statute:

Firstly, it omits the general definition of an act of aggression as "the use of armed force by a State against the sovereignty, territorial integrity or political independence of another State, or in any other manner inconsistent with the Charter of the United Nations." Secondly, it lacks the explicit reference to GA Resolution 3314

[56] See Sects. 8 to 12 of the Völkerstrafgesetzbuch; for an English translation see: http://www.department-ambos.uni-goettingen.de/index.php/forschung/projekte/translations.

[57] Critical Ambos 2014, pp. 188, 208–210.

[58] See Werle and Jeßberger 2014, p. 544; see also Ambos 2014, pp. 199, 211.

(XXIX) of 14 December 1974 which, after all, served as the—albeit problematic—starting-point for the negotiations in the Special Working Group.[59]

Thirdly, it extends the concept of an act of aggression in two ways: on the one hand, to a "group of" or "organizations of States"; on the other hand, to "non-State actor(s)" and "any foreign entity".[60] While the former extension is largely superfluous—collectivities of states refer to a plurality of states and are thus covered by the reference to "a State" –, the latter represents an important material extension of the concept that deserves critical analysis. The phrase "non-State actors" includes any armed group able to wage an act of aggression, i.e. organized armed groups within the meaning of international humanitarian law possessing a unified military command, a hierarchical structure and accompanying military capacity.[61] An obvious example would be ISIS or the Taliban. By contrast, it is unclear what is meant by a "foreign entity". It is, of course, evident that the term does not include states since these are mentioned earlier in the text. Given the criminal responsibility of corporations,[62] the phrase may refer to legal entities in the sense of legal persons, but such "entities" would certainly need military assistance to perform acts of aggression.

Fourth, as regards the individual acts of aggression, this paragraph adds a new act (subpara (a)) and makes various mainly editorial changes with regard to some of the other acts. The new subpara (a) adds as an act of aggression "[t]he use of armed forces against the sovereignty, territorial integrity and political independence of any state, or any other act inconsistent with the provisions of the Constitutive Act of the African Union and the Charter of the United Nations." This complements, in a way, the expansion of the crime's definition in para 1, omitting the reference to human security but adding "sovereignty" and "political independence" as the object of the "use of armed forces" and, in the alternative ("or"), including "any other act" "inconsistent" with the two documents mentioned. All in all, this constitutes a critical expansion as compared to the Resolution 3314 definition and will hardly find the support of major military powers.

The other changes contained in para 2 as compared to the list of Article 8*bis*(2) of the ICC Statute, i.e. Resolution 3314, are of more minor importance and may therefore be summarized in the following list containing the acts which have undergone changes. The parts in square brackets contain the text of Article 8*bis*(2)

---

[59] On this resolution see Ambos 2014, pp. 197, 202–204.

[60] The text reads (the underlined part is newly added): "The following shall constitute acts of aggression, regardless of a declaration of war by a State, group of States, organizations of States, or non-State actor(s) or by any foreign entity.".

[61] See Ambos 2014, pp. 125–126. For a non-exhaustive list of relevant factors see Lubanga, No. ICC-01/04-01/06-2842, para 537: "the force or group's internal hierarchy; the command structure and rules; the extent to which military equipment, including firearms, are available; the force or group's ability to plan military operations and put them into effect; and the extent, seriousness, and intensity of any military involvement".

[62] Article 46C of the Malabo Protocol (Annex).

of the ICC Statute omitted or replaced by the Malabo Protocol (Annex) provision (therefore crossed out in the square brackets); underlined words or parts have been added by the Malabo Protocol (Annex) and do not appear in the ICC Statute:

(b). The invasion or attack by [~~the~~] armed forces [of a State] against [~~of~~] the territory of a [another] State, or [~~any~~] military occupation however temporary, resulting from such an invasion or attack, or any annexation by the use of force of the territory of a [another] State or part thereof.

(c). <u>The</u> bombardment by the armed forces of a State against the territory of another State or the use of any weapons by a State against the territory of another State.

(e). The [an] attack by the armed forces of a State on the land, sea or air forces, or marine and fleets of another State.

(f). The use of <u>the</u> armed forces of one State which are within the territory of another State with the agreement of the receiving State, in contravention of the conditions provided for in the <u>African Union Non-Aggression and Common Defence Pact</u> [~~agreement~~] or any extension of their presence in such territory beyond the termination of the agreement.

(g). The action of a State in allowing its territory, which it has placed at the disposal of another State to be used by another [that other] State for perpetrating an act of aggression against a third State.

(h). The sending <u>or materially supporting</u> by or on behalf of a State of armed bands, groups, irregulars or mercenaries, which carry out acts of armed force against another State of such gravity as to amount to the acts listed above, or its substantial involvement therein.

The change in subpara (b) is a consequence of the extension of the act of aggression to non-state actors, although it is awkward to speak of "armed forces" when referring to such armed groups since this is a term traditionally reserved—as observed above—to state forces.

3.5.4 In any case, the most important change with regard to the above list constitutes the phrase "or *materially supporting* [emphasis added]" in subpara (h). This considerably broadens the scope of this subparagraph and arguably goes beyond the International Court of Justice's "effective control test" and, perhaps, even beyond the broader "overall control test" of the International Criminal Tribunal for the former Yugoslavia. Both tests aim to establish a standard for determining the responsibility of a state for the conduct of non-state actors, i.e., both tests pretend to propose convincing rules of attribution.

According to the International Court of Justice in the *Nicaragua* case, the decisive prerequisite for holding a state responsible for the acts of non-state actors, that is for attributing these acts to the state, is the state's *effective control* over these actors;[63] by contrast, mere material support for the non-state actor in question is not sufficient.[64] More specifically, the Court found that "to equate the Contras, for legal purposes, with an organ of the United States Government, or as acting on behalf of that Government", it would have been necessary for "the relationship of the Contras to the United States Government [...] [to have been] so much one of dependence on the one side and control on the other [...]".[65] The Court distinguished two types of non-state actors who can be considered to be acting on a state's behalf. On the one hand, those who are completely dependent on a state for money, equipment, guidance, and direction and where, therefore, the supporting state exercises almost complete control and their acts can thus be attributed to this state.[66] On the other hand, individuals who receive material support from a state but maintain a substantial amount of autonomy.[67] In the latter case, attribution under the prohibition of the use of force paradigm (Article 2(4) of the UN Charter) is possible,[68] but for attribution under international humanitarian law the Court must apply a different test.[69] Thus, the Court held that the United States must have "directed or enforced the perpetration of the acts contrary to human rights and humanitarian law."[70] According to this "effective control standard", certain knowledge as to the supply of arms or even the commission of crimes does not suffice to assume liability.[71] Rather, an ordering or forcing of the rebels to carry out specific human rights violations is necessary.[72] By contrast, there is no attribution as long as the said groups maintain some degree of autonomy without actually being explicitly ordered by the supporting state to engage in violations.[73] As a result, the

[63] International Court of Justice, *Nicaragua v. U.S.*, Judgment 27 June 1986, available under: http://www.icj-cij.org/docket/files/70/6503.pdf, para 115 ("For this conduct to give rise to legal responsibility of the United States, it would in principle have to be proved that that State had effective control of the military or paramilitary operations in the course of which the alleged violations were committed.").

[64] Ibid., para 115 ("The Court has taken the view [paragraph 110 above] that United States participation, even if preponderant or decisive, in the financing, organizing, training, supplying and equipping of the *contras*, the selection of its military or paramilitary targets, and the planning of the whole of its operation, is still insufficient in itself, on the basis of the evidence in the possession of the Court, for the purpose of attributing to the United States the acts committed by the *contras* in the course of their military or paramilitary operations in Nicaragua.").

[65] Ibid., para 109.

[66] Ibid., para 110.

[67] Ibid., para 113, 114.

[68] Ibid., para 241, 242.

[69] Ibid., para 115.

[70] Ibid.

[71] Ibid., para 116.

[72] Ibid., para 116, 119, 122.

[73] Ibid., para 114.

Court denied "effective control" of the United States over the Contras,[74] and only found a "partial dependency" through the choosing of the Contras' leaders, as well as the organizing, training, and equipping of their forces.[75] Thus, pursuant to the "effective control test", merely offering material support to non-state actors, as required by subpara (h), is not sufficient to hold a state accountable for violations committed by these groups.

Would the "*overall control* test" applied by the International Criminal Tribunal for the former Yugoslavia Appeals Chamber in the Tadić case lead to a different result? While the Tadić Trial Chamber followed the effective control test,[76] the Appeals Chamber rejected it, arguing that "the criterion for ascertaining State responsibility is different from that … for establishing individual criminal responsibility."[77] Instead, the Chamber proposed the overall control test, focusing on the persons or groups allegedly controlled by a foreign state. According to this test, an attribution regarding military or paramilitary groups can be affirmed if it is proven "that the State wields overall control over the group, not only by equipping and financing the group, but also by coordinating or helping in the general planning of its military activity."[78] The issuing of specific orders by the state or its direction of each individual operation is not necessary.[79] As far as individuals or non-military groups are concerned, specific instructions or directives aimed at the commission of specific acts or their public approval after commission are required.[80] Thus, the "overall control test" is, with regard to military groups, more flexible than the "effective control test" in that it does not require specific instructions to be given to these groups by the relevant state.[81]

According to another proposal suggested by the International Law Commission in its Draft Articles on State Responsibility,[82] a state is responsible for group actions when (1) the group is acting in accordance with the state's instructions, (2)

---

[74] Ibid., para 115.

[75] Ibid., para 106-112.

[76] See Ambos 2014, p. 136.

[77] Prosecutor v. Duško Tadić, Judgment 15 July 1999, Case No. IT-94-1-A, available under: http://www.icty.org/x/cases/tadic/acjug/en/tad-aj990715e.pdf, para 103.

[78] Ibid., para 131.

[79] Ibid., para 137 ("Under international law it is by no means necessary that the controlling authorities should plan all the operations of the units dependent on them, choose their targets, or give specific instructions concerning the conduct of military operations and any alleged violations of international humanitarian law.").

[80] See ibid., para 132; see also Ambos 2014, p. 136.

[81] Ibid., para 131 ("However, it is not necessary that, in addition, the State should also issue, either to the head or to members of the group, instructions for the commission of specific acts contrary to international law.").

[82] Draft articles on Responsibility of States for Internationally Wrongful Acts, with commentaries, 2001, available at http://legal.un.org/ilc/texts/instruments/english/commentaries/9_6_2001.pdf.

is "directed" by the state or (3) the state (otherwise) exercises control over the group.[83] This control and direction must apply to specific human rights violations. This test is, thus, in effect very similar to the one applied by the International Court of Justice in the Nicaragua case, although the term "effective control" is not explicitly used. Clearly, mere material support does not suffice. Thus, such support may only be considered sufficient under the overall control test with regard to military groups.

3.6 Conclusion

The brief inquiry has shown that the Malabo Protocol goes beyond Articles 5-8*bis* of the ICC Statute in various respects. While this may, at least in part, be accounted for by specific African concerns, for example as regards the crime of aggression and the existing common defence pact, it also seems to suggest that the drafters have a great deal of faith in criminal law's capacity to solve at least some of the ills of (African) societies. For a German scholar, such faith is not justified since criminal law can only contribute very little to the solution of what are basically socio-economic problems and should be used only *ultima ratio,* that is as a reaction to very serious rights violations. In any case, the lack of any *travaux* leaves the drafters' intent unclear.

Not all the core crimes in the Annex to the Malabo Protocol rely on a solid basis in international (criminal) law. Recourse to that somewhat numinous entity 'regional custom' cannot make up for this (partial) lack of a foundation in international law since the proposed treaty advocates broad provisions on extraterritorial jurisdiction going beyond African borders[84] and would thus entail interference in foreign (non-African) jurisdictions. Thus, many of the (core) crimes will have to be restricted or at least to be interpreted narrowly. The threshold clause of the corruption crime of Article 28I, limiting it to acts of a "serious nature affecting the stability of a state, region or the Union", may give helpful guidance in this regard.

Acknowledgments The author would like to thank Professors Ademola Abass, Florian Jeßberger, Dire Tladi, and Gerhard Werle as well as Mr. Selemani Kinyunyu for their critical comments. I also wish to thank my research assistant Ms. Jasmin Marjam Rezai-Dubiel for her invaluable assistance in preparing this chapter.

[83] Ibid., Article 8.

[84] See Article 46E*bis*(2) providing for jurisdiction based on active and passive personality and the protection principle.

References

Ambos K (2013) Treatise on international criminal law, Vol. 1: foundations and general part. Oxford University Press, Oxford

Ambos K (2014) Treatise on international criminal law, Vol. 2: the crimes and sentencing. Oxford University Press, Oxford

Drumbl MA (2007) Atrocity, Punishment and International Law. Cambridge University Press, Cambridge

Garner BA (2004) Black's Law dictionary, 8th edn. Thomson/West, St. Paul

Grabenwarter C (2014) European Convention on Human Rights: commentary. Beck, Munich

von Hebel H, Robinson D (1999) Crimes within the Jurisdiction of the Court. In: Lee RS (ed) The international criminal court: the making of the Rome Statute. Kluwer Law International, The Hague, pp 79–126

Junod S-S (1987) Article 1 Protocol II. In: Sandoz Y, Swinarski C, Zimmermann B (eds) Commentary on the Additional Protocols of 8 June 1977 to the Geneva Conventions of 12 August 1949. Martinus Nijhoff Publishers, Geneva, pp 1347–1356

Schabas WA (2009) Genocide in international law: the crime of crimes, 2nd edn. Cambridge University Press, Cambridge

Triffterer O, Ambos K (eds) (2016) The Rome Statute of the International Criminal Court: a commentary, 3rd edn. Beck et al., Munich et al., Article 7, 8, 8bis, 25

Werkmeister A (2015) Straftheorien im Völkerstrafrecht. Nomos, Baden-Baden

Werle G, Jeßberger F (2014) Principles of international criminal law, 3rd edn. Oxford University Press, Oxford

Chapter 4
The Crime of Unconstitutional Change of Government (Article 28E)

Gerhard Kemp and Selemani Kinyunyu

Abstract The crime of unconstitutional change of government does not exist as a discrete crime under international law. However, given Africa's post-colonial history, as well as a number of African regional frameworks addressing the phenomena collectively known as unconstitutional changes of government, it came as little surprise that the drafters of the Malabo Protocol decided to include this crime in the Annex to the Protocol. The historical, institutional, and normative influences informing the criminalization of unconstitutional changes of government are addressed in this chapter. We also analyze some of the key features and contentious aspects of the crime. It is submitted that the criminalization of unconstitutional changes of government is a noteworthy African response to a pervasive African problem. The criminal provision is not without some flaws, which we also highlight.

Keywords Africa · African Union · crimes under international law · unconstitutional change of government · African Charter on Democracy · elections and governance

---

The views expressed here do not represent the views of the African Court of Human and Peoples' Rights.
All internet sources in this chapter were last visited on 30 June 2016.

G. Kemp (✉)
Stellenbosch University, Stellenbosch, South Africa
e-mail: Gkemp@sun.ac.za

S. Kinyunyu
African Court on Human and Peoples' Rights, Arusha, Tanzania
e-mail: selemani@gmail.com

G. Werle and M. Vormbaum (eds.), *The African Criminal Court*, International Criminal Justice Series 10, DOI 10.1007/978-94-6265-150-0_4

Contents

4.1 Extracts from the Malabo Protocol (Annex)

Article 28E The Crime of Unconstitutional Change of Government

1. For the purposes of this Statute, 'unconstitutional change of government' means committing or ordering to be committed the following acts, with the aim of illegally accessing or maintaining power
   (a). A putsch or coup d'état against a democratically elected government
   (b). An intervention by mercenaries to replace a democratically elected government
   (c). Any replacement of a democratically elected government by the use of armed dissidents or rebels or through political assassination
   (d). Any refusal by an incumbent government to relinquish power to the winning party or candidate after free, fair and regular elections
   (e). Any amendment or revision of the Constitution or legal instruments, which is an infringement on the principles of democratic change of government or is inconsistent with the Constitution
   (f). Any substantial modification to the electoral laws in the last six (6) months before the elections without the consent of the majority of the political actors
2. For purposes of this Statute, "democratically elected government" has the same meaning as contained in AU instruments

4.2 Introduction

On 16 September 2015, members of the transitional government (including the President of the Transition) of the West-African state of Burkina Faso were kidnapped and unlawfully detained. The following day, a military coup d'état was staged by members of the elite presidential unit, the *Régiment de sécurité présidentielle*. The intention was apparently to derail the process of political transition in Burkina Faso.[1] The African Union condemned these events and, at its 544th meeting held on 18 September 2015, the African Union Peace and Security Council adopted a decision pertaining to the situation.[2] The operative part of the decision concerned the following measures:

- The immediate suspension of Burkina Faso from all African Union activities, in accordance with the African Union Constitutive Act and the African Charter on Democracy, Elections and Governance.
- The automatic imposition of certain measures against the alleged perpetrators of the coup, unless the *status quo ante* be restored within 96 h from the adoption of the African Union decision. The measures imposed included: a travel ban and asset freeze on all members of the so-called "National Committee for Democracy" put in place by the perpetrators of the coup d'état, as well as on any person participating in any Government that they might establish; the labeling as "terrorist elements" of senior officers of the *Régiment de sécurité présidentielle* involved in the kidnapping of the President of the Transition, the Prime Minister and some members of Government, all within the framework of the Organization of African Unity Convention on the Prevention and Combating of Terrorism (1999) and its Protocol (2004); the initiation of consultations with relevant African Union and international institutions with a view to bringing to justice the perpetrators in accordance with the African Charter on Democracy, Elections and Governance (2007); the launching of consultations with the West African Monetary Union with a view to denying the leaders of the coup access to the resources of the West African State Central Bank; and a request to all bilateral and multilateral partners to suspend military, security and economic cooperation with Burkina Faso, but with minimum impact on the civilian population.

It is evident from the African Union's response that the coup was viewed as an unconstitutional change of government. The African Union's reaction was unequivocal and multifaceted. It combined economic, political, security and legal responses in a coordinated effort to send a clear message. For present purposes, one aspect of the response, namely the resolve to bring to justice the perpetrators in accordance with the African Charter on Democracy, Elections and Governance, is of particular interest, as the criminalization of unconstitutional changes of government is the focus of the present chapter. The coup in Burkina Faso serves as a clear reminder that the African continent is still struggling with a scourge that has plagued the continent and its people for decades.

---

[1] See report available at http://www.abc.net.au/news/2015-09-19/african-union-condemns-burkina-faso-coup/6788636.

[2] See AU Peace and Security Council, Communiqué of 18 September 2015, PSC/PR/COMM/3. (DXLIV). http://www.peaceau.org/uploads/psc-544-comm-burkina-faso-18-9-2015.pdf.

We are concerned with the history of post-colonial efforts to deal with political instability, militarism and coups. Both the Organization of African Unity and its successor, the African Union, adopted various frameworks aimed at the eradication of unconstitutional changes of government. The most important of these is the African Charter on Democracy, Elections and Governance (2007).

Before entering into a discussion on the crime of unconstitutional change of government under the Malabo Protocol (Annex), it is important to note the institutional and normative frameworks that currently exist on the continent and that have bearing on the preservation of democracy and political stability. It will be shown that the twin ideals of democracy and political stability serve as underlying protected interests for the purpose of the criminalization of unconstitutional changes of government. This does not mean, however, that the definition of the crime as it stands is not open to criticism. The definition of the crime of unconstitutional change of government is therefore critically and contextually analyzed in the latter part of the chapter.

4.3 Unconstitutional Changes of Government and the Pan-African Ideal

Following the liberation of Africa from colonialism in the late 1950s and early 1960s, the stability and unity of the continent was tested by a colossal number of violent coups and counter-coups. Ayalew estimates there have been 80 coups and 180 attempted coups between 1956 and 2001.[3] Recent events such as the developments in Burkina Faso mentioned above add to the tally.

Africa is, of course, not unique in this respect. Many coups have also happened and continue to happen in the rest of the world, including the Americas, Eastern Europe, South East Asia and Pacific Ocean states.[4] However, it is important to remember that the vision of the then Organization of African Unity, different from any other regional grouping, was to create a United States of Africa—a federation of all African States.[5] For a region trying to establish its cohesiveness and unity, coups and the broader challenges of unconstitutional political change posed a serious challenge to this vision. It prevented Africans from speaking with one voice in the international arena and was also viewed as impeding socio-political development.

[3] Ayalew 2012, p. 4.

[4] For a comparative and empirical survey, see Galetovic and Sanhuenza 2000, pp. 183–204.

[5] For an articulation of these ideals by one of the "founding fathers" of post-colonial Africa, see Nyerere 1963, pp. 1–6.

4.4 A Brief Historical and Legislative Narrative of the Norms Against Unconstitutional Changes of Government from 1963 to Date

The Organization of African Unity's primary goal was the liberation of Africa from colonialism. The Organization subscribed to the principle of non-interference, which made sovereignty central to its agenda. However, due to the scale of the unconstitutional changes[6] taking place and the gravity of their concomitant effects, many African States came to feel that it was time to review the Organization's position on the issue. At least three factors contributed to this:

- The cyclical nature of coups and military regimes in countries deepened the appreciation that peace and stability are essential to achieving socio-economic development. There was a strong desire to encourage good governance, human rights and democracy in order to create a basis for development and true stability.
- Following the end of the Cold War, many African countries reassessed their political alliances and the need to wage proxy wars diminished.
- Technology—especially live television broadcasts from conflict hotspots—brought home the realities of wars. The images and stories of the Rwandan genocide and the Liberia and Sierra Leone wars had a profound impact on the psyche of the African region.

Due to the limited mandate of the Organization of African Unity, the institution did not have the necessary mechanisms to deal with unconstitutional changes of government and gross human rights violations. The Organization therefore relied on policy pronouncements including Article 13(1) of the African Charter on Human and Peoples' Rights which provided for the right of citizens to participate freely in their government "either directly or through freely chosen representatives."

At the Zimbabwe Summit in 1997, the Council of Ministers of the Organization of African Unity took a firm stand against unconstitutional changes of government, declaring its total rejection and condemnation of the coup d'état which occurred in Sierra Leone on 25 May 1997, and calling for the immediate restoration of constitutional order. Shortly thereafter in 2000 at Lomé, the Organization adopted the Declaration on the Framework for an Organization of African Unity Response to Unconstitutional Changes of Government popularly known as the "Lomé Declaration".[7]

[6] For a discussion of the most common forms and manifestations of unconstitutional changes of government, see Omotola 2011, pp. 20–31.

[7] For more information, see The African Union and the challenge of unconstitutional changes, ISS Paper 197 August 2009. https://www.issafrica.org/uploads/P197.PDF; Sturman 2011.

However, it was not until the formulation of the African Union Constitutive Act in 2001[8] that—for the first time outside the realm of customary practice—the African Union adopted a binding legal instrument prohibiting unconstitutional changes of government. The Constitutive Act provided for the rejection and condemnation of unconstitutional changes of government and the suspension of governments coming to power by unconstitutional means.

This was followed in 2003 by the adoption of the Protocol to the Constitutive Act Relating to the Establishment of the Peace and Security Council.[9] The Council is mandated to impose sanctions in situations of unconstitutional changes and is, in practice, the body tasked with making determinations as to whether unconstitutional changes have taken place.

In 2007, with the adoption of the African Charter on Democracy, Elections and Governance,[10] unconstitutional change of government was defined. Article 23 of the Charter lists five acts amounting *inter alia* to unconstitutional changes, namely:

1. Any putsch or coup d'état against a democratically elected government.
2. Any intervention by mercenaries to replace a democratically elected government.
3. Any replacement of a democratically elected government by armed dissidents or rebels.
4. Any refusal by an incumbent government to relinquish power to the winning party or candidate after free, fair and regular elections; or
5. Any amendment or revision of the constitution or legal instruments, which is an infringement on the principles of democratic change of government.

The Charter also imposed sanctions on perpetrators of unconstitutional changes of government. It provided that such individuals are neither allowed to participate in elections held to restore the democratic order nor to hold any position of responsibility in political institutions of their State (Article 25(4)). Further, that they might be tried before the competent court of the African Union (Article 25(5)) and be subject to additional sanctions as applied by the African Union Assembly, including punitive economic measures (Article 25(7)). Article 25(5) is especially important as it extended criminal responsibility for unconstitutional changes of government to individuals. The Charter also created an enforcement mechanism based on the principle of prosecute or extradite by barring states parties from giving sanctuary to perpetrators of unconstitutional changes of government, requiring states instead to prosecute the individuals involved or take necessary steps to effect their extradition.

---

[8] African Union Constitutive Act. www.au.int/en/sites/default/files/ConstitutiveAct_EN.pdf.

[9] Protocol to the Constitutive Act Relating to the Establishment of the Peace and Security Council. www.peaceau.org/uploads/psc-protocol-en.pdf.

[10] African Charter on Democracy, Elections and Governance. http://www.achpr.org/instruments/charter-democracy/.

The provisions of Article 23 of the African Charter on Democracy, Elections and Governance that define acts giving rise to unconstitutional changes are in *par materia* with the first five acts under Article 28E(1) of the Malabo Protocol (Annex). The sixth act giving rise to unconstitutional changes of government under Article 28E(1)(f) of the Malabo Protocol (Annex) was drawn from Article 2(1) of the Economic Community of West African States (ECOWAS) Protocol on Democracy and Good Governance.[11] It prohibits any substantial modification to the electoral laws in the last six months before the elections without the consent of the majority of the political actors.

It is evident from the historical genesis of the norm against unconstitutional changes of government that the pre-eminent regional body, first the Organization of African Unity and then the African Unity clearly recognized that unconstitutional changes of government posed a threat to the ideals of post-colonial Africa. However, it is also clear that the collective security structure was, on balance, either unwilling or unable to address this very significant problem effectively. At the same time, inaction was not a political option.

The political reaction to the problem manifested itself in the creation of a clear norm against unconstitutional changes of government, as concretized and detailed in a number of Organization of African Unity and African Union instruments, notably the African Charter on Democracy, Elections and Governance, which provides for sanctions in cases of unconstitutional changes of government. Crucially, Article 25(5) of this Charter provides that "Perpetrators of unconstitutional change of government may also be tried before the competent court of the Union." Thus, a clear criminal justice avenue is created within the scope and paradigm of a political framework to deal with unconstitutional changes of government.

Following the 2011 North African Uprisings, some North African states were worried that popular uprisings might be criminalized. Other Member States were concerned that "legitimizing" popular revolutions would encourage rebellions, instability and the breakdown of law and order. The discussion on the crime of unconstitutional change of government was highly contentious and, as a result, the drafters included a proviso to Article 28E of the draft Malabo Protocol (Annex). It read: "Any act of a sovereign people peacefully exercising their inherent right which results in a change of government shall not constitute an offence under this Article."

In June 2012, the draft Protocol was presented to the African Union Assembly. However, the Assembly requested clarification on financial and structural implications as well as on the definition of the crime of unconstitutional change of government. Its decision reads, in part, as follows:

> "STRESSES the need for the AU to adopt a definition of the crime of unconstitutional change of government and, in this regard, request the Commission in collaboration with

[11] Economic Community of West African States (ECOWAS) Protocol on Democracy and Good Governance http://www.internationaldemocracywatch.org/attachments/350_ECOWAS%20Protocol%20on%20Democracy%20and%20Good%20Governance.pdf.

> the AU Commission on International Law and the African Court on Human and Peoples' Rights to submit this definition for consideration by the policy organs at the next Summit to be held in January 2013."[12]

The June 2012 decision was particularly notable for the request to the African Union Commission to define the crime of unconstitutional change of government. This request was raised by several North African states, notably Algeria and Egypt, which had at the time undergone popular revolutions.

In December 2012, a number of stakeholders, including the African Court on Human and Peoples' Rights, the African Union Commission on International Law, and the Office of the Legal Counsel, met in Arusha, Tanzania to consult on the definition. They proposed that the Court would not exercise jurisdiction over the crime until the Peace and Security Council had adopted a definition of popular uprisings in the context of unconstitutional changes of government, and set out the conditions of exercising such criminal jurisdiction.

In April 2014, the Peace and Security Council held a session on the theme "Unconstitutional Changes of Government and Popular Uprisings in Africa, Challenges and Lessons Learnt." The objective of the session was to provide a forum for deep reflection on the elements that constitute an unconstitutional change of government on the one hand, and how to respond to popular uprisings that result in a change of government inconsistent with constitutional provisions on the other. However, despite the dialogue, no consensus on the definition of "popular uprisings" could be reached.

In May 2014, the Specialized Technical Committee on Justice and Legal Affairs amended and cleared the draft instrument before it was tabled for adoption consideration before the African Union Assembly. The Committee retained the definition of the crime of unconstitutional change of government without specific reference to popular uprisings. The criminal justice reaction to unconstitutional changes of government thus manifested itself in Article 28E of the Malabo Protocol (Annex).

4.5 The Crime of Unconstitutional Change of Government: Some Critical Observations

4.5.1 Legality and the List of Actus Reus

When a norm is transformed into a crime it is important not to lose sight of one of the foundational principles of criminal law, namely the principle of legality. This principle is so well-established that it is deemed to be part of customary international law.[13] It is also protected under international and regional human rights

[12] Decision on the Protocol on Amendments to the Protocol on the Statute of the African Court of Justice and Human Rights Doc. Assembly/Au/13(XIX)A.

[13] Werle and Jeßberger 2014, marg. number 113.

instruments, including the International Covenant on Civil and Political Rights (1966)[14] and the African Charter on Human and Peoples' Rights.[15] When a crime is defined in written form, the principle of legality entails that criminal conduct must be laid down as clearly as possible. Some commentators have pointed out that the standard of legality is less rigid under international criminal law than is generally required in, for instance, continental European law.[16]

Criminal Law ought, in principle, not be extensively construed. In case of doubt, a strict interpretation that is not to the detriment of the accused should be followed. This also entails that criminalization by analogy, where the scope of the crime becomes broader as a result of judicial interpretation, is generally unacceptable. Individuals must therefore be in a position to know from the wording of a definition what acts will lead to criminal liability. It is nonetheless conceivable that the wording of a criminalization provision require clarification. After all, cases differ in terms of their factual matrix, and where a new crime is imposed, it is even more important for courts to clarify and interpret. The principle of legality, then, permits courts to clarify the rules of criminal liability gradually, provided that the resultant development is consistent with the essence of the offence and could reasonably be foreseen.

In order to achieve the goal of foreseeability, crimes must be narrowly defined and unambiguously worded. One regional human rights court—the Inter-American Court of Human Rights—has explained the principle of legality with reference to a number of elements: First, crimes must be classified and described in precise and unambiguous language that narrowly defines the punishable offence. Second, the principle requires a clear definition of the criminalized conduct, establishing its elements and the factors that distinguish it from behavior that would not be a punishable offence. Third, ambiguity in the definition of crimes creates doubts and the opportunity for the abuse of power.[17]

The crime of unconstitutional change of government as provided for in the Malabo Protocol (Annex) contains a number of acts of varying degrees of specificity. For instance, an "intervention by mercenaries[18] to replace a democratically elected government" is, on the face of it, relatively plain and straightforward. The meaning of "democratically elected government"—insofar as this is a term the meaning of which may not be immediately obvious—is further qualified by a reference to the term's meaning under "AU instruments". We shall return to the issue of incorporation by reference later. It is however clear enough that the act here is any act by mercenaries that results in the replacement of a democratically elected government.

---

[14] Article 15(1).

[15] Article 7(2).

[16] Werle and Jeßberger 2014, marg. number 113.

[17] Inter-American Court of Human Rights, *Castillo Petruzzi* et al. *v Peru*, 30 May 1999 (Merits) par 121. http://www.univie.ac.at/bimtor/dateien/iacthr_1999_castillo-petruzzi_vs_peru.pdf.

[18] Mercenarism is also a separate crime under Article 28H of the Malabo Protocol (Annex). See on this crime the chapter by Jeßberger in this book.

It is not always possible in the definition of a crime to define in detail every aspect or element of the crime. Many instruments of international criminal law, such as the ICC Statute, for instance, provide for Elements of Crimes in order to further guide the interpretation of a crime. But for the purposes of the principle of legality it is not necessary to have a detailed exposition of the elements of a crime in an instrument, as long as the criminalized conduct is sufficiently clear. The meaning of "mercenaries", for instance, need not be further defined. Neither is it necessary to further define "intervention" here, because the context makes clear that the term cannot mean democratic and peaceful political processes to effect a change in government. The meaning of the act is, however, potentially obscured by the attempt to clarify it through the incorporated reference to other African Union instruments ostensibly dealing with the meaning of "democratically elected government".

For purposes of interpretation by a future criminal court such incorporation by reference is certainly helpful. For purposes of the principle of legality, the question is whether the "fair meaning" of the crime is clear enough. The most relevant African Union instrument to be incorporated here by reference is the African Charter on Democracy, Elections and Governance. Article 3 of the Charter provides for a number of principles that clarify the meaning of "democratically elected", including the principles of political pluralism and multi-party politics. Since the Malabo Protocol (Annex) does not provide for Elements of Crimes, the incorporation of a key African Union instrument on the underlying protected norm is indispensable. To be sure, incorporation by reference does not per se violate the principle of legality.[19] But one must also note that incorporation by reference in international criminal law normally involves the incorporation by reference of another instrument of international criminal law, in other words the incorporation of an already well-established or newly crafted *criminal framework*. Examples are the Genocide Convention, or Common Article 3 of the Geneva Conventions. Incorporating by reference instruments that are more general in nature (such as general human rights instruments or policy frameworks) can potentially undermine the legality principle. It is true that, with reference to the approach to legality, there is a more lenient tradition in international criminal law.[20] But even under a more lenient approach it is required that a criminal definition be sufficiently clear; defined with a degree of specificity; and with some legislative history or contextual materials for interpretative purposes.[21]

It is evident that there is a degree of specificity in Article 28E that delimits the notion of unconstitutional change of government for purposes of criminal liability. The article links specific acts to the *chapeau*. The incorporation by reference of the meaning of "democratically elected government" may be helpful for purposes of interpretation, especially since there is no legislative history of the provision or

---

[19] Paust 1997, p. 671.

[20] Cassese 2003, p. 143.

[21] Paust 1997, p. 668.

indeed an Elements of Crime provision to draw upon. The ultimate test from a legality point of view is whether individuals can reasonably understand the "fair meaning" of Article 28E. Some commentators have noted that draft versions of Article 28E were phrased in such broad terms that legality concerns could justifiably be raised.[22] We do not believe that Article 28E in its present form is, *as a whole,* too vague or not specific enough from a legality point of view. We do, however, think that the way in which some of the specific *actus rei* are drafted will cause problems of interpretation, thus reflecting on the legality of some of the other provisions as well. There are furthermore problems relating to the interplay between Article 28E and other provisions in the Protocol that are more problematic than legality.

An example of a badly drafted *actus reus* in Article 28E is the following: Article 28E(1)(e) provides that "unconstitutional change of government" means committing or ordering to be committed, with the aim of illegally accessing or maintaining power, "*[a]ny amendment or revision of the Constitution or legal instruments, which is an infringement on the principles of democratic change of government or is inconsistent with the Constitution*" [emphasis added]. This is certainly a provision in need of clarification and redrafting to make it more elegant and clear. The essence of this provision seems to be aimed at amendments or revisions of national constitutions and laws that significantly alter the democratic nature of the legal and political order. But why the disjunctive? The provision ought in plain terms to state what the criminalized *actus reus* is. What if an amendment to a national constitution is inconsistent with the constitution, but the aim is indeed to make it more democratic? The words "or is inconsistent with the Constitution" therefore appear to be redundant and in conflict with the general thrust of the crime created in Article 28E. Again, we do not think that badly drafted clauses in Article 28E invalidate the crime of unconstitutional change of government as a whole (there are other clauses that are plain and susceptible to fair meaning) but a clause like 28E(1)(e) does undermine the legality principle.

4.5.2 Mens Rea

The Malabo Protocol (Annex) does not provide for a general *mens rea* clause comparable to Article 30 of the ICC Statute. In the absence of a general *mens rea* clause it is necessary to interpret the language of the relevant criminalization clauses of the Protocol in order to ascertain the applicable forms of *mens rea.*

The *chapeau* of Article 28E makes reference to the various acts having been committed or ordered to be committed with "the aim of illegally accessing or maintaining power". The ordinary meaning of the word "aim" is "a purpose; an

---

[22] Du Plessis 2014, p. 202.

intention".[23] The word "aim" is also often used as a synonym for the noun "intention", as per the following explanation: "*a purpose or goal; aim: it is his intention* [...]" [emphasis added].[24] It is thus clear that the drafters created a crime of intent. The perpetrator must commit or order another person or persons to commit any of the listed acts, with the intent of illegally accessing or maintaining power. It is submitted that knowledge of unlawfulness is required. The perpetrator must know that he/she is illegally (as per one or more of the acts listed in Article 28E) accessing or maintaining power. One may ask why the drafters opted for the word "aim" instead of the more commonly used legal-technical term of "intent"? In the absence of any documented legislative history we cannot say for sure, but it is worth noting that there is little or no semantic difference between "aim" and "intent". Indeed, an *aim* is generally defined as "a clearly directed intent or purpose".[25] "Aim", which is the culpability term here,[26] means that the accused must have knowledge of the consequence of the specific *actus reus*, namely the unlawful obtainment or maintenance of political power through specified means.

An earlier draft of Article 28E provided for the following clause: "[a]ny act of a sovereign people peacefully exercising their inherent right [sic] which results in a change of government shall not constitute an offence under this article". The removal of these words from the final version of Article 28E means that the illegality of the obtainment and maintenance of power are implied by the specific acts listed. Knowledge of the nature of the specific acts can thus serve as a good indication of knowledge of unlawfulness. The ambiguity contained in Article 28E(1)(e)—as pointed out under 4.5.1 above—may cause some problems and is in need of clarification.

4.5.3 The Crime of Unconstitutional Change of Government in Context

We have noted that the establishment of the crime of unconstitutional change of government was motivated by the will to foster the twin ideals of peace and democratic governance on the African continent. At the same time, perhaps because history teaches that it is sometimes necessary to resort to less peaceful means in order to achieve political freedom, self-determination and democracy, the drafters of the Malabo Protocol (Annex) initially deemed it necessary to provide for a "democracy exception" in Article 28E (cf. 4.5.2). We have also pointed out that

[23] Oxford Advanced Learner's Dictionary (1995). An online dictionary defines it thus: "Your goal, purpose, or aim is your intention" (http://www.vocabulary.com/dictionary/intention).

[24] http://dictionary.reference.com/browse/intention.

[25] http://www.merriam-webster.com/dictionary/aim.

[26] For more on culpability terms in (international) criminal law, see in general Chap. 1 of Badar 2013.

the ambiguity in Article 28E(1)(e) may have the unfortunate consequence that the provision is not only vague (thus causing legality problems) but may also be regarded as over-criminalizing avenues of resistance against oppressive regimes or constitutional orders. One can compare this to the crime of terrorism under Article 28G. The latter contains a defence under Article 28G(C): "the struggle waged by peoples in accordance with the principles of international law for their liberation or self-determination, including armed struggle against colonialism, aggression and domination by foreign forces shall not be considered as terrorist acts." Given the inclusion of a self-determination defense in the context of the crime of terrorism, it seems even more advisable to clarify the scope of the *actus reus* under Article 28E(e).

There is one remaining matter that we would like to highlight, namely the issue of immunities. This is not something that we wish to address here in depth or detail, but it is important to note that the immunities provision in Article 46A*bis* does have the potential to undermine the effectiveness of the crime of unconstitutional change of government. Indeed, how can one reconcile the *actus reus* contained in para (d) of Article 28E ("refusal by an incumbent government to relinquish power to the winning party or candidate after free, fair and regular elections") with the broad immunity accorded to serving African Union heads of state or government, or anybody acting or entitled to act in such capacity, or other senior state officials based on their functions? The qualification "during their tenure of office" does not refer to democratic standards or any substantive meaning of what tenure entails. Does tenure end when an incumbent President refuses to leave office after a democratic and free election? If so, then the immunities provision and the crime of unconstitutional change of government are indeed compatible. If not, there seems to be a significant contradiction with the potential to render Article 28E(d) meaningless.

4.6 Concluding Remarks

A cursory reading of African political history from the early post-colonial period to the present time reveals that coups and other forms of unconstitutional changes of government are, unfortunately, pervasive, if no longer endemic. The African Union and its predecessor took a strong stance against unconstitutional changes of government. This political stance is reflected in regional instruments. The normative rationale for the criminalization of unconstitutional changes of government under the Malabo Protocol (Annex) is clear. What is less clear is the exact scope and elements of the crime. Some of the acts constituting the crime of an unconstitutional change of government are more precise than others. This raises concerns of legality. The interplay between the crime of unconstitutional change of government and some of the other provisions of the Malabo Protocol (Annex), notably the immunities clause, creates potential contradictions that may undermine the effective prosecution of the crime. Ultimately, however, it is our view that the crime of unconstitutional change of government is based on a sound normative rationale. There are weaknesses in Article 28E that may very well lead to prosecutorial difficulties. There is certainly room for better drafting. But on the whole this crime should be in the Protocol (Annex). It is our qualified view that the norm against unconstitutional change of government has been transformed into a criminal provision, the fair meaning of which should be clear to the people of Africa.

References

African Union (2003) Protocol to the Constitutive Act Relating to the Establishment of the Peace and Security Council. www.peaceau.org/uploads/psc-protocol-en.pdf

African Union (2007) African Charter on Democracy, Elections and Governance. http://www.achpr.org/instruments/charter-democracy/

Ayalew AT (2012) African Court of Justice and Human and Peoples' Rights: prospects and challenges of prosecuting unconstitutional changes of government as an international crime. LLM thesis, University of Pretoria. http://repository.up.ac.za/bitstream/handle/2263/37278/Ayalew_African_2012.pdf?sequence=1

Badar ME (2013) The concept of mens rea in international criminal law: the case for a unified approach. Hart Publishing, Oxford

Cassese A (2003) International criminal law. Oxford University Press, Oxford

Du Plessis M (2014) A (new) new regional international criminal court for Africa? South African Journal of Criminal Justice 2:199–209

Galetovic A, Sanhuenza R (2000) Citizens, autocrats, and plotters: a model and new evidence on coups d'état. Econ. Politics 12:183–204

Institute for Security Studies (2009) The AU and the challenge of unconstitutional changes. https://www.issafrica.org/uploads/P197.PDF

Nyerere JK (1963) A United States of Africa. J Mod Afr Stud 1:1–6

Omotola JS (2011) Unconstitutional changes of government in Africa—what implications for democratic consolidation. Discussion Paper 70, Nordiska Afrikainstitutet, Uppsala

Paust JJ (1997) It's no defense: Nullum crimen, international crime and the Gingerbread Man. Albany Law Rev 60:657–679

Sturman K (2011) Unconstitutional changes of government: the democrat's dilemma in Africa. Policy Briefing 30, South African Institute of International Affairs, Cape Town

Werle G, Jeßberger F (2014) Principles of international criminal law, 3rd edn. Oxford University Press, Oxford

Chapter 5
Piracy (Article 28F), Terrorism (Article 28G) and Mercenarism (Article 28H)

Florian Jeßberger

Abstract The Malabo Protocol adopted by the African Union in 2014 envisages the empowerment of the African Court of Justice and Human and People's Rights, inter alia, with international criminal jurisdiction. The chapter reflects on three specific crimes which will be subject to the jurisdiction of the Court—piracy, terrorism, and mercenarism. It explores their origins in international treaties, analyses their elements and argues that these crimes ("transnational crimes") must be distinguished from other crimes within the jurisdiction of the Court, such as genocide and war crimes ("crimes under international law"). The chapter shows that the Court will be the first international tribunal ever provided with jurisdiction over transnational crimes and concludes with the recommendation not to rashly repudiate the (perhaps: over-) ambitious project of regionalizing the enforcement of international and transnational criminal law.

Keywords Africa · African Court of Justice and Human and People's Rights · mercenarism · piracy · terrorism · transnational crimes

Contents

F. Jeßberger (✉)
Universität Hamburg, Hamburg, Germany
e-mail: florian.jessberger@uni-hamburg.de

G. Werle and M. Vormbaum (eds.), *The African Criminal Court*, International Criminal Justice Series 10, DOI 10.1007/978-94-6265-150-0_5

5.1 Extracts from the Malabo Protocol (Annex)

Article 28F Piracy
Piracy consists of any of the following acts:

(a) any illegal acts of violence or detention, or any act of depredation, committed for private ends by the crew or the passengers of a private boat, ship or a private aircraft, and directed:

   i. on the high seas, against another boat, ship or aircraft, or against persons or property on board such boat, ship or aircraft;
   ii. against a boat, ship, aircraft, persons or property in a place outside the jurisdiction of any State

(b) any act of voluntary participation in the operation of a boat, ship or of an aircraft with knowledge of facts making it a pirate boat, ship or aircraft;
(c) any act of inciting or of intentionally facilitating an act described in sub-para (a) or (b).

Article 28G Terrorism
For the purposes of this Statute, 'terrorism' means any of the following acts:

A. Any act which is a violation of the criminal laws of a State Party, the laws of the African Union or a regional economic community recognized by the African Union, or by international law, and which may endanger the life, physical integrity or freedom of, or cause serious injury or death to, any person, any number or group of persons or causes or may cause damage to public or private property, natural resources, environmental or cultural heritage and is calculated or intended to:

   1. intimidate, put in fear, force, coerce or induce any government, body, institution, the general public or any segment thereof, to do or abstain from doing any act, or to adopt or abandon a particular standpoint, or to act according to certain principles; or
   2. disrupt any public service, the delivery of any essential service to the public or to create a public emergency; or
   3. create general insurrection in a State.

B. Any promotion, sponsoring, contribution to, command, aid, incitement, encouragement, attempt, threat, conspiracy, organizing, or procurement of any person, with the intent to commit any act referred to in sub-para (a) (1) to (3).
C. Notwithstanding the provisions of paras A and B, the struggle waged by peoples in accordance with the principles of international law for their liberation or self-determination, including armed struggle against colonialism, occupation, aggression and domination by foreign forces shall not be considered as terrorist acts.

D. The acts covered by international Humanitarian Law, committed in the course of an international or non-international armed conflict by government forces or members of organized armed groups, shall not be considered as terrorist acts.
E. Political, philosophical, ideological, racial, ethnic, religious or other motives shall not be a justifiable defence against a terrorist act.

Article 28H Mercenarism

1. For the purposes of this Statute:
   (a) A mercenary is any person who:
      i. Is specially recruited locally or abroad in order to fight in an armed conflict;
      ii. Is motivated to take part in the hostilities essentially by the desire for private gain and, in fact, is promised, by or on behalf of a party to the conflict, material compensation;
      iii. Is neither a national of a party to the conflict nor a resident of territory controlled by a party to the conflict;
      iv. Is not a member of the armed forces of a party to the conflict; and
      v. Has not been sent by a State which is not a party to the conflict on official duty as a member of its armed forces.
   (b) A mercenary is also any person who, in any other situation:
      i. Is specially recruited locally or abroad for the purpose of participating in a concerted act of violence aimed at:
         1. Overthrowing a legitimate Government or otherwise undermining the constitutional order of a State;
         2. Assisting a government to maintain power;
         3. Assisting a group of persons to obtain power; or
         4. Undermining the territorial integrity of a State;
      ii. Is motivated to take part therein essentially by the desire for private gain and is prompted by the promise or payment of material compensation;
      iii. Is neither a national nor a resident of the State against which such an act is directed;
      iv. Has not been sent by a State on official duty; and
      v. Is not a member of the armed forces of the State on whose territory the act is undertaken.
2. Any person who recruits, uses, finances or trains mercenaries, as defined in para (1)(a) or (b) above commits an offence.
3. A mercenary, as defined in para (1)(a) or (b) above, who participates directly in hostilities or in a concerted act of violence, as the case may be, commits an offence.

5.2 Introduction

This chapter presents preliminary reflections on three specific crimes which will be subject to the jurisdiction of the African Court of Justice and Human Peoples' Rights—piracy, terrorism, and mercenarism. The chapter is divided into three sections. First, it presents general observations on the specific nature of these crimes and distinguishes them from the crimes under international law (also known as the "core" crimes); this analytical framework will provide the basis for the critical discussion that follows (5.3). In the second part the chapter turns to the definitions of the crimes as laid down in the Annex to the Malabo Protocol and will in particular discuss their origin in international and regional treaties (5.4). The chapter concludes with a few general remarks on the African Court of Justice and Human and Peoples' Rights in light of the previous analysis (5.5).

5.3 Piracy, Terrorism, and Mercenarism as Transnational Crimes

Compared with other international criminal courts—both past and present—the jurisdiction of the yet to be established African Court of Justice and Human and Peoples' Rights is uniquely broad. In particular, the Court's jurisdiction is not limited to crimes under international law, that is genocide, crimes against humanity, war crimes, and the crime of aggression. Rather, according to Article 28A(1) of the Malabo Protocol (Annex), the jurisdiction of the African Court of Justice and Human and Peoples' Rights includes ten additional crimes such as corruption, money laundering,[1] trafficking in drugs and persons,[2] illicit exploitation of natural resources,[3] and, notably, piracy, terrorism, and mercenarism.

These additional crimes, in particular those included in Article 28A(1) nos. 5–13, are of a specific nature and can thus be distinguished from the crimes subject to Article 28A(1) nos. 1 to 3 and 14.[4] The distinction runs along the line between transnational criminal law on the one hand and international criminal law *stricto* sensu on the other.[5]

---

[1] See the chapter by Fernandez in this book.

[2] See the chapter by Mninde-Silungwe in this book.

[3] See the chapter by Heger in this book.

[4] The crime of unconstitutional change of government, Article 28A(1) no. 4 is a pure state protection crime, i.e. it protects the interests only of the affected state, not of a group of states and not of the international community as a whole, and must therefore be distinguished from the other crimes under the jurisdiction of the Court. For a thorough analysis, see Kemp and Kinyunyu's chapter in this book.

[5] For this conceptual distinction, which today seems widely accepted although not uncontroversial, see Boister, EJIL 14 (2009), 953, 2012, p. 13; Chehtman in: van der Wilt 2016 (forthcoming); Werle and Jeßberger 2014, marg. number 125 et seq.

Today it is beyond dispute that criminal responsibility arising directly under international law exists for a limited number of crimes, those known as the crimes under international law. These crimes include genocide, war crimes, crimes against humanity, and the crime of aggression. They form part of international criminal law *stricto sensu* ("Völkerstrafrecht", "droit international pénal", "derecho penal internacional").[6] In contrast, transnational criminal law can be defined as "the indirect suppression by international law through domestic penal law of criminal activities that have actual or potential trans-boundary effects".[7] Typically, this "indirect" suppression of criminal activities refers to international and regional treaties.[8] Unlike *crimes under international law*, criminal responsibility for *transnational crimes* is not established directly under international law. Rather, the pertinent treaties describe a certain conduct (the "transnational crime") and establish legal duties for the States Party to the treaties to criminalize this conduct under their domestic law.

Within this analytical framework the three crimes discussed in this chapter—piracy, terrorism, and mercenarism—are to be categorized as transnational crimes.[9] In a nutshell, they differ from crimes under international law, including those ("core") crimes subject to the jurisdiction of the African Court of Justice and Human and Peoples' Rights, in several respects: the mode of criminalization (indirect vs. direct), the protected interest (shared interest of the states concerned vs. interest of the international community as a whole), the rationale and need for "internationalization" (enforcement gap due to a lack of transnational judicial cooperation vs. enforcement gap due to the—generally—state-sponsored nature of the crime) and, arguably, the rationale for making them subject to the jurisdiction of the new Court. As regards the latter, the establishment of the African Court of Justice and Human and Peoples' Rights primarily aims to address concerns which were voiced on several occasions by African heads of state and government through the African Union regarding the exercise of universal jurisdiction by some

[6] See Werle and Jeßberger 2014, marg. number 89 et seq.

[7] Boister 2012, p. 13. Often transnational crime will be trans-border crime. It would, however, be misleading to conceptually equate "transnational crime" and "trans-border crime". The term "transnational" refers to the type of the regulation (international treaty) and the trigger for regulation (transnational concern) rather than to the nature of the actual conduct regulated. For instance, trafficking in human beings and corruption are transnational crimes within the meaning used here although they certainly do not require, as a matter of law, that the specific act is transboundary.

[8] Because transnational criminal law "consists of horizontal treaty obligations between states" (Boister), transnational crimes have also been referred to as "treaty-based (international) crimes"; see Ambos 2013, p. 222 ("Treaty Crimes"); Currie and Rikhof 2014; Jeßberger in: Calliess 2014 , pp. 527, 528; Werle and Jeßberger 2014, marg. number 126.

[9] As regards the crime of (international) terrorism this classification is a matter of controversy. According to a minority view, which in the view of this author is not convincing, international terrorism is in fact a crime under international law; for both views see Werle and Jeßberger 2014, marg. number 129 et seq.

European states and, more particularly, the alleged "Africa bias" of the International Criminal Court.[10] The inclusion of transnational crimes, such as piracy, terrorism, and mercenarism, however, follows a different line of argument. Presumably, providing the African Court of Justice and Human and Peoples' Rights with jurisdiction over transnational crimes intends to complement and strengthen the existing treaty-based system of enforcement, which to date lies exclusively in the hands of states. In addition, addressing transnational crimes takes account of the principles of the African Union, including the "respect for the sanctity of human life, condemnation and rejection of impunity and political assassination, acts of terrorism and subversive activities".[11]

The Annex to the Malabo Protocol does not reflect the conceptual divide between transnational crimes and crimes under international law. This is unfortunate because it mixes apples with oranges which, in turn, gives rise to a number of concrete problems. For instance, it is not beyond dispute that the set of general principles applicable to crimes under international law can and should be equally valid for transnational crimes. Nevertheless, the Annex to the Malabo Protocol extends a number of legal concepts which were originally developed for crimes under international law to transnational crimes. This includes, inter alia, superior liability under Article 46B(3) and the non-applicability of statutory limitation under Article 28A(3).

A second concern relates to the provisions on immunity.[12] According to Article 46B(2) the fact that the perpetrator acted in an official capacity does not relieve him or her of criminal responsibility. There is a notable exception under Article 46A*bis* for "senior state officials" who enjoy immunity during their tenure in office. The immunity provisions are remarkable in two respects since, on the one hand (and beyond the scope of this chapter), they broaden immunity for "senior state officials" for ("core") crimes under international law when compared with immunity under customary international law.[13] On the other hand, they remove immunity for non-senior state officials for transnational crimes. The latter is the much more problematic aspect. As regards transnational crimes, such as piracy, terrorism, and mercenarism, the Annex to the Malabo Protocol takes away any

---

[10] For these concerns and their merit see, inter alia, Werle and Jeßberger 2014, marg. number 71.

[11] Article 4(o) of the Constitutive Act of the African Union; see also Malabo Protocol, Preamble.

[12] On this topic, see also Tladi's chapter in this book.

[13] Under general international law, immunity *ratione personae* for genocide, crimes against humanity, war crimes, and aggression is exclusively granted to heads of state or government and foreign ministers. The Statute, however, uses the rather vague term "senior state officials", which could be understood in a much broader way. More importantly, under customary international law, immunity *ratione personae* for "core" crimes is only granted before national courts, not international criminal courts. Thus, although *not a violation* of international law (because international law grants permission to prosecute, but does not establish an obligation), the immunity exception for "senior state officials" for core crimes under international law under Article 46A*bis* is regarded as one of the major flaws in the Malabo Protocol (Annex) and has been widely criticized.

form of immunity for *non-senior* state officials. This appears to contradict customary international law. It is a settled principle of public international law that public officials enjoy immunity *(ratione materiae)* from prosecution before foreign courts. Arguably, this rule extends to international and regional *fora*. At least in cases where the African Court of Justice and Human and Peoples' Rights exercises jurisdiction over nationals of a state not party to the Statute (see, for example, Article 46E*bis*(2)(a)), the argument that would otherwise be available—that the States Party to the Malabo Protocol have waived the immunity of their officials by way of ratification of the Protocol—does not apply.

5.4 The Definitions of Piracy, Terrorism and Mercenarism

The crimes of piracy, terrorism, and mercenarism are defined in Article 28F to Article 28H of the Malabo Protocol (Annex). A common feature of all three definitions is that none of them was newly drafted for the purpose of the Malabo Protocol. Rather, the drafters borrowed the definitions from existing international or regional treaties.

At first sight, this approach seems wise. The transfer and incorporation of definitions from treaty law ensures consistency between the law applicable to the African Court of Justice and Human and Peoples' Rights and other (domestic) courts and therefore seems to pay the highest respect to the principle of legality. On closer inspection, however, the "copy and paste" approach gives cause for concern. First, as has been explained, the treaty provisions were never meant to define crimes, i.e. to establish individual criminal responsibility for unlawful behaviour. Rather, their purpose is to describe a certain conduct which should then be criminalized under domestic law in order to enable enhanced judicial cooperation between the States Party to the treaty.[14] Second, while the drafters of the Annex to the Malabo Protocol borrowed the definitions of the crimes from the respective treaties, they did not, however, incorporate other treaty provisions, first and foremost those dealing with general principles of criminal law. With this selective cherry-picking approach, the drafters risk omitting other, crucial parts of the "system" established under the treaty. Finally, not every Member State of the African Union is a State Party to the respective treaties and not every African State Party to the respective treaty has incorporated the respective treaty provisions into its domestic legal order. Therefore the argument of consistency and respect for the *nullum crimen* principle carries less weight.

---

[14] For instance, the UN Convention on the Law of the Sea defines piracy in Article 101 in particular with a view to: the obligation of states to "cooperate to the fullest extent in the repression of piracy" (Article 100), the right of states to "seize a pirate ship", "arrest the persons on board", and the authority of "the courts of the State which carried out the seizure" to "decide upon the penalties to be imposed" (Article 105).

5.4.1 Piracy

Piracy is defined in Article 28F of the Malabo Protocol (Annex). The definition is drawn *verbatim* from Article 101 of the 1982 UN Convention of the Law of the Sea[15] and reflects customary international law.[16] As a legal concept piracy has a long history in international law. Within the analytical framework outlined above, piracy is not a crime under international law, but a transnational crime. In addition, piracy can also be classified as a 'crime of universal jurisdiction', which means that customary international law allows for the prosecution of pirates by any state. The crime of piracy protects various legal interests, in particular the interests (life, physical integrity, property) of those individuals directly affected by the act of piracy, but also the shared interests of at least a large number of states (safety of sea and air traffic on the high seas as a precondition for international trade and mobility). The expansion of the jurisdiction of the African Court of Justice and Human and Peoples' Rights over the crime of piracy is to be applauded. For a long time maritime piracy, in particular off the coast of Somalia, has been of particular relevance for the African continent. As practice has shown the prosecution of pirates by domestic courts is problematic. Therefore many have argued in favour of the establishment of an "international piracy court" or the expansion of the International Criminal Court's jurisdiction over the crime of piracy.[17] If established, the African Court of Justice and Human and Peoples' Rights would be the first international court with the mandate to try and to punish pirates.

According to Article 28F(a) of the Malabo Protocol (Annex) the *actus reus* of the crime of piracy consists of an illegal act of violence, detention or depredation carried out by the crew or passengers of a private boat, ship or aircraft and directed against (persons or property on board of) another boat, ship or aircraft ("two vessel requirement"). In cases of domestic prosecution, i.e. those situations envisaged by the UN Convention, the question under what system of law the act must be "illegal" can easily be answered. However, the answer is less obvious in the case of international prosecution of piracy. Here it can be argued that the (domestic) criminal law of the state whose flag the aircraft or vessel is flying is relevant in determining the "illegality" of the pirate act.

The territorial scope of the crime is limited to acts committed on the high seas or in other places outside the jurisdiction of any state. In addition, the act must be committed for private ends, which excludes any action sanctioned by a state authority.[18] As a separate offence, Article 28F(b) of the Malabo Protocol (Annex)

---

[15] The Convention was adopted in 1982 and entered into force in 1994. Today, 166 states, including the majority of African states (with only a few exceptions, such as Libya, Rwanda, and the Central African Republic) and the EU have joined the treaty.

[16] But see n. 16 infra.

[17] See, e.g., O'Brien 2014, p. 81.

[18] Whether the element refers to subjective motivation (and excludes politically motivated acts from piracy) or, as is suggested here, to the fact whether, objectively, a state is involved, is a matter of controversy; see Guilfoyle 2015, p. 372.

criminalizes the participation in the operation of a boat, ship, or of an aircraft with the knowledge of facts making it a pirate boat, ship or aircraft.

5.4.2 Terrorism

The crime of terrorism is set out in Article 28G. The definition is taken from Article 1 of the 1999 OAU Convention on the Prevention and Combating of Terrorism,[19] with the exception of subsection (d) which has no model in an international or regional treaty.[20] The inclusion of terrorism in the jurisdiction of the Court reflects the global trend to increasingly rely on criminal law for the suppression of terrorist violence. In Africa, terrorism is a prevalent phenomenon, particularly in the Sahel region and the Horn of Africa. In addition, terrorism has a historical dimension as the concept of "terrorism" was used by the colonial powers and apartheid South Africa to delegitimize liberation movements.

Defining terrorism is notoriously difficult. The choice by the drafters of the Annex to the Malabo Protocol to select the OAU Convention as a blueprint is not self-evident. On the international level, treaty law is "sectoral" only: the existing conventions do not address terrorism comprehensively; rather, they suppress specific types of violence commonly used by terrorists. The work on the comprehensive UN Draft Convention against International Terrorism is still ongoing, although there seems to be consensus at least as regards the elements of the crime.[21]

---

[19] The Convention was adopted in 1999 in Algiers and entered into force in 2003. 40 out of 54 AU Member States are parties to the Convention.

[20] The corresponding provision in the OAU Convention reads: "Nothing in this Convention shall be interpreted as derogating from the general principles of international law, in particular the principles of international humanitarian law, as well as the African Charter on Human and Peoples' Rights."

[21] See Saul in: Boister and Currie 2015, p. 400. Article 2 of the UN Draft Convention reads:

1. "Any person commits an offence within the meaning of the present Convention if that person, by any means, unlawfully and intentionally, causes:
   (a) Death or serious bodily injury to any person; or
   (b) Serious damage to public or private property, including a place of public use, a State or government facility, a public transportation system, an infrastructure facility or to the environment; or
   (c) Damage to property, places, facilities or systems referred to in para 1(b) of the present article resulting or likely to result in major economic loss;
   when the purpose of the conduct, by its nature or context, is to intimidate a population, or to compel a Government or an international organization to do or to abstain from doing any act.
2. Any person also commits an offence if that person makes a credible and serious threat to commit an offence as set forth in para 1 of the present article."
3. Any person also commits an offence if that person attempts to commit an offence as set forth in para 1 of the present article."

Under Article 28G Malabo Protocol (Annex), the act which forms the *actus reus* of the crime is qualified in two regards: First, the act must be unlawful. Unlike in the OAU Convention, the criterion for the determination of the "unlawfulness" is not limited to the (domestic) "criminal laws of a State Party". Rather, an act is "unlawful" under Article 28G if it violates "the laws of the African Union or a regional community recognized by the African Union, or by international law". Secondly, the act must either endanger or violate important individual interests (life, physical integrity, freedom) of a person or a group of persons or "cause or may cause damage to public or private property, natural resources or environmental or cultural heritage". The inclusion in particular of acts which may cause damage to natural resources or environmental or cultural heritage as terrorist acts significantly broadens the scope of the crime.[22] The *mens rea* of the crime of terrorism requires specific intent on part of the perpetrator ("is calculated or intended to"). According to Article 28G(a)(1)–(3) the perpetrator must either intend to intimidate or coerce a government or the general public to do or abstain from doing something or must intend to disrupt public services. Subsection (a)(1)(3) adds a third variation of the specific intent, namely the intent to "create general insurrection in a State". With the exception of the OAU Convention this third variation lacks any corresponding provision in international (treaty) law and, arguably, combines distinct legal concepts by reclassifying insurrection as terrorism.

Article 28G(D) refers to a particularly controversial issue: whether the crime of terrorism is applicable during armed conflict.[23] According to Article 28G(D) all acts covered by international humanitarian law shall not be considered terrorist acts for the purpose of the Statute. In this regard, Article 28G departs from the OAU Convention according to which the provisions of the Convention and international humanitarian law shall be applicable side by side.[24] To exclude terrorist acts committed during armed conflict from the jurisdiction of the Court may, at first sight, run counter to customary international criminal law which classifies terror against the civilian population as a prohibited method of warfare and, ultimately, a war crime.[25] However, unlike the treaty law on terrorism, the present provision must be read in connection with the provision on war crimes in Article 28D. Against this backdrop, a valid argument can be made that all acts committed in armed conflict, including acts of terrorism, are to be subsumed under the umbrella of the war crimes jurisdiction of the Court.

---

[22] This element, however, can also be found in Article 1(3) of the OAU Convention. The UN Draft Convention includes "serious damage to the environment".

[23] The difficulties in getting consensus in this matter are apparently one reason why the UN Draft Convention has not yet been adopted.

[24] Compare Article 22(1) of the OAU Convention.

[25] See, e.g., *Galic*, ICTY (TC), judgment of 5 December 2006, para 86 et seq, and Werle and Jeßberger 2014, marg. number 1301 et seq.

5.4.3 Mercenarism

Article 28H of the Malabo Protocol (Annex) defines the crime of mercenarism. Essentially, the provision is based on the 1989 UN International Convention against the Recruitment, Use, Financing, and Training of Mercenaries.[26] However, in some important aspects the provision departs from the UN Convention and takes up elements from the definition enshrined in the 1977 OAU Convention for the Elimination of Mercenarism in Africa.[27]

Africa's experience with mercenarism has been long-lasting and ambiguous. In colonial times, mercenaries were employed by the colonial powers to suppress national struggles for liberation. In more recent times, weak governments have sought help from mercenaries in order to maintain power, with the most prominent example being Sierra Leone. At present, many states, including states outside Africa, for example the United States in Iraq and Afghanistan, turn to mercenaries to perform functions traditionally carried out by a state's armed forces, making mercenarism a multi-billion dollar business. It is telling to note that today we use the term "private military contractors", which appears more neutral than "mercenaries".

The ambiguity of the concept of mercenarism is reflected in the relevant international law. While international instruments initially addressed neutral states (arguing that the status as a neutral state would not be compatible with nationals of this state fighting as mercenaries), the focus, driven by a number of UN General Assembly Resolutions, then shifted to the ban of the use of mercenaries against movements of national liberation.[28] Various (diverging) definitions of mercenarism

[26] UN Treaty Series Vol. 2163, 75. The Convention entered into force in 2001. 34 states have ratified the Convention, including seven African states and excluding, among others, Germany, France, the UK and the US.

[27] Organization of African Unity, CM/817 (XXIX), Annex II Rev. 1. The Convention entered into force in 1985. It has 30 State Parties, excluding, among others, Kenya, Sierra Leone, South Africa, and Uganda. The definition in the OAU Convention is designed differently. Article 1(2) reads:

"The crime of mercenarism is committed by the individual, group or association, representative of a State or the State itself who with the aim of opposing by armed violence a process of self-determination stability or the territorial integrity of another State, practises any of the following acts:

(a) Shelters, organises, finances, assists, equips, trains, promotes, supports or in any manner employs bands of mercenaries;
(b) Enlists, enrols or tries to enrol in the said bands;
(c) Allows the activities mentioned in para (a) to be carried out in any territory under its jurisdiction or in any place under its control or affords facilities for transit, transport or other operations of the above mentioned forces."

[28] See, e.g., GA Res. 2265 and 3103. See for details Dickinson in: Bassiouni 2008, p 355 et seq.

can be found in Additional Protocol I to the Geneva Convention,[29] a number of regional treaties, including the OAU Convention, and the UN Convention. As a consequence, the exact elements of mercenarism under international law are far from clear. Moreover, it is questionable whether mercenarism is a crime, or even prohibited at all. This inconsistency regarding the different approaches to mercenarism under international law can similarly be found in domestic legal orders.[30]

It is difficult to determine the protected interest behind the crime of mercenarism. Recourse to the underlying treaty law does not shed light on the issue. The OAU Convention classifies the crime as a "crime against peace and security in Africa".[31] Similarly, the UN Convention states that the recruitment, use, financing and training of mercenaries should be "considered as offences of grave concern to all States".[32] The classification of mercenarism as a crime against international peace and security is supported by Article 28H(1)(a) of the Malabo Protocol (Annex) which refers to "mercenaries" specially recruited to fight in an armed conflict. At the same time, however, the UN Convention holds that mercenarism "violates principles of international law such as those of sovereign equality, political independence, territorial integrity of States and self-determination of peoples."[33] The OAU Convention, on the other hand, points to "the grave threat activities of mercenaries present to the independence, sovereignty, security, territorial integrity and harmonious development of Member States of the Organization of African Unity".[34] From this perspective, mercenarism may be understood as a crime concerning state protection, a view which finds support in Article 28H(1)(b) of the Malabo Protocol (Annex), which defines as "mercenary" a person who is specially recruited to participate in a "concerted act of violence" aimed at, inter alia, a coup d'état (see subsection (1)(b)(i)).

Article 28H of the Malabo Protocol (Annex) not only distinguishes two separate types of mercenaries (subsection (1)(a) and (b) respectively) but also provides for two distinct crimes of mercenarism (subsections (2) and (3) respectively). As regards the definition of mercenaries, the common elements under (a) and (b) of subsection (1) are: Mercenaries must be specially recruited, neither nationals nor

[29] Article 47 of the Additional Protocol I to the Geneva Conventions (for completely different reasons) defines who is a mercenary, not for the purpose of prohibition or criminalization, but simply to state that "a mercenary shall not have the right to be a combatant or a prisoner of war". (Article 47(1) of the Additional Protocol I.).

[30] For instance, under German criminal law, the mere recruitment for a foreign service is a crime. Section 109 h of the German Penal Code reads: "Whosoever on behalf of a foreign power recruits a German for military service in a military or paramilitary organisation or introduces him to their recruiters or to the military service of such an organisation, shall be liable to imprisonment from three months to five years."

[31] See Article 1(3) of the OAU Convention.

[32] See UN Convention, Preamble.

[33] See UN Convention, Preamble.

[34] OAU Convention, Preamble.

residents of the state affected, and not members of the regular armed forces or sent on official duty. In addition, they have to be "motivated by private gain". With regard to the latter element, the qualifier contained in the UN Convention that the material compensation promised to the mercenary must be "substantially in excess of that promised or paid to combatants of a similar rank and functions in the armed forces",[35] has been deleted from the definition. Article 28H of the Malabo Protocol (Annex) now follows the broader definition in the OAU Convention. Furthermore, the status of a mercenary does *not* require that the person does in fact take direct part in the hostilities. Here the Malabo Protocol departs from the narrower definitions in the OAU Convention and Protocol I to the Geneva Conventions.

In addition to these common elements, Article 28H of the Malabo Protocol (Annex) sets out specific elements for two different types of mercenaries. Subsection (1)(a) defines persons specially recruited to fight in an armed conflict as mercenaries ("conflict mercenaries"). Subsection (1)(b) defines as mercenaries those specially recruited for the purpose of participating in a "concerted act of violence" ("violence mercenary"). This act of violence must be aimed at either a classic "coup d'état" (Article 28H(1)(b)(i.)1., 3. and 4.), i.e. overthrowing a legitimate government or otherwise undermining the constitutional order of a state, assisting a group of persons to obtain power, or undermining the territorial integrity of a state, or at assisting a government to maintain power (Article 28 H(1)(b)(i.)1., 2.). The latter alternative ("assisting a group of persons to maintain power") has no counterpart in existing treaty law, including the UN Convention and the OAU Convention. The same holds true for subsection (1)(b)(i.) 3. ("assisting a group of persons to obtain power"). Thus, since traditional treaty law is confined to cover coups d'état, the provisions of the Statute are again much broader. For instance, while the use of mercenaries by a government against rebels is not unlawful under the OAU Convention, it would be a crime under the Statute.

While subsection (1) of Article 28H defines "mercenary", subsections (2) and (3) set out the actual offences. Subsection (2) makes it an offence to "recruit, use, finance or train" mercenaries ("passive mercenarism"). Subsection (3) criminalizes the mercenary him or herself if he or she participates directly in hostilities or in a concerted act of violence ("active mercenarism").[36] The mere participation in the training, however, is not criminalized.

[35] See Article 2(1) of the UN Convention; see also Article 47(2)(c) of the Additional Protocol I to the Geneva Conventions.

[36] Under the OAU Convention it is unclear whether also the mercenary himself or herself commits a crime. According to Article 1(3) of the OAU Convention "any person who commits the crime of mercenarism as defined in para 1 of this Article commits an Offence". Article 1(1), however, does not contain a "crime of mercenarism" but merely defines who is a mercenary.

5.4.4 General Observations

It is beyond the scope and ambition of this chapter to discuss or even raise all concerns related to the crimes presented in the previous section. However, four general observations common to all three crimes shall briefly be pointed out.

The first concern relates to the lack of legal certainty which characterizes the definitions of piracy, terrorism, and mercenarism. The language used to define the material elements of the crimes is often vague and ambitious. For example, for the crime of terrorism the Malabo Protocol requires the intention "to coerce a body to adopt a particular standpoint", and for the crime of mercenarism recruitment "for the purpose of participating in a concerted act of violence aimed at assisting a group of persons to obtain power" or "aimed at overthrowing a legitimate Government" is required. The same holds true with regard to the determination of the "illegality" and "unlawfulness" of the act for the crimes of piracy and terrorism. To some extent, the vagueness of many elements contained in the definitions of the crimes is a result of the approach adopted by the drafters of the Malabo Protocol of borrowing the definitions from international and regional treaties. As explained above, the description of conduct in the corresponding treaties was never meant to be transferred into the definitions of actual crimes. Rather, the relevant treaty provisions describe a rather broad range of conduct and are often purposefully left ambiguous. This gives national legislators a certain degree of discretion regarding the precise conduct they want to criminalize and incorporate into their domestic criminal law system.

The second concern relates to inconsistencies as regards modes of individual criminal responsibility under the Malabo Protocol. Article 28 N of the Malabo Protocol (Annex) sets out different modes of responsibility applicable to "any of the crimes or offences provided for in this Statute".[37] The comprehensive list includes incitement, facilitation, financing, participating as a principal, a co-principal, agent or accomplice, aiding and abetting, and participation in a conspiracy. It is unclear how this provision relates to modes of responsibility laid down in the definitions of crimes. For instance, Article 28F(a) defines piracy as "any act of inciting or of intentionally facilitating an act described in subparas (a) or (b)". According to Article 28G(b) "terrorism" means, inter alia, "any promotion, sponsoring, contribution to, command, aid, incitement, encouragement, attempt, threat, conspiracy, organizing, or procurement of any person, with the intent to commit any act referred to in sub-para (a)(1) to (3)".

Thirdly, unlike for example the ICC Statute or statutes of other more recently established international or internationalized courts and tribunals, the Malabo Protocol is silent on other basic issues of criminal responsibility such as the requirements of *mens rea*. It is true that there are some elements in the definitions of specific crimes (for example, Article 28F(b) requires "knowledge of facts" and (c) criminalizes those who "intentionally facilitate" a terrorist act; under Article

[37] For more detail, see the chapter by Meloni in this book.

28G(a) an unlawful act is classified as terrorist act if it is "calculated or intended to […]"; Article 28G(b) criminalizes several actions if they are carried out "with the intent to commit any act […]."). Beyond that, however, the Annex to the Malabo Protocol does not contain any general provision as to the *mens rea* of the crimes. Again, the reason for this lack of explicit regulation is the adoption of the Statute's provisions from treaty law. Similar to the UN ad hoc tribunals, it will be up to the judges of the African Court of Justice and Human and Peoples' Rights to determine the general requirements of *mens rea*.

And finally, it is striking that the crimes discussed in this chapter—unlike other crimes under the jurisdiction of the African Court of Justice and Human and Peoples' Rights—do not ensure by way of definition that the Court's jurisdiction is focused and limited to acts of a particularly serious or transnational character. For example, according to Article 28I of the Malabo Protocol (Annex) the Court's jurisdiction for crimes of corruption is limited to "acts [which] are of a serious nature affecting the stability of a state, region or the Union". Given the nature of these crimes and their roots in international treaties, another possible qualifier would have been to require that the criminal behaviour affect more than one state. In the absence of such a formal limitation, however, the jurisdiction of the Court for the crime of terrorism includes minor incidents, such as minor damage to property if caused with the purpose to induce the general public to, say, go on strike.

5.5 Towards a Regional Court for Transnational Crimes

To conclude, three issues shall be briefly discussed which link the specific offenses discussed in this chapter with the overall idea of establishing a regional forum for the adjudication of transnational crimes.

First of all, with the establishment of criminal chambers in the African Court of Justice and Human and Peoples' Rights, it would be the first time ever that an international or regional court's criminal jurisdiction encompasses transnational crimes. Earlier efforts to establish similar institutions, either on the international or on the regional level, have failed. The most prominent example is the attempt within the framework of the League of Nations to create an international criminal court to prosecute the transnational crime of terrorism. However, the 1937 *Convention pour la Création d'une Cour Pénale Internationale* never came into effect. Similarly, the efforts to equip the International Criminal Court with jurisdiction over the transnational crimes of drug trafficking and terrorism have failed. And more recently, the UN Secretary-General considered establishing a regional judicial body to prosecute crimes of piracy off the African coast.[38]

[38] In the "Report of the Secretary-General on possible options to further the aim of prosecuting and imprisoning persons responsible for acts of piracy and armed robbery at sea off the coast of Somalia" (S/2010/394, 26 July 2010), the establishment of "a regional tribunal on the basis of a multilateral agreement among regional States, with United Nations participation" is considered as one of seven options.

Secondly, the attempt to establish an international or regional criminal court also raises a number of theoretical questions. The most fundamental of these questions relates to the source of the authority to try and to punish (*ius puniendi*) vested in, in this case, the African Court of Justice and Human and Peoples' Rights. Technically, Article 28A of the Malabo Protocol (Annex) is, at least in its wording, a purely procedural provision determining the jurisdiction of the Court over crimes that already exist ("the Court shall have power to try [...]"). In some cases, the specific provisions of the Annex to the Malabo Protocol determine the crime itself, as is the case with, for example, mercenarism (see Article 28H(2) and (3): "Any person who [...] commits an offence."; "A mercenary who [...] commits an offence"). In most cases, however, the provisions in the Annex to the Malabo Protocol only describe the conduct subject to the jurisdiction of the African Court of Justice and Human and Peoples' Rights, without declaring this conduct criminal, i.e. without establishing a crime (see, for example, Article 28F: "Piracy consists of [...]"; Article 28 G: "terrorism means [...]"). In these cases, the Annex to the Malabo Protocol seems to presume that the transnational crimes under the jurisdiction of the Court already exist somewhere, similar to the crimes of genocide, crimes against humanity, war crimes, and the crime of aggression which are established crimes under customary international law. On the other hand, Article 46B(1) of the Malabo Protocol (Annex) suggests that the amended Statute of the African Court of Justice and Human and Peoples' Rights as annexed to the Malabo Protocol itself creates these crimes ("[a] person who commits an offence under this Statute should be held individually responsible for this crime"). Similarly, according to Article 3(1) of the Malabo Protocol, the Court is "vested with original jurisdiction", which indicates that, at least in the understanding of the drafters, the Court has its own jurisdiction and authority to punish. But where does the authority to punish come from?

It seems difficult to argue that with the establishment of criminal chambers in the African Court of Justice and Human and Peoples' Rights the African Union is exercising its own inherent and genuine criminal authority. Under Article 4(h) of its Constitutive Act the African Union shall "function in accordance with", inter alia, the following principle: "the right of the Union to intervene in a Member State pursuant to a decision of the Assembly in respect of grave circumstances, namely: war crimes, genocide and crimes against humanity". This jurisdictional basis, if it can be regarded as a jurisdictional basis at all, does not include transnational crimes. As a consequence, the only remaining alternative is that the authority to punish of the African Court of Justice and Human and Peoples' Rights is based on a derivative form of authority originating in the *ius puniendi* of the States Party to the Malabo Protocol. According to this approach, the Court must be regarded as a "hybrid" institution based on different sources of authority to punish where it has jurisdiction over transnational crimes on the one hand, and jurisdiction over crimes under international law on the other.

Thirdly, and moving from theory to practice, it seems undeniable that the mandate of the African Court of Justice and Human and Peoples' Rights is highly ambitious. It includes general matters of international law and violations of human rights, as well the adjudication of an extensive list of crimes under international law and transnational crimes. Regarding specifically its criminal jurisdiction it seems rather unlikely that the Court will be able to effectively address virtually all areas of serious criminality committed all over the continent with just one trial chamber composed of three judges. The dangers of overburdening international institutions are well known and can be observed by looking at existing international criminal tribunals, which, however, have a much more limited mandate.[39] Therefore, one of the biggest concerns is that the expanded criminal jurisdiction will rapidly overload the Court and will clearly surmount its capacities. Against this backdrop, the criminal chambers in the African Court of Justice and Human and Peoples' Rights, once established, should from the outset emphasize—more than was done by the International Criminal Court in its early years—the principle of complementarity, including so-called positive complementarity, contained in Article 46A of the Malabo Protocol (Annex) which is modelled upon the corresponding provision of the Rome Statute. According to this approach, the key function of the Court would less be that of a true criminal court. Instead, the Court would serve as a pacemaker for other, more appropriate and better equipped *fora*, in particular by triggering investigations and prosecutions on the domestic level.

It is too simple to repudiate the ambitious project of an "African Criminal Court" in the face of severe flaws, such as over-criminalization, potential work overload, and technical shortcomings of the Malabo Protocol. Similar international instruments and institutions, such as the Rome Statute and the International Criminal Court, are likewise far from perfect. The idea underlying the Annex to the Malabo Protocol, to have the worst ills of the African continent adjudicated "at home" by a possibly neutral forum, deserves to be taken seriously. Time will tell whether the new "African Criminal Court" will add substantially to the existing system of international criminal justice.

Acknowledgments The author gratefully acknowledges comments by Julia Geneuss on a previous version of this chapter.

References

Ambos K (2013) Treatise on international criminal law, vol. II: the crimes and sentencing. Oxford University Press, Oxford

Bassiouni CM (2008) Perspectives on international terrorism. In: Bassiouni MC (ed) International criminal law, vol. I: sources, subjects and contents, 3rd edn. Martinus Nijhoff, The Hague, pp 697–750

Boister N (2009) Treaty crimes, international criminal court? New Crim Law Rev 12:341–365

Boister N (2012) An introduction to transnational criminal law. Oxford University Press, Oxford

[39] On the, arguably, threefold mandate of the ICC (criminal court, watchdog court, world security court) see Jeßberger and Geneuss, JICJ 10 (2012), 1081.

Chehtman A (2016) Terrorism and the conceptual divide between international and transnational criminal law. In: van der Wilt H (ed) Legal responses to transnational and international crimes: towards an integrative approach?, Edward Elgar Publishers, Cheltenham (forthcoming)

Currie R, Rikhof J (2014) International and Transnational Criminal Law, 2nd edn. Irwin Law, Toronto

Dickinson LA (2008) Mercenarism and private military contractors. In: Bassiouni MC (ed) International Criminal Law, vol. I: sources, subjects and contents, 3rd edn. Martinus Nijhoff, The Hague, pp 355–375

Guilfoyle D (2015) Piracy and the suppression of unlawful acts against the safety of maritime navigation. In: Boister N, Currie R (eds) Routledge handbook of transnational criminal law. Routledge, London, pp 364–378

Jeßberger F (2014) 'On behalf of Africa': towards the regionalization of universal jurisdiction? In: Werle G, Fernandez L, Vormbaum M (eds) Africa and the International Criminal Court. T.M.C. Asser Press, The Hague, pp 155–175

Jeßberger F, Geneuss J (2012) The many faces of the International Criminal Court. J Int Crim Justice 10:1081–1094

McIntyre A, Weiss T (2007) Weak governments in search of strength: Africa's experience of mercenaries and private military companies. In: Chesterman S, Lehnhardt C (eds) From mercenaries to market: the rise and regulation of private military companies. Oxford University Press, Oxford, pp 67–81

Mitsilegas V (2015) Regional organisations and the suppression of transnational crime. In: Boister N, Currie R (eds) Routledge handbook of transnational criminal law. Routledge, London, pp 73–88

Murungu CB (2011) Towards a criminal chamber in the African Court of Justice and Human Rights. J Int Crim Justice 9:1067–1088

Nmehielle VO (2014) 'Saddling' the new African regional human rights court with international criminal jurisdiction: innovative, obstructive, expedient? Afr J Legal Stud 7:7–42

O'Brien M (2014) Where security meets justice: prosecuting maritime piracy in the International Criminal Court. Asian J Int Law 4:81–102

Saul B (2015) Terrorism as a transnational crime. In: Boister N, Currie R (eds) Routledge handbook of transnational criminal law. Routledge, London, pp 394–408

Sundberg JWF (2008) The crime of piracy. In: Bassiouni, MC (ed) International Criminal Law, vol. I: sources, subjects and contents, 3rd edn. Martinus Nijhoff, The Hague, pp 799–813

Werle G, Jeßberger F (2014) Principles of international criminal law, 3rd edn. Oxford University Press, Oxford

Chapter 6
Corruption (Article 28I) and Money Laundering (Article 28I*bis*)

Lovell D. Fernandez

Abstract This chapter examines the feasibility of including the crimes of corruption and money laundering within the jurisdiction of the African Court of Justice and Human and Peoples' Rights. The discussion focuses on specific aspects of the two crimes, particularly their relationship to other economic crimes in and outside the crimes listed in the Malabo Protocol (Annex). The immunity granted to heads of state or government raises valid concerns about the legitimacy of the African Court of Justice and Human and Peoples' Rights in the eyes of the public. Jurisdictional issues pose major challenges as do the definitions and applicability of the crimes. Practical issues related to the ability of Member States to cooperate in criminal investigations appear to have been overlooked in adding these two crimes to the catalogue of international crimes.

Keywords Africa · African Union · transnational crimes · corruption · money laundering · human rights

Contents

All internet sources in this chapter were last visited on 30 June 2016.

L.D. Fernandez (✉)
University of the Western Cape, South African-German Centre for Transnational Criminal Justice, Bellville, South Africa
e-mail: lfernandez@uwc.ac.za

G. Werle and M. Vormbaum (eds.), *The African Criminal Court*, International Criminal Justice Series 10, DOI 10.1007/978-94-6265-150-0_6

6.1 Extracts from the Malabo Protocol (Annex)

Article 28I Corruption

1. For the purposes of this Statute, the following shall be deemed to be acts of corruption if they are of a serious nature affecting the stability of a state, region or the Union:
   (a) The solicitation or acceptance, directly or indirectly, by a public official, his/her family member or any other person, of any goods of monetary value, or other benefit, such as a gift, favour, promise or advantage for himself or herself or for another person or entity, in exchange for any act or omission in the performance of his or her public functions;
   (b) The offering or granting, directly or indirectly, to a public official, his/her family member or any other person, of any goods of monetary value, or other benefit, such as a gift, favour, promise or advantage for himself or herself or for another person or entity, in exchange for any act or omission in the performance of his or her public functions;
   (c) Any act or omission in the discharge of his or her duties by a public official, his/her family member or any other person for the purpose of illicitly obtaining benefits for himself or herself or for a third party;
   (d) The diversion by a public official, his/her family member or any other person, for purposes unrelated to those for which they were intended, for his or her own benefit or that of a third party, of any property belonging to the State or its agencies, to an independent agency, or to an individual, that such official has received by virtue of his or her position;
   (e) The offering or giving, promising, solicitation or acceptance, directly or indirectly, of any undue advantage to or by any person who directs or works for, in any capacity, a private sector entity, for himself or herself or for anyone else, for him or her to act, or refrain from acting, in breach of his or her duties;
   (f) The offering, giving, solicitation or acceptance directly or indirectly, or promising of any undue advantage to or by any person who asserts or confirms that he or she is able to exert any improper influence over the decision making of any person performing functions in the public or private sector in consideration thereof, whether the undue advantage is for himself or herself or for anyone else, as well as the request, receipt or the acceptance of the offer or the promise of such an advantage, in consideration of that influence, whether or not the influence is exerted or whether or not the supposed influence leads to the intended result;

(g) Illicit enrichment;
(h) The use or concealment of proceeds derived from any of the acts referred to in this Article.

2 For the purposes of this Statute "Illicit enrichment" means the significant increase in the assets of a public official or any other person which he or she cannot reasonably explain in relation to his or her income.

Article 28I*bis* Money Laundering

1. For the purposes of this Statute, 'Money Laundering' means: any act of
   (i) Conversion, transfer or disposal of property, knowing that such property is the proceeds of corruption or related offences for the purpose of concealing or disguising the illicit origin of the property or of helping any person who is involved in the commission of the offence to evade the legal consequences of his or her action.
   (ii) Concealment or disguise of the true nature, source, location, disposition, movement or ownership of or rights with respect to property which is the proceeds of corruption or related offences;
   (iii) Acquisition, possession or use of property with the knowledge at the time of receipt, that such property is the proceeds of corruption or related offences
   (iv) Participation in, association with or conspiracy to commit, attempts to commit and aiding, abetting, facilitating and counselling the commission of any of the offences established in accordance with this article.
2. Nothing in this article shall be interpreted as prejudicing the power of the Court to make a determination as to the seriousness of any act or offence.

6.2 Introduction

The inspirational phrases in the preamble to the Malabo Protocol reiterate the need for African states to promote peace, security and stability, and to protect human and people's rights. There is no explicit exhortation to protect African economies against economic criminality, which poses a threat to the socio-economic rights of the peoples of Africa. This omission is striking, given that at least five of the fourteen crimes over which the African Court of Justice and Human and Peoples' Rights will exercise criminal jurisdiction are overtly economic crimes. These are piracy, corruption, money laundering, trafficking in persons, and trafficking in drugs. Over the past decade several scholars have called for corruption to be made an international crime.[1] These pleas have come mainly from the United States,

[1] See, for example, Bantekas 2006, pp. 466–484; Bloom 2014, pp. 627–671, 674; Kale 2009; Global Organization of Parliamentarians Against Corruption 2013, pp. 1–10; Starr 2007, p. 1297 et seq.; Wolf 2014, pp. 1–14.

where the matter has been debated over the past few years.[2] This chapter considers the feasibility of including economic crimes as international crimes in an African setting, which has its own peculiarities. The listing of the crimes has not given rise to much debate in Africa, at least not yet. This contribution is no more than a preliminary discussion of some of the issues that could crop up in practice.

6.3 The Crime of Corruption in the Annex to the Malabo Protocol

Article 28I of the Malabo Protocol (Annex) regulates the crime of corruption. It replicates what the African Convention on Preventing and Combating Corruption lists as "acts and practices" deemed to constitute corruption.[3] But the Annex to the Malabo Protocol differs from the Convention in that it criminalizes corruption only if it is "of a serious nature affecting the stability of a state, region, or the Union." This suggests that the corruption targeted here is "grand corruption", which Transparency International defines as

> acts committed by individuals at a high level of government or executives in the private sector who have a significant impact on society by distorting policies or the functioning of the state, enabling leaders to benefit at the expense of the public good.[4]

In contrast, "petty corruption" refers to

> everyday abuse of entrusted power by low- and mid-level public officials in their interactions with ordinary citizens, who often are trying to access basic goods or services in places like hospitals, schools, police departments and other agencies.[5]

By its very nature, "grand corruption" has a transnational component, hence the Annex's reference to "a state, region or the Union". Furthermore, "grand corruption" may involve presidents, prime ministers, governors or high-level politicians who are able to hide their ill-gotten gains in foreign banks or use it to buy real estate in foreign jurisdictions.[6] They are the persons who have the capacity to destabilize countries and regions. One recent example is Zine al-Abidine Ben Ali, the former Tunisian leader who is suspected of having amassed up to USD

---

[2] See, for example, Schaefer et al. 2014.

[3] See Article 1 of the African Union Convention on Preventing and Combating Corruption, read with Article 4.

[4] Transparency International 2015a, b, p. 2. By its nature, "grand corruption" is also defined as "carried out by high-level officials who seek payment for exercising discretionary powers." See United Nations 2015, p. 9 fn 18.

[5] Transparency International 2015a, b.

[6] See Starr 2007, p. 1281. See also Kirch-Heim 2009, p. 36.

13 billion while in power, at the expense of the Tunisian people. Several of his overseas luxury assets have been seized in Canada, Switzerland and the EU.[7] Ben Ali's alleged corruption sparked Arab Spring revolutions, the devastating effects of which are reflected every day in the media.

The basic problem with the Annex to the Malabo Protocol, and one that is bound to tarnish the credibility of the African Court of Justice and Human and Peoples' Rights, is that it confers immunity from prosecution precisely on those persons who are prone to be involved in "grand corruption", namely, heads of state or government or senior state officials.[8] This means that the African Court of Justice and Human and Peoples' Rights may not exercise jurisdiction over heads of state and senior state officials, even under Article 46B(3) of the Malabo Protocol (Annex), which does not exempt a superior from criminal responsibility for failing to intervene where, as a superior, he or she knew or ought to have known that a subordinate official committed or was about to commit an act of corruption. Corruption, especially corruption by public officials, is rampant in Africa, and is usually committed while the officials are in office and have access to public funds. If officials are initially allowed to enjoy immunity whilst in office on the grounds that they will be charged with corruption once they vacate office, it may turn out that too much time has elapsed for the case to be pursued once they leave office and/or it may prove to be difficult to obtain evidence.

6.3.1 Jurisdiction

Article 46F of the Malabo Protocol (Annex) states that a State Party, the Assembly of Heads of State and Government of the African Union, or the Security Council of the African Union may refer a "situation" to the Prosecutor of the Court. What is meant by "situation" is not entirely clear. It appears that the word was borrowed from Article 14 of the ICC Statute, which states that a State Party may itself refer to the International Criminal Court a "situation" in which one or more crimes within the International Criminal Court's jurisdiction appear to have been committed, accompanied by a request that the Prosecutor investigate the "situation" to determine whether anyone should be charged with the crime or crimes. Article 46G(1) of the Malabo Protocol (Annex) authorizes the Prosecutor to initiate *proprio motu* investigations subject to the permission of the Pre-Trial Chamber. The term "situation" as used in a general sense in the Annex to the Malabo Protocol, is less suited to be applied to the crime of corruption, which is usually a crime that takes place behind closed doors, or involves secret transactions between just two persons. The conduct element of the crime is not characterized by dispersed and

---

[7] See The Economist 2013, http://www.economist.com/news/international/21577368-why-have-arab-countries-recovered-so-little-money-thought-have-been-nabbed.

[8] Article 46A*bis* of the Malabo Protocol (Annex). See also Tladi's chapter in this book.

fragmented episodes which are typical of international crimes such as war crimes, crimes against humanity or genocide. The unqualified transplantation of the term into the Annex to the Malabo Protocol is thus unfortunate insofar as it applies to the crime of corruption, in particular.

Apart from a case being referred to the African Court of Justice and Human and Peoples' Rights or initiated *proprio motu*, only African persons or African NGOs with observer status with the African Union or its organs or institutions may submit cases to the African Court of Justice and Human and Peoples' Rights, and this only if the State concerned has made a declaration accepting the Court's competence to "receive cases or applications submitted to it directly."[9] The stringent hurdles impeding direct access for individuals and NGOs were inserted into Article 16(1) following orchestrated efforts by a group of States, including Tunisia and Egypt, that were mistrustful of human rights NGOs which, traditionally, have been the main complainants at the African Commission on Human and Peoples' Rights (hereafter African Commission).[10] These claw-back clauses place the African Court of Justice and Human and Peoples' Rights virtually beyond the reach of ordinary persons who consider themselves wrongfully convicted for corruption by the courts of their respective States, or for whistleblowers whose uncovering of multi-million dollar financial scams does not lead to any action by the domestic criminal justice authorities, even where prosecutions would have a realistic prospect of success and could save a country millions of dollars.

The obstacles to direct access to the African Court of Justice and Human and Peoples' Rights for individuals contrast to the procedures at the European Court of Human Rights where, since 1998, direct access for individuals, NGOs and groups of individuals claiming to be victims of human rights violations, is now compulsory.[11]

Article 46F of the Malabo Protocol (Annex) provides also for victims making representations to the Pre-Trial Chamber. The reference to victims appears to have been taken from Article 15(3) of the ICC Statute, although the wording of the crime of corruption in Article 28I of the Malabo Protocol (Annex) does not mention victims at all. In fact, the Annex to the Malabo Protocol deals with corruption purely from a criminal law perspective, which means that the aim of the criminal proceedings is more to establish who is responsible for the crime than to determine the impact of the crime on the collective interests of the victims.[12] Thus, from the perspective of either the Prosecutor or the Court, it will be difficult to assess what impact corruption has on the security and stability of a country, region or the African Union. Perhaps the question to ask in this context is why the crime of corruption, of all the economic crimes listed in Article 28I, is the only crime in

[9] Article 16(f) of the Malabo Protocol (Annex).

[10] Sceats 2009, pp. 9–10. At the time of writing 478 NGOs are accredited with the African Commission. See African Union 2014 p. 11.

[11] Article 34 of the European Convention on Human Rights. See also Cichowski 2011, p. 85.

[12] See United Nations 2015, p. 9.

respect of which the African Court of Justice and Human and Peoples' Rights' jurisdiction is contingent upon how seriously the crime affects the stability of a state, region or the African Union. Hypothetically, there are no rational grounds for not extending this prerequisite to the other economic crimes as well. Like corruption, money laundering is not directed at a victim or a state, yet it can have the effect of shattering whole economies, undermining democratic institutions, subverting the rule of law and destroying livelihoods of peoples of a country or a region. If the national, regional or continental destabilizing effect of corruption is so determinant, why then does the Annex to the Malabo Protocol exclude other economic crimes which are not listed in the Annex, but which, by their very nature, can pose an equivalent threat to the economic stability of a nation or a region? Examples of such crimes are organized crime, illicit trade in small arms, or trading in counterfeit goods. The latter, according to the United Nations Office on Drugs and Crime (UNODC), is not only more lucrative than trafficking in persons and in drugs, but also plays havoc with the lives of people, the environment, the labor market and the economic sustainability of regions.[13]

Corruption is especially difficult to prosecute, for it involves public officials who wield power and influence, and who are able to thwart an investigation. Corruption takes place in secret and there are usually no witnesses. Investigations can last for years and are heavily dependent on undercover investigators, and also whistle-blowers or informers who, unless they are assured that they will be protected from any form of harm, are reluctant to co-operate.[14]

Article 46E*bis* of the Malabo Protocol (Annex) authorizes the African Court of Justice and Human and Peoples' Rights to exercise jurisdiction in respect of States Parties to the Protocol and Annex, but on condition that States Parties have established national jurisdiction over the crime of corruption on the basis of the territoriality principle, the active or passive personality principle, or the protection principle.[15] However, in practice, not all States Parties to international conventions on corruption exercise jurisdiction on the same grounds. While the United Nations Convention against Corruption (UNCAC) requires contracting States to exercise territorial jurisdiction, it makes it optional for states to exercise jurisdiction on other bases.[16] The African Union Convention on Preventing and Combating Corruption (AUCPCC), on the other hand, does not obligate States Parties to establish jurisdiction on any one of the grounds mentioned above.[17] Moreover, there is no single standard of implemen-

[13] United Nations Office on Drugs and Crime 2011, p. 2.

[14] Sceats 2009, p. 10.

[15] The "territoriality principle" refers to jurisdiction for offences committed on the territory of a State or on board a vessel flying the flag of the State or on board an aircraft registered under the law of the State. The "active or passive personality principle" refers to jurisdiction for offences committed by nationals of a State, or against them, and the "protection principle" refers to jurisdiction for offences committed against a State. See United Nations Office on Drugs and Crime 2009, pp. 131–132. See also the chapters of Nerlich and van der Wilt in this book.

[16] Article 42(2)(a) and (b) of the United Nations Convention Against Corruption 2003.

[17] See Article 13 of the African Union Convention on Preventing and Combating Corruption 2003.

tation, as some states apply a principle widely, others narrowly. For example, in relation to the territoriality principle, one State may take the narrow view, according to which the crime is committed in its territory if the perpetrator acted in that territory. Another State may subscribe to a wider standard, according to which the crime is considered to have been committed when at least part of the crime was carried out in that State's territory. Some other State may exercise jurisdiction based on the ubiquity theory or the principle of objective territoriality, which allows a State to exert jurisdiction if the crime has effects on that State's territory.[18]

These are some of the jurisdictional challenges that the African Court of Justice and Human and Peoples' Rights will need to overcome in fulfilling its mandate. As corruption is not a crime subject to universal jurisdiction, the Court's ability to exert jurisdiction over corruption will depend ultimately on whether a State has domesticated either UNCAC or AUCPCC, for only then will it be able to exercise derivative or representative jurisdiction. However, practice teaches that African states domesticate Organization of African Unity/African Union foundational instruments and institutions only selectively. For example, at the time of writing, 33 of the 55 African States have ratified the AUCPCC, nine years into its entry into force, but only ten have incorporated its most basic provisions into their national laws.[19]

Maluwa attributes the "modest record of ratification" to a trend which suggests that a treaty has a better chance of being ratified if it does not cause tension with the national government, and if it requires only slight changes to the existing national law. Such considerations count much in the context of Organization of African Unity/African Union treaties which, generally, do not provide for reservations that afford States Parties the "option of ratifying a treaty while making exceptions aimed at accommodating domestic legal imperatives or political interests".[20] Some authors have suggested that the AUCPCC's expansive language and use of mandatory vocabulary, is a possible reason deterring a number of countries from ratifying it, and that the lack of a follow-up mechanism that holds countries accountable might be the reason why some countries avoid or delay implementing it.[21]

6.3.2 The Need to Link Corruption to Human Rights Violations

Whereas, traditionally, corruption was dealt with purely from a criminal law perspective, it has now become a global human rights issue as well.[22] In 2012

[18] United Nations Office on Drugs and Crime 2009, p. 134.

[19] Abass 2013, p. 33.

[20] Maluwa 2012, p. 41.

[21] See Brunelle-Quraishi 2011, p. 86; Webb 2005, p. 203.

[22] United Nations 2015, p. 10. See also Alves Mendes Vieira and Varella 2014, pp. 476–493; Boles 2013/2014, pp. 841–842; Moroccan Permanent Mission to Geneva 2012; Olanyian 2014, pp. 63–66; Robinson 2014, p. 3; Sweeney 2013.

Morocco addressed the United Nations Human Rights Council on behalf of 132 States on the growing negative impact of corruption in undermining national initiatives to improve the lives of citizens.[23] Moving human rights to the center of the fight against corruption in no way diminishes the importance of criminal law as an anti-corruption measure. Rather, it opens new ways of addressing the structural problems caused by corruption.

In its 2015 final report on the negative impact of corruption on the enjoyment of human rights, the United Nations Human Rights Council Advisory Committee shows that human rights and corruption are linked in two ways, namely, (a) human rights may be violated by a corrupt act; and (b) anti-corruption measures may result in human rights violations.[24] While some acts of corruption do not impact on human rights, for example, private corruption between two people, systemic corruption in the public sector can impair the enjoyment of economic, social, cultural, civil and even political rights. Violations of human rights occur where a person has to pay a bribe in order to obtain, for instance, access to food, employment, housing, medical treatment, education or justice.[25]

Furthermore, in the area of transitional justice, the crime of corruption has been brought into sharp focus by African truth commissions. Whereas most of the truth commissions established in the 1980s and 1990s concentrated on uncovering gross violations of civil and political rights perpetrated under predecessor regimes, African truth commissions set up in Chad, Ghana, Kenya, Liberia and Sierra Leone have veered from the dominant script by analyzing the phenomenon of "economic violence", a term coined to draw attention to the socio-economic underpinning of conflict and gross human rights violations.[26] There are, however, legitimate concerns that transitional justice accountability processes should not be saddled with the additional burden of looking into socio-economic violations, for while they may record meticulously the role of economic crimes in conflicts, they are ill-suited to making targeted recommendations to remedy the wrongs.[27] Where they have done so, they have seldom addressed "economic violence" as a violation of specific socio-economic rights. However, there is no gainsaying the fact that African truth commissions have made great strides in bringing the issue of corruption into the foreground of their investigations, showing how corruption has been at the root of some of the conflicts.

---

23 Moroccan Permanent Mission to Geneva 2012.

24 United Nations 2015, p. 5.

25 Ibid p. 6.

26 Sharp 2014, p. 80 defines "economic violence" as "violations of economic and social rights, plunder of natural resources, and various forms of economic crime carried out by authorities in violation of generally applicable criminal law, including large-scale embezzlement, fraud, tax crimes, and other forms of corruption."

27 See Waldorf 2012, pp. 177–179.

However, in the African context, the AUCPCC, whose provisions on corruption inform the wording of the crime in the Malabo Protocol (Annex), fails to link "grand corruption" to widespread and systemic human right violations. The Malabo Protocol's disregard for victims' rights contrasts to the imaginative African Charter on Human and Peoples' Rights which, uniquely among human rights treaties, provides for legally enforceable group or collective rights. The African Commission, too, which has a rich history of allowing NGOs to bring cases under the African Charter on Human and Peoples' Rights before it, including cases where the NGOs themselves are not affected directly by the violation, but are acting on behalf of the poor, the illiterate, and people scared of reprisals, has handed down the world's leading decisions on economic, social and cultural rights.[28]

In 2009, the Nigerian NGO, Socio-Economic Rights and Accountability Project (SERAP), made successful use of the African Charter on Human and Peoples' Rights when it brought a case of "grand corruption" before the Economic Community of West African States (ECOWAS) Community Court of Justice. SERAP filed the suit against the State on the basis that large-scale theft and embezzlement of public funds allocated to primary education had denied Nigerian children the right to quality education. The Court held that, even if the investigation report had come to the conclusive finding that there was corruption, that itself would not amount to a denial of the right to education, without further grounds. The Court stated that it would hold the State accountable only if there was a "clear linkage between the acts of corruption and a denial of the right to education."[29] However, the Court acknowledged that corruption has a negative impact on the right to education, since it decreases the amount of money available for providing education to the people.

In the context of the present discussion, the SERAP case is significant for the fact that, besides its resulting in the recovery of the Naira 3.4 billion (USD 17,310,300) that had been stolen from the education budget, it was (a) the first time that an NGO was given *locus standi* in a sub-regional court to litigate a public interest case in respect of a justiciable public right, and (b) a pioneering case in which a sub-regional court explicitly entertained corruption as a violation of a human right.[30]

[28] For examples, see Sceats 2009, p. 7. See also Olaniyan 2004, pp. 86–87.

[29] Registered Trustees of the Socio-Economic Rights and Accountability Project (SERAP) v. Federal Republic of Nigeria and Universal Basic Education Commission (UBEC) 2010, para 19.

[30] See also Global Organization of Parliamentarians against Corruption 2013, p. 5.

6.4 Critical Commentary

The provisions on immunity from prosecution for the political elite contained in the Annex to the Malabo Protocol, coupled with the steep eligibility criteria the Annex lays down for bringing cases to the African Court of Justice and Human and Peoples' Rights, undermine its potential to serve as an effective anti-corruption mechanism. The Annex's overtly criminal law approach, which offers victims of corruption hardly any space to assert their public rights, will weaken the Court's capacity to address the negative consequences of corruption. Peters points out that a pure criminal law approach harbors the danger that "broad and indeterminate criminal offences can easily be abused to eliminate or at least discredit political opponents."[31] The Malabo Protocol Annex's threshold requirement for the Court to assert jurisdiction, namely, the geographic destabilizing effect of the corrupt act, lends itself perfectly to this kind of political manipulation.

On the other hand, the shift to combating corruption via human rights law has both its plusses and negatives. A plus is that public interest litigation can trigger compensatory action on the part of the state. Article 34 of UNCAC requires states to implement remedial measures to address the consequences of corruption. Civil law action also permits asset recovery procedures in which the burden of proof is less stringent than in criminal cases. Public interest anti-corruption litigation would help also to sensitize citizens to the need to assert their socio-economic rights more aggressively, thus making them less vulnerable to petty corruption. All three sub-regional courts in Africa, namely, the ECOWAS Court, SADC Court, and the East African Community (EAC) Court, have now been accorded competence to hear human rights cases.[32] It would therefore be practicable to take human rights-linked corruption cases to such courts. They are situated in the respective sub-regions, which makes them more readily accessible, and the costs of lodging a communication are accordingly not as high as when a case is taken to the African Commission in Banjul, the Gambia—at least for individuals from other regions of Africa. Furthermore, individuals have direct access to sub-regional courts, as there is no domestic exhaustion of remedies requirement. Their judges, too, are familiar with problems affecting the region, as they come from countries in the region.

The downside of the human rights approach has to do with the lack of enforcement. Despite its record of enlightened rulings on the safeguarding of group rights, the African Commission's decisions are not binding on states. Moreover, states have a poor record of implementing the rulings of the African Commission where it has found a state to have breached a guaranteed right. Also, civil society knows

---

[31] Peters 2015, p. 27. As to how the International Criminal Court's interventions have been misused in Uganda and Sudan to tarnish political opponents, see Nouwen and Werner 2010, pp. 941–965.

[32] Ebobrah 2009, p. 80; Murungi and Gallinetti 2010, p. 121.

little about how the Commission works and how to lodge communications, mainly because key documents are inaccessible and its website is poorly managed. The Commission suffers from a chronic lack of resources and legal officers and is dependent on an equally underfunded Secretariat for its monies. Its procedures are slow and protracted, and it can take years before a ruling is handed down. The fact that its decisions are hardly implemented "has dissuaded people from considering the African Commission as a route likely to result in change at the national level or in personal circumstances."[33] Sub-regional courts, on the other hand, render decisions that are binding on States, but these courts lack mechanisms to ensure compliance with their orders. As regards the South African Development Community (SADC) Court, the only available option in the case of non-compliance is to refer the matter to the summit of heads of state or governments.

The drawback of the human rights approach has expressed itself in the hostile reactions of the governments of the Gambia, Kenya and Zimbabwe to adverse human rights decisions made against them by the respective sub-regional courts. Attempts by these governments to curtail the human rights mandates of these courts succeeded only in the case of Zimbabwe where civil society groups were prevented from having a say in the matter. In the case of the ECOWAS and EAC Courts, the governments' attempts were repulsed successfully, mainly because of the fierce civil society resistance mobilized by the courts, with the support of neighboring governments in the respective regions.[34]

Peters makes the point that "the strength of the human rights approach to corruption is simultaneously its weakness", and that this is because of the attitudinal ambivalence in the Global South to human rights, which expresses itself in the critique that "the anti-corruption strategy is merely the imposition of a particular "Western" model of the State, a hegemonic or US-dominated strategy inspired by global capital." For her part, Peters dismisses these allegations, contending that they sound "more like an attempt to justify the behavior of elites whose power and sinecures are threatened by anti-corruption [sic] and by the demand for respect of human rights."[35]

[33] Odinkalu 2013, p. 44. See also Hansungule 2009, pp. 233–234; Robertson 2006, p. 72; Murungi and Gallinetti 2010, p. 128.

[34] For a highly enlightening analysis of the politics surrounding the cases, especially for the role of civil society in countering political hostility to the courts, see Alter et al. 2015, pp. 1–43. See also Possi 2015, pp. 192–213.

[35] Peters 2015, p. 28.

6.5 The Crime of Money Laundering in the Annex to the Malabo Protocol

Money laundering is defined variously. Essentially, it is the process of disguising the proceeds of a crime in order to make them look lawful. The crime is regulated at the international level by several conventions, namely, the 1988 UN Convention Against Illicit Traffic in Narcotic Drugs and Psychotropic Substances (Vienna Convention), the 2001 UN Convention Against Transnational Organized Crime (Palermo Convention)[36] and the 2005 UN Convention Against Corruption (Merida Convention).[37] The soft law is embodied in the 40 + 9 Recommendations of the Financial Action Task Force (FATF), an inter-governmental body which was set up by the G7 countries in 1989 to develop and promote national and international policies directed against money laundering.[38] Whilst the three international conventions are legally binding on sovereign Member States, the FATF Recommendations are not, although many countries in the world have implemented them to signal their political will to combat money laundering. In Africa, the FATF is supported

[36] Africa is the region with the largest number of signatories and parties to the Convention. See United Nations Conference of the Parties to the United Nations Convention against Transnational Organised Crime UN Doc CTOC7COP/2004/6. See Waldorf 2012, pp. 177–179.

[37] The European regional conventions are the Warsaw Convention 2005; Strasbourg Convention 1990 and the various European Parliament and Council Directives on the Prevention of the Use of the Financial System for the Purpose of Money Laundering and Terrorist Financing.

[38] The soft law is contained also in a number of various guidelines, codes and best practices issued by a host of international supervisory bodies and bodies, such as the Basel Committee on Banking Supervision, the aim of which is to improve banking supervision internationally, the Wolfsberg Group, which is an association of 13 banks worldwide, the aim of which is to formulate guidance frameworks for the management of financial crime risks, particularly with respect to the application of due diligence rules and anti-money laundering and counter-terrorist financing policies; and the European Parliament and Council Directives on the prevention of the use of the financial system for the purposes of money laundering or terrorist financing. In Africa, too, there are several cooperation initiatives at the continental and regional levels. Notable among these are the 1999 Organization of African Unity's Convention on Preventing and Combating Terrorism (the Algiers Convention), and the 2002 Plan of Action of the African Union High-level Inter-governmental Meeting on the Prevention and Combating of Terrorism in Africa, which included measures to suppress the financing of terrorism, in particular national laws to criminalize money laundering and the financing of terrorism, setting up financial intelligence units, training personnel to counter and prevent money laundering, and regulating cooperation with international financial institutions. In 2002, the African Peer Review Mechanism, an initiative of the New Partnership for Africa's Development proposed an action plan to strengthen anti-money laundering and counter-terrorism financing measures and to promote compliance with international standards.

in its work by three so-called FATF-style bodies, namely, the Eastern and Southern Africa Anti-Money Laundering Group, the Inter-governmental Action Group against Money Laundering in West Africa; and the Middle East and North Africa Financial Action Task Force against Money Laundering and Terrorist Financing.

The FATF-style bodies are meant to ensure that their respective Member States comply with the FATF's standards against money laundering and the financing of terrorism, and they do this through a system of peer reviews of each Member State on an on-going basis.

6.5.1 The Limited Ambit of the Definition of Money Laundering in the Annex to the Malabo Protocol

If there is any seriousness about the need to tackle the other serious economic crimes, then a future reform of the Statute of the African Court of Human and Peoples' Rights must make them predicate offences of money laundering, too. Mere criminalization, without any connection to the offence of money laundering, will mean that in practice only the "small fish" will be caught, but not the main culprits, the bosses, who will be left to enjoy the proceeds because of the difficulty of linking them to the predicate offence of corruption. In a sense, this defeats the purpose of the crime of money laundering, which is wide enough to catch many people, including those who have nothing to do with the commission of the predicate offence.

6.6 Why Is Corruption the Only Predicate Offence?

The Annex to the Malabo Protocol limits the predicate offence, meaning the crime that gives rise to the crime of money laundering, to the crime of corruption. Why exclude the other serious economic crimes listed in the Annex, for example, trafficking in drugs and trafficking in persons? If the Annex to the Malabo Protocol is serious about the need to combat the other serious crimes listed, which can be assumed given that they are listed together with corruption, why then not make them, too, predicate offences of money laundering as well? Mere criminalization of the other forms of conduct will in most cases lead to the arrest and conviction of only the "small fish", leaving the "kingpins", the authors of the crimes, untouched. This lacuna defeats the entire purpose of criminalizing money laundering and undermines FATF Recommendation 3, which states that "[c]ountries should apply the crime of money laundering to all serious offences, with a view to including the widest range of predicate offences."

One possible reason for the omission of other predicate offences in the definition of money laundering, is that the definition of the crime was taken from

AUCPCC, whose definition of money laundering does not meet fully the definition in Article 3 of the Vienna Convention. For example, in Article 28I*bis*(1)(ii) of the Malabo Protocol (Annex) the *mens rea* element is missing. The provision says that money laundering consists in the

> concealment or disguise of the true nature, source, location, disposition, movement or ownership of or rights with respect property which is the proceeds of corruption or related offences.

Such conduct cannot incur liability, for the simple reason that what is missing is the *mens rea* element, namely, that the person (the accused) knew or reasonably ought to have known that the property is the proceeds of unlawful activity. This is a requirement also under the definition of money laundering under the UN Convention on Transnational Organized Crime.[39]

6.7 Critical Commentary

The criminalization of money laundering in the Annex to the Malabo Protocol appears to have taken place without due regard to both the substantive law and practical challenges that the African Court of Justice and Human and Peoples' Rights will have to overcome to fulfill its mandate. The foremost obstacle that the Court will have to surmount is how to assert its jurisdiction across an uneven anti-money laundering legal landscape. Although African countries have in recent years made considerable progress in bringing their respective anti-money laundering laws in line with the FATF standards, their efforts are undermined by the lack of adequate regulatory systems.

Two major studies published in 2015, one commissioned by the Joint African Union Commission/United Nations Economic Commission for Africa Conference of African Ministers of Finance, Planning and Economic Development, and the other published by the Global Center on Cooperative Security, point to several weaknesses which continue to undermine efforts to combat money laundering.[40] These include corruption (including bribes paid to customs officers; inducements to tax inspectors; job offers; and payments to security officers, bankers and judges); lack of awareness of money laundering and terrorism financing threats; insufficient allocation of resources to address country-specific problems; lack of information sharing among institutions—a crucial necessity for the successful carrying out of transnational criminal investigations and the co-ordination of anti-money laundering strategies.

[39] For the knowledge requirement, see the House of Lords judgment in *R v Montila and others* (2004), paras 27–30.

[40] Report of the High Level Panel on Illicit Financial Flows from Africa 2015, p. 44. See also Shetret et al. 2015, p. xiv.

Without an investigative arm of its own, the African Court of Justice and Human and Peoples' Rights will have to rely wholly on the criminal justice authorities of States Parties. The widespread lack of resources and the high incidence of inadequately trained money laundering investigators constitute a huge impediment to the investigation of illicit money flows. Besides, given the fact that organized crime groups are involved in several other criminal activities, such as dealing in narcotics, wildlife poaching, dealing in counterfeit goods, or bank robberies etc., it will be difficult to separate the proceeds of corruption from those of the other crimes that the Protocol omits as predicate offence for money laundering. Also, money laundering is typically a transnational crime, with criminals being able to move their "dirty" money across several jurisdictions at the click of a computer mouse. Electronic transfers of criminal money give rise to a host of jurisdictional issues, which play havoc with traditional theories of jurisdiction based on nationality, territoriality, effect of the crime, substantial connection with the jurisdiction etc. Many countries in the world are hard put to even locate where the "dirty" money is layered or integrated into the lawful economy. Even where investigations are successful, jurisdictional conflicts could arise, resulting in long delays before actual prosecutions start. All the jurisdictional guidance the Convention on Cybercrime can offer in this regard is that "Parties involved shall [...] consult with a view to determining the most appropriate jurisdiction for prosecution".[41] At the time of writing, no African country has yet ratified the Convention, with South Africa being the only signatory.

The High Panel mentioned above found that most African countries lack prosecutors who are highly skilled in prosecuting economic crimes. The few who are competent are usually so overburdened with other work that they are unable to prepare properly for trial. Panel members heard that there were a number of cases in which law firms representing the accused had attempted to recruit or bribe competent prosecutors working on their cases. The panel observed a worrying trend in several countries, showing "that state prosecutors tend to lose key cases against powerful interests engaged in illicit financial flows to the extent that they sometimes feel that the judiciary is not supporting their efforts." These are disturbing facts, especially given that criminal asset recovery measures depend on the outcome of criminal trials. The Annex to the Malabo Protocol does not say anything about asset recovery, a critical shortcoming, since one of the main aims of anti-money laundering laws is to hit the criminal hardest where it hurts most—in the pocket.

[41] Article 22(5) of the Council of Europe Convention on Cybercrime 2001.

6.8 Conclusion

The crimes of corruption and money laundering have been inserted into the Annex to the Malabo Protocol without any theoretical underpinning in the phrases of the Preamble to the Protocol. They are thus made to appear as strangers in an inhospitable environment, recruited haphazardly to supplement an assortment of crimes made up of the classic international statutory crimes, as well as a few other economic crimes, to which they are not made to relate. The crime of money laundering is worded problematically and, inexplicably, is predicated only on corruption, to the exclusion of all the other serious economic crimes alongside which it stands. Corruption, on the other hand, is included in the list solely to protect vaguely defined national, regional and continental interests, but only when these are threatened. When, exactly, the seriousness threshold is crossed, and who decides this, has yet to be settled. Peculiarly, nowhere in the text does the Annex to the Malabo Protocol relate the crime of corruption to the violation of human rights, despite the existence of a real linkage. The credibility of the African Court of Justice and Human and Peoples' Rights is bound to be affected by the immunity from prosecutions accorded the political elite, for this privilege defeats the purpose of making corruption and money laundering economic crimes. Both crimes raise considerable and very real practical jurisdictional challenges with which the African Court of Justice and Human and Peoples' Rights will have to contend, for they are tied to the hard economic and geo-political realities of everyday African life.

References

Abass A (2013) The proposed international criminal jurisdiction for the African Court: some problematical aspects. Neth Int Law Rev 40:27–50

African Union (2014) Final African Union communiqué of the 55th Ordinary Session of the African Commission on Human and Peoples' Rights 28 April–12 May 2014. http://www.ohchr.org/Documents/HRBodies/SP/55thOrdinarySession_en.pdf

Alter KJ, Gathii JT, Helfer LR (2015) Backlash against international courts in west, east and southern Africa: causes and consequences. iCourts Working Paper Series, no. 21; Duke Law School Public Law & Legal Theory Series No. 2015-19

Alves Mendes Vieira G, Varella MD (2014) A Conexão entre os Direitos Humanos e a Corrupção. Revista de Direito Internacional 12:476–493

Bantekas I (2006) Corruption as an international crime against humanity. J Int Crim Justice 4:466–484

Bloom B (2014) Criminalizing kleptocracy? The ICC as a viable tool in the fight against grand corruption. Am Univ Int Law Rev 29:627–671

Boles (2013/2014) Criminalizing the problem of unexplained wealth: illicit enrichment offenses and human rights violations. N.Y.U. J Legislation Policy 17:835–875

Brunelle-Quraishi O (2011) Assessing the relevancy and efficacy of the United Nations Convention Against Corruption: a comparative analysis. Notre Dame J Int Comp Law 1:101–166

Cichowski RA (2011) Civil society and the European Court of Human Rights. In: Christofferson J, Madsen MR (eds) The European Court of Human Rights between law and politics. Oxford University Press, Oxford, pp 77–97

Ebobrah ST (2009) Litigating human rights before sub-regional courts in Africa: prospects and challenges. Afr J Int Comp Law 17:79–101

Global Organization of Parliamentarians against Corruption (2013) Prosecuting grand corruption as an international crime—Discussion Paper. http://gopacnetwork.org/Docs/DiscussionPaper_ProsecutingGrandCorruption_EN.pdf

Hansungule M (2009) African courts and the African Commission on Human and Peoples' Rights. In: Bösl A, Diescho J (eds) Human rights in Africa. Legal perspectives on their protection and promotion. Macmillan Education, Namibia, pp 233–271

Kale NK (2009) Economic crimes and international justice: elevating corruption to the status of a crime in positive international law. In: Keynote address, Symposium on Corruption and its Implications for Human Rights Centre for Human Rights and Democracy in Africa. Alliance Franco-Camerounaise Centre, Buea. http://fakoamerica.typepad.com/files/kofele-kale-keynote-address.pdf

Kirch-Heim C (2009) Grand corruption—A new crime under international law? Bucerius Law J 1:35–40

Maluwa T (2012) Ratification of African Union treaties by Member States: law, policy and practice. Melbourne J Int Law 13:1–46

Moroccan Permanent Mission to Geneva (2012) Cross-Regional Statement on: "Corruption and Human Rights". Delivered by Morocco on behalf of a group of 132 States at the 20th Session of the Human Right Council, Geneva, 26th June 2012. http://www.ohchr.org/Documents/Issues/Development/GoodGovernance/Corruption/StatementHRAndAntiCorruption.pdf

Murungi LN, Gallinetti J (2010) The role of sub-regional courts in the African human rights system. SUR-Int J Hum Rights 7:119–143

Nouwen SMH, Werner WG (2010) Doing justice to the political: the International Criminal Court in Uganda and Sudan. Eur J Int Law 21:941–965

Odinkalu C (2013) African Commission on Human and Peoples' Rights. Hum Rights Q 1:44–47

Olanyian K (2014) Corruption and human rights law in Africa. Hart Publishing, Oxford

Peters A (2015) Corruption and human rights. Basel Institute of Governance, Basel, Working Paper Series vol 20, pp 1–30

Possi A (2015) Striking a balance between community norms and human rights: the continuing struggle of the East African Court of Justice. Afr Hum Rights J 15:192–213

Robertson G (2006) Crimes against humanity, 3rd edn. Penguin, London

Robinson I (2014) Truth Commissions and anti-corruption: towards a complementary framework. Int J Transitional Justice 8:1–19

Sceats S (2009) Africa's New Human Rights Court: whistling in the wind? Chatham House, London

Schaefer BD, Groves S, Roberts JM (2014) Why the U.S. should oppose the creation of an international anti-corruption court, Backgrounder #2958, Heritage Foundation. http://report.heritage.org/bg2958

Sharp DN (2014) Economic violence in the practice of African Truth Commissions and beyond. In: Sharp DN (ed) Justice and economic violence in transition. Springer, Berlin et al., pp 79–104

Shetret L, Durner T, Cotter D, Tobin P (2015) Tracking progress: anti-money laundering and countering the financing of terrorism in East Africa and the Greater Horn of Africa. Global Center on Cooperative Security, Goshen

Starr S (2007) Extraordinary crimes at ordinary times: international justice beyond crisis situations. Northwest Univ Law J 101:1257–1314

Sweeney G (2013) Linking acts of corruption with specific human rights. Transparency International Presentation made to the European Parliament Sub-Committee on Human Rights. 'Corruption and Human Rights in Third Countries' Workshop, 28 Feb 2013. http://www.anagomes.eu/PublicDocs/a83f7ea0-d0d1-4711-a1e6-1f0ae76386f6.pdf

Transparency International (2015a) What is corruption? http://www.transparency.org/what-is-corruption
Transparency International (2015b) Fighting grand corruption: challenges and successes, Transparency International. http://www.transparency.org/files/content/corruptionqas/Fighting_grand_corruption_challenges_and_successes_2015.pdf
United Nations Office on Drugs and Crime (2009) Technical guide to the United Nations Convention Against Corruption. United Nations, New York
United Nations Office on Drugs and Crime (2011) The illicit trafficking of counterfeit goods and transnational organized crime. United Nations, Vienna
United Nations (2015) Final Report of the Human Rights Council Advisory Committee on the Issue of the Negative Impact of Corruption on the Enjoyment of Human Rights. UN Doc A/HRC/28/73
Waldorf L (2012) Anticipating the past: transitional justice and socio-economic wrongs. Soc Legal Stud 21:171–186
Webb P (2005) The United Nations Convention Against Corruption: global achievement or missed opportunity. J Int Econ Law 8:191–229
Wolf M (2014) The case for an international anti-corruption court. Brookings Institution, Washington

Chapter 7
Trafficking in Persons (Article 28J) and Trafficking in Drugs (Article 28K)

Fatuma Mninde-Silungwe

Abstract This chapter deals with two "transnational crimes" which the African Court of Justice and Human and Peoples' Rights will be competent to deal with, namely trafficking in drugs and trafficking in persons. The author discusses the history of these two crimes which can be traced back, partly, to the UN Convention against Illicit Traffic in Narcotic Drugs and Psychotropic Substances and to the Palermo Convention. The chapter analyzes the wording of the definitions of the two crimes in the Annex to the Malabo Protocol and considers their significance for the administration of international criminal justice in Africa. The chapter concludes by pointing out that the criminalization at the regional level is not an end in itself, and that the strengthening of national domestic laws in African states should become a priority.

Keywords Africa · African Union · trafficking in drugs · trafficking in persons · international criminal law · transnational crimes

Contents

All internet sources in this chapter were last visited on 30 June 2016.

F. Mninde-Silungwe (✉)
United Nations Development Programme, Elections Project, Lilongwe, Malawi
e-mail: fmninde@gmail.com

G. Werle and M. Vormbaum (eds.), *The African Criminal Court*, International Criminal Justice Series 10, DOI 10.1007/978-94-6265-150-0_7

7.1 Extracts from the Malabo Protocol (Annex)

Article 28J Trafficking in Persons
For the purposes of this Statute:

1. "Trafficking in persons" means the recruitment, transportation, transfer, harbouring or receipt of persons, by means of the threat or use of force or other forms of coercion, of abduction, of fraud, of deception, of the abuse of power or of a position of vulnerability or of the giving or receiving of payments or benefits to achieve the consent of a person having control over another person, for the purpose of exploitation.
2. Exploitation shall include the exploitation of the prostitution of others or other forms of sexual exploitation, forced labour or services, slavery or practices similar to slavery, servitude or the removal of organs;
3. The consent of a victim of trafficking in persons to the intended exploitation set forth in subpara (1) of this article shall be irrelevant where any of the means set forth in subpara (1) have been used;
4. The recruitment, transportation, transfer, harbouring or receipt of a child for the purpose of exploitation shall be considered "trafficking in persons" even if this does not involve any of the means set forth in subpara (1) of this article.

Article 28K Trafficking in Drugs

1. For the purposes of this Statute, trafficking in drugs means:

   (a) The production, manufacture, extraction, preparation, offering, offering for sale, distribution, sale, delivery on any terms whatsoever, brokerage, dispatch, dispatch in transit, transport, importation or exportation of drugs;
   (b) The cultivation of opium poppy, coca bush or cannabis plant;

(c) The possession or purchase of drugs with a view to conducting one of the activities listed in (a);
(d) The manufacture, transport or distribution of precursors knowing that they are to be used in or for the illicit production or manufacture of drugs.

2. The conduct described in paragraph 1 shall not be included in the scope of this Statute when it is committed by perpetrators for their own personal consumption as defined by national law.
3. For the purposes of this Article:

(A) "Drugs" shall mean any of the substances covered by the following United Nations Conventions:

(a) The 1961 Single Convention on Narcotic Drugs, as amended by the 1972 Protocol Amending the Single Convention on Narcotic Drugs of 1961;
(b) The 1971 Vienna Convention on Psychotropic Substances.

(B) "Precursors" shall mean any substance scheduled pursuant to Article 12 of the United Nations Convention against Illicit Traffic in Narcotic Drugs and Psychotropic Substances of 20 December 1988.

7.2 Introduction

The Malabo Protocol grants jurisdiction over "international crimes" to the African Court of Justice and Human and Peoples' Rights. According to Article 28A(2) of the Malabo Protocol (Annex), the Court has jurisdiction over fourteen crimes. In addition, Article 28A(2) gives the African Union Assembly the power, with the consent of the States Parties, to add additional crimes to the jurisdiction of the African Court of Justice and Human and Peoples' Rights in order "to reflect developments in International Law". It is the scope of the African Court of Justice and Human and Peoples' Rights' jurisdiction over trafficking in persons and trafficking in drugs that constitutes the focus of the present chapter. The chapter will consider, firstly, whether these two crimes can be considered as "international crimes" *stricto sensu*. Secondly, it will analyze the history and definition of the crimes, and, finally, it will address the question of whether it is, in the light of empirical realities, necessary to include these two crimes in the jurisdiction of a regional court.

7.2.1 "International" Versus "Transnational" Crimes

The classification of all fourteen crimes as "international" as the Annex to the Malabo Protocol does in Article 28A is controversial. It seems appropriate to begin by highlighting the distinction between "international" and "transnational crimes". "International crimes" or crimes under international law are any crimes that involve direct criminal liability under international law.[1] They are distinguished from treaty-based crimes or "transnational crimes" in that "international crimes" directly affect the fundamental values of the international community as a whole and, as such, establish direct criminal liability under international law.[2] By contrast, "transnational crimes" are concerned with the coordination of domestic prosecutions at an international level.[3] Historically, the concept of "transnational crime" is said to have first been used by the United Nations Crime Prevention and Criminal Justice Branch at the fifth United Nations Congress on Crime Prevention and the Treatment of Offenders in 1975 to depict "certain criminal phenomena transcending international boarders, transgressing the laws of several states or having an impact on another country."[4] Treaties on "transnational crimes" do not contain autonomous crimes as such. Rather, they oblige states to come up with domestic legislation concerning the prosecution and punishment of the crimes and, as such, their enforcement is indirect as opposed to direct.[5] Although their enforcement may involve different or multiple jurisdictions, this alone does not suffice to qualify the provisions that are the subject matter of such treaties as "international crimes". Rather, "international crimes" *stricto sensu* are genocide, crimes against humanity, war crimes and aggression, which are the core crimes under the ICC Statute.[6]

Article 3(2) of the United Nations Convention against Transnational Organized Crime (UNTOC)[7] provides that a crime be considered "transnational" if it fulfills one or more of the following four conditions: (i) the crime is committed in more than one state; (ii) it is committed in one state but the substantial preparation, planning, direction or control happened in another state; (iii) it is committed in one state but involves organized criminal groups that engage in criminal conduct in more than one state; (iv) it is committed in one state but has substantial effect in another state. This definition shows that the transnational nature of a crime is based on geographical considerations and the plurality of states involved in the commission of the crime. Trafficking in drugs and trafficking in persons do not establish direct criminal liability under international law as the treaties on these crimes oblige States Parties to incorporate the crimes in their domestic laws in

[1] Werle and Jeßberger 2014, p. 31.

[2] Ibid., p. 45.

[3] Ibid., p. 45.

[4] Boister 2012, p. 4; Mueller 2001, p. 13.

[5] Ambos 2013, p. 223; Werle and Jeßberger 2014, p. 46.

[6] Ibid.

[7] (2000) 2225 U.N.T.S. 209.

order for them to be enforceable.[8] In addition, there is no international consensus on the paramount importance and relevance of these crimes to the international community as a whole. Hence, it is not convincing to label them as "international" as opposed to "transnational crimes".

7.3 The International and Regional African Framework on Trafficking in Persons and in Drugs

7.3.1 The International Framework on Trafficking in Persons

Developing a definition for trafficking in persons was an arduous process that began in the 1990s.[9] The challenge was to find an appropriate definition that distinguished trafficking in persons or, as used interchangeably, human trafficking from other related issues such as migrant smuggling and illegal migration.[10] The history of the crime can be traced to the First Convention against White Slavery of 1904 which was aimed at suppressing the "criminal traffic" of white women or girls compulsively procured for "immoral purposes."[11] Reference to White Slavery was abandoned in 1927 on the basis that it was restricted to a specific race and as such did not encompass the full extent of the problem.[12] Other measures to combat trafficking adopted under the auspices of the League of Nations include the Convention on the Suppression of the Traffic in Women (1921),[13] and the Convention on the Suppression of the Traffic of Women of Full Age (1933).[14] These instruments did not define trafficking and focused on the movement of women abroad for purposes of prostitution.[15] In 1949 the United Nations adopted a Convention for the Suppression of the Traffic in Persons and the Exploitation of

---

[8] Article 3 of the United Nations Convention against Illicit Traffic in Narcotic Drugs and Psychotropic Substances (1988); Article 5 of the Protocol to Prevent, Suppress and Punish Trafficking in Persons Especially Women and Children, Supplementing the United Nations Convention against Transnational Organized Crime (2000) (hereinafter Trafficking in Persons Protocol).

[9] See UN General Assembly, "Traffic in Women and Girls", UN Doc. A/RES/49/166 (1994); UN General Assembly, "Traffic in Women and Girls: Report of the Secretary-General", UN Doc. A/50/369 (1995); Chuang 1998, p. 65; Gallagher 2010, pp. 12–54.

[10] Gallagher 2010, p. 11.

[11] Ibid., 13; International Convention for the Suppression of White Slavery Traffic (1904) 1 L.N.T.S 83.

[12] Gallagher 2010, p. 14.

[13] (1921) 9 L.N.T.S 415.

[14] (1933) 150 L.N.T.S 431.

[15] Gallagher 2010, p. 14.

the Prostitution of Others.[16] The Convention did not define trafficking either but had a list of prohibited forms of conduct, including *inter alia* procuring, enticing or leading another person for purposes of prostitution, regardless of whether the person procured, enticed or led consented;[17] keeping, managing or knowingly financing a brothel;[18] and knowingly letting out a building or place or part thereof for purposes of prostitution.[19] The Convention also required States to legislate for the crimes under it.[20]

It became clear that there was a need to develop a definition of trafficking in persons. This need was reflected in a United Nations General Assembly Resolution, a Report of the United Nations Secretary General on the subject and in academic literature.[21] The development of an appropriate definition for trafficking in persons required that it be distinguished from other related acts such as human smuggling. An attempt to describe the distinction between the two was made by the United Nations General Secretary Report, which posited that the main criterion for distinguishing human smuggling and human trafficking should be sought in the purpose or end goal of the movement. The report argued that the trafficking of women and girls should be defined in terms of "the end goal of forcing women and girl children into sexually or economically oppressive and exploitative situations" and the fact that it is done "for the profit of recruiters, traffickers and crime syndicates [...]".[22]

The debate as to the appropriate definition for trafficking in persons continued until the year 2000 when it was finally defined under the Protocol to the United Nations Convention on Transnational Organized Crime, officially named the Protocol to Prevent, Suppress, and Punish Trafficking in Persons, Especially Women and Children, 2000. The Protocol covers trafficking of all persons but paying particular attention to women and children.[23] The Protocol defines trafficking in persons as follows:

> The recruitment, transportation, transfer, harboring or receipt of persons, by means of the threat or use of force or other forms of coercion, of abduction, of fraud, of deception, of the abuse of power or of a position of vulnerability or of the giving or receiving of payments or benefits to achieve the consent of a person having control over another person, for the purpose of exploitation. Exploitation shall include, at a minimum, the exploitation

[16] (1949) 96 U.N.T.S 271.

[17] Article 1(1) (2) of the 1949 Convention on Suppression of Traffic in Persons.

[18] Article 2(1) of the 1949 Convention on Suppression of Traffic in Persons.

[19] Article 2(2) of the 1949 Convention on Suppression of Traffic in Persons.

[20] Article 3 of the 1949 Convention on Suppression of Traffic in Persons.

[21] See Footnote 16.

[22] Para 17 of the Report of the Secretary-General (1995).

[23] Preamble and Article 2(a) of the Protocol on Trafficking in Persons.

of the prostitution of others or other forms of sexual exploitation, forced labor or services, slavery or practices similar to slavery, servitude or the removal of organs.[24]

Trafficking in persons as defined above consists of three elements, namely, the action element, the means element, and the purpose element. The action element is part of the *actus reus* of the crime and refers to the conduct of recruitment, transportation, transferring, harboring or receipt of persons. The means element also forms part of the *actus reus* and refers to how the action element is fulfilled, that is by use of threats, use of force or other forms of coercion, abduction, fraud, deception, abuse of power amongst others.[25] The purpose element reflects the *mens rea* of the crime and refers to the purpose aimed at by the perpetrator when committing the crime.[26] The three elements of the offence are relevant in the case of trafficking of adults. In the case of persons under the age of 18, there is no need to prove the means element of the definition.[27] The consent of a victim of trafficking to the intended exploitation is irrelevant where the means set forth in the definition of the crime has been used.[28] This qualification is logical considering that the means element of the crime (e.g. threats, coercion, abduction and fraud) intrinsically vitiates consent.

Apart from defining trafficking in persons, the Protocol recognizes the need for a comprehensive international approach to trafficking in the countries of origin, transit and destination.[29] It has three goals and purposes: (i) to prevent and combat trafficking in persons, in particular women and children; (ii) to protect and assist victims of such trafficking in full respect of their human rights; and (iii) to promote cooperation among States Parties in order to achieve the objectives of curbing human trafficking.[30] The Protocol provides that trafficking in persons should be dealt with at the domestic level through the adoption of legislative instruments on human trafficking which "establish as criminal offences the conduct set forth in article 3 of this Protocol, when committed intentionally".[31]

7.3.2 *African Regional Framework on Trafficking in Persons*

Africa does not have a single regional convention on trafficking in persons. However, trafficking in persons or its related forms is prohibited under different African instruments. For example, the African Charter on Human and Peoples'

---

[24] Article 3(a) of the Protocol on Trafficking in Persons.

[25] Gallagher 2010, p. 31.

[26] Ibid., p. 34; UNDOC Anti-Trafficking Practitioners Manual (2009) Module 1 at p. 4.

[27] Article 3(c), (d) of the Protocol on Trafficking in Persons.

[28] Article 3(b) of the Protocol on Trafficking in Persons.

[29] Par 1 Preamble to the Protocol on Trafficking in Persons.

[30] Article 2 of the Protocol on Trafficking in Persons.

[31] Article 5 of the Protocol on Trafficking in Persons.

Rights prohibits slavery[32]; the Protocol on the Rights of Women in Africa obligates States Parties to take appropriate and effective measures to prevent and condemn trafficking in women, prosecute perpetrators and protect women from trafficking;[33] and the African Charter on the Rights and Welfare of the Child obliges States Parties to take appropriate measures to prevent the abduction, the sale of or traffic in children for any purpose or in any form, by any persons including the legal guardians of the child.[34] The instruments highlighted do not have a legal definition for trafficking in persons.

Apart from the regional instruments, Africa, through the African Union, has adopted some policy documents on trafficking in persons. The Ouagadougou Action Plan to Combat Trafficking in Human Beings, Especially Women and Children is an example.[35] The development of the action plan was influenced by the acknowledgment that effective actions to prevent and combat trafficking in persons, require comprehensive regional and international approaches.[36] The requisite actions to be undertaken fall into four categories: (i) prevention and awareness; (ii) victim protection and assistance; (iii) legislative framework, policy development, and law enforcement; and (iv) cooperation and coordination. In terms of the development of legislative and policy frameworks, the Action Plan calls on States to ratify and fully implement the UNTOC and the Trafficking in Persons Protocol and also calls for review and adoption of domestic legislation in order to implement the provisions of the UNTOC and the Trafficking in Persons Protocol. The Action Plan therefore echoes the importance of domestic mechanisms in the prevention and prosecution of trafficking offences. Another recent policy framework is the Khartoum Declaration on the African Union—Horn of Africa Initiative on Human Trafficking and Smuggling of Migrants.[37] It reiterates the principles under the Ouagadougou Action Plan although it was focused on States from the Horn of Africa, i.e. Djibouti, Egypt, Eritrea, Ethiopia, Libya, Sudan, South Sudan and Tunisia which have seen an increase in human smuggling and trafficking in persons in recent years. These states agreed among other things to ratify and implement instruments that address trafficking in persons and also to address socio-economic, security, and political factors that make people in the Horn of Africa vulnerable to human trafficking and migrant smuggling. Other policies at a sub-regional level include the Southern African Development Community (SADC) Regional Plan of Action on Trafficking in Persons (2009–2019) and Economic Community of West African States (ECOWAS) Declaration on the Fight against Trafficking in Persons (2001).

---

32 Article 5 of the African Charter on Human and Peoples' Rights (1981) 1520 U.N.T.S 363.

33 Article (2)(g) of the Protocol to the African Charter on Human and Peoples' Rights on the Rights of Women in Africa (2003).

34 Article 29(a) of African Charter on the Rights and Welfare of the Child (1990).

35 African Union 2006, The Ouagadougou Action Plan to Combat Trafficking in Human Beings, Especially Women and Children.

36 Preamble Ouagadougou Plan of Action.

37 African Union 2014.

7.3.3 International Framework on Trafficking in Drugs

The first attempt to regulate drug trafficking and establish a framework of procedural cooperation in drug trafficking was under the 1936 Convention for the Suppression of the Illicit Traffic in Dangerous Drugs, which, however, failed to come into force.[38] Subsequent instruments were initiated under the United Nations and aimed at regulating illicit cultivation, manufacturing, trade and use in narcotic drugs. The instruments are: the United Nations Convention against Illicit Traffic in Narcotic Drugs and Psychotropic Substances (1961)[39]; the Protocol Amending the 1961 Single Convention on Narcotic Drugs (1972)[40]; and the United Nations Convention against Illicit Traffic in Narcotic Drugs and Psychotropic Substances (Vienna Convention, 1988).[41] The instruments use what is regarded as a "control approach" by listing potentially harmful products and distinguishing their licit and illicit use.[42] Under these treaties, States are obliged to criminalize the illicit use, cultivation, and distribution of the listed drugs.[43] The Conventions arrange the drugs in schedules depending on the level of control.[44]

It is interesting to note that although drug trafficking is not a crime under the ICC Statute, the establishment of the International Criminal Court was precipitated by the request of Trinidad and Tobago to establish an international court with jurisdiction over drug-related offences.[45] The 1991 ILC Draft Code contained a drug trafficking offence but it was dropped in the subsequent drafts and in the ICC Statute.[46]

7.3.4 African Regional Framework on Trafficking in Drugs

Africa does not have a specific convention on trafficking in drugs. However, there have been different policies on drug trafficking such as the Declaration and Plan of Action on Drug Abuse and Illicit Drug Trafficking in Africa[47] and the Declaration on

---

[38] (1936) 198 L.N.T.S 300.

[39] (1961) 520 U.N.T.S 151.

[40] (1972) 976 U.N.T.S 3.

[41] (1988) 1582 U.N.T.S 95.

[42] Ambos 2013, p. 235.

[43] Ambos 2013, p. 235; Article 36(1)(a) of the Single Convention on Drug Trafficking, 1961; Article 3(1) of the Vienna Convention, 1988.

[44] See Schedules of Single Convention on Narcotic Drugs of 1961 as amended by the 1972 Protocol (9 May 2015) ST/CND/1/Add.1/Rev.1; Schedules of the Convention on Psychotropic Substances of 1971 (4 November 2015) ST/CND/1/Add.2/Rev.1.

[45] Ambos 2013, 234–235.

[46] Article 25 of the Draft Code of Crimes against Peace and Security of Mankind (1991).

[47] African Union 1996, AHG/Decl.2 (XXXII).

Control of Illicit Drug Trafficking and Abuse in Africa.[48] Currently, there is a Plan of Action for Drug Control (2013–2017). The Plan of Action highlights that trafficking and use of illicit drugs continues to be a challenge for Africa.[49] It gives a picture of the current situation and shows that illicit production in Africa is mainly focused on cannabis although there is a further emerging threat in the form of locally manufactured Amphetamine Type Stimulants.[50] In addition, cocaine trafficked from South America is stockpiled in some West African countries for shipping to Europe. The Plan of Action proposes measures for dealing with the problem at national, regional and international levels. Although regional cooperation is considered as one measure for dealing with drug trafficking, there is no indication in the Plan of Action that criminalization at the regional level was among the mechanisms considered.

7.4 The Definitions of Trafficking in Persons and Trafficking in Drugs Under the Annex to the Malabo Protocol

7.4.1 Trafficking in Persons

Under the Malabo Protocol the offence of trafficking in persons is defined in Article 28J(1) in the same manner as under the United Nations Protocol for Trafficking in Persons:

> 'Trafficking in persons' means the recruitment, transportation, transfer, harboring or receipt of persons, by means of the threat or use of force or other forms of coercion, of abduction, of fraud, of deception, of the abuse of power or of a position of vulnerability or of the giving or receiving of payments or benefits to achieve the consent of a person having control over another person, for the purpose of exploitation.

The definition thus adopts the three elements under the United Nations Protocol, i.e. the action, means and purpose elements described above. It also maintains the principle that consent is irrelevant, where the means set out in the definition has been used.[51] In addition, in cases involving children, the means element is irrelevant.[52] Of interest, however, with regard to trafficking in persons, is the absence of a gravity threshold as to which matters would fall within the jurisdiction of the African Court of Justice and Human and Peoples' Rights and which ones should be dealt with at the domestic level. The complementarity principle has

[48] African Union 2002.

[49] Para 12 of the AU Plan of Action on Drug Control (2013–2017).

[50] Ibid.

[51] Article 28J(3) of the Malabo Protocol (Annex).

[52] Article 28J(4) of the Malabo Protocol (Annex).

to be applied in deciding whether a case falls within the jurisdiction of the African Court of Justice and Human and Peoples' Rights.

7.4.2 Trafficking in Drugs

Drug trafficking is defined in Article 28K of the Malabo Protocol (Annex) in the same manner as under Article 3(1)(a)(i) to (iv) of the Vienna Convention 1988 as follows:

1. "For the purposes of this Statute, trafficking in drugs means:
   - (a) The production, manufacture, extraction, preparation, offering, offering for sale, distribution, sale, delivery on any terms whatsoever, brokerage, dispatch, dispatch in transit, transport, importation or exportation of drugs;
   - (b) The cultivation of opium poppy, coca bush or cannabis plant;
   - (c) The possession or purchase of drugs with a view to conducting one of the activities listed in (a);
   - (d) The manufacture, transport or distribution of precursors knowing that they are to be used in or for the illicit production or manufacture of drugs."

The acts constituting drug trafficking in Article 28K(1) will not fall under the jurisdiction of the Court if it is for personal consumption.[53] The Malabo Protocol (Annex) relies on the international instruments on drug trafficking for a definition of "drugs". Consequently, for a definition, recourse must be made to the 1961 Single Convention on Drugs, the 1972 Protocol amending the Single Convention, the 1971 Vienna Convention on Psychotropic Substances, and the 1988 Convention against Illicit Traffic in Narcotic Drugs and Psychotropic Substances.[54]

7.5 Analysis

7.5.1 Formulation of the Definitions

The definitions of trafficking in persons and trafficking in drugs follow the wording of international conventions and this may be a safer option in order to avoid diverting from the intention of a convention. However, it is essential to highlight that the definitions under the international conventions are not penal provisions since they do not provide for sanctions and they put the obligation on States Parties to criminalize. The approach therefore should not be to simply copy the definition under a convention, but to reformulate it and give it the constitutive

[53] Article 28K(2) of the Malabo Protocol (Annex).

[54] Article 28K(3), (4) of the Malabo Protocol (Annex).

elements of a crime i.e. *actus reus*, *mens rea* and sanction. The Malabo Protocol (Annex) has a general punishment provision for all offences in Article 43A but there is no general provision for *mens rea*.

7.5.2 Gravity Threshold

There is no gravity threshold as to the level of drug-related offences falling in the jurisdiction of the African Court of Justice and Human and Peoples' Rights as opposed to that of courts on the domestic level. It would have been favourable if the Malabo Protocol (Annex) included such a threshold specifying that the regional court should only exercise jurisdiction over the crimes if they are of so serious nature as to have an impact at the regional level. Otherwise, the jurisdiction should be exercised at the domestic level. This would reduce the workload that the African Court of Justice and Human and Peoples' Rights will have to deal with. While it could be argued that this problem could also be adequately addressed by the inclusion of the complementarity provision in Article 46H of the Malabo Protocol (Annex),[55] a gravity threshold would have the advantage of providing an intrinsic limitation within the definition of the crime, thus ensuring that only the most serious crimes with an impact at regional level would fall within the jurisdiction of the African Court of Justice and Human and Peoples' Rights.

7.5.3 Prioritizing Strengthening of Domestic Legal Frameworks

Empirical evidence point to the need to prioritize domestic legal frameworks on trafficking in persons. The UNDOC Global Report for Trafficking in Persons (2014) shows that in terms of flows, domestic trafficking accounts for 75 % of the total number of detected victims and is the main type of trafficking in Sub-Saharan Africa.[56] In the case of cross-border trafficking, the flows are mainly between states in the same sub-region, for instance most West African victims are detected in West Africa, whereas most Southern African victims are detected in Southern Africa.[57] The nature of these flows clearly shows that the most effective measure in tackling trafficking in persons in Sub-Saharan Africa would be to deal with the problem at

55 See the chapter by van der Wilt in this book.

56 Flows refers to origin country and destination country and includes domestic trafficking in which the origin and destination country coincide see UNDOC Global Report on Trafficking in Persons (2014) 37, 83.

57 Ibid., p. 83.

the domestic level, between neighboring States and at the sub-regional level.[58] There are also outbound flows to Europe and the Middle East from Sub-Saharan Africa, but mostly of West African victims. Only in this latter case does it seem necessary to adopt an inter-continental approach to deal with trafficking as well.

One of the principles under the Malabo Protocol (Annex) is that of complementarity between the domestic and regional levels. The domestic courts have primary jurisdiction over the crimes in the Annex. However, with regard to the crime of trafficking in persons, statistics show that Sub-Saharan Africa has not done well in legislating for this crime.[59] In 2003, 85 % of Sub-Saharan countries lacked legislation on human trafficking.[60] The situation has been slowly improving. Currently, more than 30 % of countries either have only partial legislation or no specific offence at all.[61] In addition, there is a lack of application of existing frameworks, as evidenced by the low number of convictions for trafficking in persons.[62] It is therefore necessary that African States take measures at the domestic level to legislate and prosecute the crime of trafficking in persons before considering regional criminalization and prosecutions.

In terms of trafficking in drugs, Africa is used as a transit route for drugs that end up in Europe.[63] Corruption and weak enforcement and judicial institutions in many countries in the region are some of the main conditions that providing a conducive environment for drug trafficking.[64] It is therefore necessary that comprehensive measures are put in place to strengthen the legislative and institutional framework at the domestic level in order to have an impact at the regional and international level.

7.6 Conclusion

7.6.1 Is It Necessary to Deal with the Crimes at the Regional Level?

It is undeniable that trafficking in persons is modern day slavery and therefore a despicable offence. Drug trafficking, too, is despicable and its negative consequences are deplorable. As such, both offences equally deserve criminalization. In

[58] This is also recommended by the AU Khartoum Declaration on AU-Horn of Africa Initiative on Human Trafficking and Smuggling of Migrants (2014).

[59] See UNDOC Global Report on Trafficking in Persons (2014) 37, p. 84.

[60] Ibid.

[61] Ibid.

[62] Ibid.

[63] Para 12 AU Plan of Action on Drug Control (2013–2017).

[64] USAID The Development Response to Drug Trafficking in Africa: Programming Guide (2013), p 3, available at https://www.ids.ac.uk/files/dmfile/Development_Response_to_Drug_Trafficking_in_Africa_Programming_Guide.pdf.

that sense, there is nothing inherently wrong with criminalization of these offences at the regional level. However, the criminalization at the regional level is not an end in itself. As the UNDOC research shows, more trafficking in persons occurs within, as opposed to between, States and at an inter-State level, the trafficking mainly occurs within the same sub-region. Equally, trafficking in drugs in Africa is promoted by weak institutions and corruption at the domestic level. It is therefore necessary that domestic legislative frameworks are strengthened to combat the crimes at that level. The regional court's jurisdiction is complementary to the national jurisdictions and, as such, the primary responsibility for prosecution of the crimes lies with the Member States whose legislative and institutional frameworks should be strengthened to enable them undertake that responsibility.

7.6.2 Nomenclature "International" or "Transnational" Crimes

Stricto sensu trafficking in persons and trafficking in drugs are "transnational" as opposed to "international" crimes. The application of wrong nomenclature leads to debates on whether the crimes fit the definition of "international crimes". The solution may lie in distinguishing between "international" and "transnational" crimes when enumerating them.

7.6.3 Cooperation for Prevention and Enforcement

Apart from domestic implementation, there is a need for legislative frameworks on cooperation in prevention and enforcement. This involves agreements on policing, mutual legal assistance, and extradition. There is also a need for cooperation between the States and the African Court of Justice and Human and Peoples' Rights. The inclusion of 14 crimes in the jurisdiction of the Court is likely to stretch its resources to the limit. Consequently, States are well advised to strengthen their domestic or sub-regional measures for dealing with crime.

References

African Union (1996) Declaration and Plan of Action on Drug Abuse and Illicit Drug Trafficking in Africa AHG/Decl.2 (XXXII). http://www.peaceau.org/uploads/ahg-decl-2-xxxii-e.pdf

African Union (2002) Declaration on Control of Illicit Drug Trafficking and Abuse in Africa. https://www.issafrica.org/uploads/DRUGS2006.PDF

African Union (2006) The Ouagadougou Action Plan to Combat Trafficking in Human Beings, Especially Women and Children. http://sa.au.int/en/content/ouagadougou-action-plan-combat-trafficking-human-beings-especially-women-and-children-0

African Union (2014) Khartoum Declaration on AU-Horn of Africa Initiative on Human Trafficking and Smuggling of Migrants. http://www.regionalmms.org/fileadmin/content/sector_publications/Final_Khartoum_Declaration_on_AU_HOA_TIP___Smuggling.docx

Ambos K (2013) Treatise on international criminal law, volume ii: the crimes and sentencing. Oxford University Press, Oxford

Boister N (2012) An introduction to transnational criminal law. Oxford University Press, Oxford

Chuang J (1998) Redirecting the debate over trafficking in women: definitions, paradigms and contexts. Harvard Hum Rights J 11:65–107

Gallagher A (2010) The international law of human trafficking. Cambridge University Press, Cambridge

Mueller G (2001) Transnational crime: definitions and concepts. In: Williams P, Vlassis D (eds) Combating transnational crime: concept, activities, responses. Frank Cass, London, pp 13–21

UN General Assembly (1994) Traffic in Women and Girls, UN Doc. A/RES/49/166. http://www.un.org/en/ga/search/view_doc.asp?symbol=A/RES/49/166

UN General Assembly (1995) Traffic in Women and Girls: Report of the Secretary-General, UN Doc. A/50/369. https://daccess-ods.un.org/TMP/9566214.08462524.html

United Nations Office on Drugs and Crime (2009) Anti-Human Trafficking Manual for Criminal Justice Practitioners. https://www.unodc.org/documents/human-trafficking/TIP_module1_Ebook.pdf

United Nations Office on Drugs and Crime (2014) Global Report on Trafficking in Persons. https://www.unodc.org/documents/data-and-analysis/glotip/GLOTIP_2014_full_report.pdf

USAID (2013) The development response to drug trafficking in Africa: a programming guide. https://www.ids.ac.uk/files/dmfile/Development_Response_to_Drug_Trafficking_in_Africa_Programming_Guide.pdf

Werle G, Jeßberger F (2014) Principles of international criminal law, 3rd edn. Oxford University Press, Oxford

Chapter 8
Trafficking in Hazardous Wastes (Article 28L) and Illicit Exploitation of Natural Resources (Article 28L*bis*)

Martin Heger

Abstract Pollution committed on a vast scale has been a problem for Africa for a long time. Frequently, it was European states which used Africa as their "trash bin". The chapter gives an overview of the international instruments that tackle this issue, and shows that, so far, the task of *criminalizing* serious acts of pollution has been left to the domestic legislator. Then, Article 28L and Article 28L*bis* of the Malabo Protocol (Annex) will be analyzed. Under these provisions, trafficking in hazardous wastes and illicit exploitation of natural resources, which have a devastating effect on the environment and the economy in Africa, are directly criminalized. The author welcomes this as a contribution to the development of international law in principle. However, in his view, the crimes in the Annex to the Malabo Protocol have some problematic features, in particular insofar as they lead to a too far-reaching criminalization. He argues that criminalization should rather take place at the domestic level and not at the international level.

Keywords Africa · African Union · trafficking in hazardous wastes · illicit exploitation of natural resources · European criminal law · environmental crimes

Contents

All internet sources in this chapter were last visited on 30 June 2016.

M. Heger (✉)
Humboldt-Universität zu Berlin, Berlin, Germany
e-mail: martin.heger@rewi.hu-berlin.de

G. Werle and M. Vormbaum (eds.), *The African Criminal Court*, International Criminal Justice Series 10, DOI 10.1007/978-94-6265-150-0_8

8.1 Extracts from the Malabo Protocol (Annex)

Article 28L: Trafficking in Hazardous Wastes

1. For the purposes of this Statute, any import or failure to reimport, transboundary movement, or export of hazardous wastes proscribed by the Bamako Convention on the Ban of the Import into Africa and the Control of Transboundary Movement and Management of Hazardous Wastes within Africa, adopted in Bamako, Mali, in January 1991 shall constitute the offence of trafficking in hazardous waste.
2. The following substances shall be "hazardous wastes" for the purpose of this statute:
   (a) Wastes that belong to any category contained in Annex I of the Bamako Convention;
   (b) Wastes that are not covered under para (a) above but are defined as, or are considered to be, hazardous wastes by the domestic legislation of the State of export, import or transit;
   (c) Wastes which possess any of the characteristics contained in Annex II of the Bamako Convention;
   (d) Hazardous substances which have been banned, cancelled or refused registration by government regulatory action, or voluntarily withdrawn from registration in the State of manufacture, for human health or environmental reasons.
3. Wastes which, as a result of being radioactive, are subject to any international control systems, including international instruments, applying specifically to radioactive materials are included in the scope of this Convention.
4. Wastes which derive from the normal operations of a ship, the discharge of which is covered by another international instrument, shall not fall within the scope of this Convention.
5. For the purposes of this Article, "failure to reimport" shall have the same meaning assigned to it in the Bamako Convention.
6. The export of hazardous waste into a Member State for the purpose of rendering it safe shall not constitute an offence under this Article.

Article 28L*bis*: Illicit Exploitation of Natural Resources

For the purpose of this Statute, "Illicit exploitation of natural resources" means any of the following acts if they are of a serious nature affecting the stability of a state, region or the Union:

(a) Concluding an agreement to exploit resources, in violation of the principle of peoples' sovereignty over their natural resources;

(b) Concluding with state authorities an agreement to exploit natural resources, in violation of the legal and regulatory procedures of the State concerned;
(c) Concluding an agreement to exploit natural resources through corrupt practices;
(d) Concluding an agreement to exploit natural resources that is clearly one-sided;
(e) Exploiting natural resources without any agreement with the State concerned;
(f) Exploiting natural resources without complying with norms relating to the protection of the environment and the security of the people and the staff; and
(g) Violating the norms and standards established by the relevant natural resource certification mechanism.

8.2 Introduction

The pollution of the natural environment and the illicit exploitation of natural resources are two of humankind´s oldest problems. But for a very long time these issues were pushed aside and ignored, both on a national and an international level. The situation changed in Western Europe and the North American states during the 1970s.[1] Africa became the place to deposit the hazardous waste industrialized countries needed to rid themselves of. The Basel Convention on the Control of Transboundary Movements of Hazardous Wastes and Their Disposal of 22 March 1989 (Basel Convention) finally turned trafficking in hazardous wastes without permission into a punishable offence according to public international law. The adoption of the Bamako Convention on the Ban on the Import into Africa and the Control of Transboundary Movement and Management of Hazardous Wastes within Africa (Bamako Convention), which was negotiated in January 1991 and entered into force in 1998, may be viewed as the reaction of several Member States of the Organization of African Unity (OAU) to the realization that less developed countries had become the "trash bin" of rich industrialized nations in the northern hemisphere. During the colonial era the colonial powers systematically exploited the natural resources of the African states. Now, decades into the process of decolonization, the northern states were using the former colonies' territories to dispose of their toxic waste.

8.3 The Background to the Environmental Crimes in the Annex to the Malabo Protocol

In the Annex to the Malabo Protocol, the African Union included two environmental crimes: trafficking in hazardous wastes and the illicit exploitation of natural resources. In both cases criminal conduct crosses national borders, making them

[1] See Radkau 2000, pp. 306–313.

typical transnational crimes. This aspect marks a significant difference when compared with other environmental crimes under national law. These scenarios are commonly characterized by the fact that it is merely the effects of criminal activity against the environment that travel across borders (for example, after the illegal emission of greenhouse gas in one country, the polluted air does not stop when it reaches the national borders).

Before I take a more detailed look at both provisions, I would like to review the concept of international and inter-regional environmental criminal law in its historical and comparative context. The crimes in the Annex to the Malabo Protocol are not the first attempt to include crimes against the natural environment into an international or regional legal framework, but in some aspects, the Annex to the Malabo Protocol goes beyond existing international and European laws. Due to the fact that the AU project might affect the competence of the International Criminal Court, I will begin my *tour d'horizon* of the international and European provisions in the field of international environmental criminal law with the Rome Statute. Then I will turn to the situation within the European Union and the Council of Europe. As a regional supranational organisation and an international organisation respectively, both institutions form a significant counterpart to the African Union.

8.3.1 Environmental Crimes in the ICC Statute

There is only one criminal offence in the ICC Statute's list of war crimes in international armed conflicts that has a connection to environmental criminal law:

> "Intentionally launching an attack in the knowledge that such attack will cause incidental loss of life or injury to civilians or damage to civilian objects or widespread, long-term and severe damage to the natural environment which would be clearly excessive in relation to the concrete and direct overall military advantage anticipated" (Article 8(2)(b)(iv) of the ICC Statute).

Viewed in light of the ICC Statute's elements of crimes, it is nearly impossible to imagine a case of widespread, long-term and severe damage to the natural environment, as the critical question of whether an attack was "clearly excessive" is not determined by objective standards.[2] On the contrary, all that is required to debunk the accusation of a clearly excessive attack is that the commander in charge at the time he gave his orders was of the opinion that the attack was not inappropriate. As Fenrick stated in a commentary on the ICC Statute, under these circumstances not even the massive bomb attacks during World War I at the western frontline, which transformed the landscape in Flanders and northern France into a moonscape, could be classified as a crime under Article 8(2)(b)(iv) of the ICC Statute.[3]

---

[2] For details see Werle and Jeßberger 2014, marg. numbers 1323 et seq.

[3] Arnold 2007, Article 8 para 60.

The provision on war crimes in Article 28D(b)(iv) of the Malabo Protocol (Annex) reads identically to Article 8(2)(b)(iv) of the ICC Statute. There is a good case to believe, therefore, that the provision in the Annex to the Malabo Protocol will also be subject to the restrictive interpretation that has been applied to the text of the ICC Statute.

Only a couple of scholars believe that severe damage to the natural environment should not only be penalized in the exceptional situation of armed conflict under international law.[4] In their view severe damage to the natural environment should equally be seen as a crime under international law when committed during non-international armed conflicts. However, to this day, most lawyers and relevant State Parties disagree with this minority opinion due to the fact that violations of the protection of the natural environment are generally not acknowledged as crimes under international law.[5]

8.3.2 European Environmental Criminal Law

Up to today a supranational environmental criminal law does not exist on a European level. This is a result of Article 83 § 2 of the Treaty of the Functioning of the European Union, which denies the European Union jurisdiction to pass legislation in the field of environmental criminal law. On the other hand, two models of harmonization have evolved, aiming at unifying environmental criminal law throughout the EU Member States as well as the countries of the Council of Europe.[6] On both levels (European Union and Council of Europe), initial measures of harmonization have already been implemented[7]: The Convention of the Council of Europe on the Protection of the Environment through Criminal Law of 4 November 1998 marked an important first step on the path to unifying environmental criminal law in Europe.[8] Thirteen Member States of the Council of Europe have signed this convention so far, however, up to today only Estonia has also ratified it. As a result, the Convention—as of yet—has not entered into force.

One reason why so many signing states refused to ratify the Convention of the Council of Europe was that the European Union initiated an independent project on the harmonization of environmental criminal law as part of the action plan of Vienna only one month later, on 3 December 1998.[9] In February 2000 Denmark

---

[4] For example, Asada 2000, p. 403, 418.

[5] See Reichart 1999, pp. 526–568; Tomuschat 2001, pp. 105–124.

[6] For details see Heger 2009, pp. 55 et seq.

[7] On the situation before the harmonization in the EU Member States, see Faure and Heine 2000, p. 9 et seq. and Criminal Penalties in EU Member States' Environmental Law, Maastricht, 2002 (www.eurocbc.org/Environmental_crime_survey_final_report.pdf).

[8] European Treaty Series (ETS) No. 172.

[9] OJ C 019, 23/01/1992, pp. 01–15.

presented a proposal for a framework decision on the protection of the environment through criminal law based on Article 31 and Article 34 of the EU Treaty,[10] and in March 2001 the EU Commission (EC) reacted with the proposal of an EC Directive on environmental criminal law based on the former Article 175 of the EC Treaty.[11] In January 2003, the EU Council refused the proposal of this EC Directive and instead adopted the EU Framework Decision 2003/80/JI on the protection of the environment through criminal law.[12] However, some two years later, in September 2005, this legal instrument was nullified by a judgment of the European Court of Justice in Luxemburg.[13] In November 2008 the European Union adopted the Directive 2008/99/EC on the protection of the environment through criminal law.[14] The EU Member States were given two years to implement the requirements of the aforementioned Directive into their national criminal codes.[15] As a result of the legislative activities on the EU level the criminal justice systems of all EU Member States now include nearly the same crimes for the protection of the natural environment.

8.4 The Environmental Crimes in the Annex to the Malabo Protocol

In view of the recent development of environmental criminal law on an international or intracontinental level I would like to focus specifically on the two provisions drafted by the African Union concerning crimes against the environment. In reference to the measures of harmonization in the EC Directive, as well as in the Convention of the Council of Europe, there is one obvious difference between them: On the one hand, trafficking in hazardous waste is a crime on both a national and European level. The Basel Convention of 1989 contains the following clause: "The Parties consider that illegal traffic in hazardous wastes or other wastes is criminal" (Article 4 § 3). This does not lead to the conclusion, however, that the State Parties to the Basel Convention, or any state for that matter, considered trafficking in hazardous waste to be a crime worth penalizing under international law. The same is to be said for the Bamako Convention of 1991. The State Parties to these international treaties were bound by the Convention to amend their national criminal law; in order for them to fulfil their international obligations

[10] OJ C 039, 11/02/2000, pp. 04–07.

[11] OJ 180 E, 26/06/2001, pp. 238–243.

[12] OJ L 029, 05/02/2003, pp. 55–58; see Faure 2004, pp. 18–29.

[13] *Commission v. Council*, Case C-176/03, ECR [2005] I-07879.

[14] OJ L 328 06/12/2008, pp. 28–37.

[15] For the example of Germany, see Heger 2012, pp. 211–223.

every State Party committed itself to implementing a provision against trafficking in hazardous waste into its national criminal code. Germany honoured this promise by introducing section 326 § 2 into the German Criminal Code in 1994.[16]

On the other hand, the illicit exploitation of natural resources is perhaps one of the most important factors for international and non-international armed conflicts in Africa. To put it in the words used by the German playwright Friedrich Schiller more than 200 years ago in his Trilogy "Wallenstein", referring to the Thirty Years War in Germany: "The war is feeding itself!"[17] Modern-day wars are commonly fuelled by exploitation of natural resources on both sides of the conflict in order to finance the costs of an army. Münkler, a political scientist at Humboldt-Universität Berlin, points out the asymmetric structure of modern armed conflicts in his book on modern wars.[18] His research shows that such asymmetric structures are a widespread phenomenon of today's armed conflicts and especially common in wars on the African continent. One very important reason for these new wars—for example in the Democratic Republic of Congo—is the fight for natural resources. Moreover, the exploitation of natural resources is one of the most important means of financing armed conflicts. Broomhall has pointed out that the illicit exploitation of natural resources is one of the big issues that international criminal law must confront in the age of globalization.[19]

---

[16] Section § 326: "§ 1 Whosoever unlawfully, outside a facility authorized therefor or in substantial deviation from the proscribed or authorized procedure, collects, ships, treats, utilizes, stores, dumps, discharges, disposes of or trades in, brokers or otherwise commercializes waste which

1. contains or can generate poisons or carriers of diseases which are dangerous to the public and are communicable to persons or animals;
2. is carcinogenic in humans, has harmful reproductive effects or can cause alterations in the genetic make-up;
3. is prone to explode, spontaneously combustible, or of more than merely minor radioactive quality; or
4. because of its nature, composition or quantity is capable of:
   (a) polluting or otherwise negatively and permanently altering a body of water, the air or the soil or
   (b) endangering an existing population of animals or plants

   shall be liable to imprisonment not exceeding five years or a fine.

   § 2 Whosoever ships into, out of or through the Federal Republic of Germany,

1. waste in significant amounts as defined by Regulation (EC) No 1013/2006 of the European Parliament and of the Council of 14 June 2006 on shipments of waste (OJ L 190, 12.7.2006,1, L 318, 28.11.2008, 15), last amended by Regulation (EU) No 135/2012 (OJ L 46, 17.11.2012, 30), provided it is a case of illegal shipment under Article 2 No 35 of Regulation (EC) No 1013/2006, or
2. other waste contrary to a prohibition or without the required permit within the meaning of subsection (1) above,

   shall incur the same penalty."

[17] Friedrich Schiller, Wallenstein, Die Piccolomini: "Der Krieg ernährt den Krieg. Gehen Bauern drauf, Ei, so gewinnt der Kaiser mehr Soldaten".

[18] Münkler 2002, pp. 48–57.

[19] Broomhall 2004, p. 163, 166.

8.4.1 Article 28L: Trafficking in Hazardous Wastes

During the last decades of the 20th century the industrialized countries of Western Europe tried to escape their emerging problem of accumulating waste by exporting unwanted substances to less developed countries in Africa. Since the 1980s several scandals have brought this reality to the public's attention. For example, it was revealed in 1987 that Italian companies had been shipping barrels of toxic waste to Nigeria, where they paid local farmers USD 100 a month in return for storing the barrels on their land.[20] While USD 100 meant a great deal to the farmers, the Italian companies hardly noticed the cost of disposing of their toxic waste.

As a result of these scandals, the State Parties to both the Basel and the Bamako Conventions agreed that illegal trafficking in hazardous waste must be made a criminal offence and implemented into each national criminal code.

The list of hazardous wastes in the current Article 28L of the Malabo Protocol (Annex) is identical to the list contained in the Bamako Convention. At first glance this seems logical, considering that the criminal offence drafted by the African Union is based on the list of prohibited wastes in the said convention. After a more thorough inspection, however, I must disagree with this premature conclusion. While there is no objection to penalizing illegal trafficking of hazardous wastes as defined in international agreements (for example, in Annex II, § 2(a) and (c) or—concerning radioactive waste—in § 3 of the Bamako Convention), I believe it is problematic that Article 28L(2)(b) bases an international criminal offence on a definition of hazardous waste that lies at the discretion of each national legislator. Article 28L(2)(b) reads as follows: "Wastes that are not covered under para (a) above but are defined as, or are considered to be, hazardous wastes by the domestic legislation of the State of export, import or transit". Such an extension of criminalization should only be incorporated into an international offence after every State Party has given its consent. Otherwise the criminalization under international law in Africa would run the risk of differing from country to country. If it is up to every Member State to define which kind of waste should be seen as hazardous, the individual state's power must be limited to penalizing the transportation of such hazardous waste only under its national law.

Another issue presents cause for concern: It is not only the perpetration of these offences that is criminalized under the Annex to the Malabo Protocol; so too is the instigation as well as the aiding and abetting of the offences. This is also the case for the other crimes in the Annex. From a European point of view this aspect is of vital importance, seeing that the number of potential instigators, aiders and abettors on the European continent is likely to be high. Let me illustrate this by means of an example: If an African enterprise or the farmers in Nigeria, to stay with the previous example, are importing or storing hazardous waste, this waste has normally been sent to Africa from industrialized countries in Europe. The initial idea of exporting toxic waste could have come from managers of European companies

[20] See wikipedia (https://en.wikipedia.org/wiki/Bamako_Convention; 1/6/2016).

or representatives from Europe, making them the instigators of trafficking in hazardous waste. The managers of the shipping companies, the captain of the ship transporting the barrels of toxic waste from Italy to Nigeria or any other person working in the harbours who helped bring the barrels onto deck could be found guilty of aiding and abetting.

8.4.2 *Article 28Lbis: Illicit Exploitation of Natural Resources*

An actual criminal offence against the illicit exploitation of natural resources exists on neither the international nor the European level. On the other hand, Article 12 of the Protocol against the Illegal Exploitation of Natural Resources of 2006 establishes the following obligation for every Member State: "each Member State shall ensure that such acts of illegal exploitation of natural resources are offences under its criminal law". The criminal conduct of the offences listed in Article 28L*bis*(a) to (g) was copied verbatim from Article 12 of the Protocol against the Illegal Exploitation of Natural Resources. However, two important differences distinguish Article 12 of the Protocol against the Illegal Exploitation of Natural Resources and Article 28L*bis* of the Annex to the Malabo Protocol: just like trafficking in hazardous waste (Article 28L), the illicit exploitation of natural resources in Article 28L*bis* no longer only states an obligation for the Member States to ensure that all acts of illegal exploitation are offences under national law. Instead, Article 28L*bis* constitutes a criminal offence in and of itself under international law.[21] On the other hand, contrary to the other environmental criminal

---

[21] http://eeas.europa.eu/top_stories/2015/270315_conflict_minerals_en.htm: The International Task Force on Illegal Exploitation of and Trade in Natural Resources in the Great Lakes Region (ITF)—originally launched by the EU in 2009—concludes inter alia:

"1.1.1 What are the main conclusions of the conference?

More than armed groups, criminal networks are now involved in illegal exploitation and trade in natural resources in the Great Lakes and their reach is regional and international. After years of weakened state authority in the eastern DRC, insurgency is predominantly economically motivated.

According to some estimates, illicit natural resources exploitation in eastern DRC is worth USD 1.25 billion per year. There is no definitive assessment of how much of this sum reaches **transnational organized criminal groups**, but it is certainly in the order of hundreds of millions of dollars. Armed groups probably see only a small percentage of the profits.

Organized crime financing is very complex, considering exploitation of gold, timber, charcoal, tin, tungsten and tantalum as well as local taxation schemes and wildlife.

Response **must include actions against impunity**, improved governance, reforming security forces, managing natural resources and promoting livelihood programmes.

Continued support for the ICGLR "Regional Certification Mechanism" is justified—but needs more attention to strengthening coordination and building trust from business.

The ITF should continue to steer stronger diplomatic engagement: by gathering those active in fighting illegal exploitation and trade in the region, the Task Force is a valuable platform to maximize efforts and avoid overlapping initiatives."

offence in the Annex to Malabo Protocol, the illicit exploitation of natural resources contains a severe restriction of criminalization, as it only classifies certain behaviour as a crime under international law if the illegal conduct is "of a serious nature affecting the stability of a state, region or the Union". The reason why the African Union has drafted this crime as a crime under international law is perhaps not to protect the natural environment and the natural resources, but to protect the affected states and the African Union.

Article 28L*bis* of the Annex to the Malabo Protocol aims to establish a crime under international law in Africa only if the act of illegal exploitation of natural resources is of a serious nature affecting the stability of a state, region or the Union.

In the alternatives (a) to (d), the conclusion of an agreement to exploit natural resources defines the *actus reus* or the objective element of the crime. As a consequence, the legal basis for penalization under international law is only the *risk* of illegal exploitation of natural resources. In my opinion the criminalization of mere preparatory acts is hard to justify, seeing as no actual harm is inflicted on the natural resources. In the end, cause for penalization is the risk alone. It seems highly problematic, however, to base an international crime on the unverifiable potential danger of the exploitation of natural resources.

Another interesting consequence, again especially from a European point of view, is that even instigating the conclusion of an agreement on the illicit exploitation of natural resources could be viewed as criminal conduct. If a European company asks its African partner to sell raw materials, for example, it is possible to prosecute the manager of the European company as well.

8.5 Some Problems

Article 28 N of the Annex to the Malabo Protocol names the various modes of responsibility.[22] I would like to focus on subpara iv., which states: Every "offence [in the Annex to the Malabo Protocol] is committed by any person who [...] attempts to commit any of the offences set forth in the present Statute". With a view to the environmental crimes, a person commits the offence of trafficking in hazardous waste (Article 28L) even when he or she only attempts to traffic it. This wording ties penalization to a very early stage of conduct. Although many national criminal justice systems, such as Germany's for example, offer the possibility of punishing the mere attempt of a crime, the Annex to the Malabo Protocol is not comparable to national legislation as it defines an international crime. It is my belief that, in light of the aforementioned EC Directive on the protection of the environment through criminal law, treating an attempted environmental crime and an accomplished offence equally is unnecessary on an international level.

---

[22] See the chapter by Meloni in this book.

Keeping in mind that the attempt of all environmental crimes marks the starting point of each criminal conduct under international law, even taking up negotiations with a foreign government on the conclusion of an agreement would lead to potential penalization under international law. I believe it is one thing if an individual state decides to criminalize preparatory acts, but it becomes problematic when the international community itself defines criminal parameters this way. I agree that in the ICC Statute even attempted genocide, crimes against humanity or war crimes should be classified as criminal conduct. But with a view to more modern crimes—such as the environmental offences—I think the African Union should be more cautious. Otherwise, in the end, criminalization on an international level will be more severe than it is in national legislation.

8.6 Conclusion

In principle we should keep the development of international environmental crimes alive. However, the international environmental crimes as drafted by the African Union don't take into consideration the limitations laid out by international law. In many cases it is sufficient to oblige the Member States to penalize certain criminal conduct in their national legal systems without it being necessary to criminalize the same behaviour on an international level. Perhaps I can conclude with the words: sometimes less is more.

Acknowledgments The author would like to thank his research assistant, Ms. Tabea Hill, for her help with the English text of the manuscript and his student assistant, Ms. Sophie Straßer, for her help with the references.

References

Arnold R (2007) In: Triffterer O (ed), Commentary on the Rome Statute, 2nd edn. Nomos, Baden-Baden, Article 8 para 60

Asada K (2000) Entstehung und Entwicklung des Umweltstrafrechts in Japan. In: Leipold (ed) Umweltschutz und Recht in Deutschland und Japan. C.F. Müller, Heidelberg, pp 403–418

Broomhall B (2004) The values, policies and goals of ICL in the age of globalization: Report. In: Association Internationale de Droit Penal (ed): International Criminal Law: Quo Vadis? Éditions érès, Ramonville Saint-Agne, pp 163–169

Faure MG (2004) European environmental criminal law: do we really need it? Eur Environm Law Rev 13:18–29

Faure MG, Heine G (2000) Environmental criminal law in the European Union, documentation of the main provisions with introductions. Edition iuscrim, Freiburg

Heger M (2009) Die Europäisierung des deutschen Umweltstrafrechts. Mohr/Siebeck, Tübingen

Heger M (2012) Das 45. Strafrechtsänderungsgesetz – Ein erstes europäisches Gesetz zur Bekämpfung der Umweltkriminalität. Höchstrichterliche Rechtsprechung in Strafsachen (HRRS) 13:211–223

Münkler H (2002) Die neuen Kriege. Rowohlt, Reinbek

Radkau J (2000) Natur und Macht. Eine Weltgeschichte der Umwelt. C.H. Beck, Munich
Reichart M (1999) Umweltschutz durch völkerrechtliches Strafrecht. Peter Lang, Frankfurt
Tomuschat C (2001), Schädigung der Umwelt als Verbrechen nach Völkerstrafrecht. In: Arndt H-W et al (eds) Völkerrecht und deutsches Recht, Festschrift für Walter Rudolf zum 70. Geburtstag. C.H. Beck, Munich, pp 105–124
Werle G, Jeßberger F (2014) Principles of international criminal law, 3rd edn. Oxford University Press, Oxford

Part III
General Principles and Rules of Procedure in the Annex to the Malabo Protocol

Chapter 9
Modes of Responsibility (Article 28N), Individual Criminal Responsibility (Article 46B) and Corporate Criminal Liability (Article 46C)

Chantal Meloni

Abstract The Annex to the Malabo Protocol contains several provisions regulating in detail the modes of liability, some of which may be inspirational for future developments of international criminal law: among these, the exclusion of the defence of superior orders for all crimes included in the Annex to the Malabo Protocol, and the inclusion of corporate criminal liability for the crimes under the jurisdiction of the African Court of Justice and Human and Peoples' Rights. Such an innovation, surely a bold one, is in line with the development of international criminal law. The real challenge will be for the (future) judges of the African Court of Justice and Human and Peoples' Rights, who will have to interpret the complex and not always coherent provisions of the Protocol. Unfortunately, it can be already anticipated that some provisions, such as the reintroduction of immunity for the African heads of state, will greatly undermine the credibility and efficacy of the Court if not amended.

Keywords Africa · African Union · International Criminal Court · modes of liability · individual criminal responsibility · Command Responsibility · corporate criminal liability · conspiracy

Contents

C. Meloni (✉)
University of Milan, Milan, Italy
e-mail: Chantal.meloni@unimi.it

G. Werle and M. Vormbaum (eds.), *The African Criminal Court*, International Criminal Justice Series 10, DOI 10.1007/978-94-6265-150-0_9

9.1 Extracts from the Malabo Protocol (Annex)

Article 28N Modes of Responsibility
An offence is committed by any person who, in relation to any of the crimes or offences provided for in this Statute:

i. Incites, instigates, organizes, directs, facilitates, finances, counsels or participates as a principal, co-principal, agent or accomplice in any of the offences set forth in the present Statute;
ii. Aids or abets the commission of any of the offences set forth in the present Statute;
iii. Is an accessory before or after the fact or in any other manner participates in a collaboration or conspiracy to commit any of the offences set forth in the present Statute;
iv. Attempts to commit any of the offences set forth in the present Statute.

Article 46B Individual Criminal Responsibility

1. A person who commits an offence under this Statute shall be held individually responsible for the crime.
2. Subject to the provisions of Article 46A*bis* (immunities, see infra) of this Statute the official position of any accused person shall not relieve such person of criminal responsibility nor mitigate the punishment.
3. The fact that any of the acts referred to in Article 28A of the present Statute was committed by a subordinate does not relieve his or her superior of criminal responsibility if he or she knew or had reason to know that the subordinate was about to commit such acts or had done so and the superior failed to take the necessary and reasonable measures to prevent such acts or to punish the perpetrators thereof.
4. The fact that an accused person acted pursuant to the order of a Government or of a superior shall not relieve him or her of criminal responsibility, but may be considered in mitigation of punishment if the Court determines that justice so requires.

Article 46C Corporate Criminal Liability

1. For the purpose of this Statute the Court shall have jurisdiction over legal persons, with the exception of States.

2. Corporate intention to commit an offence may be established by proof that it was the policy of the corporation to do the act which constituted the offence.
3. A policy may be attributed to a corporation where it provides the most reasonable explanation of the conduct of that corporation.
4. Corporate knowledge of the commission of an offence may be established by proof that the actual or constructive knowledge of the relevant information was possessed within the corporation.
5. Knowledge may be possessed within a corporation even though the relevant information is divided between corporate personnel.
6. The criminal responsibility of legal persons shall not exclude the criminal responsibility of natural persons who are perpetrators or accomplices in the same crimes.

9.2 The Principle of Individual Criminal Responsibility Under Article 46B(1) of the Malabo Protocol (Annex)

Article 46B(1) of the Malabo Protocol (Annex) provides that "[a] person who commits an offence under this Statute shall be held individually responsible for the crime." This provision expressly endorses the fundamental principle of individual criminal responsibility for those crimes falling within the jurisdiction of the African Court of Justice and Human and Peoples' Rights.

The recognition of the principle of individual criminal responsibility for the commission of crimes under international law has been one of the most revolutionary achievements of international law in the last century. Indeed, individual criminal responsibility had already started to emerge as a concept under international law at the beginning of the last century. This development was the result of the commission of crimes during the First World War that were particularly cruel and had an international dimension, which warranted adequate measures and instruments for their repression.

However, while as early as in 1919 there was, with the Treaty of Versailles, a first attempt to establish the international responsibility of individuals for what was then called "a supreme offence against international morality and the sanctity of treaties",[1] it was only with the establishment of the International Military Tribunal of Nuremberg in 1945 that the principle of individual criminal responsibility received explicit recognition in international law for the first time.[2] As is well known, in fact, it is precisely in the jurisprudence of the International Military Tribunal of Nuremberg and in the subsequent proceedings that one can find the first affirmation of the principle of individual criminal responsibility under international law.[3]

---

[1] See Meloni 2010, p 11.

[2] Werle and Jeßberger 2014, marg. number 10 et seq.

[3] Ibid.

Following the Nuremberg Trial and the subsequent proceedings, the validity of the principle was no longer questioned. Both in international criminal jurisprudence and in the international instruments that have been drafted since the Second World War—including the 1948 UN Convention on Genocide, the 1949 four Geneva Conventions, the 1984 UN Convention against Torture, and all the International Law Commission's Draft Codes on international criminal law—the principle consistently been affirmed.[4]

In particular, the principle is of course embedded in the statutes of the international criminal tribunals established during the last decade of the last century, among which are the statutes of the two ad hoc tribunals for the former Yugoslavia and for Rwanda, and of the International Criminal Court. This latter statute, after limiting the jurisdiction of the Court to natural persons, provides that: "A person who commits a crime within the jurisdiction of the court shall be individually responsible and liable for punishment in accordance with this Statute" (Article 25(2) of the ICC Statute).

Notably, not only is the wording of Article 46B(1) of the Malabo Protocol (Annex) an almost verbatim reproduction of the provision in the ICC Statute (with the exception of a few words[5]), but—similar to the ICC Statute—the Annex to the Malabo Protocol also provides for a detailed regulation of the forms of commission/modes of liability for the crimes under the jurisdiction of the African Court of Justice and Human and Peoples' Rights.[6] However, contrary to the ICC Statute, no provision in the Annex to the Malabo Protocol is dedicated specifically to the definition of the subjective elements required for the integration of the crimes under the jurisdiction of the Court. In other words, there is no provision in the Annex to the Malabo Protocol comparable with Article 30 of the ICC Statute.

Thus, while on the one hand it is clear that, as a matter of principle, collective criminal responsibility shall not apply as a mode of liability for the crimes under the jurisdiction of the African Court of Justice and Human and Peoples' Rights [listed under Article 28A of the Malabo Protocol (Annex)], on the other hand, given the absence of any general provision on the subjective element (the *mens rea*) of the crimes, it can be questioned whether the recognition of the principle of individual criminal responsibility in the Annex to the Protocol also entails the recognition of an inherent culpability principle, as has been argued with regard to the ICC Statute.[7]

There is no doubt that the principle of individual criminal responsibility in its stricter meaning is recognised as a general principle applicable at the international level for every mode of liability.[8] Furthermore, given the current stage of evolution

---

[4] Meloni 2010, p. 26.

[5] The Protocol just omits the words "and liable for punishment".

[6] See *infra* Sect. 9.3.

[7] On this issue, see Pisani 2001, p. 1370; see also Sicurella 2009, pp. 21–38.

[8] See ICTY, *Tadić* AC Judgment, para 186 et seq.

of international criminal law, it is suggested that the principle at stake should be interpreted to its full extent thus not only excluding the possibility of attributing criminal liability for acts committed by others (collective liability), but also requiring the individuals' personal culpability in order to make them accountable for a specific crime.[9]

As we shall see in the next paragraph, some modes of liability as they are listed in the Annex to the Malabo Protocol raise the question whether the principles of individual liability and culpability can be respected at all if they had to be applied by the judges of the African Court of Justice and Human and Peoples' Rights. Notably, unlike what is provided for by other international criminal tribunals, also legal persons can be criminally liable under the Annex to the Malabo Protocol.[10]

9.3 The Provisions on Modes of Liability in the Annex to the Malabo Protocol

The Annex to the Malabo Protocol includes a fairly elaborate regulation of the modes of liability for the crimes under the jurisdiction of the African Court of Justice and Human and Peoples' Rights, which comprises both forms of commission and of participation under Article 28N, and command responsibility under Article 46B(3). However, as we shall see, this detailed regulation unfortunately does not always appear as a model of coherence and systematisation.

In order to grasp the complexity of the issue, a preliminary annotation is required. In fact, the apparent lack of coherence and respect for general principles of criminal law in the Annex to the Malabo Protocol can be also seen as a by-product of the inherent fragmentation of international criminal law and of its sources.[11] Given the great number of different courts, tribunals, international instruments and various codifications, there is in fact no uniform approach with respect to the modes of liability in international criminal law. Moreover, the notion of perpetration (or commission) of a crime and, more broadly, of criminal participation differs in the various legal systems and domestic orders.

Thus, it is not surprising that each international tribunal established from Nuremberg onwards adopted and developed different rules and modes of liability to regulate criminal participation and tried to overcome the difficulties related to the attribution of individual criminal responsibility for the commission of collective, macro-crimes. To simplify, we can note that two approaches emerged from the jurisprudence of the international courts and tribunals of the last twenty years: the "unitarian model" and the "differentiated model".

---

[9] See Werle and Jeßberger 2014, marg. numbers 119–120.

[10] See *infra*, Sect. 9.5.

[11] See the various contributions collected in the volume by van den Herik and Stahn (eds) 2012, and specifically on the modes of liability, may I refer to this author's chapter, Meloni 2012, p. 481 et seq.

The first approach is based on the statutes and case law of the two ad hoc tribunals established by the UN Security Council in 1993 and 1994. Article 7(1) of the ICTY Statute, in particular, provides that a person who planned, instigated, ordered, committed or otherwise aided and abetted in the planning, preparation or execution of a crime under the Tribunal's jurisdiction shall be individually responsible for that crime.

The second approach is based instead on the statute and case law of the International Criminal Court. Article 25(3)(a) to (d) of the ICC Statute contains different modes of liability: Committing a crime individually, jointly, or through another person; ordering, soliciting, or inducing a crime; aiding, abetting, and otherwise assisting a crime; and contributing to a group crime. Scholars tend to agree that the ICC Statute overcomes the "unitarian model" of the ICTY Statute and replaces it with a differentiated model.

In fact, as has been rightly noted, it was through the jurisprudence of the ad hoc tribunals that the "unitarian approach" (or "unified perpetrator model") progressively lost ground in favour of a more differentiated one.[12] In any event, the ICC case law has from the very beginning rejected the theories and modes of liability that had been developed within the ICTY (as the joint criminal enterprise doctrine) and replaced them with a theory based on the "control over the crime" (*Tatherrschaftslehre*) approach of Germanic derivation; thus "control over the crime" became the fundamental conceptual tool to distinguish between perpetration (participation as a principal) and complicity (secondary, derivative participation).[13] Read in a systematic way, we can note that Article 25(3)(a) of the ICC Statute refers to three forms of commission as forms of principal responsibility, while Article 25(3)(b) to (d) provides forms of secondary participation, namely: ordering, soliciting, or inducing a crime (b); aiding and abetting (c); contribution in any other way to the commission of a crime by a group (d).[14]

As will be elaborated in the following section, the Protocol's drafters appear to have drawn inspiration to a certain extent from the ICC Statute, although mixing it with other elements and provisions, so that the final result is an original creation not directly traceable to any past "codification" on the issue.

9.3.1 Forms of Commission and Participation: Article 28N(I.) to (Iii.) of the Malabo Protocol (Annex)

According to Article 28N(i.) to (iii.) of the Malabo Protocol (Annex),

> [a]n offence is committed by any person who, in relation to any of the crimes or offences provided for in this Statute:

[12] Werle 2007, p. 953. See also Werle and Burghardt 2014, p. 309.

[13] See Manacorda and Meloni 2011, p. 159.

[14] Werle and Jeßberger 2014, p. 196 et seq.

i. Incites, instigates, organizes, directs, facilitates, finances, counsels or participates as a principal, co-principal, agent or accomplice in any of the offences set forth in the present Statute;
ii. Aids or abets the commission of any of the offences set forth in the present Statute;
iii. Is an accessory before or after the fact or in any other manner participates in a collaboration or conspiracy to commit any of the offences set forth in the present Statute.

As already anticipated, unlike the other provisions of the Annex to the Malabo Protocol which have been literally copied and pasted from existing international law instruments or international tribunals' statutes, Article 28N of the Malabo Protocol (Annex) appears to be an original creation of its drafters. However, one can immediately observe that the language of the provision lacks clarity and is difficult to interpret systematically. The chapeau of Article 28N is especially confusing. By affirming that "an offence is committed", it seems to imply that the modes of liability that follow are all forms of commission. In other words, if one had to interpret it literally, it would mean that all types of conduct listed in the Protocol's provision under subparagraphs (i.) to (iii.) introduce forms of principal liability, and thus entail the gravest form of responsibility in criminal law.

As this would be inconsistent with general principles on modes of liability, as well as with the Protocol's overall structure, it is advisable not to interpret the provision literally but to instead try to systematise it according to a differentiated model where, similar to the ICC Statute, distinctions are made between principal and secondary modes of liability. For simplicity, it is possible to divide the analysis according to three levels, corresponding to subparagraphs (i.) to (iii.) of Article 28N.[15]

9.3.1.1 Commission, Instigation and Forms of Complicity

Pursuant to Article 28N(i.) of the Malabo Protocol (Annex), responsibility arises under the Annex to the Protocol for those who incite, instigate, organize, direct, facilitate, finance, counsel or participate as a principal, co-principal, agent or accomplice in any of the crimes included under the Annex to the Protocol.

The provision at stake brings together types of conduct which are in fact very different to each other. The rather confusing language of the drafters puts forms of commission—giving rise to principal liability ("participates as a principal, co-principal, agent")—and forms of secondary participation in the crimes ("incites, instigates, […] facilitates, finances, counsels, […] participates as accomplice"), as well as conduct that can be considered as constituting either principal or secondary liability depending on the circumstances ("organizes, directs"), all on the same level.

The somewhat redundant nature and lack of clarity in the provision is nothing new in international criminal law: indeed, even the Rome Statute, though considered the most advanced instrument containing a sort of codification of the general part of international criminal law so far, shows deficiencies and redundancies in its

[15] See infra Sects. 9.3.1.1–9.3.1.3.

formulation, especially with regard to Article 25(3) which contains the regulation on modes of liability.

In any event, what matters is that the judges who will in the future be called to apply this provision of the Protocol shall do so being aware of and taking into consideration the inherent differences of each of the conducts outlined in such provision. Moreover, it shall be noted that the modes of liability under Article 28(N) of the Malabo Protocol (Annex) are meant to apply to all crimes under the jurisdiction of the African Court of Justice and Human and Peoples' Rights. It is puzzling, however, to observe how some of these modes of liability overlap with the definitions of the crimes.

Let us take for instance the piracy[16] definition: Article 28F(c) of the Malabo Protocol (Annex) refers to "inciting" or "intentionally facilitating" piracy as a crime, whereas Article 28N(i.) refers to inciting a crime, in general, as a mode of liability.

As inciting the incitement of a crime would amount to a double anticipation of the criminal protection/responsibility, in contrast to general principles of criminal law such as, in particular, the "harm or offence principle", the only possibility for the judges of the African Court of Justice and Human and Peoples' Rights will be to solve this apparent contradiction by evaluating the conduct of instigating a crime either pursuant to the one or the other provision, thus considering instigation either an inchoate crime or a mode of liability (but not both).

The problem, however, is not confined to piracy. With regard to the crime of terrorism, Article 28G(b) of the Malabo Protocol (Annex) defines as discrete offences many of the types of conduct which are already covered by Article 28N as general modes of liability for the crimes under the Protocol: "Any promotion, sponsoring, contribution to, command, aid, incitement, encouragement, attempt, threat, conspiracy, organizing or procurement of any person".

Similar remarks can be made with regard to other crimes as defined in the Protocol, such as mercenarism (Article 28H) and money laundering[17] (Article 28I*bis*).

Finally, one can note that some "typical" types of conduct entailing criminal responsibility for the commission of international crimes are not mentioned: in particular Article 28N of the Malabo Protocol (Annex) does not mention the conduct of "ordering". Of course this does not mean that ordering a crime will have to go unpunished before the African Court of Justice and Human and Peoples' Rights, but the judges will need to bring this typical behaviour under a different concept among those listed in the Annex to the Protocol: for instance, "directing" or "organising", or even "participat[ing] as a co-principal" in cases where the order is of a binding nature and the subordinate is only used as a tool, a gear in the machine.[18]

---

[16] On the crimes of piracy, terrorism and mercenarism see the chapter by Jeßberger in this book.

[17] On the crime of money laundering see the chapter by Fernandez in this book.

[18] This is the so-called "perpetrator behind the perpetrator" scenario by Roxin 1963, p. 93; see also—for a re-adaptation of this doctrine—ICC, PTC I Decision on Confirmation of Charges, Prosecutor against Thomas Lubanga Dyilo, 29 January 2007.

9.3.1.2 Aiding or Abetting

As for the second level of participation outlined by Article 28N(ii.), the conduct of aiding or abetting a crime—which, without doubt, entails a secondary form of liability[19]—is less problematic to interpret. In the first place, the provision is drafted in a relatively linear manner, as it only mentions one mode of liability. Moreover, without arguing that the interpretation of aiding and abetting is per se an easy one, it shall be noted that there is abundant jurisprudence stemming from the ad hoc tribunals and the ICC case law on this mode of liability, such that the elements of aiding and abetting have been rather extensively investigated. As a form of assistance, it seems to require a lower degree of involvement than those modes of liability under the previous subpara (i.).[20]

9.3.1.3 Conspiracy

The interpretation of the last provision under Article 28N(iii.) of the Malabo Protocol (Annex) is, however, more complicated. According to the wording, responsibility arises with regard to an individual who is an "accessory before or after the fact" or in any other way "participates in a collaboration or conspiracy to commit any of the offences set forth in the present Statute".

The category of "accessory after the fact" is already a very complicated and problematic one: being an "accessory after the fact" is by no means comparable with being an "accessory before the fact", notwithstanding the language of the Annex to the Protocol that seems to equate them. Moreover, the common law doctrine of accessory after the fact not only is not recognized in other legal systems (such as those of Roman-Germanic tradition), but also is considered obsolete and has been rejected as such by international criminal tribunals.[21] Indeed, the ICC Statute does not include forms of complicity after the fact.

The other problematic category envisaged by the Protocol is "conspiracy", a concept that has been controversial in international criminal law ever since Nuremberg and the post-Second World War trials. This doctrine, which once again is more familiar to the Anglo-American legal systems than to the Roman-Germanic systems, was used in particular to encompass the criminal liability of a collective of persons with regard to the commission of group crimes. Indeed, this was typically the case at Nuremberg, where the IMT Statute explicitly provided for this mode of liability for the crimes under the jurisdiction of the Tribunal.[22]

---

[19] Werle 2007, p. 953 et seq.

[20] For a recent analysis, which also gives account of counter arguments to this approach, see Werle and Burghardt 2014, pp. 315−318.

[21] See ICTY, Prosecutor v. Kordić & Čerkez (IT-95-14/2-PT), Čerkez Defence's Motion to strike portions of indictment alleging "failure to punish" liability, 11 December 1997.

[22] Meloni 2010, p. 21. On the crime of conspiracy in international criminal law see Okoth 2014.

Recourse to conspiracy, however, was then and remains now very controversial, in particular for its dubious compatibility with the principle of personal culpability.[23] The legal concept has also been challenged in the sense that it was unclear whether it created a separate offence, alongside crimes against humanity, war crimes and aggression, or just a mode of liability for these crimes.

Coming to more recent times, it can be noted that, according to the majority of scholars, the Rome Statute rejected the notion of conspiracy as it was applied in the trials after the Second World War. Nonetheless, Article 25(3)(d) of the ICC Statute provides for a residual form of responsibility that has been interpreted as a cross over between conspiracy and the offence of "criminal association" found in civil law countries.[24]

With regard to the provision at stake, it seems that conspiracy is indeed meant to be a separate offence; it would otherwise be difficult to understand how one could participate in it. What is meant by the words "participates in a collaboration" is also obscure, although it is probably just a repetition—using different words—of a concept similar to conspiracy. In any event, it makes sense to systematically interpret this provision as the criminalization of any contribution (participation) to the commission of a crime under the Court's jurisdiction by a group, and is thus in a way similar to the provision of Article 25(3)(d) of the ICC Statute.

9.3.2 Command Responsibility: Article 46B(3) of the Malabo Protocol (Annex)

Article 46B(3) of the Malabo Protocol (Annex) provides that:

> The fact that any of the acts referred to in Article 28A of the present Statute was committed by a subordinate does not relieve his or her superior of criminal responsibility if he or she knew or had reason to know that the subordinate was about to commit such acts or had done so and the superior failed to take the necessary and reasonable measures to prevent such acts or to punish the perpetrators thereof.

Even if contained in a separate article, the above-mentioned provision introduces an additional mode of liability that is traditionally called "command or superior responsibility".[25] In this regard it can be noted that the Annex to the Malabo Protocol adopted the very same language as the statutes of the ad hoc tribunals (Article 7(3) of the ICTY Statute and Article 6(3) of the ICTR Statute), departing from the most recent definition which is contained in the ICC Statute. In this sense the Protocol marks a step back from the elaborate and very precise provision of Article 28 of the ICC Statute.

---

[23] Meloni 2010, p 21.

[24] On this issue, see di Martino 2005, p 208; see also Ambos 2007, pp 172-173.

[25] For the features of this mode of liability, see extensively Burghardt 2008; Meloni 2010.

Firstly, contrary to the ICC Statute, no distinction is made in the Protocol between command responsibility (applicable to military commanders) and superior responsibility (applicable outside the military field). Nevertheless, and even in the absence of an ad hoc regulation, there can be no doubt that the provision also applies to civilian superiors. Whether command responsibility also applied outside the military sphere was one of the first issues that the ad hoc tribunals had to solve: in fact, notwithstanding some initial uncertainty, from the outset the jurisprudence of the tribunals consistently interpreted the term "superior" as including not only the military commander but also the civilian leader.[26] The reasoning was based in particular on the jurisprudence following the Second World War; more specifically, from the convictions of Japanese government officials in the Tokyo trial, the ICTY judges concluded that the applicability of command responsibility to civilian leaders was a principle of international customary law.[27] Both in the jurisprudence of the ICTY and of the ICTR there are several examples of the application of the command responsibility doctrine to non-military superiors.[28] Ultimately, what emerges from past jurisprudence is that what matters is not so much the personal status of the defendant—whether a military or civilian superior—as his or her "position of authority" over the perpetrators of the underlying crimes.[29]

Secondly, the mental element of command responsibility in the Annex to the Malabo Protocol is articulated solely around two standards (rather than the three foreseen by the Rome Statute): the actual knowledge ("knew") and the "had reason to know" standard. With regard to the latter mental standard, the ICTY judges in the seminal *Celebici* case found that the superior can be held accountable only to the extent that some specific information was actually available to him or her, information which would make the superior aware of the occurrence of the subordinates' crimes.[30] Thus, as confirmed by the ICTY Appeals Chamber, the formula "had reason to know" should be interpreted as being substantially equivalent to the meaning of Article 86(2) of the Additional Protocol I, in the part where it provides that superiors should have "information enabling—or which should have enabled—them to conclude" that crimes were being committed.[31]

In sum, it is clear that the *mens rea* standard of superior responsibility rejects any strict liability: contrary to some older judgments delivered after the Second World War, the most recent international jurisprudence does not question the

---

[26] ICTY, Čelebići TC Judgment, para 356.

[27] ICTY, Čelebići TC Judgment, paras 357–361. Notably, the ICTR judges in analysing the same post-Second World War jurisprudence had concluded that the principle of command responsibility is contentious in the civilian sphere; see ICTR, Akayesu TC Judgment, para 490.

[28] Meloni 2010, p. 93.

[29] See ICTY, Aleskovski TC judgment, para 103, upheld by the AC, para 76.

[30] ICTY, Čelebići AC Judgment.

[31] ICTY, Čelebići AC Judgment, para 233. See also ICTY, Blaškić AC Chamber Judgment, para 406: "The responsibility can be imposed for deliberately refraining from finding out but not for negligently failing to find out". See also Meloni 2010, p 113.

necessity of a requirement of culpability on the part of the superior. This implies that the required *mens rea* of the superior must be properly established at trial and must be respectful of the culpability principle as recognised in international law.

In this regard it is also interesting to note that although the text of the ad hoc tribunals' statutes, as well as the text of the Annex to the Malabo Protocol, do not distinguish between the degree of knowledge required of the military commanders and of the civilian superiors for the purposes of superior responsibility, there are a few judgments in which this difference has been introduced. For example, borrowing the wording of the Rome Statute, the judges of the International Criminal Tribunal for Rwanda decided that for a civilian superior to be responsible it has to be proved that he knew or "consciously disregarded information which clearly indicated or put him on notice that his subordinates had committed, or were about to commit" crimes.[32]

Thus, notwithstanding the fact that the Annex to the Malabo Protocol does not explicitly entail any difference in the regulation of command responsibility (in the military field) *vis-à-vis* superior responsibility (in the civilian context), it can be foreseen that such differences will emerge and have to be taken into consideration at the interpretation stage.

Similarly to what happened before the ad hoc tribunals, the fact that the defendant is a civilian superior, rather than a military commander, surely will be ripe with consequences. Indeed, the following statement seems to still be valid, even after the entry into force of the ICC Statute: "Civilian superiors undoubtedly bear responsibility for subordinate offences under certain conditions, but whether their responsibility contains identical elements to that of military commanders is not clear in customary law".[33]

9.4 Superior Orders

Pursuant to Article 46B(4) of the Malabo Protocol (Annex), "[t]he fact that an accused person acted pursuant to the order of a Government or of a superior shall not relieve him or her of criminal responsibility, but may be considered in mitigation of punishment if the Court determines that justice so requires."

This provision reproduces verbatim Article 7(4) of the ICTY Statute and the parallel Article 6(4) of the ICTR Statute. It regulates one of the most problematic issues regarding the attribution of criminal liability for international crimes, namely the defence of superior orders. As before the ad hoc tribunals, the Protocol excludes the applicability of such a defence with regard to the commission of all crimes under the jurisdiction of the African Court of Justice and Human and Peoples' Rights. This is in line with customary international law, which prescribes

---

32 ICTR, Kayishema and Ruzindana TC Judgment, paras 227–228.

33 ICTY, Čelebići AC Judgment, para 240. Meloni 2010, p. 128.

that acting under orders cannot in principle free a person from criminal liability for the commission of crimes under international law.[34] The "absolute liability principle" thus replaced the "*respondeat superior*" principle, which found application until the Second World War: pursuant to the latter principle, superior orders always excluded the criminal liability of the subordinate who had acted pursuant to those orders or instructions.[35]

The ICC Statute, on the contrary, adopted a third, intermediate position, which has been described as the "manifest illegality principle", prescribing that superior orders can only amount to a criminal defence under specific circumstances, namely: (i) that the order was binding; (ii) that it was not manifestly unlawful; and (iii) that the person did not know that it was unlawful (Article 33 of the ICC Statute). Moreover, under the Rome Statute, an order to commit genocide or crimes against humanity is always manifestly unlawful, thus leaving some limited room for the applicability of the defence only with regard to war crimes. Nevertheless, such a provision has been criticised by some scholars, as it would represent a step back *vis-à-vis* the evolution of international criminal law, which, as anticipated, seems to completely exclude the relevance of superior orders with regard to the commission of the core crimes.[36]

In this sense, the provision of the Annex to the Malabo Protocol appears more in line with the customary law standard. However, it can be noted that Article 46B(4) applies to every offence under the jurisdiction of the African Court of Justice and Human and Peoples' Rights, and thus much more broadly than the core crimes usually falling under the jurisdiction of international courts and tribunals. One could question whether the absolute liability principle is in fact appropriate also with regard to other crimes listed in the Annex to the Protocol, such as corruption or money laundering, which are of course very serious offences but lack the "monstrosity" character[37] of genocide, crimes against humanity, war crimes and the crimes of aggression.

Obeying superior orders can undoubtedly still play a role under the Statute and can be taken into consideration as a mitigating factor in determining the sentence.

9.5 Corporate Criminal Liability: Article 46C of the Malabo Protocol (Annex)

One of the most important innovations of the Annex to the Malabo Protocol, compared to the ICC Statute and other international criminal tribunals' statutes, is the inclusion of a provision on corporate criminal liability for international crimes.

34 Werle and Jeßberger 2014, marg. number 658 et seq.

35 Ibid., p. 249.

36 Gaeta 1999, p. 172.

37 Werle and Jeßberger 2014, marg. number 665.

According to Article 46C(1) of the Malabo Protocol (Annex), "[f]or the purpose of this Statute the Court shall have jurisdiction over legal persons, with the exception of States." Thus, contrary to other international criminal law institutions established so far, which have jurisdiction only over natural persons (see in particular Article 25(3)(1) of the ICC Statute), the African Court of Justice and Human Peoples' Rights will also have the power to adjudicate the responsibility of legal persons.

It is in fact not surprising that, currently, no international court or tribunal can exercise criminal jurisdiction over transnational business corporations. Indeed, corporate criminal responsibility is a very complex issue, which has not yet found any uniform regulation in the various legal systems, not even on a regional level. In Europe, for instance, there is no consensus on whether corporations can commit and therefore be liable for crimes. Some states, such as Switzerland, do admit this possibility, while others, like Germany and Italy, do not. Indeed, one of the biggest obstacles to the recognition of the criminal liability of corporations, especially in those systems of Roman-Germanic tradition, is a strict interpretation of the principle of culpability: evidently no legal person can be said to have the "intent and knowledge", thus to be acting with *dolus*, in a naturalistic sense. Therefore, many legal systems do not admit the possibility of having a corporation criminally liable for the commission of crimes, envisaging at most a corporate responsibility of an administrative or civil nature.

The drafters of the Annex to the Malabo Protocol also had to deal with this crucial issue. In this regard, the Annex provides in Article 46C(2) that "[c]orporate intention to commit an offence may be established by proof that it was the policy of the corporation to do the act which constituted the offence." Moreover, the Protocol specifies [in Article 46C(3) to (4)] that "[a] policy may be attributed to a corporation where it provides the most reasonable explanation of the conduct of that corporation. Corporate knowledge of the commission of an offence may be established by proof that the actual or constructive knowledge of the relevant information was possessed within the corporation."

That transnational corporations are often indirectly involved in massive human rights violations amounting to international crimes is beyond dispute. In this sense, the attempt by the drafters to hold corporations directly accountable under international criminal law for the commission of those international and transnational crimes under the jurisdiction of the African Court has to be welcomed. In fact, as has been noted, even if the efforts to hold military and political leaders accountable for the commission of international crimes have become increasingly successful in the recent past, the prosecution and punishment of their business accomplices has remained an exception.[38] Therefore, the restriction of the jurisdiction of the ICC, the ad hoc tribunals, and other international or hybrid criminal courts to natural persons leaves gaps of impunity. Notably, a proposal to extend the ICC's jurisdiction to legal persons was presented at the time of the diplomatic conference in Rome, but was ultimately not included in the Statute.[39]

---

38 Jeßberger and Geneuss 2010, p. 1.

39 Nerlich 2010, p. 896.

It remains to be seen how the provision of Article 46C of the Malabo Protocol (Annex) will be interpreted by the future judges of the African Court of Justice and Human and Peoples' Rights: in the absence of specific case law and jurisprudence on the issue, difficulties can be foreseen in developing solid criteria for the attribution of criminal responsibility to corporations/legal persons, a responsibility which is always derived from conduct of natural persons and is thus imputed liability.

Moreover, taking into consideration the different features of the crimes under the jurisdiction of the African Court of Justice and Human and Peoples' Rights, while it appears easier to attribute responsibility to corporations for those crimes that have an economic dimension or involve some kind of business activity, as in the case of, for instance, corruption, money laundering, and the various forms of trafficking or exploitation of natural resources, it will be more difficult to attribute responsibility with regard to those crimes that have no such economic underpinning, such as killing, rape or other war crimes and crimes against humanity of a similar nature.[40] As regards the crime of aggression, liability of transnational business corporations appears to be even more limited, and conceivable only in very restricted circumstances.

9.6 Conclusions

If, on the on the one hand, one can express some criticism with regard to the regulation of the modes of liability included in the Annex to the Malabo Protocol, on the other hand, the Annex also presents some interesting provisions on modes of liability that may be inspirational for future developments in international criminal law. In addition to the exclusion of the defence of superior orders for all crimes included in the Annex to the Malabo Protocol, I am referring in particular to the inclusion of corporate criminal liability for the crimes under the jurisdiction of the African Court of Justice and Human and Peoples' Rights. Such an innovation, surely a bold one, is in line with the development of international criminal law and not in breach of the principle of *nullum crimen sine lege*.

In fact, although, as we have seen, the Annex to the Malabo Protocol is the first international instrument to extend liability for international crimes to legal persons, scholars have noted that a rule of substantive international law providing for the punishment of legal persons for core crimes does in fact already exist.

---

[40] Ibid, pp. 900–901: "Some of the post-World War II cases seem to confirm this approach: in *Flick*, the defendants were charged with war crimes and crimes against humanity for their participation in the slave-labour programme, the spoliation of public and private property, the exercise of anti-Semitic economic pressure to obtain property, and the financing of the SS. All these crimes had a clear economical underpinning. Similarly, in *Krupp*, agents of the Krupp industrial conglomerate were held responsible for participation in the slave labour programme and for plunder and spoliation."

According to some authors, international customary law would provide for criminal punishment of transnational businesses for core international crimes.[41] Such a position, however, is difficult to sustain in the absence of any state practice and *opinio juris* in that respect. It is certainly true that some post Second World War crimes against humanity and war crimes cases involved corporations (as, for instance, in the *Flick*, *Krupp* and *IG Farben* cases), yet the defendants in these cases were always natural persons. A more moderate position thus appears to be more convincing. As it was observed by one author (a few years before the drafting of the Annex to the Malabo Protocol): "It is conceivable that a norm exists even though there is currently no forum where it could be enforced. The norm thus would lie dormant, but it could be activated, without breach of the *nullum crimen* principle, through the establishment of a court or tribunal vested with jurisdiction over transnational business corporations."[42] Moreover: "To argue that transnational business corporations are bound by the prohibitions underlying international crimes is in line with a general trend in international law to broaden its scope of application: traditionally, international law applied only to the relationships among states and state-like entities. The rise of international human rights law, and indeed international criminal law itself, changed this dramatically."[43] It was indeed with the criminal proceedings that took place after the Second World War that the major paradigm shift happened, and that shift did not lie as much in the fact that rules of international law were found to apply to natural persons, but that subjects that were non-state private actors were considered to be bound by international law norms directly.[44] According to the same author, whether these non-state actors are natural or legal persons would conceptually be only of secondary relevance: "legal persons are but a man-made legal construction to facilitate social interaction. Why, then, should not the same basic rules apply to them as to natural persons?"[45]

In sum, it remains to be seen how the judges of the African Court of Justice and Human and Peoples' Rights will interpret the complex provisions of the Protocol; surely some of them, such as the reintroduction of immunity for the African heads of state,[46] will greatly undermine the credibility and efficacy of the Court if not amended. Other provisions, such as the criminal responsibility of corporations, will on the contrary, represent a progressive and positive development for international criminal law and could perhaps serve as an inspiration for future amendments of the ICC Statute.

---

41 More thorougly in this regard, Nerlich 2010, p. 898, with references in particular no. 7.

42 Ibid.

43 Ibid.

44 Ibid.

45 Ibid.

46 See the chapter by Tladi in this book.

References

Ambos K (2007) Joint Criminal Enterprise and Command Responsibility. J Int Crim Justice 5:159–183

Burghardt B (2008) Die Vorgesetztenverantwortlichkeit im völkerrechtlichen Straftatsystem. Berliner Wissenschafts-Verlag, Berlin

Burghardt B (2010) Modes of participation and their role in a general concept of crimes under international law. In: Burchard C, Triffterer O, Vogel J (eds) The ICC Review Conference and the Future of the International Criminal Court. Wolters Kluwer, Köln, pp 81–94

di Martino A (2005) La disciplina del concorso di persone. In: Cassese A, Chiavario M and De Francesco G (eds) Problemi attuali della giustizia penale internazionale, Giappichelli, pp 189–214

Gaeta P (1999) The defence of superior orders, the Statute of the International Criminal Court versus customary international law. Eur J Int Law 10:172–191

Jeßberger F, Geneuss J (2010) Introduction to Special Issue Transnational Business and International Criminal Law. J Int Crim Justice 8:1–4

Manacorda S, Meloni C (2011) Indirect perpetration versus joint criminal enterprise. Concurring approaches in the practice of international criminal law? J Int Crim Justice 9:159–178

Meloni C (2010) Command Responsibility in international law. T.M.C Asser Press, The Hague

Meloni C (2012) Fragmentation of the notion of co-perpetration in international criminal law? In: van den Herik L, Stahn C (eds) The diversification and fragmentation of international criminal law. Martinus Nijhoff Publishers, Leiden, pp 481–502

Nerlich V (2010) Core crimes and transnational business corporations. J Int Crim Justice 8:895–908

Okoth J (2014) The crime of conspiracy in international criminal law. T.M.C. Asser Press, The Hague

Pisani N (2001) L'elemento psicologico del crimine internazionale nella parte generale dello Statuto della Corte Internazionale Penale, Rivista Italiana di Diritto e Procedura Penale, pp 1370–1392

Roxin C (1963) Straftaten im Rahmen organisatorischer Machtapparate. Goltdammer's Archiv für Strafrecht 110:193–207

Sicurella R (2009) Per una teoria della colpevolezza nel sistema dello Statuto della Corte Penale Internazionale, Giuffré

van den Herik L, Stahn C (eds) (2012) The diversification and fragmentation of international criminal law. Martinus Nijhoff Publishers, Leiden

van Sliedregt E (2012) Individual criminal responsibility in international criminal law. Oxford University Press, Oxford

Werle G (2007) Individual criminal responsibility in Article 25 ICC Statute. J Int Crim Justice 5:953–975

Werle G, Burghardt B (2014) Establishing degrees of responsibility: modes of participation in Article 25 of the ICC Statute. In: van Sliedregt E, Vasiliev S (eds) Pluralism in international criminal law. Oxford University Press, Oxford, pp 301–319

Werle G, Jeßberger F (2014) Principles of international criminal law, 3rd edn. Oxford University Press, Oxford

Chapter 10
Preconditions to the Exercise of Jurisdiction (Article 46E*bis*), Exercise of Jurisdiction (Article 46F) and the Prosecutor (Article 46G)

Volker Nerlich

Abstract Articles 46E*bis* to 46G define the conditions under which the African Court of Justice and Human and Peoples' Rights may exercise its jurisdiction over the crimes set out in Articles 28A to 28M of the Malabo Protocol (Annex). As such, the provisions are of key importance to the jurisdictional reach of the African Court of Justice and Human and Peoples' Rights. Articles 46E*bis* to 46G are largely modeled upon the respective provisions of the ICC Statute, including the provision on the opening of *proprio motu* investigations by the Office of the Prosecutor. Nevertheless, compared to the International Criminal Court, the jurisdictional reach of the African Court of Justice and Human and Peoples' Rights is significantly broadened by the inclusion of jurisdiction based on the passive personality and protective principles. Some of the provisions, however, are in important aspects incomplete and become functional only if interpreted with reference to the corresponding provision of the ICC Statute. Generally, additional procedural rules are likely to be needed to make the African Court of Justice and Human and Peoples' Rights' jurisdictional regime fully operational in practice.

Keywords Africa · African Union · Territoriality Principle · Active and Passive Personality Principles · Protective Principle · Trigger Mechanism · *Proprio motu* investigation · Jurisdiction · Sovereignty · Vienna Convention on the Law of Treaties · Universal jurisdiction · Non-retroactivity · Appeal · Challenges to jurisdiction · Acceptance of jurisdiction

The views expressed are those of the author and cannot be attributed to the United Nations or to the International Criminal Court.
All internet sources in this chapter were last visited on 30 June 2016.

V. Nerlich (✉)
Legal Adviser, International Criminal Court, The Hague, The Netherlands;
Humboldt-Universität zu Berlin, Berlin, Germany
e-mail: volker.nerlich.jicj@gmail.com

G. Werle and M. Vormbaum (eds.), *The African Criminal Court*, International Criminal Justice Series 10, DOI 10.1007/978-94-6265-150-0_10

Contents

10.1 Extracts from the Malabo Protocol (Annex)

Article 46E*bis* Preconditions to the exercise of Jurisdiction

1. A State which becomes a Party to this Protocol and Statute thereby accepts the jurisdiction of the Court with respect to the crimes referred to in Article 28A.
2. The Court may exercise its jurisdiction if one or more of the following conditions apply:

   (a) The State on the territory of which the conduct in question occurred or, if the crime was committed on board a vessel or aircraft, the State of registration of that vessel or aircraft.
   (b) The State of which the person accused of the crime is a national.
   (c) When the victim of the crime is a national of that State.
   (d) Extraterritorial acts by non-nationals which threaten a vital interest of that State.

3. If the acceptance of a State which is not a Party to this Statute is required under para 2, that State may, by declaration lodged with the Registrar, accept the exercise [sic, end of sentence].

Article 46F Exercise of Jurisdiction

The Court may exercise its jurisdiction with respect to a crime referred to in Article 28A in accordance with the provisions of this Statute if:

1. A situation in which one or more of such crimes appears to have been committed is referred to the Prosecutor by a State Party.
2. A situation in which one or more of such crimes appears to have been committed is referred to the Prosecutor by the Assembly of Heads of State and Government of the African Union or the Peace and Security Council of the African Union.
3. The Prosecutor has initiated an investigation in respect of such a crime in accordance with Article 46G.

Article 46G The Prosecutor

1. The Office of the Prosecutor may initiate investigations proprio motu on the basis of information on crimes within the jurisdiction of the Court.
2. The Office of the Prosecutor shall analyze the seriousness of information received. For this purpose, he or she may seek additional information from States, organs of the African Union or United Nations, intergovernmental or non-governmental organizations, or other reliable sources that he or she deems appropriate, and may receive written or oral testimony.
3. If the Office of the Prosecutor concludes that there is a reasonable basis to proceed with an investigation, it shall submit to a Pre-Trial Chamber a request for authorization of an investigation, together with any supporting material collected. Victims may make representations to the Pre-Trial Chamber, in accordance with the Rules of the Court.
4. If the Pre-Trial Chamber, upon examination of the request and supporting material, considers that there is a reasonable basis to proceed with an investigation, and that the case appears to fall within the jurisdiction of the Court, it shall authorize the commencement of the investigation, without prejudice to subsequent determinations by the Court with regard to the jurisdiction and admissibility of a case.
5. The refusal of the Pre-Trial Chamber to authorize the investigation shall not preclude the presentation of a subsequent request by the Office of the Prosecutor based on new facts or evidence regarding the same situation.
6. If, after the preliminary examination referred to in paras 1 and 2, the Office of the Prosecutor concludes that the information provided does not constitute a reasonable basis for an investigation, it shall inform those who provided the information. This shall not preclude the Office of the Prosecutor from considering further information submitted to him or her regarding the same situation in the light of new facts or evidence.

10.2 Introduction

Articles 46E*bis* ("Preconditions for the Exercise of Jurisdiction"), 46F ("Exercise of Jurisdiction") and 46G ("The Prosecutor") of the Malabo Protocol (Annex), regulate the conditions under which the African Court of Justice and Human and Peoples' Rights may exercise its jurisdiction over the crimes set out in Articles 28A to 28M of the Malabo Protocol (Annex). As such, the three provisions are of central importance to the Court's criminal jurisdiction. They are inspired by, and modeled upon, Articles 13 to 15 of the ICC Statute, which for that reason may serve as a useful reference point in the interpretation and application of Articles 46E*bis* to 46G. This appears to be all the more necessary as there are significant *lacunae* in particular in the text of Article 46E*bis*, which render the provision (almost) dysfunctional.

The present chapter seeks to analyze the Articles 46E*bis* to 46G of the Malabo Protocol (Annex) and propose an interpretation thereof.

10.3 Article 46E*bis:* Defining the Extent of the Criminal Jurisdiction of the African Court of Justice and Human and Peoples' Rights

10.3.1 Criminal Jurisdiction and Respect for Other States' Sovereignty

In addition to defining the substantive crimes—either through legislation or case law—any criminal jurisdiction has to determine the extent of its competence to prescribe and to try such crimes. While the latter can be framed either as a question of the reach of the substantive law,[1] or as a question of the powers of a given court to exercise jurisdiction and therefore as a matter of procedural law,[2] the underlying issue in terms of public international law remains the same: to what extent may states legislate and apply their criminal laws in cases that involve a foreign element—for instance when the crime was not, or not exclusively, committed on a given state's territory, or was committed by or against a foreign national? The competence to legislate and to adjudicate criminal behavior is an aspect of a state's sovereignty, which must, however, also respect the sovereignty of other states.[3]

[1] See, for instance, Sections 3–7 of the German Criminal Code, which determines the applicability of that Code to conduct occurring inside and outside Germany. These provisions are complemented by procedural rules governing the exercise of jurisdiction over crimes committed outside Germany by the German prosecutorial authorities; see Sections 153c et seq. of the German Code of Criminal Procedure. See also Ambos 2014, p. 3 et seq.

[2] See Ambos 2014, p. 3.

[3] See generally Brownlie 2008, p. 291; Ambos 2014, p. 24 et seq.; Cassese 2005, p. 49 et seq.

For an international criminal jurisdiction, in particular one established by way of a multilateral treaty ("enabling treaty"), two principal relationships need to be distinguished: that between the international criminal jurisdictions and States Parties to the enabling treaty (the "internal relationship"); and that between the international criminal jurisdiction and states not party to the enabling treaty (the "external relationship"). As regards the "internal relationship", the matter appears to be straightforward in terms of international law: a state's decision to vest an international entity with the power to adjudicate crimes committed on that state's territory and by that state's nationals does not per se involve any other state's sovereign interests and would thus be in line with general public international law.[4] Similarly, the principle of sovereignty would appear to be undisturbed if an enabling treaty allows for the prosecution of crimes that involve more than one State Party. For example, and irrespective of the more specific rules of international law regarding the exercise of criminal jurisdiction, no issue of sovereignty would arise if states vested an international criminal jurisdiction with the competence to try crimes committed by any of their own nationals on any of their national territories. To the extent that the exercise of jurisdiction by an international court may be construed as an (indirect) interference by all States Parties to the enabling treaty in the internal affairs of the State Party concerned, the sovereign power to enter into treaties provides sufficient grounds for justification. By entering into the enabling treaty, the State Party concerned accepted such interference.

As regards the "external relationship", however, the matter is more complicated. Does an international criminal jurisdiction have to respect the same limitations in the exercise of jurisdiction as states have to in their relations with each other? Or does the international character of the criminal jurisdiction allow for a broader interference with a state's internal affairs, even if the state in question is not party to the enabling treaty? In international criminal law, this question is often addressed in the context of discussions on immunities from prosecution.[5]

[4] Note, however, that issues of municipal law (in particular, constitutional law) may arise, including in relation to a potential *jus de non evocando*. Furthermore, it is also perceivable that issues of international human rights law may arise if the international criminal jurisdiction in question does not comply fully with fair trial standards as set out, for example, Article 14 of the ICCPR. In such a situation, exposing a state's nationals to that international criminal jurisdiction may amount to an (indirect) breach of the human rights obligations of the state in question.

[5] See International Court of Justice, Case Concerning the Arrest Warrant of 11 April 2000 (Democratic Republic of the Congo vs. Belgium), Judgment, 14 February 2002, I.C.J. Reports 2002, 3, at para 61, where the International Court of Justice held that, while incumbent foreign ministers enjoy immunity from prosecution by third states, "an incumbent or former Minister for Foreign Affairs may be subject to criminal proceedings before certain International Criminal Courts, where they have jurisdiction." This finding does not, however, imply that immunities or other restrictions to the exercise of criminal jurisdiction are generally inapplicable as concerns *any* International Criminal Court. In this regard see further Gaeta 2009, pp. 320–321: "International Criminal Courts are not organs of a particular state; they act on behalf of the international community as a whole to protect collective or universal values, and thus to repress very

Nevertheless, it equally arises with regard to the exercise of criminal jurisdiction in respect of cases involving a foreign element concerning a state not party to the enabling treaty. Arguably, the general rules regarding the exercise of criminal jurisdiction in cases involving a foreign element must be applied *mutatis mutandis.* This is because states acting through an international institution may not assume powers vis-à-vis third states that they could not exercise individually, at least to the extent that the international institution in question—such as the African Court of Justice and Human and Peoples' Rights—is neither universal nor even destined to be universal:[6] it bears reminding that the Malabo Protocol is open for ratification to Member States of the African Union only,[7] which is, in turn, open only to African states.[8]

Accordingly, in drafting the provisions of the Annex to the Malabo Protocol regarding the extent of jurisdiction of the African Court of Justice and Human and Peoples' Rights, the rules of general international law regarding the exercise by states of criminal jurisdiction had to be borne in mind. This is reflected, if imperfectly, in Article 46E*bis*(2) of the Malabo Protocol (Annex), which will be discussed in more detail below. In contrast, Article 46E*bis*(1) is primarily concerned with the internal relationship, while Article 46E*bis*(3) regulates the specific situation of those states, which, while not being party to the Statute of the African Court of Justice and Human and Peoples' Rights as contained in the Annex to the Malabo Protocol, have accepted the Court's criminal jurisdiction.

Footnote 5 (continued)
serious international crimes. Therefore, their jurisdiction cannot be conceived as an expression of the sovereign authority of a state upon that of another state, nor can their judicial activity be considered as a form of 'unduly' interfering with the sovereign prerogatives of another state." It is, however, questionable, whether a court that is an organ of a *regional* organisation and that is per se not accessible to all states may rely on the same argument in rejecting immunities from prosecution or other limitations of the exercise of criminal jurisdiction under customary international law. For a general critique of this line of argument see Wardle 2011, p. 185 et seq.

[6] This distinguishes the African Court of Justice and Human and Peoples' Rights from the International Criminal Court, which, in terms of Article 125(3) of the ICC Statute, is open to accession by *all* states, which includes states not members of the United Nations Organization. Accordingly, the International Criminal Court is potentially a universal institution. Indeed, achieving the universality of the ICC Statute is one of the declared objectives of the Assembly of States Parties to the ICC Statute: see, for example, Assembly of States Parties, "Strengthening the International Criminal Court and the Assembly of States Parties", 17 December 2014, Resolution ICC/ASP/13/Res.5, op. paras 1 et seq.

[7] See Article 9(1) of the Malabo Protocol.

[8] See Articles 27 and 29 of the Constitutive Act of the African Union, adopted 11 July 2000, entered into force 26 May 2001, UNTS 2158, I-37733.

10.3.2 Article 46Ebis(1)—General Acceptance of the Jurisdiction of the African Court of Justice and Human and Peoples' Rights

Article 46E*bis*(1) of the Malabo Protocol (Annex) contains a rule, the simplicity of which is striking: if a state decides to become party to the Statute of the African Court of Justice and Human and Peoples' Rights, it accepts the Court's criminal jurisdiction over the crimes listed in Article 28A. The import of the provision, however, becomes apparent if one considers the drafting history of Article 12(1) of the ICC Statute, which closely resembles Article 46E*bis*(1) and has almost certainly served as a model.

One of the many contentious issues in the negotiations of the ICC Statute was the extent of the International Criminal Court's jurisdiction. The proposals ranged from a broad competence, based on the principle of universal jurisdiction and allowing the International Criminal Court to prosecute the crimes under its jurisdiction irrespective of whether the states concerned were parties to the ICC Statute, to a strictly consent-based system, according to which states would have to consent to the International Criminal Court's exercise of jurisdiction in respect of each case, thus potentially resulting in a weakened International Criminal Court and a system of jurisdiction *à la carte*.[9]

The compromise that is reflected in Article 12 et seq. of the ICC Statute included, first of all, the principle that by joining the ICC Statute, a state accepts the International Criminal Court's jurisdiction. No further consent is required, which means that States Parties to the ICC Statute may be exposed to International Criminal Court investigations and prosecutions even in circumstances in which a state does not wish the International Criminal Court to intervene. Given that the adoption of the Malabo Protocol appears to have been, at least in part, a reaction to what was perceived to be an unwanted and unwarranted intervention by the International Criminal Court in respect of the Kenyan cases,[10] the adoption of the same model in Article 46E*bis*(1) of the Malabo Protocol (Annex) may come as a surprise. At the same time, this is to be welcomed because, together with the *propio motu* powers of the Prosecutor under Article 46G of the Malabo Protocol (Annex), it provides a safeguard against potential political manipulation and abuse of the African Court of Justice and Human and Peoples' Rights as regards its criminal jurisdiction.[11]

---

[9] On the drafting of Article 12 of the ICC Statute, see Kaul 2002, p. 593 et seq.; Williams and Schabas 2008a, marg. numbers 1–12.

[10] See Du Plessis 2012, pp. 3–4; Murithi 2014, p. 188 et seq.; see also Materu 2014, p. 211 et seq.

[11] See also, in relation to Article 12(1) of the ICC Statute, Kaul 2002, pp. 605–606.

10.3.3 Article 46Ebis(2)—An Incomplete Core Provision

Article 46E*bis*(2) contains the regulatory core of Article 46E*bis* and is of relevance, in particular, to the external relationship of the African Court of Justice and Human and Peoples' Rights, i.e. its relationship vis-à-vis states not party to the Malabo Protocol. Strikingly, however, the text of the provision is so incomplete that it may be considered almost dysfunctional.[12] Given the significance of the provision, this is deplorable, as it is likely to give rise to extensive litigation with uncertain results.[13]

Article 46E*bis*(2) contains four sub-paragraphs, which, according to the *chapeau* of the provision, set out the conditions under which the African Court of Justice and Human and Peoples' Rights may exercise its jurisdiction. The *chapeau* reads as follows:

> The Court may exercise its jurisdiction if one or more of the following conditions apply:

The *chapeau* thus clarifies that the conditions set out in the sub-paragraphs that follow are in the alternative ("one or more of the following conditions"); it is therefore sufficient to establish that the African Court of Justice and Human and Peoples' Rights may exercise its jurisdiction based on one of the four options. When read together with the sub-paragraphs, however, it becomes clear that the *chapeau* (or the text in the sub-paragraphs) is incomplete, for the sub-paragraphs do not actually stipulate any real conditions. Rather, they simply refer to the state on the territory of which a crime occurred, of which the accused is a national or a victim, or whose vital interests are threatened.

Significantly, the text of Article 46E*bis*(2) does not require that the states mentioned in the four sub-paragraphs must be parties to the Malabo Protocol. A comparison with Article 12(2) of the ICC Statute indicates that this is (presumably) precisely what was intended by Article 46E*bis*(2): The *chapeau* of Article 12(2) of the ICC Statute provides in relevant part as follows:

> [...] the Court may exercise its jurisdiction if one or more of the following conditions apply States *are Parties to this Statute or have accepted the jurisdiction of the Court* in accordance with paragraph 3 [emphasis added]:[14]

[12] The text version of Article 46E*bis* upon the present analysis is based is the one posted on the official website of the African Union. It is noteworthy that the French version of Article 46E*bis* contains the same language, lending further support to the assumption that the gaps in the English version of Article 46E*bis* are not merely the result of an editorial mistake, but reflect the authentic version of the Malabo Protocol (Annex).

[13] See also Kemp 2014, p. 18, who notes that "the legislative history of the Draft Protocol is rather thin and did not benefit from the input of a diversity of academics, civil society and other interested individuals and groups", and Du Plessis 2012, p. 11, who notes that "the draft protocol appears to have been rushed into existence, and the result is a legal instrument that raises more questions than it provides answers to Africa's vast human rights needs."

[14] Emphasis added.

The italicized text is missing in the *chapeau* of Article 46E*bis*(2). In order to render the latter provision operational, it is suggested that the italicized text should be read into it, replacing the reference to "conditions", and so resulting in an introductory sentence that would read as follows:

> "The Court may exercise its jurisdiction if one or more of the following conditions apply *States are Parties to the Statute or have accepted the jurisdiction of the Court in accordance with paragraph 3 with respect to the crimes referred to in Article 28A*:"[15]

That the addition of the phrase suggested above would be in keeping with the intent of the drafters of the Malabo Protocol is confirmed by the text of Article 46E*bis*(3), which speaks of a state whose acceptance of jurisdiction is required, thus echoing the language of the introductory sentence of Article 12(2) of the ICC Statute, which is missing in Article 46E*bis*(2).

While interpreting the provision by reading into it the additional phrase suggested above may provide a workable solution, and one which would arguably be in line with the principles of treaty interpretation as stipulated in the Vienna Convention on the Law of Treaties,[16] it is nevertheless regrettable that a key provision of the Annex to the Malabo Protocol is incomplete and becomes understandable only if interpreted by reference to the ICC Statute. To remedy this situation, the text of Article 46E*bis*(2) should be corrected using the procedure set out in Article 79 of the Vienna Convention on the Law of Treaties.

10.3.4 The Sub-paragraphs of Article 46Ebis(2)—From Conservative to Progressive

The sub-paragraphs of Article 46E*bis*(2) of the Malabo Protocol (Annex) set out the conditions under which the African Court of Justice and Human and Peoples' Rights may exercise its criminal jurisdiction. In doing so, the Annex relies on well-established grounds for states' claims to criminal jurisdiction as accepted under customary international law. A comparison with Article 12(2) of the ICC Statute shows that the conditions set out in the sub-paragraphs of Article 46E*bis*(2) range from the conservative (in the sense that they correspond to the conditions outlined in Article 12(2) of the ICC Statute) to the more progressive.

[15] The reference to the Article 28A is required because, unlike the situation at the International Criminal Court, states may accept the jurisdiction of the African Court of Justice and Human and Peoples' Rights with regard to human rights and other matters, but not its criminal jurisdiction.

[16] Adopted on 23 May 1969 and entered into force on 27 January 1980, UNTS 1155, I-18232. In particular, it could be said that Article 12(2) of the ICC Statute may serve as a supplementary means of interpretation in terms of Article 32 of the Vienna Convention, to which recourse may be had in the circumstances, given that without such recourse, the meaning of Article 46E*bis*(2) remains obscure and leads to a result that would be manifestly absurd.

10.3.4.1 Article 46E*bis*(2)(a)—Territoriality

Perhaps the most basic rule of customary international law regarding the exercise of criminal jurisdiction is the principle of territoriality: it is the right of each state to investigate and prosecute crimes committed on its territory as an expression of the particular state's sovereignty.[17] In keeping with this principle, Article 46E*bis*(2)(a) (if interpreted as suggested above) provides that the African Court of Justice and Human and Peoples' Rights may exercise its jurisdiction if the crime in question was committed on the territory of a State Party to the Malabo Protocol. A corresponding rule is contained in Article 12(2)(a) of the ICC Statute, of which it has been observed that the exercise of jurisdiction based on the territoriality principle "is not a case of a non-State Party being bound and the International Criminal Court overreaching its jurisdiction, but rather the individual being amendable to the jurisdiction of the International Criminal Court where crimes are committed in the territory of a State Party."[18]

The principle of territoriality extends to crimes committed on vessels or aircraft flying that state's flag, a rule accepted in international law since at least the Lotus case before the Permanent Court of International Justice.[19] This may lead to competing jurisdictional claims based on the territoriality principle, for instance in situations where a vessel flying the flag of a State Party to the Statute finds itself in the territorial waters of a third state. Claims to jurisdiction based on the state where a vessel or aircraft is registered could be of relevance, in particular, when it comes to the prosecution of the crime of piracy, which falls under the jurisdiction of the African Court of Justice and Human and Peoples' Rights as per Article 28F of the Malabo Protocol (Annex), and which requires criminal acts "on the high seas" or "in a place outside the jurisdiction of any State".[20]

Generally, given the broad acceptance of the principle of territoriality as a ground for exercise of jurisdiction, the application of Article 43E*bis*(2)(a) of the Malabo Protocol (Annex) should not raise significant problems in practice.

10.3.4.2 Article 46E*bis*(2)(b)—Active Personality

Article 46E*bis*(2)(b) of the Malabo Protocol (Annex) provides for jurisdiction based on the active personality principle: the African Court of Justice and Human and Peoples' Rights may exercise jurisdiction in situations where the accused

---

[17] See for instance, Cassese 2005, p. 451; Dugard 2005, p. 151 et seq.

[18] Williams and Schabas 2008a, marg. number 15. Similarly, Kaul 2002, p. 608: "the argument that giving the Court jurisdiction over a crime committed in the territory of a State Party by a suspected national of a non-State Party would conflict irreconcilably with the fundamental principle of treaty law that only States that are parties to a treaty are bound by its terms, has been examined intensively and generally been rejected."

[19] The Case of the S.S. "Lotus" (France vs. Turkey), Judgment of 7 September 1927, Collection of Judgments, Series A No. 10.

[20] Article 28F(a)(i) and (ii) of the Malabo Protocol (Annex).

person is a national of a State Party to the Statute. This ground for a claim to jurisdiction by states is universally accepted and finds its equivalent in Article 12(2)(b) of the ICC Statute.[21] It appears that domestic jurisdictions following the Romano-Germanic tradition rely on the active personality principle more frequently than common law jurisdictions, which is a corollary of the former's general reluctance to extradite their own nationals to other states.[22] As a basis for the jurisdiction of the African Court of Justice and Human and Peoples' Rights, this provision should prove uncontroversial.

10.3.4.3 Article 46E*bis*(2)(c)—Passive Personality

With Article 46E*bis*(2)(c), the Annex to the Malabo Protocol departs from the grounds for jurisdictional claims outlined in the ICC Statute. The provision gives the of the African Court of Justice and Human and Peoples' Rights jurisdiction over crimes in situations where the *victim* is a national of a State Party to the Statute (so-called passive personality principle); Article 12(2) of the ICC Statute contains no corresponding provision. Though many states rely on the passive personality principle, there is some debate surrounding it.[23] There is, however, no reason of principle why an international court should not be entrusted with jurisdiction on this ground. Nonetheless, it should be noted that the inclusion of the passive personality principle significantly broadens the potential reach of the jurisdiction of the African Court of Justice and Human and Peoples' Rights. The implications of this are discussed in more detail below.

10.3.4.4 Article 46E*bis*(2)(d)—Protection of Vital State Interests

Article 46E*bis*(2)(d) of the Malabo Protocol (Annex) gives the African Court of Justice and Human and Peoples' Rights jurisdiction over "[e]xtraterritorial acts by non-nationals which threaten a vital interest of that State" (read: "of a State Party to the Statute"). Just like the territoriality and the active and passive personality principles, the so-called protective principle is broadly accepted in customary international law. It allows states, for instance, to try treason and espionage even if the relevant conduct did not take place on the state's territory, and is also invoked in relation to certain immigration and economic offences.[24] Nevertheless, in the context of an international court and given the subject-matter jurisdiction of the

---

[21] See Kaul 2002, pp 609–610.

[22] See Williams and Schabas 2008a, marg. number 16.

[23] See, for instance, Dugard 2005, p. 304: "This is the least justifiable, as a general principle, of the various bases of jurisdiction […]." See also Ambos 2014, pp. 57 et seq., with further references.

[24] See Brownlie 2008, pp. 304–305; Dugard 2005, p. 154.

African Court of Justice and Human and Peoples' Rights, certain questions arise. Notably, it has to be considered whether jurisdiction based on this provision may be invoked in relation to all crimes over which the African Court of Justice and Human and Peoples' Rights has jurisdiction, or whether its scope of application should be limited to crimes genuinely and primarily concerned with the security and safety of states (as opposed to that of the individuals living in those states). It seems conceivable that only crimes such as unconstitutional change of government, aggression, and, potentially, mercenarism, terrorism and corruption should fall into this category. Alternatively, it could be argued that in respect of each individual case in which the protective principle is relied upon to claim jurisdiction, the impact on the "vital interests" of a State Party to the Malabo Protocol has to be assessed. The problem arising here is that the formulation in Article 46E*bis*(2)(d) and, indeed, of the protective principle as such, are rather vague[25] and therefore potentially open to abuse.

Another issue that could arise is that the notion of "vital interests" of a state almost automatically involves a political assessment. This is unproblematic if a domestic jurisdiction undertakes the task because internal mechanisms usually provide a sufficient safeguard to ensure proper assessment of what a given state's vital interests are and whether it is advisable to assert jurisdiction on that ground in relation to a given case.[26] In contrast, the African Court of Justice and Human and Peoples' Rights appears to be ill-equipped to make such an assessment on behalf of the States Parties to the Malabo Protocol. For that reason, it could be argued that, as a matter of policy, if not as a matter of law, jurisdiction on the basis of the protective principle should only be exercised if the state whose vital interests are supposedly affected refers a situation to the African Court pursuant to Article 46F(1) of the Malabo Protocol (Annex).

10.3.4.5 Assessment

The fact that Article 46E*bis*(2) relies on accepted principles regarding the exercise of criminal jurisdiction by states is evidence of a cautious approach employed by the drafters of the Malabo Protocol: rather than emphasizing the international character of the African Court of Justice and Human and Peoples' Rights and arguing that, for that reason, it may exercise broad jurisdiction, the jurisdictional regime of the African Court of Justice and Human and Peoples' Rights is grounded in well-established principles of criminal jurisdiction, which are part of customary international law. Thus, the African Court of Justice and Human and Peoples'

---

[25] See Brownlie 2008, p. 305: "the interpretation of the concept of protection may vary widely."

[26] See, for instance, Sections 153c and 153d of the German Code of Criminal Procedure, which provides the prosecution service with discretion not to institute prosecutions regarding crimes committed outside Germany, as well as generally regarding crimes that affect the security of the state ("*Staatsschutzdelikte*").

Rights has been granted jurisdiction that each State Party to the Malabo Protocol could also have exercised individually. This step seems designed to disperse fears that the jurisdictional regime of the African Court of Justice and Human and Peoples' Rights might prejudice the sovereignty of states not parties to the Malabo Protocol.

Nevertheless, the jurisdictional regime is rather far-reaching, in particular when compared to that of the International Criminal Court: the adoption of the passive personality principle allows for the investigation and prosecution of crimes committed across the world, as long as the victim is a national of a State Party to the Malabo Protocol. Given the broad range of crimes over which the African Court of Justice and Human and Peoples' Rights has jurisdiction, which include not only the core international crimes, but also conduct that is arguably significantly less serious, this may not always be appropriate.[27] In this respect, it must be noted that the intervention by an international court is arguably more weighty and will attract more attention than domestic investigation and prosecution: if a crime is prosecuted domestically on the basis of the passive personality principle, it remains, from an international relations perspective, a bilateral, horizontal matter between the state of which the victim is a national and the state of which the accused is a national. Bilateral extradition agreements etc. may govern the cooperation of those states; the matter may also be the subject of diplomatic negotiations. In contrast, if an investigation and prosecution is carried out based on the passive personality principle at the level of the African Court of Justice and Human and Peoples' Rights and the accused is a national of a state not party to the Malabo Protocol, it is an international institution facing an individual third state, with whom there will, typically, be no agreements in place as to cooperation in criminal matters. There will also be no established diplomatic channels that could be used to overcome any difficulties in this regard. Thus, the exercise of jurisdiction by the African Court of Justice and Human and Peoples' Rights based on the passive personality principle may lead to challenges that would not necessarily arise if a state exercised jurisdiction on that basis.

The exercise of jurisdiction based on the protective principle [Article 46E*bis*(d) of the Malabo Protocol (Annex)] could lead to the same situation. The problem would arguably be exacerbated by the fact that the protective principle covers crimes that are likely to have a strong political dimension. For instance, allegations that members of the government of a third state were involved in an unconstitutional change of government in one of the states parties to the Malabo Protocol could, theoretically, be investigated by and prosecuted before the African Court of Justice and Human and Peoples' Rights based on Article 28E, read with Articles 28N and 46E*bis*(d) of the Malabo Protocol (Annex). The same applies to

27 See also Kemp 2014, p. 18, who speaks, in relation to the African Court's subject-matter jurisdiction, of a "jurisdictional overreach", which raises, in addition to legal problems, financial and logistical problems.

allegations of the crime of aggression [Article 28M of the Malabo Protocol (Annex)]. The investigation and prosecution of members of government and other state officials of third states in such situations would arguably be particularly problematic, given that the (controversial) immunity clause of Article 46A*bis* covers only heads of state and government and senior state officials of Member States of the African Union.[28] If it was felt that the immunity clause was necessary to protect international relations, it begs the question as to why it was not extended to officials of other states as well.

10.3.4.6 (Lack of) Universal Jurisdiction

It is noteworthy that Article 46E*bis*(2) does not rely on the principle of universal jurisdiction, i.e. the notion that in respect of certain crimes, criminal jurisdiction may be exercised despite the absence of any of the traditional grounds for a claim to jurisdiction. Arguably, there are two reasons for this. First, universal jurisdiction is usually found to apply only in relation to core international crimes, notably genocide, crimes against humanity and war crimes, as well as piracy.[29] The African Court of Justice and Human and Peoples' Rights, by contrast, has subject-matter jurisdiction over a number of non-core international crimes, such as corruption, money laundering, trafficking in human beings and drugs, as well as some crimes not (yet) universally accepted as international crimes. Extending jurisdiction to such crimes on the basis of the principle of universal jurisdiction would be tenuous at best (although it must be recalled that the African Union Model Law on Universal Jurisdiction over International Crimes includes under its scope not only genocide, crimes against humanity, war crimes and piracy, but trafficking in drugs and terrorism[30]).

Second, the African Union has been highly critical regarding what is said to be an "abusive" exercise of universal jurisdiction by certain European states in respect of "African leaders" and state officials, and the desire to curb reliance on universal jurisdiction appears to have been one of the motives for vesting criminal jurisdiction in the African Court of Justice and Human and Peoples' Rights.[31] Indeed, the 15th preambular paragraph of the Malabo Protocol expressly refers to

[28] On the immunity clause see Tladi's chapter in this book.

[29] The exact extent of universal jurisdiction regarding these crimes and whether it also extends to the crime of aggression is subject to scholarly debate. See, for instance, Geneuss 2009; Jeßberger 2014, 2015; Lafontaine 2012; Langer 2015; O'Keefe 2004; van der Wilt 2011.

[30] See Sections 4(a) read with 12, 13 and 14 of the African Union Model National Law on Universal Jurisdiction over International Crimes, 12 July 2012, EX.CL/731(XXI)c (available at: www.peaceau.org/uploads/ex-cl-731-xxi-e.pdf).

[31] See Asaala 2014, p. 43 et seq., Murungu 2011, p. 1069 et seq.

the African Union Assembly's "Decision on the Implementation of the Assembly Decision on the Abuse of the Principle of Universal Jurisdiction".[32] It would have been inconsistent with the African Union's position as regards universal jurisdiction to give the African Court of Justice and Human and Peoples' Rights jurisdiction based on that principle and would, potentially, have undermined the African Union's argument that the principle should not be relied upon, particularly in relation to state officials.[33]

10.3.5 Article 46Ebis(3)—Yet Another Incomplete Provision

Article 46E*bis*(3) contains a provision that is, yet again, curiously incomplete. It provides as follows:

> If the acceptance of a State which is not a Party to this Statute is required under paragraph 2, that State may, by declaration lodged with the Registrar, accept the exercise [sic!]

The provision in its current form has no meaningful content. As with Article 46E*bis*(2), reference to Article 12 of the ICC Statute may shed light on what was intended. Article 12(3) of the ICC Statute provides as follows:

> If the acceptance of a State which is not party to this Statute is required under paragraph 2, that State may, by declaration lodged with the Registrar, accept the exercise *of jurisdiction by the Court with respect to the crimes in question. The accepting State shall cooperate with the Court without any delay or exception in accordance with Part 9* [emphasis added].

It is suggested that Article 46E*bis*(3) of the Malabo Protocol (Annex) should be read as though it contained the text of Article 12(3) of the ICC Statute italicized in the above quote. However, the reference in the second sentence would have to be adapted to the provisions of the Annex: instead of referring to Part 9 of the ICC Statute (which contains the legal regime for cooperation with the International Criminal Court), reference should be made to Article 46L of the Malabo Protocol (Annex), which addresses cooperation with the African Court of Justice and Human and Peoples' Rights. Accordingly, by reference to Article 12(3) of the ICC Statute, Article 46E*bis*(3) should be interpreted as though it read as follows:

> If the acceptance of a State which is not party to this Statute is required under paragraph 2, that State may, by declaration lodged with the Registrar, accept the exercise *of jurisdiction by the Court with respect to the crimes in question. The accepting State shall cooperate with the Court without any delay or exception in accordance with Article 46L.*

---

[32] 1–3 February 2009, Doc. Assembly/AU/Dec.213(XII) (available at: http://www.au.int/en/sites/default/files/decisions/9559-assembly_en_1_3_february_2009_auc_twelfth_ordinary_session_decisions_declarations_message_congratulations_motion.pdf).

[33] See Geneuss 2009; Jeßberger 2015; van der Wilt 2011.

Again, recourse to the correction procedure of Article 79 of the Vienna Convention on the Law of Treaties would provide an opportunity to fix what appears to be an unfortunate oversight in the current text of the provision.

Article 46E*bis*(3) of the Malabo Protocol (Annex), as interpreted and completed above, allows states to avail themselves of the African Court of Justice and Human and Peoples' Rights in respect of its criminal jurisdiction without or before becoming a party to the Court's Statute. The utility of such a provision has been demonstrated by the corresponding provision of the ICC Statute: before joining the ICC Statute, Côte d'Ivoire lodged a declaration under Article 12(3) of the ICC Statute, thereby giving the International Criminal Court jurisdiction over certain alleged crimes.[34] Similarly, Ukraine and Palestine lodged declarations under Article 12(3) before or without joining the ICC Statute.[35] Declarations under Article 12(3) of the ICC Statute may in particular be of use to overcome the limitation of the International Criminal Court's temporal jurisdiction: according to Article 11(2) of the ICC Statute, if a state becomes party to the ICC Statute after its entry into force, the International Criminal Court may "exercise its jurisdiction only with respect to crimes committed after the entry into force of [the Rome Statute] for that State, unless that State has made a declaration under Article 12, para 3." The last part of this provision has been interpreted to allow for the retroactive acceptance of jurisdiction under Article 12(3) of the ICC Statute.[36] Thus, by making a declaration under Article 12(3), a state not party to the ICC Statute may not only give the International Criminal Court jurisdiction prior to ratifying or acceding to the Statute, but also prior to the making of the declaration of acceptance of jurisdiction itself.

It bears noting that Article 46E of the Malabo Protocol (Annex), which regulates the temporal jurisdiction of the African Court of Justice and Human and Peoples' Rights, does not make reference to the acceptance of jurisdiction under Article 46E*bis*(3) in the way Article 11(2) of the ICC Statute does. Nevertheless, it would arguably be in line with the overall purpose of Article 46E*bis*(3) to adopt such an interpretation for Article 46E of the Malabo Protocol (Annex) as well. Thus, declarations of acceptance of jurisdictions could potentially be used as a

---

[34] See Republic of Côte d'Ivoire, *Déclaration de reconnaissance de la Compétence de la Cour Pénal Internationale*, 18 April 2003 (available at: http://www.icc-cpi.int/NR/rdonlyres/FF9939C2-8E97-4463-934C-BC8F351BA013/279779/ICDE1.pdf).

[35] See Ukraine, Declaration on the recognition of jurisdiction, 9 April 2014 (available at: https://www.icc-cpi.int/itemsDocuments/997/declarationRecognitionJuristiction09-04-2014.pdf&ln=en); Ukraine, Declaration of recognition of jurisdiction, 8 September 2015 (available at: http://www.icc-cpi.int/iccdocs/other/Ukraine_Art_12-3_declaration_08092015.pdf); Government of the State of Palestine, Declaration Accepting the Jurisdiction of the International Criminal Court, 31 December 2014 (available at: http://www.icc-cpi.int/iccdocs/PIDS/press/Palestine_A_12-3.pdf).

[36] See ICC, Pre-Trial Chamber III, Situation in the Republic of Côte d'Ivoire, "Decision Pursuant to Article 15 of the Rome Statute on the Authorisation of an Investigation into the Situation in the Republic of Côte d'Ivoire", 3 October 2011, ICC-01/11-14, para 15; Williams and Schabas 2008a, marg. number 17.

vehicle to provide retroactive jurisdiction over alleged crimes, should the state in question so desire. Such an interpretation would appear not to be in conflict with the principle of non-retroactivity of criminal laws, as stipulated by Article 15 of the ICCPR, as far as core international crimes are concerned.[37] This is because Article 15(2) of the ICCPR contains an exception to the rule of non-retroactivity for conduct that was "criminal according to the general principles of law recognized by the community of nations".[38] Nevertheless, problems could arise as regards other crimes over which the African Court of Justice and Human and Peoples' Rights has jurisdiction: it is doubtful whether crimes such as unconstitutional change of government, corruption, money laundering, trafficking in drugs, trafficking in human beings etc. are criminal under "general principles of law". To find so would arguably lead to an unjustified erosion of the principle of non-retroactivity, which is a core aspect of human rights in the context of criminal trials. It must also be noted in this regard that Article 7(2) of the African Charter of Human and Peoples' Rights, which contain the principle of non-retroactivity for the African human rights system, does not contain any exception comparable to Article 15(2) of the ICCPR for international crimes. Accordingly, and given that the mandate of the African Charter of Human and Peoples' Rights is also to uphold the African Charter of Human and Peoples' Rights, it would be difficult to justify retroactive application of the Annex to the Malabo Protocol by way of a declaration under Article 46E*bis*(3) of the Malabo Protocol (Annex).

A question arises as to which states may lodge a declaration under Article 46E*bis*(3): clearly, this mechanism is open to Member States of the African Union which have decided not to ratify the Malabo Protocol and are therefore not subject to the criminal jurisdiction of the African Court of Justice and Human and Peoples' Rights.[39] It is, however, questionable whether states that are not members of the African Union can also lodge a declaration accepting the criminal jurisdiction of the African Court of Justice and Human and Peoples' Rights. As far as African states are concerned, this question could arise in relation to Morocco, which left the African Union in 1984, while all other states on the African

[37] Notably, genocide, crimes against humanity and war crimes, as well as the crime of aggression.

[38] Note also that Article 15(1) of the ICCPR refers to criminal offences under either "national or international law", raising the question of whether the "exception" in Article 15(2) of the ICCPR is actually required; see Joseph et al. 2004, 469.

[39] See in this regard Article 6*bis* of the Malabo Protocol, according to which upon entry into force of the Malabo Protocol and the Statute as amended by it, the African Court shall exercise the functions of the African Court on Human and Peoples' Rights or the African Court of Justice and Human Rights (the court to be created by the Protocol on the Statute of the African Court of Justice and Human Rights, 1 July 2008, the so-called "Merger Protocol", see in the Annex to this book) in relation to Member States of the African Union that have not ratified the Malabo Protocol.

continent and adjacent islands are members of the African Union.[40] Since Morocco could rejoin the African Union under the terms of the Constitutive Act of the African Union, Morocco should arguably also be entitled to accept the jurisdiction of the African Court of Justice and Human and Peoples' Rights.

More difficult is the situation in relation to states located outside Africa. The terms of Article 46E*bis*(3) would appear to allow for the making of such a declaration. Given that the African Court of Justice and Human and Peoples' Rights has jurisdiction over a significantly broader range of crimes than the International Criminal Court, non-African states may have reason to accept the jurisdiction of the African Court of Justice and Human and Peoples' Rights—namely to avail themselves of an international (albeit regional) institution to investigate, prosecute and adjudicate crimes such as terrorism, money laundering and trafficking in human beings and drugs.[41] Nevertheless, it appears doubtful whether the African Court of Justice and Human and Peoples' Rights, which is an organ of the African Union, could potentially become an "African criminal court for the rest of the world", in particular in respect of all those crimes not falling under the International Criminal Court's jurisdiction. Accordingly, the reference to a "state" in Article 46E*bis*(3) of the Malabo Protocol (Annex) should be interpreted restrictively, so as to include only Member States of the African Union, or, at the most, African states. This is further confirmed by the first sentence of Article 29(2) of the Malabo Protocol (Annex), which provides as follows: "The Court shall not be open to States, which are not members of the Union."

10.3.6 Challenges to Jurisdiction and Possibility of Appeal

Article 46E*bis* of the Malabo Protocol (Annex) contains detailed provisions regarding the jurisdiction of the African Court of Justice and Human and Peoples' Rights. What is missing—in Article 46E*bis* and elsewhere in the Annex to the Malabo Protocol—are rules that govern how this jurisdictional regime is to be enforced procedurally. By contrast, Article 19 of the ICC Statute provides for a set of procedures in this regard: Article 19(1) stipulates that the International Criminal Court "shall satisfy itself that it has jurisdiction"; Article 19(2) sets out who may challenge the International Criminal Court's jurisdiction (namely, an accused or a person in respect of whom a warrant of arrest or summons to appear has been issued, as well as states "from which acceptance of jurisdiction is required"); Article 19(3) provides for the ICC Prosecutor's right to seek a ruling on jurisdiction; Article 19(4) to (11) contains a set of further rules regarding proceedings in

[40] An exception applies to the Canary Islands and the territories of Ceuta and Mellila, which are geographically in Africa but held by Spain, which is not a member of the African Union.

[41] In this regard, it is recalled that attempts to extend the International Criminal Court's jurisdiction to crimes such as terrorism and drug trafficking have so far failed.

respect of the International Criminal Court's jurisdiction.[42] The absence of such rules in the Annex to the Malabo Protocol does not undermine the proposed Statute as a whole. Nonetheless, similar provisions ought to be incorporated into the Rules of Court. Arguably, in the Rules of Court, the right to challenge the jurisdiction should be provided not only to the accused person, but also, in keeping with the approach of the ICC Statute, to persons who are the subject of warrants of arrest and to those states which ordinarily would exercise jurisdiction over a given case (i.e. the territorial state and the state of nationality of the perpetrator and, potentially, the victim).

It is not entirely clear which Chamber of the African Court of Justice and Human and Peoples' Rights would issue decisions on jurisdiction. Article 19*bis*(1) of the Malabo Protocol (Annex) provides that the "Pre-Trial Chamber shall exercise the functions provided for in Article 46F of this Statute". Strictly speaking, however, Article 46F does not provide for any "functions", but merely sets out the conditions under which the African Court of Justice and Human and Peoples' Rights may exercise its jurisdiction. Nevertheless, it is suggested that Article 19*bis*(1) should be understood as implying that it is indeed the Pre-Trial Chamber that is primarily tasked with determining whether the African Court of Justice and Human and Peoples' Rights has jurisdiction over a given case. This appears to be all the more logical as jurisdiction is a requirement even for the opening of an investigation (see further below). Even so, it cannot be excluded that other Chambers of the African Court of Justice and Human and Peoples' Rights will also be compelled to rule on the existence of jurisdiction.

As to the possibility of seeking a review of a decision on jurisdiction, Article 18(3) of the Malabo Protocol (Annex) provides *inter alia* for appeals against decisions on jurisdiction. Decisions taken under Article 46E*bis* fall squarely under this provision and are therefore subject to an appeal as of right; Article 18(2) stipulates that on appeal, an appellant may raise errors of procedure, law and fact, thereby allowing for a broad review of the first-instance decision. The right to appeal, however, appears to be limited to the Prosecutor and the accused; states potentially affected by the exercise of jurisdiction by the African Court of Justice and Human and Peoples' Rights do not have a right to appeal. This contrasts with the provisions of the ICC Statute: pursuant to Article 19(2)(c) read with Article 82(1)(a) of the ICC Statute, appeals in respect of a decision on jurisdiction may also be brought by states whose acceptance of jurisdiction is required. Again, it may be possible to amend the procedure in the Rules of Court, granting states a right to appeal.

As to the appeal itself, there is some doubt as to which Chamber would hear appeals: clearly, if the Trial Chamber renders a decision on jurisdiction, the Appellate Chamber[43] has appellate jurisdiction.[44] However, it is less clear what

---

[42] On the interpretation of Article 19 of the ICC Statute see, for example, Hall 2008.

[43] Note that the terminology of the Statute is inconsistent: Articles 16(2), 18(4) and 21(5) speak of the "Appellate Chamber", while Article 19*bis*(6) refers to the "Appeals Chamber".

[44] See Article 19*bis*(6) of the Malabo Protocol (Annex).

will happen if the Pre-Trial Chamber issues a decision on jurisdiction, which is likely to be the most frequent case. Article 19*bis*(5) of the Malabo Protocol (Annex) provides that it is the *Trial Chamber* that "shall receive and conduct appeals from the Pre-Trial Chamber in accordance with Article 18 of this Statute", thus vesting appellate jurisdiction in the Trial Chamber and not the Appellate Chamber, including in respect of decisions of the Pre-Trial Chamber on jurisdiction. Strangely, however, Article 18(4) does not refer to the Trial Chamber when determining the powers of the appellate level. Rather, it simply provides that: "The Appellate Chamber may affirm, reverse or revise the decision appealed against. The decision of the Appellate Chamber shall be final". It could be argued that this provision must be applied *mutatis mutandis* to appeals against decisions of the Pre-Trial Chamber before the Trial Chamber. Furthermore, it is open to question whether the resulting decision of the Trial Chamber on appeal is likewise liable to appeal before the Appellate Chamber, leading to a two-level appellate review in respect of the Pre-Trial Chamber's decisions. The advantage of such a system would be that the Appellate Chamber would remain at the apex of the jurisdictional system of the African Court of Justice and Human and Peoples' Rights, though the benefits gained from first having an appeal heard before the Trial Chamber remain unclear. In general, further clarification and elaboration of the appeals procedure in the Rules of Court appear desirable, if not strictly necessary.

10.4 Articles 46F and 46G: Balancing State Party Supervision of the Exercise of Jurisdiction with Prosecutorial Independence

While Article 46E*bis* of the Malabo Protocol (Annex) is concerned with the conditions under which the African Court of Justice and Human and Peoples' Rights has criminal jurisdiction, Articles 46F and 46G determine when it may actually exercise this jurisdiction, or, in other words, how the jurisdiction is "triggered". In a municipal setting, the police, prosecution authorities etc. are usually charged with investigating and prosecuting crimes as part of their daily business. The exercise of their duties does not require a specific "trigger" beyond the suspicion that a crime has been committed. Opening an investigation in a domestic jurisdiction is a routine act that will usually go unnoticed by society at large. In contrast, the decision by an international court to exercise its criminal jurisdiction in respect of alleged criminal behavior, even if only by opening an investigation, is of great significance and may have serious repercussions in the state concerned and beyond. Accordingly, there is a need to regulate further under which conditions an international court may actually commence investigating a case. This is even more so for international criminal jurisdictions primarily or exclusively adjudicating crimes committed after their establishment: unlike, for instance, the ad hoc tribunals of the United Nations for the former Yugoslavia[45] and for Rwanda, it is uncertain over which future events courts like the International Criminal Court and the African Court of Justice and Human and Peoples' Rights may come to exercise their jurisdiction. For that reason, states establishing an international court may wish to retain some influence over its exercise of jurisdiction. Naturally, this requires careful balancing with the principle of prosecutorial independence, so as to avoid political abuse.

Article 46F and 46G seek to strike this balance by allowing for referrals to the Prosecutor by States Parties to the Court's Statute and by certain organs of the African Union, but also providing for *proprio motu* investigations by the Prosecutor, which are, however, subject to authorization by the Pre-Trial Chamber. The two provisions are modeled upon Articles 13 and 15 of the ICC Statute.

10.4.1 Article 46F: Entities Entitled to Trigger the Jurisdiction of the African Court of Justice and Human and Peoples' Rights

Article 46F sets out in its three paragraphs when the jurisdiction of the African Court of Justice and Human and Peoples' Rights may be exercised. "Exercise of jurisdiction" must be understood broadly in this context: it covers not only the actual prosecution of a case before the Chambers of the African Court of Justice and Human and Peoples' Rights, but also the investigation of alleged crimes by the Prosecutor. This results from the interplay between Articles 46F and 46G: the latter provision stipulates in its first paragraph that the Office of the Prosecutor may open an investigation on its own initiative and sets out in the subsequent paragraphs under which conditions it may do so. It follows that even an investigation is dependent on the jurisdiction of the African Court of Justice and Human and Peoples' Rights having been "triggered" in accordance with Article 46F. This is in line with the interpretation of Articles 13 and 15 of the ICC Statute.[46]

The "trigger" of the jurisdiction of the African Court of Justice and Human and Peoples' Rights must thus be distinguished from the institution of proceedings before the International Criminal Law Section of the African Court of Justice and Human and Peoples' Rights, which is regulated in Article 34A of the Malabo

---

[45] It is noteworthy that the ICTY has assumed jurisdiction also over crimes committed after its establishment: Article 1 of the ICTY Statute, which was adopted in 1993, provides for jurisdiction over crimes committed on the territory of the former Yugoslavia "after 1991". Both the ICTY Prosecutor and the UN Security Council found that this included jurisdiction over crimes committed in Kosovo, which commenced in 1998; see Krieger 2001, p. 501. In contrast, the jurisdiction of the ICTR, which was established on 8 November 1994, is limited to crimes committed between 1 January 1994 and 31 December 1994 (Article 1 ICTR-Statute).

[46] On the triggering procedure before the International Criminal Court see generally Olásolo 2005.

Protocol (Annex). The latter covers the actual bringing of a case before a Chamber of the African Court of Justice and Human and Peoples' Rights and thus occurs after the Court's jurisdiction has been triggered.

According to Article 46F(1) of the Malabo Protocol (Annex), states that are parties to it have the right to refer to the Prosecutor of the African Court of Justice and Human and Peoples' Rights "[a] situation in which one or more [...] crimes [referred to in Article 28A] appears to have been committed". The wording is borrowed from Article 13 of the ICC Statute. Of note is the use of the term "situation", which has been defined as "a crisis, defined by personal, territorial and temporal parameters, in the course of which crimes under Article 5 [ICC Statute] are alleged to have been committed".[47] Accordingly, states may only refer a "situation" to the African Court of Justice and Human and Peoples' Rights, but not target specific individuals for investigation. The International Criminal Court has developed jurisprudence on the scope of a "situation" and the International Criminal Court's Office of the Prosecutor has been careful to highlight that there are limits as to how States Parties can define a situation in a referral.[48]

It is also worth noting that in the practice of the International Criminal Court so far, State Party referrals have come in the form of so-called "self-referrals", i.e. by a State Party referring a "situation" in its own territory to the International Criminal Court. It is now accepted that such a practice is in compliance with the ICC Statute.[49] It is to be expected that the African Court of Justice and Human and Peoples' Rights will also be confronted with "self-referrals".

The right to refer a "situation" to the African Court of Justice and Human and Peoples' Rights under Article 46F(1) is limited to States Parties to the Court's Statute. Member States of the African Union that are not party to the Statute (or, for that matter, any other third states) are not entitled to refer a situation to the African Court of Justice and Human and Peoples' Rights (though they may arguably make information about alleged crimes available to the Prosecutor with a view to triggering the *proprio motu* powers of the Prosecutor under Article 46G).

Furthermore, the acceptance of the jurisdiction of the African Court of Justice and Human and Peoples' Rights under Article 46E*bis*(3) does not entail the right to refer a "situation" to the Court under Article 46F(1) and so to trigger the Court's jurisdiction. The practice of the International Criminal Court is instructive in this regard: when Côte d'Ivoire accepted the International Criminal Court's jurisdiction prior to becoming a State Party to the ICC Statute, the International Criminal Court's jurisdiction had to be triggered by a *proprio motu* investigation by the ICC Prosecutor pursuant to Article 15 of the ICC Statute.

---

[47] Olásolo 2005, 74. See also, ICC, Pre-Trial Chamber I, *Situation in the Democratic Republic of the Congo*, Decision on the Applications for Participation in the Proceedings of VPRS 1, VPRS 2, VPRS 3, VPRS 4, VPRS 5 and VPRS 6, 22 March 2006, ICC-01/04-101-tEN-Corr, para 65; Rastan 2012.

[48] *See* Rastan (2012) for further details.

[49] On the discussion surrounding "self-referrals" see, for example, Akhavan 2010, Gaeta 2004, Kleffner 2009, Müller and Stegmiller 2010.

Article 46F(2) of the Malabo Protocol (Annex) stipulates that two organs of the African Union may trigger the criminal jurisdiction of the African Court of Justice and Human and Peoples' Rights: the Assembly of Heads of State and Government and the Peace and Security Council. The Assembly of Heads of State and Government is the "supreme organ" of the African Union and brings together the heads of state and government of the African Union Member States.[50] Decisions at the level of the Assembly of Heads of State and Government require at least a two-thirds majority of the Member States.[51] This would appear to also apply to decisions to refer a given situation to the African Court of Justice and Human and Peoples' Rights. The Peace and Security Council was established by a protocol as an organ of the African Union with specific tasks in the field of peacekeeping and security.[52]

As such, it appears logical that the Peace and Security Council should be entitled to refer a situation to the Prosecutor of the African Court of Justice and Human and Peoples' Rights. It must be noted, however, that despite the similarity in name, the Peace and Security Council does not have as broad-ranging powers as the Security Council of the United Nations. Notably, the Peace and Security Council does not have the power, recognized for the United Nations Security Council under Chapter VII of the UN Charter, to make binding decisions in respect of Member States in case of any threat to or breach of peace. It follows that, unlike the United Nations Security Council with respect to the International Criminal Court,[53] the Peace and Security Council cannot, by referring a situation to the African Court of Justice and Human and Peoples' Rights, give it jurisdiction over states that are not parties to the Court's Statute.

African individuals or African non-governmental organizations with observer status with the African Union or its organs or institutions do not have the right to refer a situation to the African Court of Justice and Human and Peoples' Rights with a view to it exercising its criminal jurisdiction, even in respect of states that have made a declaration under Article 30(f) of the Malabo Protocol (Annex). While the wording of the *chapeau* of Article 30 would potentially lend itself to such an interpretation, as international crimes generally qualify as violations of human rights, it would appear that Article 46F is the *lex specialis* regarding the criminal jurisdiction of the African Court of Justice and Human and Peoples' Rights. The same goes for the interpretation of Article 29 of the Malabo Protocol (Annex): while, according to its para (1)(c), *inter alia* the Pan-African Parliament and "other organs of the Union authorized by the Assembly" generally have the right to bring cases before the African Court of Justice and Human and Peoples'

[50] See Article 6 of the Constitutive Act of the African Union.

[51] Article 7(1) of the Constitutive Act of the African Union.

[52] On the Peace and Security Council see Cilliers and Sturman 2004.

[53] See Williams and Schabas 2008b, marg. number 16.

Rights, this does not comprise the right to the trigger the Court's criminal jurisdiction, which is vested only in the entities listed in Article 46F.[54]

Finally, Article 46F(3) provides for the right of the Prosecutor of the African Court of Justice and Human and Peoples' Rights to initiate investigations on his or her own initiative. This important aspect of the trigger mechanisms is discussed in more detail below, in respect of Article 46G of the Malabo Protocol (Annex).

What is missing in Article 46F (and elsewhere in the Annex to the Malabo Protocol) is a provision clarifying what should happen once a State Party to the Malabo Protocol, the Assembly of Heads of State and Government or the Peace and Security Council has referred a situation to the Prosecutor of the African Court of Justice and Human and Peoples' Rights. Is the Prosecutor required to open an investigation? For referrals to the ICC Prosecutor, Article 53(1) of the ICC Statute clarifies that this is not the case. Rather, the Prosecutor it entitled to review the information received and makes an independent decision whether there are sufficient grounds to proceed to an investigation. This "preliminary examination" is an important element of the ICC Prosecutor's independence: the decision to investigate should not be based on political considerations, which may have informed the decision to refer a situation to the International Criminal Court, but on a judicial assessment based on criteria such as the availability of evidence and the interests of justice.[55] For that reason, it is suggested that criteria such as those in Article 53(1) of the ICC Statute should also guide the African Court's Prosecutor's decision whether or not to open an investigation following a referral. Ideally, provisions to that effect should be included in the Rules of Court.

Another "candidate" for inclusion in the Rules of Court are provisions for a—potentially limited—judicial review of a prosecutorial decision not to open an investigation. Again, Article 53 of the ICC Statute may be a model in this regard: its para (3) provides for the possibility of a review of a decision not to open an investigate by the Pre-Trial Chamber at the request of the entity that referred a given situation to the ICC Prosecutor and, under certain conditions, also *proprio motu* by the Pre-Trial Chamber.[56]

[54] In this regard, it appears that the amendments to Article 29 of the Statute by Article 15 of the Malabo Protocol (Annex), including the references to the Peace and Security Council and to the Office of the Prosecutor, were meant to make Article 29 of the Statute consistent with the powers that those entities were given in respect of the African Court's criminal jurisdiction; however, the Peace and Security Council and the Office of the Prosecutor arguably have no power to bring cases before the African Court that concern its jurisdiction over human rights or general matters.

[55] See Bergsmo and Kruger 2008, marg. number 6.

[56] See Bergsmo and Kruger 2008, marg. numbers 32 et seq.

10.4.2 Article 46G: Proprio Motu Investigations by the Office of the Prosecutor

Article 46G of the Malabo Protocol (Annex) further elaborates on the power of the Prosecutor to open an investigation *proprio motu*. Apart from small changes in the terminology and an omission of text in one of the paragraphs,[57] the provision is a *verbatim* copy of Article 15 of the ICC Statute. At the Rome Conference, the *proprio motu* power of the Prosecutor to open an investigation was one of the main bones of contention[58]—while many states were in favor of a strong and independent ICC Prosecutor who could open an investigation not only if a State Party or the United Nations Security Council made a request to that effect, other states were concerned that vesting too much power in the Prosecutor could give rise to abuses. The compromise found provides for judicial control of the Prosecutor's decision: a *proprio motu* investigation may be opened only if authorized by the ICC Pre-Trial Chamber.[59] Thus, whereas in case of a State Party or United Nations Security Council referral, the Pre-Trial Chamber potentially comes into play only when the Prosecutor decides *not* to open an investigation, prior judicial authorization is a pre-requisite for a *proprio motu* investigation.[60]

Copying the procedural regime of Article 15 of the ICC Statute for *proprio motu* investigations of the African Court's Prosecutor appears to have been both a wise and surprising decision of the drafters. Wise because Article 15 of the ICC Statute is the result of lengthy negotiations and reflects a compromise between opposing positions; there was no reason to open up the debate again in respect of the African Court of Justice and Human and Peoples' Rights. Surprising because the *proprio motu* powers of the ICC Prosecutor appeared to have been one of the reasons for the African Union's criticism of the International Criminal Court;[61] it

[57] Article 46G of the Malabo Protocol (Annex) refers throughout to the "Office of the Prosecutor" and not to the "Prosecutor" though in the second sentences of paras (2) and (6), the pronouns "he or she"/"him or her" instead of "it" are used. The change in terminology does not appear to be of any significance. Further, while Article 15(2), second sentence, of the ICC Statute provides that the Prosecutor may receive written or oral testimony "at the seat of the Court", this last phrase is missing in Article 46G(2) of the Malabo Protocol (Annex). It is unclear whether this omission has any practical importance. Finally, Article 46G(2) of the Malabo Protocol (Annex) includes a reference to organs of the African Union as one of the sources of additional information; given that the Prosecutor in any event has the power to seek additional information from "intergovernmental organizations", this appears to be merely a clarification that does not add any powers.

[58] See Bergsmo and Pejić 2008, marg. numbers 1 et seq.

[59] Note that as far as the crime of aggression is concerned, Article 15*bis* of the ICC Statute provides for a special procedure in case of referrals by a State Party or *proprio motu* investigations: unless the UN Security Council has made a determination that an act of aggression has occurred, the investigation may only proceed if authorized by the judges of the Pre-Trial Division sitting *en banc*.

[60] See Nerlich 2009, 349.

[61] See Asaala 2014, 49.

is therefore somewhat incongruent with the African Union's position that the Prosecutor of the African Court of Justice and Human and Peoples' Rights should be vested with the same powers.

The procedure regarding the opening of an investigation *proprio motu* may be summarized as follows: the first step is the Prosecutor's review of information received regarding crimes falling under the jurisdiction of the African Court of Justice and Human and Peoples' Rights.[62] For the purposes of this preliminary examination, the Prosecutor may seek additional information from a variety of sources and may also "receive written or oral testimony". However, the preliminary examination is not a full-blown investigation; accordingly, the States Parties' duties of co-operation and judicial assistance under Article 46L do not yet arise.[63]

The second step involves the decision of the Prosecutor as to whether there is "a reasonable basis to proceed with an investigation", in which case he or she shall request the Pre-Trial Chamber to authorize the investigation.[64] The term "reasonable basis to proceed" is not further defined, nor is there any indication in the Statute as to the criteria according to which the Prosecutor's decision should be made. A comparison with the International Criminal Court is instructive in this regard: rule 48 of the International Criminal Court's Rules of Procedure and Evidence makes applicable the criteria in Article 53(1) of the ICC Statute. Thus, when determining whether there is a reasonable basis to proceed with an investigation, the Prosecutor will have to consider whether there is a "reasonable basis to believe" that crimes within the International Criminal Court's jurisdiction have been committed, and that the case would be admissible as well as in the interests of justice.[65] It is suggested that the decision of the Prosecutor of the African Court of Justice and Human and Peoples' Rights should be based on the same criteria.

The use of the word "shall" suggests that the Prosecutor enjoys no discretion as to whether to open an investigation once it has been established that there is a reasonable basis to proceed. Nevertheless, it appears that the criteria for determining whether there is a "reasonable basis to proceed" actually include elements of discretion or a margin of appreciation. Notably, the concept of "interests of justice" suggests that there may be situations where, despite sufficient evidence of crimes, an investigation may nevertheless not be opened.[66] It is of note, however, that Article 53(1)(c) of the ICC Statute contains a presumption *in favour of* the opening of an investigation.

If the Prosecutor decides that there is no reasonable basis to proceed on the basis of the information received, he or she shall inform "those who provided the information" of the decision. This would appear to include only those who provided the initial information that triggered the preliminary examination, but not

[62] Article 46G(2) of the Malabo Protocol (Annex).

[63] See in respect of Article 15 of the ICC Statute Kreß and Prost (2008), marg. number 11.

[64] Article 46G(3) of the Malabo Protocol (Annex).

[65] See also Bergsmo and Pejić 2008, marg. numbers 19–20.

[66] See Bergsmo and Pejić 2008, marg. number 22.

those from whom additional information was obtained in the course of the preliminary examination.[67]

Once seized of a request for authorization, the Pre-Trial Chamber will have to make the same determination, namely whether there is a reasonable basis to proceed with the investigation.[68] The decision will also have to address whether "the case appears to fall within the jurisdiction of the Court", though this criterion is arguably redundant: if the African Court of Justice and Human and Peoples' Rights does not have jurisdiction, there is clearly no "reasonable basis to proceed".[69] In the interpretation of the standard "reasonable basis to proceed", the jurisprudence of the ICC Pre-Trial Chambers may be of significance. According to the ICC Pre-Trial Chambers, this standard is the "lowest evidentiary standard provided by the [Rome] Statute" and requires that the Chamber is "satisfied that a sensible or reasonable justification exists for the belief that a crime falling within the jurisdiction of the Court 'has been or is being committed'."[70]

If the Pre-Trial Chamber concludes that there is a reasonable basis to proceed with an investigation, it shall authorize the investigation [Article 46G(4) of the Malabo Protocol (Annex)]. There is no discretion in this regard.[71]

A decision not to authorize the opening of an investigation does not bar future requests by the Prosecutor for an authorization of an investigation in respect of the same situation "based on new facts or evidence".[72]

In the proceedings before the Pre-Trial Chamber, victims may make representations, "in accordance with the Rules of the Court".[73] Thus, further elaboration of the procedure in the Rules of Court is mandatory. In this regard, it is noteworthy that Rules 46–50 of the ICC Rules of Procedure and Evidence provide for further procedural rules in relation to proceedings on requests for the authorization of *propio motu* investigations, which may serve as a model for the rules of the African Court of Justice and Human and Peoples' Rights in this regard.

---

[67] See Bergsmo and Pejić 2008, marg. number 30.

[68] Article 46G(4) of the Malabo Protocol (Annex).

[69] See also Pre-Trial Chamber II, Situation in the Republic of Kenya, "Decision Pursuant to Article 15 of the Rome Statute on the Authorization of an Investigation into the Situation in the Republic of Kenya", 31 March 2010, ICC-01/09-19-Corr, paras 66 et seq.

[70] Pre-Trial Chamber II, Situation in the Republic of Kenya, "Decision Pursuant to Article 15 of the Rome Statute on the Authorization of an Investigation into the Situation in the Republic of Kenya", 31 March 2010, ICC-01/09-19-Corr, para 35; Pre-Trial Chamber III, Situation in the Republic of Côte d'Ivoire, "Decision Pursuant to Article 15 of the Rome Statute on the Authorisation of an Investigation into the Situation in the Republic of Côte d'Ivoire", 3 October 2011, ICC-01/11-14, para 24. Note that these decisions refer to the "reasonable basis to believe" standard of Article 53(1) of the ICC Statute, which they consider to be incorporated in the "reasonable basis to proceed" standard of Article 15 of the ICC Statute.

[71] See Bergsmo and Pejić 2008, marg. number 27: "the reasonable basis standard in para 4 is purely evidentiary and not one of appropriateness."

[72] Article 46G(5) of the Malabo Protocol (Annex).

[73] Article 46G(3), second sentence, of the Malabo Protocol (Annex).

An interesting question arises from an inconsistent use of terminology in Article 46G of the Malabo Protocol (Annex) (as well as in Article 15 of the ICC Statute): the provision speaks in its para (4) of "the case [which] appears to fall within the jurisdiction of the Court", which suggests that the object of the authorization of an investigation is a specific case. In contrast, paras (5) and (6) refer to subsequent action in respect of the same "situation". Thus, there is some ambiguity as to whether an investigation is authorized in respect of a specific case or in respect of a situation as whole. In case of the former, the Pre-Trial Chamber's oversight of the Prosecutor's investigations would be much tighter, which arguably is in line with the intention of some of the drafters to have tight judicial control over *propio motu* investigations. Nevertheless, according to the jurisprudence of the Pre-Trial Chambers of the International Criminal Court, the authorization of an investigation is made in respect of a given situation and not in respect of individual cases arising from the situation.[74]

10.5 Conclusion

Overall, Articles 46E*bis* to 46G provide for a workable regime regarding the scope of and exercise of jurisdiction by the African Court of Justice and Human and Peoples' Rights, which is largely modeled on the respective provisions of the ICC Statute. It is nevertheless regrettable that Article 46E*bis* is in important aspects incomplete. Additional procedural rules are likely to be needed to make the jurisdictional regime fully functional in practice. Provisions of the ICC Statute and the ICC Rules of Procedure and Evidence may serve as sources of inspiration, if not models, in that regard.

It should be emphasized that, compared to the International Criminal Court, the jurisdictional reach of the African Court of Justice and Human and Peoples' Rights is significantly broadened by the inclusion of jurisdiction based on the passive personality and protective principles. Particularly in light of the broad subject-matter jurisdiction of the African Court of Justice and Human and Peoples' Rights, this wide jurisdictional scope is not unproblematic and the African Court of Justice and Human and Peoples' Rights may be well advised to exercise jurisdiction based on these principles but cautiously.

[74] See Pre-Trial Chamber II, Situation in the Republic of Kenya, "Decision Pursuant to Article 15 of the Rome Statute on the Authorization of an Investigation into the Situation in the Republic of Kenya", 31 March 2010, ICC-01/09-19-Corr, paras 40 et seq.; Pre-Trial Chamber III, Situation in the Republic of Côte d'Ivoire, "Decision Pursuant to Article 15 of the Rome Statute on the Authorisation of an Investigation into the Situation in the Republic of Côte d'Ivoire", 3 October 2011, ICC-01/11-14, para 18.

References

Akhavan P (2010) Self-referrals before the International Criminal Court: are states the villains or the victims of atrocities? Crim Law Forum 10:103–120

Ambos K (2014) Internationales Strafrecht, 4th edn. C.H Beck, Munich

Asaala EO (2014) The African Court of Justice and Human and Peoples' Rights: an opportunity for international criminal justice? In: Van der Merwe B (ed) International criminal justice in Africa: challenges and opportunities. Konrad Adenauer Stiftung, Nairobi, pp 33–56

Bergsmo M, Kruger P (2008) Article 53 initiation of an investigation. In: Triffterer O (ed) Commentary on the Rome Statute of the International Criminal Court: observers' notes, article by article, 2nd edn. C.H. Beck, Munich, pp 1065–1078

Bergsmo M, Pejić J (2008) Article 15 Prosecutor. In: Triffterer O (ed) Commentary on the Rome Statute of the International Criminal Court: observers' notes, article by article, 2nd edn. C.H. Beck, Munich, pp 581–593

Brownlie I (2008) Principles of public international law, 7th edn. Oxford University Press, Oxford

Cassese A (2005) International Law. Oxford University Press, Oxford

Cilliers J, Sturman K (2004) Challenges facing the AU's Peace and Security Council. Afr Secur Rev 13:97–104

Du Plessis M (2012) Implications of the AU decision to give the African Court jurisdiction over international crimes. Institute for Security Studies Paper 235

Dugard J (2005) International law, a South African perspective, 3rd edn. Juta & Co., Landsdowne

Gaeta P (2004) Is the practice of 'self-referrals' a sound start for the ICC? J Int Crim Justice 2:949–952

Gaeta P (2009) Does President Al Bashir enjoy immunity from arrest? J Int Crim Justice 7:315–332

Geneuss J (2009) Fostering a better understanding of universal jurisdiction: a comment on the AU-EU Expert Report on the Principle of Universal Jurisdiction. J Int Crim Justice 7:945–962

Hall CK (2008) Article 19 challenges to the jurisdiction of the court or the admissibility of a case. In: Triffterer O (ed) Commentary on the Rome Statute of the International Criminal Court: observers' notes, article by article, 2nd edn. C.H. Beck, Munich, pp 637–667

Jeßberger F (2014) 'On behalf of Africa': towards the regionalization of universal jurisdiction? In: Werle G, Fernandez L, Vormbaum M (eds) Africa and the International Criminal Court. T.M.C. Asser Press, The Hague, pp 155–175

Jeßberger F (2015) 'Litigating universal jurisdiction'—introduction. J Int Crim Justice 13:205–208

Joseph S, Schultz J, Castan M (2004) The International Covenant on Civil and Political Rights, 2nd edn. Oxford University Press, Oxford

Kaul H-P (2002) Preconditions to the exercise of jurisdiction. In: Cassese A et al (eds) The Rome Statute of the International Criminal Court: a commentary, vol I. Oxford University Press, Oxford, pp 583–618

Kemp G (2014) Taking stock of international criminal justice in Africa—three inventories considered. In: van der Merwe B (ed) International criminal justice in Africa: challenges and opportunities. Konrad Adenauer Stiftung, Nairobi, pp 7–32

Kleffner JK (2009) Auto referrals and the complementary nature of the ICC. In: Stahn C, Sluiter G (eds) The emerging practice of the International Criminal Court. Nijhoff, Leiden, pp 41–54

Kreß C, Prost K (2008) Article 86 General Obligation to Cooperate. In: Triffterer O (ed) Commentary on the Rome Statute of the International Criminal Court: observers' notes, article by article, 2nd edn. C.H. Beck, Munich, pp 1513–1516

Krieger H (2001) The Kosovo conflict and international law: an analytical documentation 1974–1999. Cambridge University Press, Cambridge

Lafontaine F (2012) Universal jurisdiction-the realistic Utopia. J Int Crim Justice 11:1277–1302

Langer M (2015) Universal jurisdiction is not disappearing: the shift from 'global enforcer' to 'no safe haven' universal jurisdiction. J Int Crim Justice 13:245–256

Materu SF (2014) A strained relationship: reflections on the African Union's stand towards the International Criminal Court from the Kenyan experience. In: Werle G, Fernandez F, Vormbaum M (eds) Africa and the International Criminal Court. T.M.C. Asser Press, The Hague, pp 211–228

Müller AT, Stegmiller I (2010) Self-referrals on trial: from panacea to patient. J Int Crim Justice 8:1267–1294

Murithi T (2014) Between political justice and judicial politics: charting a way forward for the African Union and the International Criminal Court. In: Werle G, Fernandez F, Vormbaum M (eds) Africa and the International Criminal Court. T.M.C. Asser Press, The Hague, pp 179–193

Murungu CB (2011) Towards a Criminal Chamber in the African Court of Justice and Human Rights. J Int Crim Justice 9:1065–1088

Nerlich V (2009) ICC (Pre-Trial Proceedings). In: Cassese A (ed) Oxford companion to international criminal justice. Oxford University Press, Oxford, pp 349–350

O'Keefe R (2004) Universal jurisdiction: clarifying the basic concept. J Int Crim Justice 2:735–760

Olásolo H (2005) The triggering procedure of the International Criminal Court. Martinus Nijhoff, Leiden

Rastan R (2012) The jurisdictional scope of situations before the International Criminal Court. Crim Law Forum 23:1–34

van der Wilt H (2011) Universal jurisdiction under attack: an assessment of African misgivings towards international criminal justice as administered by Western States. J Int Crim Justice 9:1043–1066

Wardle P (2011) The survival of head of state immunity at the International Criminal Court. Aust Int Law J 18:181–205

Williams SA, Schabas WA (2008a) Article 12 Preconditions to the Exercise of Jurisdiction. In: Triffterer O (ed) Commentary on the Rome Statute of the International Criminal Court: observers' notes, article by article, 2nd edn. C.H. Beck, Munich, pp 547–561

Williams SA, Schabas WA (2008b) Article 13 Exercise of Jurisdiction. In: Triffterer O (ed) Commentary on the Rome Statute of the International Criminal Court: observers' notes, article by article, 2nd edn. C.H. Beck, Munich, pp 563–574

Chapter 11
Complementary Jurisdiction (Article 46H)

Harmen van der Wilt

Abstract The jurisdictional relationship between African states and the African Court of Justice and Human and Peoples' Rights and between the latter Court and the International Criminal Court is not entirely clear. While the Malabo Protocol (Annex) has borrowed the complementarity principle from the Rome Statute, the Protocol does not indicate that states' investigations or prosecutions should be *genuine*, in order to render a case inadmissible. Moreover, the Malabo Protocol (Annex) is completely silent on the African Court's relationship to the International Criminal Court. This chapter first discusses whether the leaving out of the term "genuinely" bears any consequences on the assessment of the quality of the performance of states in respect of investigation and prosecution of international crimes. Next, it considers two alternative scenario's—one in which the International Criminal Court is hierarchically superior to the African Court of Justice and Human and Peoples' Rights and one in which both courts cooperate as equal partners. The author concludes that the latter model would be feasible if the International Criminal Court and the African Court of Justice and Human and Peoples' Rights move towards a "division of labor".

Keywords Africa · African Union · African Court of Justice and Human and Peoples' Rights · International Criminal Court · complementarity · "genuinely" · cooperation

All internet sources in this chapter were last visited on 30 June 2016.
The author is obliged to his Master-student, Mr. Timothy Kanyogonya, who wrote an interesting thesis on the proposed Criminal Chamber of the African Court, with an emphasis on complementarity issues.

H. van der Wilt (✉)
University of Amsterdam, Amsterdam, The Netherlands
e-mail: H.G.vanderWilt@uva.nl

G. Werle and M. Vormbaum (eds.), *The African Criminal Court*, International Criminal Justice Series 10, DOI 10.1007/978-94-6265-150-0_11

Contents

11.1 Extracts from the Malabo Protocol (Annex)

Article 46H Complementary Jurisdiction

1. The jurisdiction of the Court shall be complementary to that of the National Courts, and to the Courts of the Regional Economic Communities where specifically provided for by the Communities.
2. The Court shall determine that a case is inadmissible where:
   (a) The case is being investigated or prosecuted by a State which has jurisdiction over it, unless the State is unwilling or unable to carry out the investigation or prosecution;
   (b) The case has been investigated by a State which has jurisdiction over it and the State has decided not to prosecute the person concerned, unless the decision resulted from the unwillingness or inability of the State to prosecute;
   (c) The person concerned has already been tried for conduct which is the subject of the complaint;
   (d) The case is not of sufficient gravity to justify further action by the Court.
3. In order to determine that a State is unwilling to investigate or prosecute in a particular case, the Court shall consider, having regard to the principles of due process recognized by international law, whether one or more of the following exist, as applicable:
   (a) The proceedings were or are being undertaken or the national decision was made for the purpose of shielding the person concerned from criminal responsibility for crimes within the jurisdiction of the Court;
   (b) There has been an unjustified delay in the proceedings which in the circumstances is inconsistent with an intent to bring the person concerned to justice;
   (c) The proceedings were not or are not being conducted independently or impartially, and they were or are being conducted in a manner which, in the circumstances, is inconsistent with an intent to bring the person concerned to justice.

4. In order to determine that a State is unable to investigate or prosecute in a particular case, the Court shall consider whether, due to a total or substantial collapse or unavailability of its national judicial system, the State is unable to obtain the accused or the necessary evidence and testimony or otherwise unable to carry out its proceedings.

11.2 Introduction

It is generally acknowledged that the efforts of the African Union to add an International Criminal Law Section to the African Court of Justice and Human and Peoples' Rights very much stem from feelings of discontent at the exercise of universal jurisdiction over African people by—mainly—Western states and the selective policy of the International Criminal Court, which is often perceived to be exclusively interested in targeting African countries.

The concrete event that prompted mounting tensions between the African Union and the International Criminal Court was the latter's decision to issue an arrest warrant for Sudan's incumbent president Al Bashir.[1] The general feeling was that the initiative was ill-timed and thwarted attempts to achieve peace by political means, thereby revealing callous disregard for African solutions.[2] In a Resolution issued in July 2009 the African Union referred to the "unfortunate consequences that the indictment has had on the delicate peace processes underway in the Sudan and the fact that it continues to undermine the ongoing efforts aimed at facilitating the early resolution of the conflict in Darfur." The Resolution enjoined African Union Member States not to cooperate with the Court when asked to surrender Al Bashir and requested the Security Council to defer the situation in Darfur in conformity with Article of the 16 ICC Statute, a request that was largely ignored.[3] In connection with the excessive exercise of universal jurisdiction against African high officials by European courts, the African Union acknowledged that "universal jurisdiction is a principle of international law whose purpose is to ensure that individuals who commit grave offences such as war crimes and crimes against humanity do not do so with impunity and are brought to justice", but it pointed to an "abuse of the principle of universal jurisdiction by judges from some non-African

[1] International Criminal Court, Situation in Darfur, Sudan, Prosecutor v. Omar Hassan Ahmad Al Bashir, Decision on the Prosecution's Application for a Warrant of Arrest against Omar Hassan Ahmad Al Bashir, ICC-02/05-01/09-3, 4 March 2009.

[2] See, amongst others, Murungu 2011; Obel Hansen 2012; Ssenyonyo 2013.

[3] Decision on the Meeting of African States Parties to the Rome Statute of the International Criminal Court (ICC) Doc. Assembly/AU/13(XIII), 3 July 2009.

States against African leaders."[4] More specific allegations were uttered against European states, revealing old grievances:

> Indictments issued by European states against officials of African states have the effect of subjecting the latter to the jurisdiction of European states, contrary to the sovereign equality and independence of states. For African states, this evokes memories of colonialism.[5]

The African Union's decision to vest the African Court of Justice and Human and Peoples' Rights with criminal jurisdiction cannot be viewed in isolation from such deep-rooted misgivings.[6] It is plainly an attempt to preempt both the (universal) jurisdiction of European states and of the International Criminal Court. It is telling in this regard that the Preamble of the Malabo Protocol explicitly refers to the African Union Assembly's Decision on the Abuse of the Principle of Universal Jurisdiction.[7]

While the Annex to the Malabo Protocol endorses the ideal that Africans are only to be exposed to African justice and that the African Court of Justice and Human and Peoples' Rights is expected—at least to a large extent—to substitute the International Criminal Court, it hardly seems realistic to expect the International Criminal Court to quit the African scene entirely. After all, 34 African countries have ratified the ICC Statute and if they have no intention whatsoever of enabling the International Criminal Court to exercise its jurisdiction, they should withdraw from the Court.[8] Of course, such a withdrawal would probably toll the death knell for the International Criminal Court. It is therefore fair to assume that the African Court of Justice and Human and Peoples' Rights and the International Criminal Court will coexist.

This raises a number of interesting questions concerning the three-way relationship between African states, the African Court of Justice and Human and Peoples' Rights and the International Criminal Court, and it is the objective of this chapter to examine these relations more closely. It is worth pointing out from the outset that the jurisdictional relationships between African states on the one hand, and the International Criminal Court and the African Court of Justice and Human and

[4] Decision on the Report of the Commission on the Abuse of the Principle of Universal Jurisdiction, Doc. Assembly/AU/14 (XI), Assembly/AU/Dec. 199 (XI), Eleventh Ordinary Session 30 June–1 July 2008, Sharm El-Sheikh, Egypt, §§ 3–5.

[5] Assembly/AU/Dec. 199(XI), no. 5, § 5(iv).

[6] In a similar vein, Ssenyonyo 2013, pp. 415–416, who identifies the objections against universal jurisdiction and the displeasure with the International Criminal Court's prosecutorial strategy as two of the four factors giving impetus to the African Union's decision. See also Du Plessis 2012, p. 1, observing that "the process [of amending the Statute of the African Court] occurs against the backdrop of the AU's open hostility to the ICC."

[7] African Union, First Meeting of the Specialized Technical Committee on Justice and Legal Affairs, Draft Protocol on Amendments to the Protocol on the Statute of the African Court of Justice and Human Rights (hereafter: Malabo Protocol), STC/Legal/Min/7(I) Rev. 1, Addis Ababa, Ethiopia, 15–16 May 2014, § 13.

[8] Kenya's threat to withdraw from the International Criminal Court on 5 September 2013 has—at least temporarily—been averted by the dropping of criminal proceedings against Kenya's incumbent President, Kenyatta.

Peoples' Rights on the other, are both mined by the complementarity principle.[9] This principle implies that both regional and international criminal courts are only allowed to intervene whenever a state is either unable or unwilling to carry out investigations or prosecutions. The first question that will be addressed in Sect. 11.3 is whether the African Court of Justice and Human and Peoples' Rights has to observe the same threshold of (in)admissibility in relation to African states as the International Criminal Court.

While the Annex to the Malabo Protocol regulates the division of labor between states and the African Court of Justice and Human and Peoples' Rights, the latter's relationship with the International Criminal Court is not dealt with explicitly at all. By the same token, the ICC Statute makes no mention of "regional criminal courts", an omission, which need not, however, surprise us, because such courts did not exist when the Statute came into being. It is odd, though, as has also been observed before by Du Plessis, that the Annex to the Malabo Protocol is entirely silent on the International Criminal Court.[10] Against the backdrop of this apparent *lacuna* in the ICC Statute and the Annex to the Malabo Protocol, Sect. 11.4 discusses a hierarchical model in which the International Criminal Court would remain at the apex of international criminal law enforcement. In other words, it envisages a situation in which a judgment by the African Court of Justice and Human and Peoples' Rights might be superseded by one of the International Criminal Court if the former's judgment be found not to measure up to the standards of the ICC Statute and therefore to exemplify the inability (or unwillingness) of the African Court of Justice and Human and Peoples' Rights to exercise effective jurisdiction in a particular case.

Such a hierarchical scenario would no doubt perpetuate the discontent of African states and is therefore neither desirable, nor likely to emerge. Precisely because the relationship between the African Court of Justice and Human and Peoples' Rights and the International Criminal Court is not carved in stone, it rather seems desirable to devise a "flatter", more horizontal model of mutual cooperation between the African Court of Justice and Human and Peoples' Rights and the International Criminal Court. Such a model ought to be based on the rule that states have primary jurisdiction and that the African Court of Justice and Human and Peoples' Rights and International Criminal Court must confer as to who should intervene whenever a particular state should show itself incapable of taking on a case. The delineation of jurisdiction between the African Court of Justice and Human and Peoples' Rights and the International Criminal Court should be made dependent on the nature of the crimes and their geographical scope. Section 11.5 will assess the viability of such a collaborative model. Section 11.6 offers some concluding reflections on the subject.

---

[9] Paragraph 15 of the Preamble of the Malabo Protocol: "Convinced that the present Protocol will *complement* national, regional and continental bodies and institutions in preventing serious and massive violations of human and peoples' rights in keeping with Article 58 of the Charter and ensuring accountability for them whenever they occur [emphasis added]." Complementarity is corroborated in Article 46H of the Malabo Protocol (Annex).

[10] Du Plessis 2012, p. 12.

11.3 Complementarity and the African Court of Justice and Human and Peoples' Rights: The Relevance of the Adverb "Genuinely"

As indicated in the introduction, the jurisdictional relations between African states and the African Court of Justice and Human and Peoples' Rights, viz. between African states and the International Criminal Court are both governed by the principle of complementarity. Article 46H(1) of the Malabo Protocol (Annex) stipulates that the jurisdiction of the African Court of Justice and Human and Peoples' Rights be complementary to that of the national courts and the courts of the regional economic communities where specifically provided for by the communities. The provision goes on to echo Article 17 of the ICC Statute *almost* verbatim, referring to the successive stages of the criminal proceedings and elucidating the concepts of "unwillingness" and "inability".[11] Of special interest is the second paragraph of Article 46H that indeed reads nearly—but not entirely!—the same as Article 17(1) of the ICC Statute. When one compares both provisions, it is immediately obvious that the qualification "genuinely"—in relation to the carrying out of investigations or prosecution—is lacking in Article 46H. Is this a grave omission? Maybe. In my opinion, we need to distinguish between "genuine" activities or efforts on the part of an unwilling and of an unable state.

For a better understanding of the difference between these two cases, it seems useful to consider the dynamics of the interaction between states, the International Criminal Court and the African Court of Justice and Human and Peoples' Rights, in the light of the objectives of international criminal justice. In case of "unwillingness", the purpose of the state is to perpetuate "impunity" and prevent the African Court of Justice and Human and Peoples' Rights or International Criminal Court from intervening. After all, if the state wishes the regional or international court to "take over", it can simply sit still and do nothing. Both in Katanga and in Al Senussi, the (Pre-)Trial Chamber held that the issue of admissibility only arises, if a state deploys *action of some sort*.[12] There is no reason why the African

[11] For the text of Article 46H see above.

[12] Situation in the Democratic Republic of the Congo, Prosecutor v. Germain Katanga and Mathieu Ngudjolo Chui; Judgement on the Appeal of Mr. Germain Katanga against the Oral Decision of trial Chamber II of 12 June 2009 on the Admissibility of the Case, No. ICC-01/04-01/07 OA8, 25 September 2009, § 78: "It follows that in case of inaction, the question of unwillingness or inability does not arise; inaction on the part of the State having jurisdiction [...] renders a case admissible before the Court, subject to Article 17(1)(d) of the Statute." The Pre-Trial Chamber in the case of the Prosecutor v. Saif Al-Islam Gaddafi and Abdullah Al-Senussi (Decision on the admissibility of the case against Abdullah Al-Senussi, No.: ICC-01/11-01/11, 11 October 2013, § 26) confirmed the finding of the Appeals Chamber, adding that Article 17(1)(a) of the Statute involved a two-step test "according to which the Chamber, in considering whether a case is admissible before the Court, shall address in turn two questions: (i) whether, at the time of the proceedings in respect of the admissibility of a case, there is an ongoing investigation or prosecution of the case at the national level (first limb); and, in case the answer to the first question is in the affirmative, (ii) whether the State is unwilling or unable genuinely to carry out such investigation or prosecution (second limb)."

Court of Justice and Human and Peoples' Rights should take another position in this respect. A state intending to outsmart the African Court of Justice and Human and Peoples' Rights or the International Criminal Court could thus start a token or fraudulent investigation, claiming that it is willing and able to prosecute the accused. In case of "inability", however, the stakes are rather different. The question is not whether impunity will prevail, but rather which entity, namely the state, the regional court or the International Criminal Court, will carry out investigations and prosecute the accused.

The qualifying adverb "genuinely" may have different connotations when applied by the International Criminal Court to assess the "willingness" or "ability" of a state. Several scholars have observed that the exact meaning of "genuinely" is both elusive and controversial. Kleffner questions "whether the term 'genuinely' modifies the verb 'to carry out' or the words 'is willing or unable'."[13] In a slightly different vein, Sadat and Carden inquire whether "[...] 'genuinely' refers to situations where the State's *motives* are not 'genuine' (id est are duplicitous or disingenuous) or situations where the State is 'really' unable or unwilling to prosecute."[14] One is inclined to associate motives primarily with an "unwilling" state. And because motives and intentions are difficult to gauge, it may not be easy for the International Criminal Court to assess their sincerity. These problems of interpretation are reflected in the *indiciae* for "unwillingness" (Article 17(2) of the ICC Statute and Article 46H of the Malabo Protocol (Annex)). After all, it may be hard to determine whether criminal proceedings are undertaken for the purpose of shielding a person from criminal responsibility or have not been conducted independently or impartially. And while a delay in the proceedings can be more easily established, the International Criminal Court would have difficulty in finding out whether such tardiness is "inconsistent with an *intent* to bring the person concerned to justice [emphasis added]."[15] For in the context of admissibility proceedings under the ICC Statute, it is not sufficient to render proof that the state is "unwilling". Rather, proof is necessary to the effect that the state in question is "genuinely" unwilling. Thus, the onus of proof on the Prosecutor is aggravated by the insertion of the qualifier "genuinely". This situation is compounded by the fact that (insincere) motives are hard to detect. In other words, the addition of the word "genuinely" increases the threshold of admissibility.[16] Leaving out the term "genuinely" would, therefore, ease the admissibility of a case.

In case of "inability", the emphasis of the term "genuine" shifts the focus from the motives to the actual performance of the state—does the state really lack the resources to conduct criminal investigations or is it simply convenient for the state to outsource a difficult job? "Genuinely" suggests the introduction of an objective

---

[13] Kleffner 2008, p. 114.

[14] Sadat and Carden 2000, pp. 381, 418.

[15] Article 17(2)(b) of the ICC Statute and Article 46H(3)(b) of the Malabo Protocol (Annex).

[16] Kleffner 2008, p. 114.

standard against which the performance of the state can be assessed.[17] El Zeidy argues convincingly that "the inclusion of the term 'genuinely' clearly raises the threshold of *objective* scrutiny in testing the quality of states' national proceedings."[18] Obviously, the introduction of such a standard only makes sense if a situation lends itself to objective verification. The criteria for "(in)ability"—whether the state is (un)able to capture the accused or to obtain the necessary evidence and testimony [Article 17(3) of the ICC Statute/Article 46H(4) of the Malabo Protocol (Annex)]—can indeed be more easily verified objectively. Holmes correctly observes that "the inability of the state to effect an investigation or prosecution is not due to lack of good faith but rather to other, more *objective*, factors [emphasis added]."[19] Moreover, in the context of the assessment of the state's ability, "genuine" implies that the state must make a real effort to bring a criminal case to completion. In the case of *Paniagua Morales* et al. the Inter-American Court of Human Rights clarified and specified the meaning of "genuine and effective investigations", requiring the state to use "all the legal means at its disposal in the conduct of a serious criminal process that identifies the suspects involved and leads to actual trial and appropriate punishment if necessary."[20]

The effects of the application of the "genuinely" standard in the context of "inability" are difficult to predict. The introduction of an objective check gravitates towards a mean. On the one hand, it may prevent a rash presumption of "ability" by a state, by pointing out its poor performance.[21] In such situations, the

[17] Compare Holmes 2002, pp. 673–674: "[…] the delegations [to the Rome Conference] were mindful that the ICC was not envisaged as an appellate body to review decisions of domestic courts. To avoid this result, it was said that the criteria permitting ICC intervention should be as *objective* as possible. […] The negotiations finally settled on the term 'genuinely', even though there was no precedent quoted for the utilization of this word. The term captured the concerns of some delegations by being the *least subjective* concept considered [emphasis added]."

[18] El Zeidy 2008, p. 165.

[19] Holmes 2002, p. 674.

[20] *Paniagua Morales* et al. ("Panel Blanca", Judgment of 8 March 1998, Inter-American Court of Human Rights (series C) No. 37 (1998), para 94.

[21] A fairly good example of the standards that the International Criminal Court is applying is the Decision on Côte d'Ivoire's challenge to the admissibility of the case against Simone Gbagbo (Situation in the Republic of Côte d'Ivoire in the case of the Prosecutor v. Simone Gbagbo), Case No.: ICC-02/11-01/12, 11 December 2014. The Pre-Trial Chamber explained that "for the Admissibility Challenge to succeed, it must be established that tangible and progressive investigative steps are being undertaken in order to ascertain whether Simone Gbagbo is criminally responsible for the conduct alleged in the proceedings before the Court", adding that "from the documentation provided by Côte d'Ivoire, it appears that the investigative activities undertaken by the domestic authorities are not tangible, concrete and progressive, but, on the contrary, sparse and disparate."(§ 65). Later on, the Pre-Trial Chamber specified that "The investigative steps into Simone Gbagbo's criminal responsibility are not only scarce in quantity and lacking in progression. They also appear disparate in nature and purpose to the extent that the overall factual contours of the alleged domestic investigations (as part of which these individual investigative steps

insertion of "genuinely", when connected to the actual performance of states in the realm of criminal investigations and prosecution, introduces a quality check that indeed increases the threshold of *in*admissibility.[22] On the other hand, it may enable the Court to counter unnecessary self-referrals, in that the Court, in line with the *Paniagua* judgment, could urge the state concerned fully to employ its resources and make a real effort. In view of the current situation in Africa, where states have predominantly claimed "inability" and have subsequently referred situations to the International Criminal Court (*vide* Uganda, Democratic Republic of Congo, Central African Republic, Mali), the omission of the term "genuinely" in the Malabo Protocol (Annex) may indeed be a cause for some concern. Leaving out the word "genuinely" may allow African states to "throw the garbage over the fence" and saddle the African Court of Justice and Human and Peoples' Rights with a considerable caseload.[23]

11.4 A Hierarchical Relationship Between the International Criminal Court and the African Court of Justice and Human and Peoples' Rights?

In the previous section, we addressed the potential complementary relationship between the African Court of Justice and Human and Peoples' Rights and states, leaving the International Criminal Court out of the equation entirely. Such an approach is, however, of course not realistic because the International Criminal Court is here to stay. What form might, then, the three-way relationship between

Footnote 21 (continued)
were undertaken) remain indiscernible. In this sense, the Chamber is unable to establish whether these limited steps undertaken at the national level are together directed at ascertaining Simone Gbagbo's criminal responsibility for the same conduct as that alleged in the proceedings before the Court."(§ 70). Although the Pre-Trial Chamber concluded that the national proceedings did not even reveal sufficient "action" to ascertain whether Ivory Coast was "willing and able", it gives a pretty good impression of the quality that the Court requires. The Pre-Trial Chamber's findings were confirmed by the Appeals Chamber in its judgment on the appeal of Côte d'Ivoire against the decision of Pre-Trial Chamber I of 11 December 2014 entitled "Decision on "Côte d'Ivoire's challenge to the admissibility of the case against Simone Gbagbo" No. ICC-02/11-01/12 OA, 27 May 2015.

[22] Kleffner 2008, p. 114.

[23] For similar apprehensions, see Abass 2013, pp. 27, 44: "The omission of the word 'genuinely' in the Draft Protocol's version has the disastrous implication of lowering the evidential standard of 'inability to prosecute' required before African states can refer a case to the Court. African states could easily exploit this lacuna to turn the Court into a clearinghouse for crimes otherwise prosecutable by their courts. Insofar as only evidence of an 'inability to prosecute' and not evidence of an 'inability to *genuinely* prosecute' is required under Article 46(2)(b), the Court should expect the floodgates to be opened by opportunistic states which will effectively turn the Court into a court of 'first recourse', not of 'last resort.'" [emphasis original].

states, International Criminal Court and African Court of Justice and Human and Peoples' Rights take? Is it, for instance, conceivable that states may be able to choose freely to refer a situation to either the African Court of Justice and Human and Peoples' Rights or the International Criminal Court if they consider themselves unable to exercise jurisdiction in a given case? As the Annex to the Malabo Protocol is silent on the International Criminal Court, it is difficult—if not impossible—to say. For its part, the ICC Statute does not envisage any criminal law enforcement by a regional court.

The most pressing question is, however, what, if any, hierarchy would govern the relationship between the two courts if they were to find themselves at odds on a certain legal issue. Would the International Criminal Court be authorized to scrutinize and assess the performance of the African Court of Justice and Human and Peoples' Rights if, in the former's opinion, the regional court did not come up with the right solution? At first glance, it may be quite difficult to conceive of any situation in which the African Court of Justice and Human and Peoples' Rights would turn out to be "unwilling" or "unable" to carry out investigations or prosecution. However, there is one conspicuous aspect in which the ICC Statute and the Annex to the Malabo Protocol differ, resulting in a limitation of the jurisdiction of the African Court of Justice and Human and Peoples' Rights. The Annex to the Malabo Protocol explicitly introduces the—severely criticized—personal immunity of any serving head of state or government of the African Union. Article 46A*bis* stipulates that "No charges shall be commenced or continued before the Court against any serving AU Head of State or Government, or anybody acting or entitled to act in such capacity, or other senior state officials based on their functions, during their tenure of office."[24] This is clearly at variance with the corresponding provision in the ICC Statute (Article 27) that does not allow any exclusion of criminal responsibility on the basis of official capacity, as the Al Bashir case made abundantly clear.[25]

Now one may imagine a situation in which a state, in order to deliberately bypass the International Criminal Court, refers a situation of gross and flagrant human rights violations in which the incumbent president of that state is involved as well, to the African Court of Justice and Human and Peoples' Rights. If the African Court of Justice and Human and Peoples' Rights were to decline to exercise jurisdiction over the President, invoking Article 46A*bis*, the International Criminal Court would arguably be allowed to intervene and consider the case admissible, in view of the "inability" of the African Court to carry out investigations. However, such hierarchical supremacy of the International Criminal Court over the regional court cannot easily be construed by legal arguments, precisely

[24] On this contested provision, see the chapter by Tladi in this book.

[25] Situation in Darfur, Sudan, Prosecutor v. Omar Hassan Ahmad Al Bashir, Decision on the Prosecution's Application for a Warrant of Arrest against Omar Hassan Ahmad Al Bashir, Case No. ICC-902/05-01/09-3, 4 March 2009.

because the ICC Statute and the African Court of Justice and Human and Peoples' Rights make no mention of the other institution.[26] In respect of the specific topic of (personal) immunities, the supremacy of the International Criminal Court can be defended by resorting to the assumption that the abolition of immunities before international criminal courts has solidified into a rule of customary international law.[27] However, that does not entail a general authority of the International Criminal Court to intervene whenever the African Court is "unable" or "unwilling" to carry out investigations or prosecutions.

To be sure, it is not very likely that the situation described above will emerge. As is well known, the situations in Sudan/Darfur and Libya, in which the prosecution of a sitting head of state was at stake, were referred to the International Criminal Court by a Resolution of the Security Council.[28] Article 15 of the Malabo Protocol (Annex) authorizes the African Union Peace and Security Council to submit cases to the African Court of Justice and Human and Peoples' Rights, but the Protocol does not envisage a role for the UN Security Council. The UN Security Council is therefore likely to bypass the African Court and call upon the International Criminal Court directly, whenever it decides that widespread and systematic violence, including the involvement of heads of states, constitutes a threat or breach of the peace and requires action by the Court. Self-referrals, on the other hand, have usually emanated from situations in which the authorities were unable to cope with rebel forces.

Nonetheless, it cannot be ruled out that the African Court of Justice and Human and Peoples' Rights will be unable to prosecute perpetrators of core crimes, simply because it lacks the proper legal tools and concepts to accomplish this. In this context, one might observe that the modes of responsibility, as enunciated in Article 28N of the Malabo Protocol (Annex), are different from and less sophisticated than the concepts of criminal responsibility, detailed in the Rome Statute.[29] In these situations, the International Criminal Court must be available as a default option. And because there is no proper legal arrangement for such—admittedly

---

[26] The Vienna Convention on the Law of Treaties (Vienna 23 May 1969, UN Treaties Series 1980, No. 18231) offers no solution. Article 30 suggests that the younger treaty (Annex to the Malabo Protocol) should prevail, but only in the relations between states that are party to both treaties. Moreover, Article 27 of the ICC Statute and Article 46A*bis* of the Malabo Protocol (Annex) only regulate the scope of the jurisdiction of both courts. They do not urge States Parties to comply with conflicting obligations.

[27] Compare for this approach, ICC, Situation in Darfur, Sudan, Prosecutor v. Omar Ahmad Al Bashir, Decision Pursuant to Article 87(7) of the Rome Statute on the Failure by the Republic of Malawi to Comply with the Cooperation Requests Issued by the Court with Respect to the Arrest and Surrender of Omar Hassan Ahmad Al Bahir, No.: ICC-02/05—011/09, 12 December 2011.

[28] See, respectively, Resolution 1593 (2005); Adopted by the Security Council at its 5158th meeting, on 31 March 2005, S/RES/1593 (2005) (Darfur) and Resolution 1970 (2011); Adopted by the Security Council at its 6401st meeting, on 26 February 2011, S/RES/ 1970 (2011).

[29] See the chapter by Meloni in this book.

rare—situations, the hierarchical relationship between the International Criminal Court and the African Court of Justice and Human and Peoples' Rights urgently requires attention.

11.5 Towards a Cooperative Model

The scenario that has been described in the previous section is predicated on a hierarchical relationship between the International Criminal Court and the African Court of Justice and Human and Peoples' Rights and contains the seeds of antagonism and conflict. However, the African states and the International Criminal Court need not necessarily remain embarked on a collision course. There is plenty of potential for fruitful and enduring cooperation in the future. The concept of "positive complementarity" may serve as a useful model. In its "Prosecutorial Strategy", the ICC Office of the Prosecutor has repeatedly emphasized the relevance of a positive approach to complementarity, meaning that "the Office will encourage genuine national proceedings where possible, including in situation countries, relying on its various networks of cooperation, but without involving the Office directly in capacity building or financial or technical assistance."[30] Analogously, the International Criminal Court and the African Court of Justice and Human and Peoples' Rights might agree to enter into a working relationship, dividing the investigation and prosecution of international (and transnational) crimes between them and rendering mutual assistance by exchanging information and evidence. The prime incentive to establish such a relationship is to improve the effectiveness of international criminal law enforcement by broadening the opportunities for prosecution.[31] Obviously, this aspiration stems from the limited resources of the International Criminal Court that compel the Prosecutor to make difficult choices in selecting appropriate situations and cases. Selectivity is probably one of the greatest challenges for international criminal justice and the topic exceeds the limits of this modest contribution.[32] However, we cannot entirely ignore the issue either because any constructive cooperation between the International Criminal Court and the African Court of Justice and Human and Peoples' Rights requires a reflection on the proper division of labor between the

[30] International Criminal Court, Office of the Prosecutor, Prosecutorial Strategy 2009–2012, The Hague, 1 February 2010, § 17, available at: http://www.icc-cpi.int/NR/rdonlyres/66A8DCDC-3650-4514-AA62-D229D1128F65/281506/OTPProsecutorialStrategy20092013.pdf.

[31] On positive complementarity cf. Burke-White 2008, p. 73: "The most immediate implication of a policy of proactive complementarity is to increase the number of available judicial fora through which to prosecute international crimes."

[32] See for interesting discussions on the issue: Cryer 2005; Damaška 2008, pp. 329, 360–363; de Guzman 2012, p. 265; Schabas 2010, p. 535.

Courts and, therefore, a decision on which cases, crimes and situations to select and which ones to leave to the other Court. Some brief observations will suffice for the moment.

First of all, one could envisage a selection and division of cases on the basis of gravity. Article 17(1)(d) of the ICC Statute stipulates that a case is inadmissible if it is not of sufficient gravity. Parallel to the division of labor between the Court and domestic jurisdictions, the International Criminal Court could opt for prosecution of the gravest crimes, while leaving others to the African Court of Justice and Human and Peoples' Rights.[33] The distribution of cases requires careful consultation and orchestration. In the case against Saif Al-Islam Gaddafi, the Appeals Chamber explained that such a distribution could even involve distinctions at the level of specific incidents:

> "[t]he 'conduct' that defines the 'case' is both that of the suspect, Mr Gaddafi, and that described in the incidents under investigation which is imputed to the suspect. 'Incident' is understood as referring to a historical event, defined in time and place, in the course of which crimes within the jurisdiction of the Court were allegedly committed by one or more direct perpetrators."[34]

However, the gravity criterion is not very precise and is, therefore, difficult to apply, especially since the Appeals Chamber in the case against Ntaganda has rejected the parameters that the Pre-Trial Chamber had advanced to accentuate the standard.[35]

A stronger case can arguably be advanced for selection on the basis of the nature of the crime. In this volume, Fernandez, Heger, Jeßberger, Kemp, Kinyunyu, and Mninde-Silungwe have analyzed the transnational crimes that belong to the subject matter jurisdiction of the African Court of Justice and Human and Peoples' Rights. Such crimes, for example trafficking in human beings or exploitation of natural resources, are beyond the jurisdictional grasp of the International Criminal Court and may particularly qualify for prosecution by the African Court of Justice and Human and Peoples' Rights. The regional court would, therefore, be well-advised to focus on transnational crimes, while leaving

---

33 Burke-White ibid., no. 32, p. 101: "[...] a division of labor may also arise where the OTP seeks to prosecute those crimes meeting the gravity threshold articulated in Article 17 and a state seeks accountability (whether criminal or non-criminal) for lower level offenders who are not likely to be the subjects of an ICC investigation."

34 ICC, Situation in Libya, Prosecutor v. Saif Al-Islam Gaddafi and Abdullah Al-Senussi, Judgment on the appeal of Libya against the decision of Pre-Trial Chamber I of 31 May 2013 entitled "Decision on the admissibility of the case against Saif Al-Islam Gaddaffi, Case No. ICC-01/11-01/11 OA 4, 21 May 2014, § 62.

35 ICC, Situation in the Democratic Republic of the Congo, Judgment on the Prosecutor's appeal against the decision of Pre-Trial Chamber I entitled: Decision on the Prosecutor's Application for Warrants of Arrest, Article 58", Case No. ICC-01/04, 13 July 2006, §§ 68–82. The three-pronged test of the Pre-Trial Chamber included the social alarm caused to the community, the fact that the suspect was one of the most senior leaders in the situation under investigation and the role played by the state in the overall commission of crimes.

the prosecution of the perpetrators of core crimes to the International Criminal Court. Such a division of labor finds surprisingly broad support from African scholars on the African Court of Justice and Human and Peoples' Rights.[36] There are several arguments in favor of this mode of distribution. Obviously, it goes a long way to preventing conflict between the International Criminal Court, and reduces the risk of *bis in idem* and double jeopardy. More importantly, it enables the African Court of Justice and Human and Peoples' Rights to take charge of huge problems that cannot be adequately addressed by the International Criminal Court. The African continent is plagued by several man-made disasters. Rampant corruption paralyzes the public sector. Poachers exploit and destroy with dazzling speed the last remnants of African wildlife. By prosecuting the perpetrators of such transnational crimes, the African Court of Justice and Human and Peoples' Rights could demonstrate the special value of regional criminal courts. Indeed, there is one field in particular in which the African Court of Justice and Human and Peoples' Rights can make an interesting contribution. The Court's jurisdiction covers corruption and money laundering.[37] It is well-known that large corporations from Western countries are often involved in these white-collar crimes. Multi-national corporations succeed in evading taxes in developing states and rob countries like Malawi on a yearly basis of tens of millions of dollars, money that should go into the development of the public sector. Unlike the ICC Statute, which limits the jurisdiction of the International Criminal Court to natural persons, the African Court of Justice and Human and Peoples' Rights provides for corporate criminal liability.[38] The African Court of Justice and Human and Peoples' Rights could, therefore, decide to open investigations against corporations, including Western entities, whenever they can be located on the territory of an African State Party to the Malabo Protocol.

As indicated above, the African Court of Justice and Human and Peoples' Rights and the International Criminal Court could bolster each other's effectiveness by working closely together, for instance, by engaging in mutual exchange of evidence. The Annex to the Malabo Protocol and the ICC Statute would require

---

[36] Cf. Abass 2013, pp. 27, 49: "the fact that the Rome Statute does not cover such crimes as corruption, unconstitutional changes of governments, mercenarism and so on, which affect the majority of African states, is perhaps the strongest case in favour of the prosecution of international crimes by the African Court."; Murungu 2011, p. 1085: "[…] perhaps it would be good for the Criminal Chamber to show its distinctive features by dealing with the crime of aggression and certain common crimes in Africa (that do not all amount to international crimes) such as election-rigging, unconstitutional change of governments, human trafficking, acts of terrorism, piracy, drug trafficking, slave practices and slavery."

[37] Cf. Fernandez's chapter in this book.

[38] Article 46C(1) of the Malabo Protocol (Annex): "For the purpose of this Statute, the Court shall have jurisdiction over legal corporations, with the exception of States." See also Meloni's chapter in this book.

but small amendments in order to enable such forms of assistance.[39] Such cooperation is not necessarily dependent on the assisting court having jurisdiction over the crime or perpetrator. The International Criminal Court could, for instance, assist the African Court of Justice and Human and Peoples' Rights by sharing information obtained in the context of the investigations of war crimes, if that information were to reveal possible complicity of *legal entities* in these war crimes or other offences. These are the kinds of concerted action and cooperation that would surely prove conducive to effective criminal law enforcement.

11.6 Some Final Reflections

Relations between the African states and the International Criminal Court have been strained. The efforts to establish criminal chambers in the African Court of Justice and Human and Peoples' Rights have—at least partially—been fueled by spite and resentment. In the first part of the present contribution I focused on the problematic aspects of the three-way relationship between African states, the African Court of Justice and Human and Peoples' Rights and the International Criminal Court. I tried to demonstrate that the current phrasing of the complementarity principle in the Malabo Protocol (Annex) invites states to outsource the prosecution of crimes to the regional court. Moreover, the assumption of a hierarchical relationship between the International Criminal Court and the African Court of Justice and Human and Peoples' Rights would be likely to perpetuate the mutual tensions.

The second part of this chapter strikes a more positive note. In it, I explored the possibilities for a constructive relationship between the International Criminal Court and the African Court of Justice and Human and Peoples' Rights, predicated on a division of labor based on the nature of the crime and mutual assistance. One should be cautious not to burden the courts with exaggerated expectations. Even the international and regional court working in tandem can obviously not solve all societal problems. Criminal courts cannot alleviate the suffering of all victims and I am personally not convinced of the deterrent effect of international criminal justice. However, criminal trials issue powerful normative messages that vastly exceed their capacity for concrete problem-solving. This norm-expressive function of international criminal justice is best served by a modest but determined

[39] Article 46L of the Malabo Protocol (Annex) provides that "The Court shall be entitled to seek the cooperation or assistance of regional or international courts, non-State Parties or cooperating partners of the African Union and may conclude Agreements for that purpose." In other words, it envisages the reception but not the rendering of assistance. Article 93(10) ICC Statute allows the Court to co-operate with and provide assistance to a State Party, but does not contemplate the cooperation with regional courts or institutions.

selection of strong and symbolic cases. The International Criminal Court's attention is legally restricted to the core crimes, while the African Court of Justice and Human and Peoples' Rights ought, in my view, to focus on transnational crimes such as illicit exploitation of natural resources, corruption, trafficking in human beings etc. This seems particularly desirable in such cases where the crimes affect multiple jurisdictions and are, therefore, difficult for individual states to counter on their own. The distribution of jurisdiction on the basis of the nature of the crime reflects the notion that some crimes are of concern to the entire international community, while others have but a regional import. Be that as it may, the urge for greater synergy and collaboration between the Courts symbolizes the increasing fusion of core and transnational crimes. Their cooperation may contribute to a better understanding of this relationship, a subject which has hitherto not received sufficient scholarly attention.

References

Abass A (2013) The proposed international criminal jurisdiction for the African Court, some problematic aspects. Neth Int Law Rev 60:27–50

Burke-White W (2008) Proactive complementarity: the International Criminal Court and national courts in the Rome system of international justice. Harvard Int Law J 49:53–108

Cryer R (2005) Prosecuting international crimes: selectivity and the International Criminal Court. Cambridge University Press, Cambridge

Damaška M (2008) What is the point of international criminal justice? Chicago-Kent Law Rev 83:329–365

De Guzman M (2012) Choosing to prosecute: expressive selections at the International Criminal Court. Mich J Int Law 33:265–320

Du Plessis M (2012) Implications of the AU decision to give the African Court jurisdiction over international crimes. Institute for Security Studies Paper 235

El Zeidy M (2008) The principle of complementarity in international criminal law; origin development and practice. Martinius Nijhoff Publishers, Leiden

Holmes J (2002) Complementarity: national courts versus the ICC. In: Cassese et al. (eds) The Rome Statute of the International Criminal Court: a commentary. Oxford University Press, Oxford

Kleffner J (2008) Complementarity in the Rome Statute and national criminal jurisdictions. Oxford University Press, Oxford

Murungu CB (2011) Towards a criminal court in the African Court of Justice and Human Rights. J Int Crim Justice 9:1067–1088

Obel Hansen T (2012) Africa and the International Criminal Court. In: Murithi T (ed) A Handbook of Africa's International Relations. Routledge, Oxford, pp 165–179

Sadat L, Carden R (2000) The new international criminal court: an uneasy revolution. Georgetown Law J 88:381–459

Schabas W (2010) Victor's justice: selecting "situations" at the International Criminal Court. John Marshall Law Rev 43:535–552

Ssenyonyo M (2013) The rise of the African Union opposition to the International Criminal Court's investigations and prosecutions of African leaders. Int Crim Law Rev 13:385–428

Chapter 12
Immunities (Article 46A*bis*)

Dire Tladi

Abstract Article 46 A*bis* of the Malabo Protocol (Annex) which provides for the immunity of state officials from the jurisdiction of the African Court of Justice and Human and Peoples' Rights has attracted the widest and most negative attention in the debate concerning the African Union and international criminal justice. This is partly because the Malabo Protocol is seen as a protest against the International Criminal Court's exercise of jurisdiction over African heads of state. This chapter considers whether, as a matter of international law, the arguments against Article 46 A*bis* are valid. In particular, the chapter assesses whether customary international either requires or rejects immunity before international courts.

Keywords Africa · African Union · International Criminal Court · immunity · customary international law · jurisdiction · impunity · heads of state and government · State officials · Treaty interpretation · conflict of norms

Contents

This chapter is an updated version of an article that first appeared as Tladi 2015.

D. Tladi (✉)
Member of the UN International Law Commission,
Minister of International Relations and Cooperation,
University of Pretoria, Pretoria, South Africa
e-mail: diretladi2012@gmail.com

G. Werle and M. Vormbaum (eds.), *The African Criminal Court*, International Criminal Justice Series 10, DOI 10.1007/978-94-6265-150-0_12

12.1 Extracts from the Malabo Protocol (Annex)

Article 46A*bis* Immunities
No charges shall be commenced or continued before the Court against any serving AU Head of State or Government, or anybody acting or entitled to act in such capacity, or other senior state officials based on their functions, during their tenure of office.

12.2 Statement of the Issues

For many, Article 46A*bis* is *the* defining feature of the Annex of the Malabo Protocol and the provision has for that reason attracted the widest attention—much of it negative. This is partly because the provision has prompted a view of the Malabo Protocol as a "protest treaty" against the International Criminal Court.[1] The debates surrounding it have centered on both legal and policy issues. The focus has, in particular, been on the consistency of Article 46A*bis* with customary international law and the ubiquitous fight against impunity.

Much of the debate has tended to reflect the hero-villain trend that has so characterized African Union-International Criminal Court debates in recent years.[2] As with other debates in which one side is portrayed as a hero and the other as a villain, most of the positions on both sides of the divide ignore the nuances of what is, in fact, a complex area of law. Amidst the jockeying for positions, the distinctions between doctrinal positions and normative policy assertions often become blurred. Sometimes they disappear altogether. The doctrinal question of whether immunities of certain officials before international courts is consistent with modern international law is very often answered by the normative policy postulation that the African Union ought not to have included the immunities provision in the Annex of the Malabo Protocol. Conversely, the normative postulation questioning the wisdom prosecuting heads of state is met by a reference to a provision in the ICC Statute. Added to the mix is very often an empirical assertion, either that a position will result in impunity or will lead to the destabilization of a country or region. The discourse is further complicated by the recourse had by commentators to the political rationale or objective behind the Malabo Protocol, i.e. the assertion

[1] See also Abass's chapter in this book.

[2] See Tladi 2014, p. 381, where the author described debates on the International Criminal Court as being "characterised by an ideological chasm that has pitted villains against protagonists—with both sides casting the other villains intent on wanton destruction and themselves as protagonists fighting the good fight."

that the Annex to the Malabo Protocol, and the immunity provision in particular, was a response to the prosecutions conducted by the International Criminal Court against African heads of state.

In this chapter, I assess the merits of some of the arguments that have been advanced both in support of and against Article 46A*bis*. I begin, in the next section, by identifying the various propositions underlying the arguments for and against Article 46A*bis*. I then evaluate these propositions on the basis of the rules of international law before offering some concluding remarks.

12.3 Immunity Before the African Court of Justice and Human and Peoples' Rights: Unpacking the Case for and Against

12.3.1 Scope of Immunity in the Annex of the Malabo Protocol

First of all, and irrespective of doctrinal and normative issues, the text of Article 46A*bis* is ambiguous and poorly drafted. For example, what is meant by "or anybody [...] entitled to act in such capacity", a phrase which first appeared in the decision of the African Union Extraordinary Summit of October 2014,[3] is not at all clear. One possible reading is that the phrase refers to any number of persons including potentially all ministers and even all members of parliament in some states.[4] This very broad interpretation is inherently relative and would result in different rules being applicable to officials from different states since whether a person enjoyed immunity before the African Court of Justice and Human and Peoples' Rights would depend on the constitutional system of each state. At its narrowest, however, the provision could be limited to the deputy head of state or government.[5] This second, narrower interpretation is more objective and altogether more consistent with the objective of the decision in which the phrase first

[3] Paragraph 10(j) AU Decision on Africa's Relationship with the International Criminal Court (ICC), Ext/Assembly/AU/Dec.1 (October 2013).

[4] Section 90 of the Constitution of the Republic of South Africa, 1996, provides that the deputy president, a minister designated by the president, a minister designated by other members of the cabinet, and the speaker of parliament until the parliament designates one of its members, may act as head of state.

[5] Under section 147(3) of the Constitution of Kenya, only the deputy president may hold the office of the acting president in the absence of the president. See also Article II section 6 of the Constitution of the United States.

appeared, i.e. to prevent the prosecution of Kenya's head of state and his deputy. For the purpose of the analysis below, the narrower meaning of the phrase is assumed although the broader interpretation cannot be ruled out.

The second ambiguity relates to whether Article 46A*bis* aims at providing two different regimes of immunity i.e. immunity *ratione personae* and immunity *ratione materiae*, or only one.[6] Moreover, if the aim is to establish only one regime, it is unclear whether the regime would be immunity *ratione materiae* or immunity *ratione personae.* An ordinary meaning of Article 46A*bis* appears to support two separate categories.[7] The first category, approximating immunity *ratione personae*, would be applicable to "Heads of State or Government" and "anybody acting or entitled to act in such capacity." The second category, approximating immunity *ratione materiae*, applies to "other senior officials based on their functions". The phrase "based on their functions" in Article 46A*bis* appears to only qualify "other senior officials" and not "Heads of State or Government, or anybody acting or entitled to act in such capacity." An interpretation of Article 46A*bis* as establishing two categories of immunities would also be consistent with applicable principles of international law.[8] Assuming this interpretation were the more correct interpretation, it would mean that, contrary to the conclusions of the International Law Commission and the decision of the International Court of Justice in the Arrest Warrant case, immunity *ratione personae* under the Malabo

[6] At its 65th Session, in the context of its work on Immunity of State Officials from Foreign Criminal Jurisdiction, the International Law Commission adopted Draft Articles 3 and 4 on immunity *ratione personae* as covering all acts, whether in private or official capacity, performed by heads of state, heads of government and ministers for foreign affairs. See Chapter 5 of the Report of the International Law Commission on the Work of its Sixty-Fifth Session (6 May–7 June and 8 July–9 August 2013), General Assembly Official Records Sixty-Eighth Session, Supplement 10 (A/68/10). At its 66th Session, in the context of its work on Immunity of State Officials from Foreign Criminal Jurisdiction, the ILC adopted Draft Article 5 on immunity *ratione materiae* as applicable to state officials acting as such. See Chap. 9 of the Report of the International Law Commission on the Work of its Sixty-Sixth Session (5 May–6 June and 7 July–8 August 2014), General Assembly Official Records Sixty-Ninth Session, Supplement 10 (A/69/10).

[7] The general rule on interpretation of treaties, in Article 31(1) of the Vienna Convention on the Law of Treaties, requires the terms of a treaty to be given their ordinary meaning in context and in the light of the treaty's object and purpose.

[8] Under the Vienna rules of interpretation, in particular Article 31(3)(c) of the Vienna Convention on the Law of Treaties, "relevant rules of international law applicable in the relations between the parties" are to be taken into account in the interpretation of treaties. On the notion of two categories of immunities under international law, see the work of the International Law Commission cited, supra no. 6.

Protocol (Annex) would not be extended to Ministers for Foreign Affairs.[9] Other senior officials, including Ministers for Foreign Affairs, would then be entitled to immunity *ratione materiae* for acts performed in their official capacity.

An alternative interpretation of Article 46A*bis* is that it establishes only immunity *ratione personae*. Under such an interpretation, "based on their functions" does not qualify the extent of immunity but rather forms part of the description of the senior officials. In other words, senior officials, defined in terms of their functions, enjoy the same type of immunity as heads of state or governments and anyone else acting or entitled in that capacity. Indeed, the phrase "based on their functions" appears to have been drawn from the International Court of Justice's reasoning in extending immunity *ratione personae* to Ministers for Foreign Affairs in the Arrest Warrant case.[10] This interpretation is supported mainly by the fact that in its earlier decisions leading to the adoption of Article 46A*bis*, the African Union has never distinguished between the immunities of heads of state and those of other senior state officials.[11] Moreover, such an interpretation would resolve the inconsistency between the first interpretation and the decision of the International Court of Justice in the Arrest Warrant case identified above. Although Article 46A*bis* could be read as establishing two categories of immunities, namely immunity *ratione materiae* and immunity *ratione personae*, on balance it appears that this second alternative is likely what was meant by the African Union. It is unnecessary to resolve this interpretative ambiguity, save to recognize these two possible readings of the provisions. Under this second interpretation, however, other officials whose functions do not exhibit the characteristics identified by the International Court of Justice in the Arrest Warrant case as indicating immunity *ratione personae* would not have immunity before the criminal law section of the African Court of Justice and Human and Peoples' Rights.

[9] See Case Concerning the Arrest Warrant of 11 April 2000 (*Democratic Republic of the Congo v Belgium*), Judgement of 14 February 2002, 2002 ICJ Reports 3 at para 54 where the International Court of Justice held that ministers for foreign affairs enjoy immunity *ratione personae*. Whether the ministers for foreign affairs should enjoy immunity *ratione personae* was a matter of intense debate during the International Law Commission's consideration of the topic. Although the International Law Commission decided to include ministers for foreign Affairs, at para 5 of the Commentary to Draft Article 3, the Commission states as follows: "On the one hand, some members of the Commission pointed out that the Court's judgment [in the Arrest Warrant case was not sufficient grounds for concluding that a customary rule existed, as it did not contain a thorough analysis of the practice and that several judges expressed opinions that differed from the majority view. One member of the Commission who considered that the Court's judgment did not, at the time it was made, reflect customary law, nevertheless said that, in view of the fact that Court's judgement in that case had not been opposed by States, the absence of a customary rule does not prevent the Commission from including [ministers for foreign affairs] among the persons enjoying immunity *ratione personae*."

[10] In the Arrest Warrant case, supra no. 9 at para 53, the Court states that to determine the extent of the immunities of ministers for foreign affairs it "must first consider the nature of the functions exercised by a Minister for Foreign Affairs."

[11] See, e.g. para 9 of the Decision on Africa's Relationship with the International Criminal Court (ICC), Ext/Assembly/AU/Dec.1 (October 2013).

Linked to these questions is the question of how the immunity provision impacts on the exercise of jurisdiction over specific crimes. The first interesting question relates to the crime of unconstitutional change of government.[12] Presumably, other than in unsuccessful attempts at unconstitutional change in government, the perpetrators of the crime would in every conceivable case have immunity. This raises the question whether the African Court of Justice and Human and Peoples' Rights would be able to exercise jurisdiction only in situations of unsuccessful attempts. In truth, how the African Court of Justice and Human and Peoples' Rights would, as it develops its jurisprudence, deal with such matters remains to be seen. One likely approach would be to withhold recognition from any government that comes to power through unconstitutional means, such that officials of that government are denied immunity. Such a presumption is more difficult, but still possible, in cases involving incumbent governments.[13] However, as noted by Ambos, one may expect that the African Court of Justice and Human and Peoples' Rights, if it becomes operational, will manage to come to an interpretation of the relevant provisions and give them meaning.[14]

12.3.2 Arguments on the Immunity Provisions in the Annex of the Malabo Protocol

As a normative proposition, arguments against the immunity provision in the Annex of the Malabo Protocol are numerous and include arguments based on the fight against impunity. However, as a doctrinal question, arguments against this provision have tended to revolve around its (in)consistency with international law and the ICC Statute in particular. Njeri Kariri, for example, puts forward primarily normative arguments against the immunity provision. She observes, for example, that the immunity provision is a "setback to advancing democracy and the rule of law" and provides a "protective veil that denies justice to victims and is detrimental to accountability."[15] These are all normative arguments that suggest that the African Union *should not* have included the immunity provision. Although not focused on the legal doctrinal question about the place of immunity in international (and domestic) law, Njeri Kariri postulates, as a legal position, that "the immunity provision flouts international law and is contrary to the national laws of African states like Kenya and South Africa."[16]

---

[12] See Articles. 28A and 28E of the Malabo Protocol (Annex) and the chapter by Kemp and Kinyunyu in this book.

[13] See Article 28E(1)(d), (e) and (f) of the Malabo Protocol (Annex).

[14] See the chapter by Ambos in this book.

[15] Njeri Kariri 2014.

[16] Ibid.

The doctrinal argument, questioning the legal basis of an immunity provision in the Annex of the Malabo Protocol can be illustrated by a reference to Murungu's observations on the African Court.[17] Murungu asserts, citing Article 27 of the ICC Statute, that "immunity of state officials is no longer a valid defence for the commission of international crimes."[18] This position is also one that appears to have been advanced by the International Criminal Court in its decisions in the Malawi and Chad non-cooperation cases.[19] More to the point, Murungu questions whether extending the jurisdiction of the African Court of Justice and Human and Peoples' Rights to cover ICC Statute crimes (along with Article 46A*bis*) "has a legal basis under the ICC Statute".[20] The ICC Statute, he asserts, "does not expressly allow or even imply that regional courts [...] be conferred with jurisdiction" over ICC Statute crimes.[21] On the basis of his analysis, he concludes that "it is difficult to establish a clear legal basis" for extending the jurisdiction of the African Court of Justice and Human and Peoples' Rights in the ICC Statute.[22] Indeed, Murungu suggests that the very process of establishing the International Criminal Law Section of the African Court of Justice and Human and Peoples' Rights was "contrary to the provisions of the ICC Statute" in relation to cooperation.[23] Murungu's critique of the extension of the jurisdiction of the African Court of Justice and Human and Peoples' Rights is based on the issues of immunity of African heads of state raised by the African Union. He states, for example, that the only purpose behind the expansion of the jurisdiction of the African Court of Justice and Human and Peoples' Rights is the African Union's attempts to "protect some of its leaders."[24]

Murungu's arguments are reflective of the whispers in the corridors of International Criminal Court meetings, even if not always captured in the literature. This argument can be reduced to three related propositions. First, customary international law does not provide for immunity of officials before international courts. Second, the provision of immunity in Article 46A*bis* is inconsistent with

[17] Murungu 2011, p. 1067.

[18] Ibid. at 1077.

[19] See e.g. paras 18 and 36 of the Decision Pursuant to Article 87(7) on the Failure of the Republic of Malawi to Comply with the Cooperation Request Issued by the Court with respect to the Arrest and Surrender of Omar Hassan Ahmed Al Bashir, Al Bashir (ICC-02/05-01/09), Pre-Trial Chamber I, 12 December 2011; Décision Rendue en Application de l'Article 87(7) de la Statut de Rome concernant le refus de la République du Tchad d'accéder aux demandes de cooperation délivrées par la Cour concernant l'arrestation et la remise d'Omar Hassan Ahmed Al Bashir, Al Bashir (ICC-02/05-01/09), Pre-Trial Chamber I, 12 December 2011.

[20] See Murungu 2011, p. 1077.

[21] Ibid.

[22] Ibid.

[23] Ibid.

[24] Ibid.

international law or, at best, goes against the trend of practice. Finally, the argument postulates that Article 46A*bis* undermines the ICC Statute. These legal propositions about immunity for ICC Statute crimes are very often based on normative statements about the effect of immunity on the fight against impunity. The granting of immunity is said to be contrary to the African Union commitment to protecting the sanctity of life, and condemning and rejecting impunity.[25] Lamony of the Coalition for the International Criminal Court is quoted as saying "Africa should be moving forward in the fight against impunity, not regressing."[26] Similarly Belay of Amnesty International has said that the decision "undermines the integrity of the African Court".[27]

The African Union itself has defended the need for immunities both on normative and doctrinal grounds. According to the African Union, under customary international law, "Heads of state and other senior state officials are granted immunities during their tenure of office."[28] As a doctrinal proposition, the African Union has maintained that "immunities provided for by international law apply not only to proceedings in foreign domestic courts but also to international tribunals."[29] Providing for immunities of heads of state and other officials in the Annex of the Malabo Protocol is, therefore, from the African Union's perspective, acting in furtherance of international law.

The African Union does not dispute the legality of arrangements such as those in Article 27 of the ICC Statute, which provides that neither immunity nor other special procedural rules attaching to the official capacity of a person constitute an obstacle to the International Criminal Court in exercising jurisdiction over a person.[30] The African Union instead approaches Article 27 as a treaty rule applicable only to State Parties, while for non-State Parties the rules of customary international law relating to immunities are said to remain intact. In response to the

---

[25] International Justice Resource Centre 2014.

[26] Ibid.

[27] Ibid.

[28] See para 9 of the Decision on Africa's Relationship with the International Criminal Court (ICC), Ext/Assembly/AU/Dec.1 (October 2013).

[29] See Press Release 02/2012 on the Decision of Pre-Trial Chamber of the International Criminal Court (ICC) Pursuant to Article 87(7) of the Rome Statute on the Alleged Failure by the Republic of Chad and the Republic of Malawi to Comply with the Cooperation Requests Issued By the Court With Respect to the Arrest and Surrender of President Omar Hassan Al Bashir of the Republic of the Sudan, 9 January 2012.

[30] Article 27(1) of the ICC Statute provides that the "Statute shall apply equally to all persons without distinction any distinction based on official capacity. In particular, official capacity as a Head of State or Government, member of a Government [...] shall in no case exempt a person from criminal responsibility under this Statute, nor shall it, in and of itself, constitute a ground for reduction of sentence." Article 27(2) provides that "[I]mmunities or special procedural rules which may attach to the official capacity of a person, whether under national or international law, shall not bar the Court from exercising jurisdiction over such a person."

decisions of the International Criminal Court on non-cooperation by Malawi and Chad, the African Union issued a press release which stated, in part, that:

> "[…] immunities of State officials are rights of the State concerned and a treaty only binds parties to the treaty. A treaty may not deprive non-Party States of rights which they ordinarily possess."[31]

This position essentially presents Article 27 of the ICC Statute and similar provisions in the statutes of international tribunals, as being exceptions to the rules of customary international law relating to immunities, and as applying only between parties to the constitutive treaties. The immunities provision in the Annex to the Malabo Protocol is, from this perspective, seen not only as acceptable but as reflecting customary international law. This has been the legal basis of the African Union's call for non-cooperation with the International Criminal Court's appeal for the arrest and surrender of Al Bashir.[32] According to the African Union, Article 27 leaves customary international law on immunities intact, and the waiver of immunities implied by Article 27 applies only between States Parties to the ICC Statute. Thus, while there may be a duty on States Parties to the ICC Statute to cooperate in the arrest and surrender of a head of a State Party, no such a duty exists in relation to the arrest and surrender of a head of a non-State Party.[33] To the extent that there is such a duty under the ICC Statute, compliance with it results in a breach of international law obligations under customary international law, thus engaging the responsibility of the cooperating state. While this aspect of immunity is not directly relevant to the debate on Article 46A*bis*, it does serve to illustrate the African Union's understanding of immunities under customary international law and, more to the point, the perceived exceptionality of Article 27 of the ICC Statute.

Both the positions supporting the immunities provision and the position opposing it are based on doctrinal assumptions about the rules of general international law relating to immunities. I turn now to an evaluation of these doctrinal assumptions.

---

[31] Press Release 02/2012 on the Decision of Pre-Trial Chamber of the International Criminal Court (ICC) Pursuant to Article 87(7) of the Rome Statute on the Alleged Failure by the Republic of Chad and the Republic of Malawi to Comply with the Cooperation Requests Issued By the Court With Respect to the Arrest and Surrender of President Omar Hassan Al Bashir of the Republic of the Sudan, 9 January 2012.

[32] In its first decision on non-cooperation with respect to Omar Al Bashir, for example, the AU Summit requests the Commission and African states to engage in a process to clarify "the Immunities of officials whose States are not party to the [Rome] Statute." See para 8 of the AU Decision on the Meeting of African States Parties to the Rome Statute of the International Criminal Court (ICC), Assembly/AU/Dec. 245(XIII) Rev. 1. See especially para 6 of the AU Decision on the Progress Report of the Commission on the Implementation of the Assembly Decisions on the International Criminal Court (ICC), Assembly/AU/Dec.397 (XVIII) in which the AU Assembly reaffirms "its understanding that Article 98(1) was included in the Rome Statute […] out of a recognition that the Statute is not capable of removing an immunity which international law grants to officials of States that are not parties to the Rome Statute."

[33] See Press Release 20/2012, supra no. 29.

12.4 Evaluating the Doctrinal Argument Concerning the Immunity Provision

I begin with an assessment of the African Union position. First, it goes without saying that the duty to cooperate under the ICC Statute cannot deprive non-States Parties of their rights in respect of immunities under customary international law. Treaties create rights and obligations only as between parties to the treaty and the rights of non-parties cannot be affected by the treaty.[34] Whether this means, as argued by the African Union, that there is no duty to cooperate in the arrest and surrender of Al Bashir is dependent on other legal questions beyond the scope of the present enquiry, such as the effect of a Security Council referral of a situation to the International Criminal Court and the interpretation of Article 98 of the ICC Statute.[35]

While the assertion that the rights relating to immunities under customary international law for a non-State Party cannot be affected by the duty to cooperate under the ICC Statute is indisputable, what does require closer scrutiny is the assertion that under customary international law heads of state (and other officials entitled to immunity *ratione personae*) enjoy immunity before international courts and tribunals. This assertion seems to ignore the dictum by the International Court of Justice in the Arrest Warrant case where the Court stated that, notwithstanding the customary international law rules on immunity of officials from foreign criminal jurisdiction, a state official may still be prosecuted before an international court under certain circumstances.[36] But there is another far more fundamental problem with the African Union's postulation. The immunity of state officials, whether *ratione personae* or *ratione materiae*, under customary international law means, in essence, the immunity of state officials from the jurisdiction of courts of *foreign states*. This immunity is an extension of the immunity of the state from the jurisdiction of other states based on the principle of sovereign equality of states.[37] International tribunals, like the International Criminal Court and the African Court of Justice and Human and Peoples' Rights, are not foreign states. The rationale for immunity of states and their officials, namely the sovereign equality of states, does not apply to the exercise of jurisdiction of international courts and tribunals since, though created by states, they are not themselves states. Moreover, while the immunity of officials from the jurisdiction of the courts of *foreign states* can be shown to exist in the practice of states accepted as law, extending this immunity

[34] See generally Article 34 of the Vienna Convention on the Law of Treaties.

[35] This aspect of the immunities debate has been considered in various articles. See, e.g. Akande 2009 and Gaeta 2009. See also Tladi 2013.

[36] Arrest Warrant case no. 9, at para 61.

[37] See, e.g. para 6 of the commentary to Draft Article 4 of the International Law Commission's Draft Articles on the Immunity of State Officials from Foreign Criminal Jurisdiction, supra no. 6.

also to international courts and tribunals would require evidence of practice of states accepted as law to this effect. Such practice does not, however, exist.[38] On the contrary, if anything, given the history of international criminal law described in, for example, the International Criminal Court decisions in Malawi and Chad, there appears to be practice in the other direction.[39] Therefore, the argument from the African Union that the insertion of Article 46A*bis* is not only consistent with, but is reflective of, customary international law is doctrinally flawed.

Does the fact that the African Union proposition concerning immunity before international courts is incorrect, mean that the counter-proposition, i.e. that customary international law rejects immunity, is correct? This was essentially the argument advanced by the International Criminal Court in Malawi and Chad.[40] The experience with the Nuremberg Tribunals, the Tokyo Tribunals, the International Criminal Tribunal for the former Yugoslavia, the International Criminal Tribunal for Rwanda, the Special Court for Sierra Leone and the Lebanon Tribunals constitutes practicing denial of immunity. However, to transform an empirical fact, "practice" in legal terms, into a rule of customary international law requires that the practice be accompanied by a sense of obligation to the effect that the practice is required by law.[41] No evidence of such an acceptance of the practice is present as regards the immunity of state officials before international courts and tribunals, and none is presented by the International Criminal Court in Malawi and Chad. Indeed, in the debate over the arrest and surrender of Al Bashir, those arguing that there was indeed a duty to arrest have advanced as a legal reason, not the fact that the court was an international one but rather that the situation was referred to the court by the Security Council, which, so the argument goes, has the power to override customary international law.[42]

Proponents of the view that there is a rule under customary international law denying immunity before international courts and tribunals may point to the Arrest Warrant case.[43] In the Arrest Warrant case, the International Court of Justice famously made the following observations:

> [...] immunities enjoyed under international law by an [official] do not represent a bar to criminal prosecution in certain instances.
>
> [...]

---

[38] In this regard, the International Court of Justice in the Arrest Warrant case, supra no. 9 at paras 58 and 59, where the Court makes it clear that the rules relating jurisdiction of national courts, including immunities applicable before them, should be distinguished from the same relating to international courts.

[39] Malawi decision, supra no. 19 at para 23 et seq.

[40] Ibid.

[41] See generally para 169 of the Report of the International Law Commission at Sixty-Sixth Session (Chap. 10), supra no. 6.

[42] See, e.g. Akande 2009. See contra, Tladi 2013.

[43] Malawi decision, supra no. 198, at para 34.

Fourthly, an [official enjoying immunity in national courts] may be subject to criminal proceedings before certain international criminal courts, [sic] where they have jurisdiction.[44]

The extract quoted does not, however, suggest anything about the status of immunities before international courts under customary international law. The International Court of Justice was not laying down a rule of international law but the Court was simply referring to *possible* avenues that may be followed for the prosecution of officials with immunity *if certain conditions are met.* The first avenue provided by the International Court of Justice, for example, refers to the possibility of a person being tried before the courts of their own state.[45] Yet this can only happen if the national court in question has jurisdiction and the official in question has no immunity under domestic law. Similarly, an international court or tribunal can only try an individual if there is no jurisdictional obstacle, including immunity, to trying the individual. Whether or not the international court or tribunal will have jurisdiction and whether or not there is a bar to the exercise of such jurisdiction will depend on the constitutive instrument establishing the court or tribunal.[46] The argument that customary international law denies immunity before international courts is, therefore, unconvincing. At any rate, as a matter of customary international law, it is difficult to see how a rule of customary international law can form when the African Union, representing more than a quarter of states, rejects the said rule.

That there is no legal rule under customary international law denying immunity to state officials does not, of course, mean that a state official can plead immunity before a tribunal having jurisdiction which, by its constitutive instrument, has removed immunity as in, for example, Article 27 of the ICC Statute.[47] By the same token, however, the exclusion of immunity in a treaty establishing an international court or tribunal does not affect the relationship between a non-State Party to the treaty and States Parties. Thus, the fact that a state is party to the ICC Statute does not imply that such a state is no longer obliged to respect the immunity of an official from a state that is not a party to the ICC Statute. Indeed, even if the assertion that customary international law excludes immunities in respect of proceedings before international courts were correct—and I have argued that it isn't—this would apply only as between the state officials and the international court or tribunal concerned, and would not, of itself, affect the relationship between states *inter se.*[48]

---

44 Arrest Warrant case, supra no. 9, at para 61.

45 Ibid.

46 See *id.* where the International Court of Justice refers to the constitutive instruments establishing the International Criminal Court, the International Criminal Tribunal for the former Yugoslavia and the International Criminal Tribunal for Rwanda.

47 Id.

48 In the context of the ICC Statute, this distinction is explained in Tladi 2013, at p. 211 noting that Article 27 "applies to defences, substantive or jurisdictional, that an individual *may raise before the ICC.* It does not, in any way, address the relationship between states nor does it address the relationship between the ICC and states parties [emphasis in the original]."

If neither the African Union's argument that customary international law requires international courts to respect immunity nor the argument advanced by, *inter alia*, the International Criminal Court that customary international law denies immunity before international courts is correct, then how is Article 46A*bis* of the Malabo Protocol (Annex) to be understood from the perspective of customary international law? If customary international law neither requires nor rejects immunity before international courts and tribunals, then, as a matter of law, the African Union is free to include or exclude immunities as a bar to prosecution as it deems fit. Whether this is desirable or not is a different question. Thus, Article 46A*bis* is neither reflective of, nor inconsistent with, customary international law. The question may well be asked whether, under a treaty that is silent on immunities, state officials are entitled to claim immunity. Subject to the normal rules of interpretation, a court, national or international, having jurisdiction is entitled to exercise that jurisdiction unless there is a rule of international law prohibiting such exercise. This is not the same as saying, however, that there is a rule of international law excluding immunity.

A related question is whether Article 46A*bis* of the Malabo Protocol (Annex) undermines the fight against impunity. The argument on which this is based appears to be that the extension of the jurisdiction of the African Court of Justice and Human and Peoples' Rights to international crimes, while also expressly including immunity, will shield perpetrators from the reaches of justice. However, this argument does not follow. The effect of the extension of the jurisdiction of the African Court of Justice and Human and Peoples' Rights is, *potentially*, to expand the reach of international criminal justice. It does not, as the argument may suggest, reduce this reach. Assuming African states that are not party to the ICC Statute become party to the expanded African Court of Justice and Human and Peoples' Rights, then the reach of the international courts to potential situations and perpetrators becomes enlarged. On the other hand, regardless of the number of states that fall within the jurisdiction of the expanded African Court of Justice and Human and Peoples' Rights, the reach of the International Criminal Court will remain unaffected.

The idea that Article 46A*bis* of the Malabo Protocol (Annex) affects the reach of international criminal justice can only be based on a misconstruction of the relationship between the African Court of Justice and Human and Peoples' Rights and the International Criminal Court. Under Article 46A*bis* the African Court of Justice and Human and Peoples' Rights will not have the competence to try persons having immunity but this will not prevent the International Criminal Courts from exercising jurisdiction over such persons where it has jurisdiction. Under the principle of complementarity, the International Criminal Court is, of course, barred from proceeding with trials where a court with competence is willing and able to exercise jurisdiction.[49] This procedural bar applies, however, only to state

[49] See Articles 17, 18 and 19 of the ICC Statute.

prosecution and/or investigations, and does not extend to the exercise of jurisdiction by regional courts. Although an amendment to the ICC Statute to recognize the competence of regional courts for the purposes of complementarity has been transmitted to the Secretary-General by Kenya,[50] this amendment is unlikely to be adopted by the Assembly of States Parties. At any rate, until such a time as an amendment has been passed, from the perspective of the International Criminal Court, Article 46A*bis* should be a non-issue.

12.5 Conclusion

The expansion of the jurisdiction of the African Court of Justice and Human and Peoples' Rights to include also international crimes has generated much controversy in international criminal justice circles, both diplomatic and academic. Even more controversial has been the decision by the African Union to make provision for immunity of certain officials before the African Court of Justice and Human and Peoples' Rights in the form of Article 46A*bis*. In the back-and-forth of arguments for and against Article 46A*bis*, normative policy arguments, empirical statements and doctrinal positions have been lumped together in a way bound to result in confusion. This confusion has aided in the perpetuation of the hero-villain trend in which supporters of the International Criminal Court see themselves as heroes and the African Union as villains and vice versa.

In the eagerness to put on the white hat and fight the evil, basic principles of international law have been conveniently covered in a heap of rhetoric and slightly distorted doctrine. Much of the confusion created by the debate arises from the failure by commentators to make a distinction between the law relating to immunity and the wisdom (or desirability) of Article 46A*bis* of the Malabo Protocol (Annex). Supporters of Article 46A*bis* present it as salvaging international law and reclaiming the foundational international principle of sovereignty by preserving immunity. What is overlooked in this narrative is that international law rules on immunity apply to the exercise of jurisdiction by domestic courts over officials of a foreign state, and that customary international law neither requires immunity before international courts nor prevents it. Opponents of Article 46A*bis*, on the other hand, present it as harming the fight against impunity by protecting officials from the reach of international courts. What is ignored here is that the expansion of the jurisdiction of the African Court of Justice and Human and Peoples'

---

50 See ICC Working Group on Amendments Informal Compilation of Proposals to Amend the Rome Statute (on file with the author). It should be noted, that the Kenyan proposal only seeks to amend to the Preambular paragraph relating to complementarity and does not address the substantive provisions in Articles 17, 18 and 19. As currently drafted, it is therefore unlikely to be sufficient to establish a complementarity role for the African Court.

Rights does not in any way affect the jurisdiction of other courts, including the International Criminal Court, and can in no way prevent the exercise of jurisdiction by those courts over individuals who may be immune from prosecution before the African Court of Justice and Human and Peoples' Rights by virtue of Article 46A*bis*.

References

Akande D (2009) The legal nature of the Security Council Referrals to the ICC and its impact on Bashir's immunities. J Int Crim Justice 7:333–352

Gaeta P (2009) Does President Al Bashir enjoy immunity from arrest? J Int Crim Justice 7:315–332

International Justice Resource Centre (2014) African Union approves immunity for government officials in amendment to African Court of Justice and Human Rights Statute. http://www.ijrcenter.org/2014/07/02/african-union-approves-immunity-for-heads-of-state-in-amendment-to-african-court-of-justice-and-human-rights-statute/

Murungu C (2011) Towards a criminal chamber in the African Court of Justice and Human Rights. J Int Crim Justice 9:1067–1088

Njeri Kariri J (2014) Can the new African court truly deliver justice for serious crimes? ISS Today. http://www.issafrica.org. Accessed 19 July 2015

Tladi D (2013) The ICC decisions in Chad and Malawi: on cooperation, immunities, and Article 98. J Int Crim Justice 11:199–221

Tladi D (2014) When elephants collide it is the grass that suffers: cooperation and the Security Council in the context of the AU/ICC dynamic. Afr J Legal Stud 7:298–381

Tladi D (2015) The immunity provision in the AU Amendment Protocol: separating the (doctrinal) wheat from the (normative) chaff. J Int Crim Justice 13:3–17

Annexes

Documents

1. Protocol on Amendments to the Protocol on the Statute of the African Court of Justice and Human Rights, adopted in the 25th Ordinary Session of the AU's Assembly of Heads of State and Governments, Malabo, Equatorial Guinea, 27 June 2014 (Malabo Protocol).
2. Definitions of Crimes in the Annex to the Malabo Protocol and their Sources in International Instruments.
3. Protocol on the Statute of the African Court of Justice and Human Rights, adopted in Sharm El-Sheikh, Egypt, on 1 July 2008 (Merger Protocol).
4. Protocol of the Court of Justice of the African Union, Maputo, Mozambique, 11 July 2003 (Maputo Protocol).
5. Protocol to the African Charter on Human and Peoples' Rights on the Establishment of an African Court on Human and Peoples' Rights, 9 June 1998.
6. African Union Decisions Regarding the Creation of a Criminal Section in the African Court of Justice and Human and Peoples' Rights.

PROTOCOL ON AMENDMENTS TO THE PROTOCOL ON THE STATUTE OF THE AFRICAN COURT OF JUSTICE AND HUMAN RIGHTS

27 June 2014

(Malabo Protocol)

PREAMBLE

The Member States of the African Union parties to the Constitutive Act of the African Union;

G. Werle and M. Vormbaum (eds.), *The African Criminal Court*, International Criminal Justice Series 10, DOI 10.1007/978-94-6265-150-0

RECALLING the objectives and principles enunciated in the Constitutive Act of the African Union, adopted on 11 July 2000 in Lome, Togo, in particular the commitment to settle their disputes through peaceful means;

FURTHER RECALLING the provisions of the Protocol on the Statute of the African Court of Justice and Human Rights and the Statute annexed to it adopted on 1 July 2008 in Sharm-El-Sheikh, Egypt;

RECOGNIZING that the Protocol on the Statute of the African Court of Justice and Human Rights had merged the African Court on Human and Peoples' Rights and the Court of Justice of the African Union into a single Court;

BEARING IN MIND their commitment to promote peace, security and stability on the continent, and to protect human and people's rights in accordance with the African Charter on Human and Peoples' Rights and other relevant instruments;

FURTHER RECOGNIZING the efforts and contribution of the African Commission on Human and Peoples' Rights in the promotion and protection of human and peoples' rights since its inception in 1987;

NOTING the steady growth of the African Court on Human and Peoples' Rights and the contribution it has made in protecting human and people's rights on the African continent as well as the progress towards the establishment of the African Court of Justice and Human and Peoples' Rights;

FURTHER BEARING IN MIND the complementary relationship between the African Commission on Human and Peoples' Rights and the African Court on Human and Peoples' Rights, as well as its successor, the African Court of Justice and Human and Peoples' Rights;

FURTHER RECALLING their commitment to the right of the Union to intervene in a Member State pursuant to a decision of the Assembly in respect of grave circumstances, namely: war crimes, genocide and crimes against humanity as well as a serious threat to legitimate order to restore peace and stability to the Member State of the Union upon the recommendation of the Peace and Security Council;

REITERATING their respect for democratic principles, human and people's rights, the rule of law and good governance;

FURTHER REITERATING their respect for the sanctity of human life, condemnation and rejection of impunity and political assassination, acts of terrorism and subversive activities, unconstitutional changes of governments and acts of aggression;

FURTHER REITERATING their commitment to fighting impunity in conformity with the provisions of Article 4(o) of the Constitutive Act of the African Union;

ACKNOWLEDGING the pivotal role that the African Court of Justice and Human and Peoples' Rights can play in strengthening the commitment of the African Union to promote sustained peace, security and stability on the Continent and to promote justice and human and peoples' rights as an aspect of their efforts to promote the objectives of the political and socio-economic integration and development of the Continent with a view to realizing the ultimate objective of a United States of Africa;

FURTHER RECALLING Assembly Decision Assembly/AU/Dec.213 (XII) adopted by the Twelfth Ordinary Session of the Assembly in Addis Ababa, Federal Democratic Republic of Ethiopia, on 3 February 2009 on the implementation of the Assembly's Decision on the Abuse of the Principle of Universal Jurisdiction;

FURTHER RECALLING Assembly Decision Assembly/AU/Dec.263 (XIII) adopted by the Thirteenth Ordinary Session of the Assembly in Sirte, Libya, on 3 July 2009 on the transformation of the African Union Commission to the African Union Authority;

FURTHER RECOGNIZING the need to take the necessary measures to amend the legal instruments of the principal organs of the African Union in the light of the aforementioned Assembly Decisions;

CONVINCED that the present Protocol will complement national, regional and continental bodies and institutions in preventing serious and massive violations of human and peoples' rights in keeping with Article 58 of the Charter and ensuring accountability for them wherever they occur;

HAVE AGREED to adopt the present amendments to the Protocol on the Statute of the African Court of Justice and Human Rights and the Statute annexed thereto as follows: -

CHAPTER I

In CHAPTER 1 of the Protocol (MERGER OF THE AFRICAN COURT ON HUMAN AND PEOPLES' RIGHTS AND THE COURT OF JUSTICE OF THE AFRICAN UNION) the deletion of the existing title, Articles and their provisions in their entirety and the insertion in their place of the following:

CHAPTER I
GENERAL PROVISIONS

Article 1
Definitions

In this Protocol:

"Assembly" means the Assembly of Heads of State and Government of the African Union;
"Chairperson" means the Chairperson of the Assembly;
"Charter" means the African Charter on Human and Peoples' Rights;
"Commission" means the Commission of the African Union;
"Court" means the African Court of Justice and Human and Peoples' Rights;
"Member State" means a Member State of the Union;
"President" means the President of the Court;
"Protocol" means the Protocol on the Statute of the African Court of Justice and Human Rights;
"Single Court" has the same meaning as the Court;
"Statute" means the present Statute;
"Union" means the African Union established by the Constitutive Act of the African Union;
"Vice President" means the Vice President of the Court.

Article 2
Organs of the Court

The Court shall be composed of the following organs:

1. The Presidency;
2. The Office of the Prosecutor;
3. The Registry;
4. The Defence Office.

Article 3
Jurisdiction of the Court

1. The Court is vested with an original and appellate jurisdiction, including international criminal jurisdiction, which it shall exercise in accordance with the provisions of the Statute annexed hereto.
2. The Court has jurisdiction to hear such other matters or appeals as may be referred to it in any other agreements that the Member States or the Regional Economic Communities or other international organizations recognized by the African Union may conclude among themselves, or with the Union.

Article 4
Relationship between the Court and the African Commission on Human and Peoples' Rights

The Court shall, in accordance with the Charter and this Protocol, complement the protective mandate of the African Commission on Human and Peoples' Rights.

CHAPTER II
TRANSITIONAL PROVISIONS

Article 5
Term of Office of the Judges of the African Court on Human and Peoples' Rights

In Article 4 (Term of Office of the Judges of the African Court on Human and Peoples' Rights), replace the existing provision including its title, with:

"Article 4
Term of Office of the Judges of the African Court on Human and Peoples' Rights

1. Upon the coming into force of the Protocol on the Statute of the African Court of Justice and Human Rights, the terms and appointment of the Judges of the African Court on Human and Peoples' Rights shall terminate.

2. Without prejudice to para 1, the Judges of the African Court on Human and Peoples' Rights shall remain in office until the judges of the African Court of Justice and Human and Peoples' Rights are sworn in."

Article 6
Pending Cases

At the entry into force of this Protocol, where any matter affecting any State had already been commenced before either the African Court on Human and Peoples' Rights or the African Court of Justice and Human Rights, if in force, such a matter shall be continued before the relevant Section of the African Court of Justice and Human and Peoples' Rights, pursuant to such Rules as may be made by the Court.

Article 6*bis*
Temporary Jurisdiction

At the entry into force of this Protocol, until a Member State ratifies it, any jurisdiction which has hitherto been accepted by such Member State with respect to either the African Court on Human and Peoples' Rights or the African Court of Justice and Human Rights shall be exercisable by this Court.

Article 7
Registry of the Court

1. The Registrar of the African Court on Human and Peoples' Rights shall remain in office until the appointment of a new Registrar for the African Court of Justice and Human and Peoples' Rights.
2. The staff of the African Court on Human and Peoples' Rights shall be absorbed into the Registry of the African Court of Justice and Human and Peoples' Rights, for the remainder of their subsisting contracts of employment.

CHAPTER III
FINAL PROVISIONS

Article 8
Nomenclature

In the Protocol and the Statute wherever it occurs "African Court of Justice and Human Rights" is deleted and replaced with "African Court of Justice and Human and Peoples' Rights."

Article 9
Signature, Ratification and Accession

1. This Protocol and the Statute annexed to it shall be open for signature, ratification or accession by Member States, in accordance with their respective constitutional procedures.
2. The instruments of ratification or accession to this Protocol and the Statute annexed to it shall be deposited with the Chairperson of the Commission.
3. Any Member State may, at the time of signature or when depositing its instrument of ratification or accession, or at any time thereafter, make a declaration accepting the competence of the Court to receive cases under Article 30(f).

Article 10
Depository Authority

1. This Protocol and the Statute annexed to it, drawn up in four (4) original texts in the Arabic, English, French and Portuguese languages, all four (4) texts being equally authentic, shall be deposited with the Chairperson of the Commission, who shall transmit a certified true copy to the Government of each Member State.
2. The Chairperson of the Commission, shall notify all Member States of the dates of deposit of the instruments of ratification or accession, and shall, upon the entry into force of this Protocol, register the same with the Secretariat of the United Nations.

Article 11
Entry into force

1. This Protocol and the Statute annexed to it shall enter into force thirty (30) days after the deposit of instruments of ratification by fifteen (15) Member States.
2. For each Member State which shall accede to it subsequently, this Protocol and Annexed Statute shall enter into force on the date on which the instruments of ratification or accession are deposited.
3. The Chairperson of the Commission shall notify all Member States of the entry into force of this Protocol.

Article 12
Amendments

1. This Protocol and the Statute annexed to it may be amended if a State Party to the Protocol makes a written request to that effect to the Chairperson of the Commission. The Assembly may adopt, by simple majority, the draft amendment after all the States parties to the present Protocol have been duly informed of it and the Court has given its opinion on the amendment.

2. The Court shall also be entitled to propose such amendments to the present Protocol or the Statute annexed to it as it may deem necessary, through the Chairperson of the Commission.
3. The amendments shall come into force for each State Party which has accepted it thirty (30) days after the Chairperson of the Commission has received notice of the acceptance.

ADOPTED BY THE TWENTY-THIRD ORDINARY SESSION OF THE ASSEMBLY, HELD IN MALABO, EQUATORIAL GUINEA

27th JUNE 2014

Annex
Statute of the African Court of Justice and Human and Peoples' Rights

Article 1
Definitions

1. In Article 1 of the Statute (Definitions), the deletion from the chapeau of the words "except otherwise indicated, the following shall mean"
2. The insertion of the following words and the definitions ascribed to them

"Chairperson" means the Chairperson of the Commission;
"Child" means any person under eighteen years of age;
"Court" means the African Court of Justice and Human and Peoples' Rights;
"Full Court" means the three Sections of the Court sitting together in plenary;
"Person" means a natural or legal person;
"President" means the President of the Court unless otherwise specified; "Section" means the General Affairs or Human and Peoples' Rights or International Criminal Law Section of the Court;
"Statute" means the Statute of the African Court of Justice and Human and Peoples' Rights;
"Vice President" means the Vice President of the Court.

Article 2
Composition

In Article 3 of the Statute (Composition), add the following para 4:
"The Assembly shall ensure that there is equitable gender representation in the Court."

Article 3
Qualifications of Judges

Article 4 of the Statute (Qualifications of Judges) is replaced with the following:
"The Court shall be composed of impartial and independent Judges elected from among persons of high moral character, who possess the qualifications required

in their respective countries for appointment to the highest judicial offices, or are juris-consults of recognized competence and experience in international law, international human rights law, international humanitarian law or international criminal law."

Article 4
List of Candidates

Article 6 of the Statute (List of Candidates) is replaced with the following: -

"1. For the purpose of election, the Chairperson of the Commission shall establish three (3) alphabetical lists of candidates presented as follows:

   i. List A containing the names of candidates having recognized competence and experience in International law;
   ii. List B containing the names of candidates having recognized competence and experience in international human rights law and international humanitarian law; and
   iii. List C containing the names of candidates having recognized competence and experience in international criminal law.

2. States Parties that nominate candidates possessing the competences required on the three (3) lists shall choose the list on which their candidates may be placed.
3. At the first election, five (5) judges each shall be elected from amongst the candidates on lists A and B, and six (6) judges shall be elected from amongst the candidates of list C respectively.
4. The Chairperson of the Commission shall communicate the three lists to Member States, at least thirty (30) days before the Ordinary Session of the Assembly or of the Council during which the elections shall take place."

Article 5
Term of Office

Article 8 of the Statute (Term of Office) is replaced with the following: -

"1. The Judges shall be elected for a single, non-renewable term of nine (9) years. The terms of office of five (5) of the judges elected at the first election shall end after three (3) years, and the terms of another five (5) of the judges shall end after six (6) years.
2. The Judges whose term of office shall end after the initial periods of three (3) and six (6) years shall be determined by lot drawn by the Chairperson of the Assembly or the Executive Council, immediately after the first election.
3. A Judge elected to replace another whose term of office has not expired shall complete the term of office of his or her predecessor.
4. All the Judges, except the President and the Vice President, shall perform their functions on a part-time basis.

5. The Assembly shall, on the recommendation of the Court, decide the time when all the Judges of the Court shall perform their functions on a full time basis."

Article 6
Structure of the Court

Article 16 of the Statute (Sections of the Court) is replaced with the following: -

"Article 16
Structure of the Court

1. The Court shall have three (3) Sections: a General Affairs Section, a Human and Peoples' Rights Section and an International Criminal Law Section.
2. The International Criminal Law Section of the Court shall have three (3) Chambers: a Pre-Trial Chamber, a Trial Chamber and an Appellate Chamber.
3. The allocation of Judges to the respective Sections and Chambers shall be determined by the Court in its Rules."

Article 7
Assignment of matters to Sections of the Court

Article 17 of the Statute (Assignment of matters to Sections) is replaced with the following:

"Article 17
Assignment of matters to Sections of the Court

1. The General Affairs Section shall be competent to hear all cases submitted under Article 28 of the Statute except those assigned to the Human and Peoples' Rights Section and the International Criminal Law Section as specified in this Article.
2. The Human and Peoples' Rights Section shall be competent to hear all cases relating to human and peoples' rights.
3. The International Criminal Law Section shall be competent to hear all cases relating to the crimes specified in this Statute."

Article 8
Revision and Appeal

Article 18 (Referral of matters to the Full Court) is replaced with the following:

"Article 18
Revision and Appeals

1. In the case of the General Affairs Section and the Human and People's Rights Section, a revision of a judgement shall be made in terms of the provisions of Article 48.
2. In the case of the International Criminal Law Section, a decision of the Pre-Trial Chamber or the Trial Chamber may be appealed against by the Prosecutor or the accused, on the following grounds:

   (a) A procedural error;
   (b) An error of law;
   (c) An error of fact.

3. An appeal may be made against a decision on jurisdiction or admissibility of a case, an acquittal or a conviction.
4. The Appellate Chamber may affirm, reverse or revise the decision appealed against. The decision of the Appellate Chamber shall be final."

Article 9
Chambers of the Court

Article 19 of the Statute (Chambers) is replaced with the following:

"Chambers of the Court

1. The General Affairs Section, Human and Peoples' Rights Section or International Criminal Law Section may, at any time, constitute one or more Chambers in accordance with the Rules of Court.
2. A Judgment given by any Chamber shall be considered as rendered by the Court."

Article 9 Bis
Powers and Functions of the Chambers of the International Criminal Law Section

After Article 19 of the Statute (Chambers) add the following as Article 19 *Bis*:

"Article 19 Bis
Powers and Functions of the Chambers of the International Criminal Law Section

1. The Pre-Trial Chamber shall exercise the functions provided for in Article 46F of this Statute.
2. In addition, the Pre-Trial Chamber may also at the request of the Prosecutor issue such orders and warrants as may be required for an investigation or prosecution.

3. The Pre-Trial Chamber may issue such orders as may be required to provide for the protection and privacy of witnesses and victims, the presentation of evidence and the protection of arrested persons.
4. The Trial Chamber shall conduct trials of accused persons in accordance with this Statute and the Rules of Court.
5. The Trial Chamber shall receive and conduct appeals from the Pre-Trial Chamber in accordance with Article 18 of this Statute.
6. The Appeals Chamber shall receive and conduct appeals from the Trial Chamber in accordance with Article 18 of this Statute."

Article 10
Quorum

Article 21 of the Statute (Quorum) is replaced with the following:

1. The General Affairs Section of the Court shall be duly constituted by three (3) judges.
2. The Human and Peoples' Rights Section of the Court shall be duly constituted by three (3) judges.
3. The Pre-Trial Chamber of the International Criminal Law Section of the Court shall be duly constituted by one (1) judge.
4. The Trial Chamber of the International Criminal Law Section of the Court shall be duly constituted by three (3) judges.
5. The Appellate Chamber of the International Criminal Law Section of the Court shall be duly constituted by five (5) judges.

Article 11
Presidency and Vice Presidency

Article 22 (Presidency, Vice-Presidency and Registry) is replaced with the following: -

"Article 22
Presidency and Vice Presidency

1. At its first ordinary session after the election of the Judges, the Full Court shall elect a President and a Vice President of the Court.
2. The President and Vice President shall serve for a period of two (2) years, and may be re-elected once.
3. The President and Vice President shall, in consultation with the Members of the Court and as provided for in the Rules of Court, assign Judges to the Sections.
4. The President shall preside over all sessions of the Full Court. In the event of the President being unable to sit during a session, the session shall be presided over by the Vice President.
5. The President and Vice President shall reside at the seat of the Court."

Article 12
Presidency and Vice Presidency

After Article 22 (Presidency and Vice-Presidency) add the following as Articles 22A and 22B:

"Article 22A
The Office of the Prosecutor

1. The Office of the Prosecutor shall comprise a Prosecutor and two Deputy Prosecutors.
2. The Prosecutor and Deputy Prosecutors shall be elected by the Assembly from amongst candidates who shall be nationals of States Parties nominated by States Parties.
3. The Prosecutor shall serve for a single, non-renewable term of seven (7) years.
4. The Deputy Prosecutors shall serve for a term of four (4) years, renewable once.
5. The Prosecutor and the Deputy Prosecutors shall be persons of high moral character, be highly competent in and have extensive practical experience in the conduct of investigations, trial and prosecution of criminal cases.
6. The Office of the Prosecutor shall be responsible for the investigation and prosecution of the crimes specified in this Statute and shall act independently as a separate organ of the Court and shall not seek or receive instructions from any State Party or any other source.
7. The Office of the Prosecutor shall have the power to question suspects, victims and witnesses and collect evidence, including the power to conduct on-site investigations.
8. The Prosecutor shall be assisted by such other staff as may be required to perform the functions of the Office of the Prosecutor effectively and efficiently.
9. The staff of the Office of the Prosecutor shall be appointed by the Prosecutor in accordance with the Staff Rules and Regulations of the African Union.
10. The remuneration and conditions of service of the Prosecutor and Deputy Prosecutors shall be determined by the Assembly on the recommendation of the Court made through the Executive Council.

Article 22B
The Registry

1. The Registry shall comprise of a Registrar and three Assistant Registrars.
2. The Court shall appoint the Registrar and Assistant Registrars, in accordance with the Staff Rules and Regulations of the African Union.
3. The Registrar shall serve for a single, non-renewable term of seven years.
4. The Assistant Registrars shall serve for a term of four (4) years, renewable once.
5. The Registry shall be headed by a Registrar who, under the direction of the President, shall be responsible for the non-judicial aspects and servicing of

the Court. The Registrar shall be the principal administrative and accounting officer of the Court, and shall ensure that proper books of accounts are kept in accordance with the financial rules and regulations of the African Union.

6. The Registrar and Assistant Registrars shall be persons of high moral character, be highly competent in and have extensive practical managerial experience.
7. The Registrar shall be assisted by such other staff as may be necessary for the effective and efficient performance of the functions of the Registry.
8. The staff of the Registry shall be appointed by the Court in accordance with the Staff Rules and Regulations of the African Union.
9. The Registrar shall set up, within the Registry:

   (a) A Victims and Witnesses Unit, which shall provide, in consultation with the Court and the Office of the Prosecutor, as appropriate, protective measures and security arrangements, counselling and other appropriate assistance for witnesses, victims who appear before the Court and others who are at risk on account of testimony given by such witnesses. The Unit personnel shall include experts in the management of trauma.
   (b) A Detention Management Unit, which shall manage the conditions of detention of suspects and accused persons.

10. The salaries and conditions of service of the Registrar, Assistant Registrars and other staff of the Registry shall be determined by the Assembly on the proposal of the Court, through the Executive Council.

Article 22C
The Defence Office

1. The Court shall establish, maintain and develop a Defence Office for the purpose of ensuring the rights of suspects and accused and any other person entitled to legal assistance.
2. The Defence Office, which may also include one or more public defenders, shall act independently as a separate organ of the Court. It shall be responsible for protecting the rights of the defence, providing support and assistance to defence counsel and to the persons entitled to legal assistance, including, where appropriate, legal research, collection of evidence and advice, and appearing before the Chamber in respect of specific issues.
3. The Defence Office shall ensure that there are adequate facilities to defence counsel and persons entitled to legal assistance in the preparation of a case, and shall provide any additional assistance ordered by a Judge or Chamber.
4. The Defence Office shall be headed by a Principal Defender, who shall be appointed by the Assembly, and shall be a person of high moral character and possess the highest level of professional competence and extensive experience in the defence of criminal cases. He shall be admitted to the practice of law in a recognised jurisdiction and shall have practised criminal law before a national or international criminal court for a minimum of ten years.

5. The Principal Defender shall, in order to ensure that the fair trial rights of suspects and accused are protected, adopt such regulations and practice directions as may be necessary to effectively carry out the functions of the Defence Office.
6. The Principal Defender shall be assisted by such other staff as maybe required to perform the functions of the Defence Office effectively and efficiently. The staff of the Defence Office shall be appointed by the Principal Defender in accordance with the Staff Rules and Regulations of the African Union.
7. The Principal Defender shall, for all purposes connected with pre-trial, trial and appellate proceedings, enjoy equal status with the Prosecutor in respect of rights of audience and negotiations *inter partes*.
8. At the request of a Judge or Chamber, the Registry, Defence or where the interests of justice so require, *proprio motu*, the Principal Defender or a person designated by him shall have rights of audience in relation to matters of general interest to defence teams, the fairness of the proceedings or the rights of a suspect or accused."

Article 12Bis
Conditions of Service of the Registrar and Members of the Registry

Article 24 of the Statute (Conditions of Service of the Registrar and Members of the Registry) is deleted.

Article 13

Under Chapter lll (Competence of the Court) In Article 28 of the Statute (Jurisdiction of the Court), the insertion of a new sub-para (d) as follows, with consequential renumbering of the existing paras (d) to (h).

"…

(d) The crimes contained in this Statute, subject to a right of appeal.

…"

Article 14
International Criminal Jurisdiction of the Court

Immediately after Article 28 (Jurisdiction of the Court), the insertion of new Articles 28A, 28B, 28C, 28D, 28E, 28F, 28G, 28H, 28I, 28I *Bis*, 28J, 28K, 28L, 28L *Bis*, 28M and 28N **as follows:**

"Article 28A
International Criminal Jurisdiction of the Court

1. Subject to the right of appeal, the International Criminal Law Section of the Court shall have power to try persons for the crimes provided hereunder:

(1) Genocide
(2) Crimes Against Humanity
(3) War Crimes
(4) The Crime of Unconstitutional Change of Government;
(5) Piracy
(6) Terrorism
(7) Mercenarism
(8) Corruption
(9) Money Laundering
(10) Trafficking in Persons
(11) Trafficking in Drugs
(12) Trafficking in Hazardous Wastes
(13) Illicit Exploitation of Natural Resources
(14) The Crime of Aggression

2. The Assembly may extend upon the consensus of States Parties the jurisdiction of the Court to incorporate additional crimes to reflect developments in international law.
3. The crimes within the Jurisdiction of the Court shall not be subject to any statute of limitations.

Article 28 B
Genocide

For the purposes of this Statute, 'genocide' means any of the following acts committed with intent to destroy, in whole or in part, a national, ethnical, racial or religious group, as such:

(a) Killing members of the group;
(b) Causing serious bodily or mental harm to members of the group;
(c) Deliberately inflicting on the group conditions of life calculated to bring about its physical destruction in whole or in part;
(d) Imposing measures intended to prevent births within the group;
(e) Forcibly transferring children of the group to another group;
(f) Acts of rape or any other form of sexual violence.

Article 28 C
Crimes Against Humanity

1. For the purposes of this Statute, 'crime against humanity' means any of the following acts when committed as part of a widespread or systematic attack or enterprise directed against any civilian population, with knowledge of the attack or enterprise:

   (a) Murder;
   (b) Extermination;

(c) Enslavement;
(d) Deportation or forcible transfer of population;
(e) Imprisonment or other severe deprivation of physical liberty in violation of fundamental rules of international law;
(f) Torture, cruel, inhuman and degrading treatment or punishment;
(g) Rape, sexual slavery, enforced prostitution, forced pregnancy, enforced sterilization, or any other form of sexual violence of comparable gravity;
(h) Persecution against any identifiable group or collectivity on political, racial, national, ethnic, cultural, religious, gender or other grounds that are universally recognized as impermissible under international law;
(i) Enforced disappearance of persons;
(j) The crime of apartheid;
(k) Other inhumane acts of a similar character intentionally causing great suffering, or serious injury to body or mental or physical health.

2. For the purpose of para 1:

(a) 'Attack directed against any civilian population' means a course of conduct involving the multiple commission of acts referred to in para 1 against any civilian population, pursuant to or in furtherance of a State or organizational policy to commit such attack;
(b) 'Extermination' includes the intentional infliction of conditions of life, *inter alia* the deprivation of access to food and medicine, calculated to bring about the destruction of part of a population;
(c) 'Enslavement' means the exercise of any or all of the powers attaching to the right of ownership over a person and includes the exercise of such power in the course of trafficking in persons, in particular women and children;
(d) 'Deportation or forcible transfer of population' means forced displacement of the persons concerned by expulsion or other coercive acts from the area in which they are lawfully present, without grounds permitted under international law;
(e) 'Torture' means the intentional infliction of severe pain or suffering, whether physical or mental, upon a person in the custody or under the control of the accused; except that torture shall not include pain or suffering arising only from, inherent in or incidental to, lawful sanctions;
(f) 'Forced pregnancy' means the unlawful confinement of a woman forcibly made pregnant, with the intent of affecting the ethnic composition of any population or carrying out other grave violations of international law. This definition shall not in any way be interpreted as affecting national laws relating to pregnancy;
(g) 'Persecution' means the intentional and severe deprivation of fundamental rights contrary to international law by reason of the identity of the group or collectivity;
(h) 'The crime of apartheid' means inhumane acts of a character similar to those referred to in para 1, committed in the context of an institutionalized regime of systematic oppression and domination by one racial group

over any other racial group or groups and committed with the intention of maintaining that regime;

(i) 'Enforced disappearance of persons' means the arrest, detention or abduction of persons by, or with the authorization, support or acquiescence of, a State or a political organization, followed by a refusal to acknowledge that deprivation of freedom or to give information on the fate or whereabouts of those persons, with the intention of removing them from the protection of the law for a prolonged period of time.

Article 28 D
War Crimes

For the purposes of this Statute, 'war crimes' means any of the offences listed, in particular when committed as part of a plan or policy or as part of a large scale commission of such crimes.

(a) Grave breaches of the Geneva Conventions of 12 August 1949, namely, any of the following acts against persons or property protected under the provisions of the relevant Geneva Convention:

- (i) Wilful killing;
- (ii) Torture or inhuman treatment, including biological experiments;
- (iii) Wilfully causing great suffering, or serious injury to body or health;
- (iv) Extensive destruction and appropriation of property, not justified by military necessity and carried out unlawfully and wantonly;
- (v) Compelling a prisoner of war or other protected person to serve in the forces of a hostile Power;
- (vi) Wilfully depriving a prisoner of war or other protected person of the rights of fair and regular trial;
- (vii) Unlawful deportation or transfer or unlawful confinement;
- (viii) Taking of hostages.

(b) Grave breaches of the First Additional Protocol to the Geneva Conventions of 8 June 1977 and other serious violations of the laws and customs applicable in international armed conflict, within the established framework of international law, namely, any of the following acts:

- (i) Intentionally directing attacks against the civilian population as such or against individual civilians not taking direct part in hostilities;
- (ii) Intentionally directing attacks against civilian objects, that is, objects which are not military objectives;
- (iii) Intentionally directing attacks against personnel, installations, material, units or vehicles involved in a humanitarian assistance or peacekeeping mission in accordance with the Charter of the United Nations, as long as they are entitled to the protection given to civilians or civilian objects under the international law of armed conflict;

(iv) Intentionally launching an attack in the knowledge that such attack will cause incidental loss of life or injury to civilians or damage to civilian objects or widespread, long-term and severe damage to the natural environment which would be clearly excessive in relation to the concrete and direct overall military advantage anticipated;

(v) Intentionally launching an attack against works or installations containing dangerous forces in the knowledge that such attack will cause excessive loss of life, injury to civilians or damage to civilian objects which will be excessive in relation to the concrete and direct overall military advantage anticipated;

(vi) Attacking or bombarding, by whatever means, towns, villages, dwellings or buildings which are undefended and which are not military objectives;

(vii) Killing or wounding a combatant who, having laid down his arms or having no longer means of defence, has surrendered at discretion;

(viii) Making improper use of a flag of truce, of the flag or of the military insignia and uniform of the enemy or of the United Nations, as well as of the distinctive emblems of the Geneva Conventions, resulting in death or serious personal injury;

(ix) The transfer, directly or indirectly, by the Occupying Power of parts of its own civilian population into the territory it occupies, or the deportation or transfer of all or parts of the population of the occupied territory within or outside this territory;

(x) Intentionally directing attacks against buildings dedicated to religion, education, art, science or charitable purposes, historic monuments, hospitals and places where the sick and wounded are collected, provided they are not military objectives;

(xi) Subjecting persons who are in the power of an adverse party to physical mutilation or to medical or scientific experiments of any kind which are neither justified by the medical, dental or hospital treatment of the person concerned nor carried out in his or her interest, and which cause death to or seriously endanger the health of such person or persons;

(xii) Killing or wounding treacherously individuals belonging to the hostile nation or army;

(xiii) Declaring that no quarter will be given;

(xiv) Destroying or seizing the enemy's property unless such destruction or seizure be imperatively demanded by the necessities of war;

(xv) Declaring abolished, suspended or inadmissible in a court of law the rights and actions of the nationals of the hostile party;

(xvi) Compelling the nationals of the hostile party to take part in the operations of war directed against their own State, even if they were in the belligerent's service before the commencement of the war;

(xvii) Pillaging a town or place, even when taken by assault;

(xviii) Employing poison or poisoned weapons;

(xix) Employing asphyxiating, poisonous or other gases, and all analogous liquids, materials or devices;

(xx) Employing bullets which expand or flatten easily in the human body, such as bullets with a hard envelope which does not entirely cover the core or is pierced with incisions;

(xxi) Employing weapons, projectiles and material and methods of warfare which are of a nature to cause superfluous injury or unnecessary suffering or which are inherently indiscriminate in violation of the international law of armed conflict

(xxii) Committing outrages upon personal dignity, in particular humiliating and degrading treatment;

(xxiii) Committing rape, sexual slavery, enforced prostitution, forced pregnancy, enforced sterilization, or any other form of sexual violence also constituting a grave breach of the Geneva Conventions;

(xxiv) Utilizing the presence of a civilian or other protected person to render certain points, areas or military forces immune from military operations;

(xxv) Intentionally directing attacks against buildings, material, medical units and transport, and personnel using the distinctive emblems of the Geneva Conventions in conformity with international law;

(xxvi) Intentionally using starvation of civilians as a method of warfare by depriving them of objects indispensable to their survival, including wilfully impeding relief supplies as provided for under the Geneva Conventions;

(xxvii) Conscripting or enlisting children under the age of eighteen years into the national armed forces or using them to participate actively in hostilities;

(xxviii) Unjustifiably delaying the repatriation of prisoners of war or civilians;

(xxix) Willfully committing practices of apartheid and other inhuman and degrading practices involving outrages upon personal dignity, based on racial discrimination.

(xxx) Making non-defended localities and demilitarised zones the object of attack;

(xxxi) Slavery and deportation to slave labour;

(xxxii) Collective punishments;

(xxxiii) Despoliation of the wounded, sick, shipwrecked or dead;

(c) In the case of an armed conflict not of an international character, serious violations of Article 3 common to the four Geneva Conventions of 12 August 1949, namely, any of the following acts committed against persons taking no active part in the hostilities, including members of armed forces who have laid down their arms and those placed hors de combat by sickness, wounds, detention or any other cause:

(i) Violence to life and person, in particular murder of all kinds, mutilation, cruel treatment and torture;

- (ii) Committing outrages upon personal dignity, in particular humiliating and degrading treatment;
- (iii) Taking of hostages;
- (iv) The passing of sentences and the carrying out of executions without previous judgment pronounced by a regularly constituted court, affording all judicial guarantees which are generally recognized as indispensable.

(d) Paragraph (c) applies to armed conflicts not of an international character and thus does not apply to situations of internal disturbances and tensions, such as riots, isolated and sporadic acts of violence or other acts of a similar nature.

(e) Other serious violations of the laws and customs applicable in armed conflicts not of an international character, within the established framework of international law, namely, any of the following acts:

- (i) Intentionally directing attacks against the civilian population as such or against individual civilians not taking direct part in hostilities;
- (ii) Intentionally directing attacks against buildings, material, medical units and transport, and personnel using the distinctive emblems of the Geneva Conventions in conformity with international law;
- (iii) Intentionally directing attacks against personnel, installations, material, units or vehicles involved in a humanitarian assistance or peacekeeping mission in accordance with the Charter of the United Nations, as long as they are entitled to the protection given to civilians or civilian objects under the international law of armed conflict;
- (iv) Intentionally directing attacks against buildings dedicated to religion, education, art, science or charitable purposes, historic monuments, hospitals and places where the sick and wounded are collected, provided they are not military objectives;
- (v) Pillaging a town or place, even when taken by assault;
- (vi) Committing rape, sexual slavery, enforced prostitution, forced pregnancy, enforced sterilization, and any other form of sexual violence also constituting a serious violation of Article 3 common to the four Geneva Conventions;
- (vii) Conscripting or enlisting children under the age of eighteen years into armed forces or groups or using them to participate actively in hostilities;
- (viii) Ordering the displacement of the civilian population for reasons related to the conflict, unless the security of the civilians involved or imperative military reasons so demand;
- (ix) Killing or wounding treacherously a combatant adversary;
- (x) Declaring that no quarter will be given;
- (xi) Subjecting persons who are in the power of another party to the conflict to physical mutilation or to medical or scientific experiments of any kind which are neither justified by the medical, dental or hospital treatment of the person concerned nor carried out in his or her interest, and which cause death to or seriously endanger the health of such person or persons;

(xii) Destroying or seizing the property of an adversary unless such destruction or seizure be imperatively demanded by the necessities of the conflict;
(xiii) Employing poison or poisoned weapons;
(xiv) Employing asphyxiating, poisonous or other gases, and all analogous liquids, materials or devices;
(xv) Employing bullets which expand or flatten easily in the human body, such as bullets with a hard envelope which does not entirely cover the core or is pierced with incisions;
(xvi) Intentionally using starvation of civilians as a method of warfare by depriving them of objects indispensable to their survival, including wilfully impeding relief supplies;
(xvii) Utilizing the presence of a civilian or other protected person to render certain points, areas or military forces immune from military operations;
(xviii) Launching an indiscriminate attack resulting in death or injury to civilians, or an attack in the knowledge that it will cause excessive incidental civilian loss, injury or damage;
(xix) Making non-defended localities and demilitarised zones the object of attack;
(xx) Slavery;
(xxi) Collective punishments;
(xxii) Despoliation of the wounded, sick, shipwrecked or dead.

(f) Para e) applies to armed conflicts not of an international character and thus does not apply to situations of internal disturbances and tensions, such as riots, isolated and sporadic acts of violence or other acts of a similar nature. It applies to armed conflicts that take place in the territory of a State when there is protracted armed conflict between governmental authorities and organized armed groups or between such groups.
(g) Using nuclear weapons or other weapons of mass destruction

Article 28E
The Crime of Unconstitutional Change of Government

1. For the purposes of this Statute, 'unconstitutional change of government' means committing or ordering to be committed the following acts, with the aim of illegally accessing or maintaining power:

   (a) A putsch or coup d'état against a democratically elected government;
   (b) An intervention by mercenaries to replace a democratically elected government;
   (c) Any replacement of a democratically elected government by the use of armed dissidents or rebels or through political assassination;

(d) Any refusal by an incumbent government to relinquish power to the winning party or candidate after free, fair and regular elections;
(e) Any amendment or revision of the Constitution or legal instruments, which is an infringement on the principles of democratic change of government or is inconsistent with the Constitution;
(f) Any substantial modification to the electoral laws in the last six (6) months before the elections without the consent of the majority of the political actors.

2. For purposes of this Statute, "democratically elected government" has the same meaning as contained in AU instruments.

Article 28F
Piracy

Piracy consists of any of the following acts:

(a) any illegal acts of violence or detention, or any act of depredation, committed for private ends by the crew or the passengers of a private boat, ship or a private aircraft, and directed:
    i. on the high seas, against another boat, ship or aircraft, or against persons or property on board such boat, ship or aircraft;
    ii. against a boat, ship, aircraft, persons or property in a place outside the jurisdiction of any State

(b) any act of voluntary participation in the operation of a boat, ship or of an aircraft with knowledge of facts making it a pirate boat, ship or aircraft;
(c) any act of inciting or of intentionally facilitating an act described in subpara (a) or (b).

Article 28 G
Terrorism

For the purposes of this Statute, 'terrorism' means any of the following acts:

A. Any act which is a violation of the criminal laws of a State Party, the laws of the African Union or a regional economic community recognized by the African Union, or by international law, and which may endanger the life, physical integrity or freedom of, or cause serious injury or death to, any person, any number or group of persons or causes or may cause damage to public or private property, natural resources, environmental or cultural heritage and is calculated or intended to:
1. intimidate, put in fear, force, coerce or induce any government, body, institution, the general public or any segment thereof, to do or abstain from doing any act, or to adopt or abandon a particular standpoint, or to act according to certain principles; or

2. disrupt any public service, the delivery of any essential service to the public or to create a public emergency; or
3. create general insurrection in a State.

B. Any promotion, sponsoring, contribution to, command, aid, incitement, encouragement, attempt, threat, conspiracy, organizing, or procurement of any person, with the intent to commit any act referred to in sub-para (a)(1) to (3).
C. Notwithstanding the provisions of paragraphs A and B, the struggle waged by peoples in accordance with the principles of international law for their liberation or self-determination, including armed struggle against colonialism, occupation, aggression and domination by foreign forces shall not be considered as terrorist acts.
D. The acts covered by international Humanitarian Law, committed in the course of an international or non-international armed conflict by government forces or members of organized armed groups, shall not be considered as terrorist acts.
E. Political, philosophical, ideological, racial, ethnic, religious or other motives shall not be a justifiable defence against a terrorist act.

Article 28H
Mercenarism

1. For the purposes of this Statute:

   (a) A mercenary is any person who:

   i. Is specially recruited locally or abroad in order to fight in an armed conflict;
   ii. Is motivated to take part in the hostilities essentially by the desire for private gain and, in fact, is promised, by or on behalf of a party to the conflict, material compensation;
   iii. Is neither a national of a party to the conflict nor a resident of territory controlled by a party to the conflict;
   iv. Is not a member of the armed forces of a party to the conflict; and
   v. Has not been sent by a State which is not a party to the conflict on official duty as a member of its armed forces.

   (b) A mercenary is also any person who, in any other situation:

   i. Is specially recruited locally or abroad for the purpose of participating in a concerted act of violence aimed at:

      1. Overthrowing a legitimate Government or otherwise undermining the constitutional order of a State;
      2. Assisting a government to maintain power;
      3. Assisting a group of persons to obtain power; or
      4. Undermining the territorial integrity of a State;

ii. Is motivated to take part therein essentially by the desire for private gain and is prompted by the promise or payment of material compensation;
iii. Is neither a national nor a resident of the State against which such an act is directed;
iv. Has not been sent by a State on official duty; and
v. Is not a member of the armed forces of the State on whose territory the act is undertaken.

2. Any person who recruits, uses, finances or trains mercenaries, as defined in para (*1*) (*a*) *or* (*b*) above commits an offence.
3. A mercenary, as defined in para (*1*)(*a*) *or* (*b*) above, who participates directly in hostilities or in a concerted act of violence, as the case may be, commits an offence.

Article 28I
Corruption

1. For the purposes of this Statute, the following shall be deemed to be acts of corruption if they are of a serious nature affecting the stability of a state, region or the Union:

(a) The solicitation or acceptance, directly or indirectly, by a public official, his/her family member or any other person, of any goods of monetary value, or other benefit, such as a gift, favour, promise or advantage for himself or herself or for another person or entity, in exchange for any act or omission in the performance of his or her public functions;
(b) The offering or granting, directly or indirectly, to a public official, his/ family member or any other person, of any goods of monetary value, or other benefit, such as a gift, favour, promise or advantage for himself or herself or for another person or entity, in exchange for any act or omission in the performance of his or her public functions;
(c) Any act or omission in the discharge of his or her duties by a public official. His/her family member or any other person for the purpose of illicitly obtaining benefits for himself or herself or for a third party;
(d) The diversion by a public official, his/her family member or any other person, for purposes unrelated to those for which they were intended, for his or her own benefit or that of a third party, of any property belonging to the State or its agencies, to an independent agency, or to an individual, that such official has received by virtue of his or her position;
(e) The offering or giving, promising, solicitation or acceptance, directly or indirectly, of any undue advantage to or by any person who directs or works for, in any capacity, a private sector entity, for himself or herself or for anyone else, for him or her to act, or refrain from acting, in breach of his or her duties;

(f) The offering, giving, solicitation or acceptance directly or indirectly, or promising of any undue advantage to or by any person who asserts or confirms that he or she is able to exert any improper influence over the decision making of any person performing functions in the public or private sector in consideration thereof, whether the undue advantage is for himself or herself or for anyone else, as well as the request, receipt or the acceptance of the offer or the promise of such an advantage, in consideration of that influence, whether or not the influence is exerted or whether or not the supposed influence leads to the intended result;
(g) Illicit enrichment;
(h) The use or concealment of proceeds derived from any of the acts referred to in this Article.

2. For the purposes of this Statute "Illicit enrichment" means the significant increase in the assets of a public official or any other person which he or she cannot reasonably explain in relation to his or her income.

Article 28I Bis
Money Laundering

1. For the purposes of this Statute, 'Money Laundering' means: any act of—

(i) Conversion, transfer or disposal of property, knowing that such property is the proceeds of corruption or related offences for the purpose of concealing or disguising the illicit origin of the property or of helping any person who is involved in the commission of the offence to evade the legal consequences of his or her action.
(ii) Concealment or disguise of the true nature, source, location, disposition, movement or ownership of or rights with respect to property which is the proceeds of corruption or related offences;
(iii) Acquisition, possession or use of property with the knowledge at the time of receipt, that such property is the proceeds of corruption or related offences
(iv) Participation in, association with or conspiracy to commit, attempts to commit and aiding, abetting, facilitating and counselling the commission of any of the offences established in accordance with this article.

2. Nothing in this article shall be interpreted as prejudicing the power of the Court to make a determination as to the seriousness of any act or offence.

Article 28J
Trafficking in persons

For the purposes of this Statute:

1. "Trafficking in persons" means the recruitment, transportation, transfer, harbouring or receipt of persons, by means of the threat or use of force or other

forms of coercion, of abduction, of fraud, of deception, of the abuse of power or of a position of vulnerability or of the giving or receiving of payments or benefits to achieve the consent of a person having control over another person, for the purpose of exploitation.

2. Exploitation shall include the exploitation of the prostitution of others or other forms of sexual exploitation, forced labour or services, slavery or practices similar to slavery, servitude or the removal of organs;
3. The consent of a victim of trafficking in persons to the intended exploitation set forth in subpara (1) of this article shall be irrelevant where any of the means set forth in subpara (1) have been used;
4. The recruitment, transportation, transfer, harbouring or receipt of a child for the purpose of exploitation shall be considered "trafficking in persons" even if this does not involve any of the means set forth in subpara (1) of this article;

Article 28K
Trafficking in drugs

1. For the purposes of this Statute, trafficking in drugs means:

   (a) The production, manufacture, extraction, preparation, offering, offering for sale, distribution, sale, delivery on any terms whatsoever, brokerage, dispatch, dispatch in transit, transport, importation or exportation of drugs;
   (b) The cultivation of opium poppy, coca bush or cannabis plant;
   (c) The possession or purchase of drugs with a view to conducting one of the activities listed in (a);
   (d) The manufacture, transport or distribution of precursors knowing that they are to be used in or for the illicit production or manufacture of drugs.

2. The conduct described in para 1 shall not be included in the scope of this Statute when it is committed by perpetrators for their own personal consumption as defined by national law.
3. For the purposes of this Article:

(A) "Drugs" shall mean any of the substances covered by the following United Nations Conventions:

   (a) The 1961 Single Convention on Narcotic Drugs, as amended by the 1972 Protocol Amending the Single Convention on Narcotic Drugs of 1961;
   (b) The 1971 Vienna Convention on Psychotropic Substances.

(B) "Precursors" shall mean any substance scheduled pursuant to Article 12 of the United Nations Convention against Illicit Traffic in Narcotic Drugs and Psychotropic Substances of 20 December 1988.

Article 28L
Trafficking in Hazardous Wastes

1. For the purposes of this Statute, any import or failure to re-import, transboundary movement, or export of hazardous wastes proscribed by the Bamako Convention on the Ban of the Import into Africa and the Control of Transboundary Movement and Management of Hazardous Wastes within Africa, adopted in Bamako, Mali, in January 1991 shall constitute the offence of trafficking in hazardous waste.
2. The following substances shall be "hazardous wastes" for the purpose of this statute:

   (a) Wastes that belong to any category contained in Annex I of the Bamako Convention;
   (b) Wastes that are not covered under para (a) above but are defined as, or are considered to be, hazardous wastes by the domestic legislation of the State of export, import or transit;
   (c) Wastes which possess any of the characteristics contained in Annex II of the Bamako Convention;
   (d) Hazardous substances which have been banned, cancelled or refused registration by government regulatory action, or voluntarily withdrawn from registration in the State of manufacture, for human health or environmental reasons.

3. Wastes which, as a result of being radioactive, are subject to any international control systems, including international instruments, applying specifically to radioactive materials are included in the scope of this Convention.
4. Wastes which derive from the normal operations of a ship, the discharge of which is covered by another international instrument, shall not fall within the scope of this Convention.
5. For the purposes of this Article, "failure to re-import" shall have the same meaning assigned to it in the Bamako Convention.
6. The export of hazardous waste into a Member State for the purpose of rendering it safe shall not constitute an offence under this Article.

Article 28L Bis
Illicit Exploitation of Natural Resources

For the purpose of this Statute, "Illicit exploitation of natural resources" means any of the following acts if they are of a serious nature affecting the stability of a state, region or the Union:

(a) Concluding an agreement to exploit resources, in violation of the principle of peoples' sovereignty over their natural resources;
(b) Concluding with state authorities an agreement to exploit natural resources, in violation of the legal and regulatory procedures of the State concerned;

(c) Concluding an agreement to exploit natural resources through corrupt practices;
(d) Concluding an agreement to exploit natural resources that is clearly one-sided;
(e) Exploiting natural resources without any agreement with the State concerned;
(f) Exploiting natural resources without complying with norms relating to the protection of the environment and the security of the people and the staff; and
(g) Violating the norms and standards established by the relevant natural resource certification mechanism.

Article 28M
Crime of Aggression

A. For the purpose of this Statute, "Crime of Aggression" means the planning, preparation, initiation or execution, by a person in a position effectively to exercise control over or to direct the political or military action of a state or organization, whether connected to the state or not of an act of aggression which, by its character, gravity and scale, constitutes a manifest violation of the Charter of the United Nations or the Constitutive Act of the African Union and with regard to the territorial integrity and human security of the population of a State Party."

B. The following shall constitute acts of aggression, regardless of a declaration of war by a State, group of States, organizations of States, or non-State actor(s) or by any foreign entity:

   (a) The use of armed forces against the sovereignty, territorial integrity and political independence of any state, or any other act inconsistent with the provisions of the Constitutive Act of the African Union and the Charter of the United Nations.
   (b) The invasion or attack by armed forces against the territory of a State, or military occupation however temporary, resulting from such an invasion or attack, or any annexation by the use of force of the territory of a State or part thereof.
   (c) The bombardment by the armed forces of a State against the territory of another State or the use of any weapons by a State against the territory of another State.
   (d) The blockade of the ports, coasts or airspace of a State by the armed forces of another State.
   (e) The attack by the armed forces of a State on the land, sea or air forces, or marine and fleets of another State.
   (f) The use of the armed forces of one State which are within the territory of another State with the agreement of the receiving State, in contravention of the conditions provided for in the African Union Non-Aggression and Common Defence Pact or any extension of their presence in such territory beyond the termination of the agreement.

(g) The action of a State in allowing its territory, which it has placed at the disposal of another State to be used by another State for perpetrating an act of aggression against a third State.
(h) The sending or materially supporting by or on behalf of a State of armed bands, groups, irregulars or mercenaries, which carry out acts of armed force against another State of such gravity as to amount to the acts listed above, or its substantial involvement therein.

Article 28N
Modes of Responsibility

An offence is committed by any person who, in relation to any of the crimes or offences provided for in this Statute:

i. Incites, instigates, organizes, directs, facilitates, finances, counsels or participates as a principal, co-principal, agent or accomplice in any of the offences set forth in the present Statute;
ii. Aids or abets the commission of any of the offences set forth in the present Statute;
iii. Is an accessory before or after the fact or in any other manner participates in a collaboration or conspiracy to commit any of the offences set forth in the present Statute;
iv. Attempts to commit any of the offences set forth in the present Statute."

Article 15
Entities Eligible to Submit Cases to the Court

In para 1(b) of Article 29 of the Statute (Entities Eligible to Submit Cases to the Court), immediately after the words "The Assembly" insert:
"the Peace and Security Council"

Add a new para (d)

(d) "The Office of the Prosecutor"

Article 16
Other Entities Eligible to Submit Cases to the Court

The deletion of para (f) of Article 30 of the Statute (Other Entities Eligible to Submit Cases to the Court), and the insertion of the following new paragraph:

(f) African individuals or African Non-Governmental Organizations with Observer Status with the African Union or its organs or institutions, but only with regard to a State that has made a Declaration accepting the competence of the Court to receive cases or applications submitted to it directly. The Court shall not receive any case or application involving a State Party which has not made a Declaration in accordance with Article 9(3) of this Protocol.

Article 17
Institution of Proceedings before the International Criminal Law Section

UNDER CHAPTER FOUR (PROCEDURE), immediately after Article 34 of the Statute (Institution of Proceedings before the Human Rights Section, the insertion of new Articles 34A and 34B as follows:

"Article 34A
Institution of Proceedings before the International Criminal Law Section

1. Subject to the provisions of Articles 22A and 29, cases brought before the International Criminal Law Section of the Court shall be brought by or in the name of the Prosecutor.
2. The Registrar shall forthwith give notice of the case to all parties concerned, as well as the Chairperson of the Commission.

Article 34B
Institution of Proceedings before the Appellate Chamber

The Court shall define the procedures for appeals in its Rules."

Article 18
Representation of Parties

In Article 36 of the Statute (Representation of the Parties), the insertion of a new para (6) as follows, with consequential renumbering of the existing para 6:

"…

6. A person accused under the international criminal jurisdiction of this Court shall have the right to represent himself or herself in person or through an agent.

……"

Article 19
Sentences and Penalties

Immediately after Article 43 of the Statute (Judgments and Decisions) the insertion of a new Article 43A as follows:

"Article 43A
Sentences and Penalties under the International Criminal Jurisdiction of the Court

1. Without prejudice to the provisions of Article 43, the Court shall pronounce judgment and impose sentences and/or penalties, other than the death penalty, for persons convicted of international crimes under this Statute.
2. For the avoidance of doubt, the penalties imposed by the Court shall be limited to prison sentences and/or pecuniary fines.

3. The sentences and/or penalties shall be pronounced in public and, wherever possible, in the presence of the accused.
4. In imposing the sentences and/or penalties, the Court should take into account such factors as the gravity of the offence and the individual circumstances of the convicted person.
5. In addition to the sentences and/or penalties, the Court may order the forfeiture of any property, proceeds or any asset acquired unlawfully or by criminal conduct, and their return to their rightful owner or to an appropriate Member State."

Article 20
Compensation and Reparations to Victims

Article 45 of the Statute (Compensation), including its title, is deleted in its entirety and substituted with the following:

"Article 45
Compensation and Reparations to Victims

1. Without prejudice to the provisions of para (i) of Article 28, the Court shall establish in the Rules of Court principles relating to reparations to, or in respect of, victims, including restitution, compensation and rehabilitation. On this basis, in its decision the Court may, either upon request or on its own motion in exceptional circumstances, determine the scope and extent of any damage, loss or injury to, or in respect of, victims and will state the principles on which it is acting.
2. With respect to its international criminal jurisdiction, the Court may make an order directly against a convicted person specifying appropriate reparations to, or in respect of, victims, including restitution, compensation and rehabilitation.
3. Before making an order the Court may invite and take account of representations from or on behalf of the convicted person, victims, other interested persons or interested States.
4. Nothing in this article shall be interpreted as prejudicing the rights of victims under national or international law."

Article 21
Binding Force and Execution of Judgments

Paragraph 2 of Article 46 of the Statute (Binding Force and Execution of Judgments) is deleted and substituted with the following: -

"…

2. Subject to the provisions of Article 18 (as amended) and para 3 of Article 41 of the Statute, the judgment of the Court is final.
3. ……"

Article 22
Provisions Specific to the International Criminal Jurisdiction of the Court

Under Chapter lV (PROCEDURE), immediately at the end of Article 46 (Binding Force and Execution of Judgments), the insertion of a new CHAPTER IVA and new Articles 46A to 46L as follows:

"CHAPTER IVA: PROVISIONS SPECIFIC TO THE INTERNATIONAL CRIMINAL JURISDICTION OF THE COURT

Article 46A
Rights of Accused

1. All accused shall be equal before the Court.
2. The accused shall be entitled to a fair and public hearing, subject to measures ordered by the Court for the protection of victims and witnesses.
3. The accused shall be presumed innocent until proven guilty according to the provisions of this Statute.
4. In the determination of any charge against the accused pursuant to this Statute, he or she shall be entitled to the following minimum guarantees, in full equality:

   (a) To be informed promptly and in detail in a language that he or she understands of the nature and cause of the charge against him or her;
   (b) To have adequate time and facilities for the preparation of his or her defence and to communicate freely with counsel of his or her own choosing;
   (c) To be tried without undue delay;
   (d) To be tried in his or her presence, and to defend himself or herself in person or through legal assistance of his or her own choosing; to be informed, if he or she does not have legal assistance, of this right; and to have legal assistance assigned to him or her, in any case where the interests of justice so require, and without payment by him or her in any such case if he or she does not have sufficient means to pay for it;
   (e) To examine, or have examined, the witnesses against him or her and to obtain the attendance and examination of witnesses on his or her behalf under the same conditions as witnesses against him or her;
   (f) To have the free assistance of an interpreter if he or she cannot understand or speak the language used in the Court;
   (g) Not to be compelled to testify against himself or herself or to confess guilt.
   (h) To have the judgment pronounced publicly
   (i) To be informed of his/her right to appeal.

Article 46A bis
Immunities

No charges shall be commenced or continued before the Court against any serving AU Head of State or Government, or anybody acting or entitled to act in such capacity, or other senior state officials based on their functions, during their tenure of office.

Article 46B
Individual Criminal Responsibility

1. A person who commits an offence under this Statute shall be held individually responsible for the crime.
2. Subject to the provisions of Article 46A*bis* of this Statute, the official position of any accused person shall not relieve such person of criminal responsibility nor mitigate punishment.
3. The fact that any of the acts referred to in Article 28A of the present Statute was committed by a subordinate does not relieve his or her superior of criminal responsibility if he or she knew or had reason to know that the subordinate was about to commit such acts or had done so and the superior failed to take the necessary and reasonable measures to prevent such acts or to punish the perpetrators thereof.
4. The fact that an accused person acted pursuant to the order of a Government or of a superior shall not relieve him or her of criminal responsibility, but may be considered in mitigation of punishment if the Court determines that justice so requires.

Article 46C
Corporate Criminal Liability

1. For the purpose of this Statute, the Court shall have jurisdiction over legal persons, with the exception of States.
2. Corporate intention to commit an offence may be established by proof that it was the policy of the corporation to do the act which constituted the offence.
3. A policy may be attributed to a corporation where it provides the most reasonable explanation of the conduct of that corporation.
4. Corporate knowledge of the commission of an offence may be established by proof that the actual or constructive knowledge of the relevant information was possessed within the corporation.
5. Knowledge may be possessed within a corporation even though the relevant information is divided between corporate personnel.
6. The criminal responsibility of legal persons shall not exclude the criminal responsibility of natural persons who are perpetrators or accomplices in the same crimes.

Article 46D
Exclusion of Jurisdiction over Persons under the age of eighteen

The Court shall have no jurisdiction over any person who was under the age of eighteen (18) years at the time of the alleged commission of a crime.

Article 46E
Temporal Jurisdiction

1. The Court has jurisdiction only with respect to crimes committed after the entry into force of this Protocol and Statute.
2. If a State becomes a Party to this Protocol and Statute after its entry into force, the Court may exercise its jurisdiction only with respect to crimes committed after the entry into force of this Protocol and Statute for that State.

Article 46E bis
Preconditions to the exercise of Jurisdiction

1. A State which becomes a Party to this Protocol and Statute thereby accepts the jurisdiction of the Court with respect to the crimes referred to in Article 28A.
2. The Court may exercise its jurisdiction if one or more of the following conditions apply:

   (a) The State on the territory of which the conduct in question occurred or, if the crime was committed on board a vessel or aircraft, the State of registration of that vessel or aircraft.
   (b) The State of which the person accused of the crime is a national.
   (c) When the victim of the crime is a national of that State.
   (d) Extraterritorial acts by non-nationals which threaten a vital interest of that State.

3. If the acceptance of a State which is not a Party to this Statute is required under para 2, that State may, by declaration lodged with the Registrar, accept the exercise

Article 46F
Exercise of Jurisdiction

The Court may exercise its jurisdiction with respect to a crime referred to in Article 28A in accordance with the provisions of this Statute if: -

1. A situation in which one or more of such crimes appears to have been committed is referred to the Prosecutor by a State Party;
2. A situation in which one or more of such crimes appears to have been committed is referred to the Prosecutor by the Assembly of Heads of State and

Government of the African Union or the Peace and Security Council of the African Union.

3. The Prosecutor has initiated an investigation in respect of such a crime in accordance with Article 46G.

Article 46G
The Prosecutor

1. The Office of the Prosecutor may initiate investigations *proprio motu* on the basis of information on crimes within the jurisdiction of the Court.
2. The Office of the Prosecutor shall analyze the seriousness of information received. For this purpose, he or she may seek additional information from States, organs of the African Union or United Nations, intergovernmental or non-governmental organizations, or other reliable sources that he or she deems appropriate, and may receive written or oral testimony.
3. If the Office of the Prosecutor concludes that there is a reasonable basis to proceed with an investigation, it shall submit to a Pre-Trial Chamber a request for authorization of an investigation, together with any supporting material collected. Victims may make representations to the Pre-Trial Chamber, in accordance with the Rules of the Court.
4. If the Pre-Trial Chamber, upon examination of the request and supporting material, considers that there is a reasonable basis to proceed with an investigation, and that the case appears to fall within the jurisdiction of the Court, it shall authorize the commencement of the investigation, without prejudice to subsequent determinations by the Court with regard to the jurisdiction and admissibility of a case.
5. The refusal of the Pre-Trial Chamber to authorize the investigation shall not preclude the presentation of a subsequent request by the Office of the Prosecutor based on new facts or evidence regarding the same situation.
6. If, after the preliminary examination referred to in paras 1 and 2, the Office of the Prosecutor concludes that the information provided does not constitute a reasonable basis for an investigation, it shall inform those who provided the information. This shall not preclude the Office of the Prosecutor from considering further information submitted to him or her regarding the same situation in the light of new facts or evidence.

Article 46H
Complementary Jurisdiction

1. The jurisdiction of the Court shall be complementary to that of the National Courts, and to the Courts of the Regional Economic Communities where specifically provided for by the Communities.
2. The Court shall determine that a case is inadmissible where:

(a) The case is being investigated or prosecuted by a State which has jurisdiction over it, unless the State is unwilling or unable to carry out the investigation or prosecution;
(b) The case has been investigated by a State which has jurisdiction over it and the State has decided not to prosecute the person concerned, unless the decision resulted from the unwillingness or inability of the State to prosecute;
(c) The person concerned has already been tried for conduct which is the subject of the complaint;
(d) The case is not of sufficient gravity to justify further action by the Court.

3. In order to determine that a State is unwilling to investigate or prosecute in a particular case, the Court shall consider, having regard to the principles of due process recognized by international law, whether one or more of the following exist, as applicable:

(a) The proceedings were or are being undertaken or the national decision was made for the purpose of shielding the person concerned from criminal responsibility for crimes within the jurisdiction of the Court;
(b) There has been an unjustified delay in the proceedings which in the circumstances is inconsistent with an intent to bring the person concerned to justice;
(c) The proceedings were not or are not being conducted independently or impartially, and they were or are being conducted in a manner which, in the circumstances, is inconsistent with an intent to bring the person concerned to justice.

4. In order to determine that a State is unable to investigate or prosecute in a particular case, the Court shall consider whether, due to a total or substantial collapse or unavailability of its national judicial system, the State is unable to obtain the accused or the necessary evidence and testimony or otherwise unable to carry out its proceedings.

Article 46I
Non bis in idem

1. Except as provided in this Statute, no person shall be tried before the Court with respect to conduct which formed the basis of crimes for which the person has been convicted or acquitted by the Court.
2. Except in exceptional circumstances, no person who has been tried by another court for conduct proscribed under Article 28A of this Statute shall be tried by the Court with respect to the same conduct unless the proceedings in the other Court:

(a) Were for the purpose of shielding the person concerned from criminal responsibility for crimes within the jurisdiction of the Court;

(b) Otherwise were not conducted independently or impartially in accordance with the norms of due process recognized by international law and were conducted in a manner which, in the circumstances, was inconsistent with an intent to bring the person concerned to justice.

3. In considering the penalty to be imposed on a person convicted of a crime under the present Statute, the Court shall take into account the extent to which any penalty imposed by another Court on the same person for the same act has already been served.

Article 46J
Enforcement of Sentences

1. A sentence of imprisonment shall be served in a State designated by the Court from a list of States which have indicated to the Court their willingness to accept sentenced persons.
2. Such imprisonment shall be as provided for in a prior agreement between the Court and a receiving State and in accordance with the criteria as set out in the Rules of Court.

Article 46J bis
Enforcement of fines and forfeiture measures

1. States Parties shall give effect to fines or forfeitures ordered by the Court without prejudice to the rights of bona fide third parties, and in accordance with the procedure provided for in their national law.
2. If a State Party is unable to give effect to an order for forfeiture, it shall take measures to recover the value of the proceeds, property or assets ordered by the Court to be forfeited, without prejudice to the rights of bona fide third parties.
3. The Court shall determine in its Rules how real or movable property obtained by a State as a result of its enforcement of a judgment or order may be dealt with.

Article 46K
Pardon or Commutation of Sentences

If, pursuant to the applicable law of the State in which the convicted person is imprisoned, he or she is eligible for pardon or commutation of sentence, the State concerned shall notify the Court accordingly. There shall only be pardon or commutation of sentence if the Court so decides on the basis of the interests of justice and the general principles of law.

Article 46L
Co-operation and Judicial Assistance

1. States Parties shall co-operate with the Court in the investigation and prosecution of persons accused of committing the crimes defined by this Statute.
2. States Parties shall comply without undue delay with any request for assistance or an order issued by the Court, including but not limited to:

   (a) The identification and location of persons;
   (b) The taking of testimony and the production of evidence;
   (c) The service of documents;
   (d) The arrest, detention or extradition of persons;
   (e) The surrender or the transfer of the accused to the Court."
   (f) The identification, tracing and freezing or seizure of proceeds, property and assets and instrumentalities of crimes for the purpose of eventual forfeiture, without prejudice to the rights of bona fide third parties.
   (g) Any other type of assistance which is not prohibited by the law of the requested State, with a view to facilitating the investigation and prosecution of crimes within the jurisdiction of the court.

3. The Court shall be entitled to seek the co-operation or assistance of regional or international courts, non-States Parties or co-operating partners of the African Union and may conclude Agreements for that purpose.

Article 46M
Trust Fund

1. The Assembly shall, by a Decision, establish, within the jurisdiction of the Court, a Trust Fund for legal aid and assistance and for the benefit of victims of crimes or human rights violations and their families.
2. The Court may order money and other property collected through fines or forfeiture to be transferred, by order of the Court, to the Trust Fund.
3. The Trust Fund shall be managed according to criteria to be determined by the Assembly."

Article 23
Annual Activity Report

Article 57 of the Statute (Annual Activity Report) is deleted and substituted with the following:

"The Court shall submit to the Assembly an annual report on its work during the previous year. The report shall specify, in particular, the pending and concluded investigations, prosecutions and decisions and the cases in which a party has not complied with the judgment, sentence, order or penalty of the Court."

Definitions of Crimes in the Annex to the Malabo Protocol and their Sources in International Instruments

Crimes in the Annex to the Malabo Protocol	**Sources**
Article 28B	**Article 6 of the ICC Statute**
Genocide	**Genocide**
For the purposes of this Statute, 'genocide' means any of the following acts committed with intent to destroy, in whole or in part, a national, ethnical, racial or religious group, as such	For the purpose of this Statute, 'genocide' means any of the following acts committed with intent to destroy, in whole or in part, a national, ethnical, racial or religious group, as such
(a) Killing members of the group	(a) Killing members of the group
(b) Causing serious bodily or mental harm to members of the group	(b) Causing serious bodily or mental harm to members of the group
(c) Deliberately inflicting on the group conditions of life calculated to bring about its physical destruction in whole or in part	(c) Deliberately inflicting on the group conditions of life calculated to bring about its physical destruction in whole or in part
(d) Imposing measures intended to prevent births within the group	(d) Imposing measures intended to prevent births within the group
(e) Forcibly transferring children of the group to another group	(e) Forcibly transferring children of the group to another group
(f) Acts of rape or any other form of sexual violence	
Article 28C	**Article 7 of the ICC Statute**
Crimes Against Humanity	**Crimes Against Humanity**
1. 'For the purposes of this Statute, 'crime against humanity' means any of the following acts when committed as part of a widespread or systematic attack or enterprise directed against any civilian population, with knowledge of the attack or enterprise	1. For the purpose of this Statute, 'crime against humanity' means any of the following acts when committed as part of a widespread or systematic attack directed against any civilian population, with knowledge of the attack
(a) Murder	(a) Murder
(b) Extermination	(b) Extermination
(c) Enslavement	(c) Enslavement
(d) Deportation or forcible transfer of population	(d) Deportation or forcible transfer of population
(e) Imprisonment or other severe deprivation of physical liberty in violation of fundamental rules of international law	(e) Imprisonment or other severe deprivation of physical liberty in violation of fundamental rules of international law
(f) Torture, cruel, inhuman and degrading treatment or punishment	(f) Torture

Crimes in the Annex to the Malabo Protocol	**Sources**
(g) Rape, sexual slavery, enforced prostitution, forced pregnancy, enforced sterilization, or any other form of sexual violence of comparable gravity	(g) Rape, sexual slavery, enforced prostitution, forced pregnancy, enforced sterilization, or any other form of sexual violence of comparable gravity
(h) Persecution against any identifiable group or collectivity on political, racial, national, ethnic, cultural, religious, gender as defined in para 3, or other grounds that are universally recognized as impermissible under international law	(h) Persecution against any identifiable group or collectivity on political, racial, national, ethnic, cultural, religious, gender as defined in para 3, or other grounds that are universally recognized as impermissible under international law, in connection with any act referred to in this paragraph or any crime within the jurisdiction of the Court
(i) Enforced disappearance of persons	(i) Enforced disappearance of persons
(j) The crime of apartheid	(j) The crime of apartheid
(k) Other inhumane acts of a similar character intentionally causing great suffering, or serious injury to body or to mental or physical health	(k) Other inhumane acts of a similar character intentionally causing great suffering, or serious injury to body or to mental or physical health
2. For the purpose of para 1	2. For the purpose of para 1
(a) 'Attack directed against any civilian population' means a course of conduct involving the multiple commission of acts referred to in para 1 against any civilian population, pursuant to or in furtherance of a State or organizational policy to commit such attack	(a) 'Attack directed against any civilian population' means a course of conduct involving the multiple commission of acts referred to in para 1 against any civilian population, pursuant to or in furtherance of a State or organizational policy to commit such attack
(b) 'Extermination' includes the intentional infliction of conditions of life, inter alia the deprivation of access to food and medicine, calculated to bring about the destruction of part of a population	(b) 'Extermination' includes the intentional infliction of conditions of life, inter alia the deprivation of access to food and medicine, calculated to bring about the destruction of part of a population
(c) 'Enslavement' means the exercise of any or all of the powers attaching to the right of ownership over a person and includes the exercise of such power in the course of trafficking in persons, in particular women and children	(c) 'Enslavement' means the exercise of any or all of the powers attaching to the right of ownership over a person and includes the exercise of such power in the course of trafficking in persons, in particular women and children
(d) 'Deportation or forcible transfer of population' means forced displacement of the persons concerned by expulsion or other coercive acts from the area in which they are lawfully present, without grounds permitted under international law	(d) 'Deportation or forcible transfer of population' means forced displacement of the persons concerned by expulsion or other coercive acts from the area in which they are lawfully present, without grounds permitted under international law

Crimes in the Annex to the Malabo Protocol	Sources
(e) 'Torture' means the intentional infliction of severe pain or suffering, whether physical or mental, upon a person in the custody or under the control of the accused; except that torture shall not include pain or suffering arising only from, inherent in or incidental to, lawful sanctions	(e) 'Torture' means the intentional infliction of severe pain or suffering, whether physical or mental, upon a person in the custody or under the control of the accused; except that torture shall not include pain or suffering arising only from, inherent in or incidental to, lawful sanctions
(f) 'Forced pregnancy' means the unlawful confinement of a woman forcibly made pregnant, with the intent of affecting the ethnic composition of any population or carrying out other grave violations of international law. This definition shall not in any way be interpreted as affecting national laws relating to pregnancy	(f) 'Forced pregnancy' means the unlawful confinement of a woman forcibly made pregnant, with the intent of affecting the ethnic composition of any population or carrying out other grave violations of international law. This definition shall not in any way be interpreted as affecting national laws relating to pregnancy
(g) 'Persecution' means the intentional and severe deprivation of fundamental rights contrary to international law by reason of the identity of the group or collectivity	(g) 'Persecution' means the intentional and severe deprivation of fundamental rights contrary to international law by reason of the identity of the group or collectivity
(h) 'The crime of apartheid' means inhumane acts of a character similar to those referred to in para 1, committed in the context of an institutionalized regime of systematic oppression and domination by one racial group over any other racial group or groups and committed with the intention of maintaining that regime	(h) 'The crime of apartheid' means inhumane acts of a character similar to those referred to in para 1, committed in the context of an institutionalized regime of systematic oppression and domination by one racial group over any other racial group or groups and committed with the intention of maintaining that regime
(i) 'Enforced disappearance of persons' means the arrest, detention or abduction of persons by, or with the authorization, support or acquiescence of, a State or a political organization, followed by a refusal to acknowledge that deprivation of freedom or to give information on the fate or whereabouts of those persons, with the intention of removing them from the protection of the law for a prolonged period of time	(i) 'Enforced disappearance of persons' means the arrest, detention or abduction of persons by, or with the authorization, support or acquiescence of, a State or a political organization, followed by a refusal to acknowledge that deprivation of freedom or to give information on the fate or whereabouts of those persons, with the intention of removing them from the protection of the law for a prolonged period of time
	3. For the purpose of this Statute, it is understood that the term 'gender' refers to the two sexes, male and female, within the context of society. The term 'gender' does not indicate any meaning different from the above
Article 28D	**Article 8 of the ICC Statute**
War crimes	**War crimes**

Crimes in the Annex to the Malabo Protocol	Sources
For the purposes of this Statute, 'war crimes' means any of the offences listed, in particular when committed as part of a plan or policy or as part of a large scale commission of such crimes	1. The Court shall have jurisdiction in respect of war crimes in particular when committed as part of a plan or policy or as part of a large-scale commission of such crimes
(a) Grave breaches of the Geneva Conventions of 12 August 1949, namely, any of the following acts against persons or property protected under the provisions of the relevant Geneva Convention	2. For the purpose of this Statute, 'war crimes' means: (a) Grave breaches of the Geneva Conventions of 12 August 1949, namely, any of the following acts against persons or property protected under the provisions of the relevant Geneva Convention
(i) Wilful killing	(i) Wilful killing
(ii) Torture or inhuman treatment, including biological experiments	(ii) Torture or inhuman treatment, including biological experiments
(iii) Wilfully causing great suffering, or serious injury to body or health	(iii) Wilfully causing great suffering, or serious injury to body or health
(iv) Extensive destruction and appropriation of property, not justified by military necessity and carried out unlawfully and wantonly	(iv) Extensive destruction and appropriation of property, not justified by military necessity and carried out unlawfully and wantonly
(v) Compelling a prisoner of war or other protected person to serve in the forces of a hostile Power	(v) Compelling a prisoner of war or other protected person to serve in the forces of a hostile Power
(vi) Wilfully depriving a prisoner of war or other protected person of the rights of fair and regular trial	(vi) Wilfully depriving a prisoner of war or other protected person of the rights of fair and regular trial
(vii) Unlawful deportation or transfer or unlawful confinement	(vii) Unlawful deportation or transfer or unlawful confinement
(viii) Taking of hostages	(viii) Taking of hostages
(b) Grave breaches of the First Additional Protocol to the Geneva Conventions of 8 June 1977 and other serious violations of the laws and customs applicable in international armed conflict, within the established framework of international law, namely, any of the following acts	(b) Other serious violations of the laws and customs applicable in international armed conflict, within the established framework of international law, namely, any of the following acts
(i) Intentionally directing attacks against the civilian population as such or against individual civilians not taking direct part in hostilities	(i) Intentionally directing attacks against the civilian population as such or against individual civilians not taking direct part in hostilities
(ii) Intentionally directing attacks against civilian objects, that is, objects which are not military objectives	(ii) Intentionally directing attacks against civilian objects, that is, objects which are not military objectives

Crimes in the Annex to the Malabo Protocol	**Sources**
(iii) Intentionally directing attacks against personnel, installations, material, units or vehicles involved in a humanitarian assistance or peacekeeping mission in accordance with the Charter of the United Nations, as long as they are entitled to the protection given to civilians or civilian objects under the international law of armed conflict	(iii) Intentionally directing attacks against personnel, installations, material, units or vehicles involved in a humanitarian assistance or peacekeeping mission in accordance with the Charter of the United Nations, as long as they are entitled to the protection given to civilians or civilian objects under the international law of armed conflict
(iv) Intentionally launching an attack in the knowledge that such attack will cause incidental loss of life or injury to civilians or damage to civilian objects or widespread, long-term and severe damage to the natural environment which would be clearly excessive in relation to the concrete and direct overall military advantage anticipated	(iv) Intentionally launching an attack in the knowledge that such attack will cause incidental loss of life or injury to civilians or damage to civilian objects or widespread, long-term and severe damage to the natural environment which would be clearly excessive in relation to the concrete and direct overall military advantage anticipated
(v) Intentionally launching an attack against works or installations containing dangerous forces in the knowledge that such attack will cause excessive loss of life, injury to civilians or damage to civilian objects which will be excessive in relation to the concrete and direct overall military advantage anticipated	
(vi) Attacking or bombarding, by whatever means, towns, villages, dwellings or buildings which are undefended and which are not military objectives	(v) Attacking or bombarding, by whatever means, towns, villages, dwellings or buildings which are undefended and which are not military objectives
(vii) Killing or wounding a combatant who, having laid down his arms or having no longer means of defence, has surrendered at discretion	(vi) Killing or wounding a combatant who, having laid down his arms or having no longer means of defence, has surrendered at discretion
(viii) Making improper use of a flag of truce, of the flag or of the military insignia and uniform of the enemy or of the United Nations, as well as of the distinctive emblems of the Geneva Conventions, resulting in death or serious personal injury	(vii) Making improper use of a flag of truce, of the flag or of the military insignia and uniform of the enemy or of the United Nations, as well as of the distinctive emblems of the Geneva Conventions, resulting in death or serious personal injury
(ix) The transfer, directly or indirectly, by the Occupying Power of parts of its own civilian population into the territory it occupies, or the deportation or transfer of all or parts of the population of the occupied territory within or outside this territory	(viii) The transfer, directly or indirectly, by the Occupying Power of parts of its own civilian population into the territory it occupies, or the deportation or transfer of all or parts of the population of the occupied territory within or outside this territory

Crimes in the Annex to the Malabo Protocol	Sources
(x) Intentionally directing attacks against buildings dedicated to religion, education, art, science or charitable purposes, historic monuments, hospitals and places where the sick and wounded are collected, provided they are not military objectives	(ix) Intentionally directing attacks against buildings dedicated to religion, education, art, science or charitable purposes, historic monuments, hospitals and places where the sick and wounded are collected, provided they are not military objectives
(xi) Subjecting persons who are in the power of an adverse party to physical mutilation or to medical or scientific experiments of any kind which are neither justified by the medical, dental or hospital treatment of the person concerned nor carried out in his or her interest, and which cause death to or seriously endanger the health of such person or persons	(x) Subjecting persons who are in the power of an adverse party to physical mutilation or to medical or scientific experiments of any kind which are neither justified by the medical, dental or hospital treatment of the person concerned nor carried out in his or her interest, and which cause death to or seriously endanger the health of such person or persons
(xii) Killing or wounding treacherously individuals belonging to the hostile nation or army	(xi) Killing or wounding treacherously individuals belonging to the hostile nation or army;
(xiii) Declaring that no quarter will be given	(xii) Declaring that no quarter will be given
(xiv) Destroying or seizing the enemy's property unless such destruction or seizure be imperatively demanded by the necessities of war	(xiii) Destroying or seizing the enemy's property unless such destruction or seizure be imperatively demanded by the necessities of war
(xv) Declaring abolished, suspended or inadmissible in a court of law the rights and actions of the nationals of the hostile party	(xiv) Declaring abolished, suspended or inadmissible in a court of law the rights and actions of the nationals of the hostile party
(xvi) Compelling the nationals of the hostile party to take part in the operations of war directed against their own State, even if they were in the belligerent's service before the commencement of the war	(xv) Compelling the nationals of the hostile party to take part in the operations of war directed against their own country, even if they were in the belligerent's service before the commencement of the war
(xvii) Pillaging a town or place, even when taken by assault	(xvi) Pillaging a town or place, even when taken by assault
(xviii) Employing poison or poisoned weapons	(xvii) Employing poison or poisoned weapons
(xix) Employing asphyxiating, poisonous or other gases, and all analogous liquids, materials or devices	(xviii) Employing asphyxiating, poisonous or other gases, and all analogous liquids, materials or devices
(xx) Employing bullets which expand or flatten easily in the human body, such as bullets with a hard envelope which does not entirely cover the core or is pierced with incisions	(xix) Employing bullets which expand or flatten easily in the human body, such as bullets with a hard envelope which does not entirely cover the core or is pierced with incisions

Crimes in the Annex to the Malabo Protocol	Sources
(xxi) Employing weapons, projectiles and material and methods of warfare which are of a nature to cause superfluous injury or unnecessary suffering or which are inherently indiscriminate in violation of the international law of armed conflict	(xx) Employing weapons, projectiles and material and methods of warfare which are of a nature to cause superfluous injury or unnecessary suffering or which are inherently indiscriminate in violation of the international law of armed conflict, provided that such weapons, projectiles and material and methods of warfare are the subject of a comprehensive prohibition and are included in an annex to this Statute, by an amendment in accordance with the relevant provisions set forth in Articles 121 and 123
(xxii) Committing outrages upon personal dignity, in particular humiliating and degrading treatment	(xxi) Committing outrages upon personal dignity, in particular humiliating and degrading treatment
(xxiii) Committing rape, sexual slavery, enforced prostitution, forced pregnancy, enforced sterilization, or any other form of sexual violence also constituting a grave breach of the Geneva Conventions	(xxii) Committing rape, sexual slavery, enforced prostitution, forced pregnancy, as defined in Article 7, para 2(f), enforced sterilization, or any other form of sexual violence also constituting a grave breach of the Geneva Conventions
(xxiv) Utilizing the presence of a civilian or other protected person to render certain points, areas or military forces immune from military operations	(xxiii) Utilizing the presence of a civilian or other protected person to render certain points, areas or military forces immune from military operations
(xxv) Intentionally directing attacks against buildings, material, medical units and transport, and personnel using the distinctive emblems of the Geneva Conventions in conformity with international law	(xxiv) Intentionally directing attacks against buildings, material, medical units and transport, and personnel using the distinctive emblems of the Geneva Conventions in conformity with international law
(xxvi) Intentionally using starvation of civilians as a method of warfare by depriving them of objects indispensable to their survival, including wilfully impeding relief supplies as provided for under the Geneva Conventions	(xxv) Intentionally using starvation of civilians as a method of warfare by depriving them of objects indispensable to their survival, including wilfully impeding relief supplies as provided for under the Geneva Conventions

Crimes in the Annex to the Malabo Protocol	Sources
(xxvii) Conscripting or enlisting children under the age of eighteen years into the national armed forces or using them to participate actively in hostilities	(xxvi) Conscripting or enlisting children under the age of fifteen years into the national armed forces or using them to participate actively in hostilities
(xxviii) Unjustifiably delaying the repatriation of prisoners of war or civilians	
(xxix) Willfully committing practices of apartheid and other inhuman and degrading practices involving outrages upon personal dignity, based on racial discrimination	
(xxx) Making non-defended localities and demilitarised zones the object of attack	
(xxxi) Slavery and deportation to slave labour	
(xxxii) Collective punishments	
(xxxiii) Despoliation of the wounded, sick, shipwrecked or dead	
(c) In the case of an armed conflict not of an international character, serious violations of Article 3 common to the four Geneva Conventions of 12 August 1949, namely, any of the following acts committed against persons taking no active part in the hostilities, including members of armed forces who have laid down their arms and those placed hors de combat by sickness, wounds, detention or any other cause	(c) In the case of an armed conflict not of an international character, serious violations of Article 3 common to the four Geneva Conventions of 12 August 1949, namely, any of the following acts committed against persons taking no active part in the hostilities, including members of armed forces who have laid down their arms and those placed hors de combat by sickness, wounds, detention or any other cause
(i) Violence to life and person, in particular murder of all kinds, mutilation, cruel treatment and torture	(i) Violence to life and person, in particular murder of all kinds, mutilation, cruel treatment and torture
(ii) Committing outrages upon personal dignity, in particular humiliating and degrading treatment	(ii) Committing outrages upon personal dignity, in particular humiliating and degrading treatment
(iii) Taking of hostages	(iii) Taking of hostages
(iv) The passing of sentences and the carrying out of executions without previous judgment pronounced by a regularly constituted court, affording all judicial guarantees which are generally recognized as indispensable	(iv) The passing of sentences and the carrying out of executions without previous judgement pronounced by a regularly constituted court, affording all judicial guarantees which are generally recognized as indispensable
(d) Paragraph (c) applies to armed conflicts not of an international character and thus does not apply to situations of internal disturbances and tensions, such as riots, isolated and sporadic acts of violence or other acts of a similar nature	(d) Paragraph 2(c) applies to armed conflicts not of an international character and thus does not apply to situations of internal disturbances and tensions, such as riots, isolated and sporadic acts of violence or other acts of a similar nature

Crimes in the Annex to the Malabo Protocol	Sources
(e) Other serious violations of the laws and customs applicable in armed conflicts not of an international character, within the established framework of international law, namely, any of the following acts	(e) Other serious violations of the laws and customs applicable in armed conflicts not of an international character, within the established framework of international law, namely, any of the following acts
(i) Intentionally directing attacks against the civilian population as such or against individual civilians not taking direct part in hostilities	(i) Intentionally directing attacks against the civilian population as such or against individual civilians not taking direct part in hostilities
(ii) Intentionally directing attacks against buildings, material, medical units and transport, and personnel using the distinctive emblems of the Geneva Conventions in conformity with international law	(ii) Intentionally directing attacks against buildings, material, medical units and transport, and personnel using the distinctive emblems of the Geneva Conventions in conformity with international law
(iii) Intentionally directing attacks against personnel, installations, material, units or vehicles involved in a humanitarian assistance or peacekeeping mission in accordance with the Charter of the United Nations, as long as they are entitled to the protection given to civilians or civilian objects under the international law of armed conflict	(iii) Intentionally directing attacks against personnel, installations, material, units or vehicles involved in a humanitarian assistance or peacekeeping mission in accordance with the Charter of the United Nations, as long as they are entitled to the protection given to civilians or civilian objects under the international law of armed conflict
(iv) Intentionally directing attacks against buildings dedicated to religion, education, art, science or charitable purposes, historic monuments, hospitals and places where the sick and wounded are collected, provided they are not military objectives	(iv) Intentionally directing attacks against buildings dedicated to religion, education, art, science or charitable purposes, historic monuments, hospitals and places where the sick and wounded are collected, provided they are not military objectives
(v) Pillaging a town or place, even when taken by assault	(v) Pillaging a town or place, even when taken by assault
(vi) Committing rape, sexual slavery, enforced prostitution, forced pregnancy, enforced sterilization, and any other form of sexual violence also constituting a serious violation of Article 3 common to the four Geneva Conventions	(vi) Committing rape, sexual slavery, enforced prostitution, forced pregnancy, as defined in Article 7, para 2(f), enforced sterilization, and any other form of sexual violence also constituting a serious violation of Article 3 common to the four Geneva Conventions
(vii) Conscripting or enlisting children under the age of eighteen years into armed forces or groups or using them to participate actively in hostilities	(vii) Conscripting or enlisting children under the age of fifteen years into armed forces or groups or using them to participate actively in hostilities
(viii) Ordering the displacement of the civilian population for reasons related to the conflict, unless the security of the civilians involved or imperative military reasons so demand	(viii) Ordering the displacement of the civilian population for reasons related to the conflict, unless the security of the civilians involved or imperative military reasons so demand

Crimes in the Annex to the Malabo Protocol	Sources
(ix) Killing or wounding treacherously a combatant adversary	(ix) Killing or wounding treacherously a combatant adversary
(x) Declaring that no quarter will be given	(x) Declaring that no quarter will be given
(xi) Subjecting persons who are in the power of another party to the conflict to physical mutilation or to medical or scientific experiments of any kind which are neither justified by the medical, dental or hospital treatment of the person concerned nor carried out in his or her interest, and which cause death to or seriously endanger the health of such person or persons	(xi) Subjecting persons who are in the power of another party to the conflict to physical mutilation or to medical or scientific experiments of any kind which are neither justified by the medical, dental or hospital treatment of the person concerned nor carried out in his or her interest, and which cause death to or seriously endanger the health of such person or persons
(xii) Destroying or seizing the property of an adversary unless such destruction or seizure be imperatively demanded by the necessities of the conflict	(xii) Destroying or seizing the property of an adversary unless such destruction or seizure be imperatively demanded by the necessities of the conflict
(xiii) Employing poison or poisoned weapons	
(xiv) Employing asphyxiating, poisonous or other gases, and all analogous liquids, materials or devices	
(xv) Employing bullets which expand or flatten easily in the human body, such as bullets with a hard envelope which does not entirely cover the core or is pierced with incisions	
(xvi) Intentionally using starvation of civilians as a method of warfare by depriving them of objects indispensable to their survival, including wilfully impeding relief supplies	
(xvii) Utilizing the presence of a civilian or other protected person to render certain points, areas or military forces immune from military operations	
(xviii) Launching an indiscriminate attack resulting in death or injury to civilians, or an attack in the knowledge that it will cause excessive incidental civilian loss, injury or damage	
(xix) Making non-defended localities and demilitarised zones the object of attack	

Crimes in the Annex to the Malabo Protocol	**Sources**
(xx) Slavery	
(xxi) Collective punishments	
(xxii) Despoliation of the wounded, sick, shipwrecked or dead	
(f) Paragraph (e) applies to armed conflicts not of an international character and thus does not apply to situations of internal disturbances and tensions, such as riots, isolated and sporadic acts of violence or other acts of a similar nature. It applies to armed conflicts that take place in the territory of a State when there is protracted armed conflict between governmental authorities and organized armed groups or between such groups	(f) Paragraph 2(e) applies to armed conflicts not of an international character and thus does not apply to situations of internal disturbances and tensions, such as riots, isolated and sporadic acts of violence or other acts of a similar nature. It applies to armed conflicts that take place in the territory of a State when there is protracted armed conflict between governmental authorities and organized armed groups or between such groups
(g) Using nuclear weapons or other weapons of mass destruction	3. Nothing in paras 2(c) and (e) shall affect the responsibility of a Government to maintain or re-establish law and order in the State or to defend the unity and territorial integrity of the State, by all legitimate means
Article 28E	**Article 23 of the African Charter on Democracy, Election and Governance**
Unconstitutional Change of Government	
1. For the purpose of this statute 'unconstitutional change of government' means committing or ordering to be committed the following acts, with the aim of illegally accessing or maintaining power	State Parties agree that the use of, inter alia, the following illegal means of accessing or maintaining power constitute an unconstitutional change of government and shall draw appropriate sanctions by the Union
(a) A putsch or coup d'état against a democratically elected government	1. Any putsch or coup d'Etat against a democratically elected government
(b) An intervention by mercenaries to replace a democratically elected government	2. Any intervention by mercenaries to replace a democratically elected government
(c) Any replacement of a democratically elected government by the use of armed dissidents or rebels or through political assassination	3. Any replacement of a democratically elected government by armed dissidents or rebels
(d) Any refusal by an incumbent government to relinquish power to the winning party or candidate after free, fair and regular elections	4. Any refusal by an incumbent government to relinquish power to the winning party or candidate after free, fair and regular elections; or

Crimes in the Annex to the Malabo Protocol	Sources
(e) Any amendment or revision of the Constitution or legal instruments, which is an infringement on the principles of democratic change of government or is inconsistent with the Constitution	5. Any amendment or revision of the constitution or legal instruments, which is an infringement on the principles of democratic change of government
(f) Any substantial modification to the electoral laws in the last six (6) months before the elections without the consent of the majority of the political actors	
2. For purposes of this Statute, "democratically elected government" has the same meaning as contained in AU instruments."	
Article 29F	**Article 101 of the United Nations Convention on the Law of the Sea (1982)**
Piracy	**Definition of Piracy**
Piracy consists of any of the following acts	Piracy consists of any of the following acts
(a) any illegal acts of violence or detention, or any act of depredation, committed for private ends by the crew or the passengers of a private boat, ship or a private aircraft, and directed: i. on the high seas, against another boat, ship or aircraft, or against persons or property on board such boat, ship or aircraft; ii. against a boat, ship, aircraft, persons or property in a place outside the jurisdiction of any State	(a) any illegal acts of violence or detention, or any act of depredation, committed for private ends by the crew or the passengers of a private ship or a private aircraft, and directed: (i) on the high seas, against another ship or aircraft, or against persons or property on board such ship or aircraft; (ii) against a ship, aircraft, persons or property in a place outside the jurisdiction of any State
(b) any act of voluntary participation in the operation of a boat, ship or of an aircraft with knowledge of facts making it a pirate boat, ship or aircraft	(b) any act of voluntary participation in the operation of a ship or of an aircraft with knowledge of facts making it a pirate ship or aircraft
(c) any act of inciting or of intentionally facilitating an act described in subpara (a) or (b)	(c) any act of inciting or of intentionally facilitating an act described in subpara (a) or (b)."
Article 28G Terrorism	**Article1(3) cum Article 2 of the Organization of African Unity Convention on the Prevention and Combating of Terrorism (1999)**
For the purposes of this Statute, 'terrorism' means any of the following acts	"Terrorist act" means

Crimes in the Annex to the Malabo Protocol	Sources
A. Any act which is a violation of the criminal laws of a State Party, the laws of the African Union or a regional economic community recognized by the African Union, or by international law, and which may endanger the life, physical integrity or freedom of, or cause serious injury or death to, any 27 person, any number or group of persons or causes or may cause damage to public or private property, natural resources, environmental or cultural heritage and is calculated or intended to	(a) any act which is a violation of the criminal laws of a State Party and which may endanger the life, physical integrity or freedom of, or cause serious injury or death to, any person, any number or group of persons or causes or may cause damage to public or private property, natural resources, environmental or cultural heritage and is calculated or intended to
1. intimidate, put in fear, force, coerce or induce any government, body, institution, the general public or any segment thereof, to do or abstain from doing any act, or to adopt or abandon a particular standpoint, or to act according to certain principles; or	(i) intimidate, put in fear, force, coerce or induce any government, body, institution, the general public or any segment thereof, to do or abstain from doing any act, or to adopt or abandon a particular standpoint, or to act according to certain principles; or
2. disrupt any public service, the delivery of any essential service to the public or to create a public emergency; or	(ii) disrupt any public service, the delivery of any essential service to the public or to create a public emergency; or
3. create general insurrection in a State	(iii) create general insurrection in a State
B. Any promotion, sponsoring, contribution to, command, aid, incitement, encouragement, attempt, threat, conspiracy, organizing, or procurement of any person, with the intent to commit any act referred to in sub-para (a) (1) to (3)	(b) any promotion, sponsoring, contribution to, command, aid, incitement, encouragement, attempt, threat, conspiracy, organizing, or procurement of any person, with the intent to commit any act referred to in para (a) (i) to(iii)
[…]	
Article 28H **Mercenarism**	**Article 1 of the Organization of African Unity Convention for the Elimination of Mercenarism in Africa (1977)**
1. For the purposes of this Statute: (a) A mercenary is any person who i. Is specially recruited locally or abroad in order to fight in an armed conflict	1. A mercenary is any person who (a) is specially recruited locally or abroad in order to fight in an armed conflict (b) does in fact take a direct part in the hostilities
ii. Is motivated to take part in the hostilities essentially by the desire for private gain and, in fact, is promised, by or on behalf of a party to the conflict, material compensation	(c) is motivated to take part in the hostilities essentially by the desire for private gain and in fact is promised by or on behalf of a party to the conflict material compensation
iii. Is neither a national of a party to the conflict nor a resident of territory controlled by a party to the conflict	(d) is neither a national of a party to the conflict nor a resident of territory controlled by a party to the conflict

Crimes in the Annex to the Malabo Protocol	Sources
iv. Is not a member of the armed forces of a party to the conflict; and	(e) is not a member of the armed forces of a party to the conflict; and
v. Has not been sent by a State which is not a party to the conflict on official duty as a member of its armed forces	(f) is not sent by a state other than a party to the conflict on official mission as a member of the armed forces of the said state
(b) A mercenary is also any person who, in any other situation	2. The crime of mercenarism is committed by the individual, group or association, representative of a State and the State itself who with the aim of opposing by armed violence a process of self-determination stability or the territorial integrity of another State, that practises any of the following acts
i. Is specially recruited locally or abroad for the purpose of participating in a concerted act of violence aimed at	(a) Shelters, organises, finances, assists, equips, trains, promotes, supports or in any manner employs bands of mercenaries
1. Overthrowing a legitimate Government or otherwise undermining the constitutional order of a State	
2. Assisting a government to maintain power	(b) Enlists, enrols or tries to enrol in the said bands
3. Assisting a group of persons to obtain power; or	(c) Allows the activities mentioned in para (a) to be carried out in any territory under its jurisdiction or in any place under its control or affords facilities for transit, transport or other operations of the above mentioned forces
4. Undermining the territorial integrity of a State; ii. Is motivated to take part therein essentially by the desire for private gain and is prompted by the promise or payment of material compensation; [...]	
2. Any person who recruits, uses, finances or trains mercenaries, as defined in para (1) (a) or (b) above commits an offence. 3. A mercenary, as defined in para (1)(a) or (b) above, who participates directly in hostilities or in a concerted act of violence, as the case may be, commits an offence	3. Any person, natural or juridical who commits the crime of mercenarism as defined in para 1 of this Article commits an offence considered as a crime against peace and security in Africa and shall be punished as such
Article 28I	**Article 4 of the African Union Convention on Preventing and Combating Corruption (2003)**
Corruption	
For the purposes of this Statute, the following shall be deemed to be acts of corruption if they are of a serious nature affecting the stability of a state, region or the Union	1. This Convention is applicable to the following acts of corruption and related offences

Crimes in the Annex to the Malabo Protocol	**Sources**
(a) The solicitation or acceptance, directly or indirectly, by a public official, his/her family member or any other person, of any goods of monetary value, or other benefit, such as a gift, favour, promise or advantage for himself or herself or for another person or entity, in exchange for any act or omission in the performance of his or her public functions	(a) the solicitation or acceptance, directly or indirectly, by a public official or any other person, of any goods of monetary value, or other benefit, such as a gift, favour, promise or advantage for himself or herself or for another person or entity, in exchange for any act or omission in the performance of his or her public functions
(b) The offering or granting, directly or indirectly, to a public official, his/family member or any other person, of any goods of monetary value, or other benefit, such as a gift, favour, promise or advantage for himself or herself or for another person or entity, in exchange for any act or omission in the performance of his or her public functions	(b) the offering or granting, directly or indirectly, to a public official or any other person, of any goods of monetary value, or other benefit, such as a gift, favour, promise or advantage for himself or herself or for another person or entity, in exchange for any act or omission in the performance of his or her public functions
(c) Any act or omission in the discharge of his or her duties by a public official. his/her family member or any other person for the purpose of illicitly obtaining benefits for himself or herself or for a third party	(c) any act or omission in the discharge of his or her duties by a public official or any other person for the purpose of illicitly obtaining benefits for himself or herself or for a third party
(d) The diversion by a public official, his/her family member or any other person, for purposes unrelated to those for which they were intended, for his or her own benefit or that of a third party, of any property belonging to the State or its agencies, to an independent agency, or to an individual, that such official has received by virtue of his or her position	(d) the diversion by a public official or any other person, for purposes unrelated to those for which they were intended, for his or her own benefit or that of a third party, of any property belonging to the State or its agencies, to an independent agency, or to an individual, that such official has received by virtue of his or her position
(e) The offering or giving, promising, solicitation or acceptance, directly or indirectly, of any undue advantage to or by any person who directs or works for, in any capacity, a private sector entity, for himself or herself or for anyone else, for him or her to act, or refrain from acting, in breach of his or her duties	(e) the offering or giving, promising, solicitation or acceptance, directly or indirectly, of any undue advantage to or by any person who directs or works for, in any capacity, a private sector entity, for himself or herself or for anyone else, for him or her to act, or refrain from acting, in breach of his or her duties
(f) The offering, giving, solicitation or acceptance directly or indirectly, or promising of any undue advantage to or by any person who asserts or confirms that he or she is able to exert any improper influence over the decision making of any person performing functions in the public or private sector in consideration thereof, whether the undue advantage is for himself or herself or for anyone else, as well as the request, receipt or the acceptance of the offer or the promise of such an advantage, in consideration of that influence, whether or not the influence is exerted or whether or not the supposed influence leads to the intended result	(f) the offering, giving, solicitation or acceptance directly or indirectly, or promising of any undue advantage to or by any person who asserts or confirms that he or she is able to exert any improper influence over the decision making of any person performing functions in the public or private sector in consideration thereof, whether the undue advantage is for himself or herself or for anyone else, as well as the request, receipt or the acceptance of the offer or the promise of such an advantage, in consideration of that influence, whether or not the influence is exerted or whether or not the supposed influence leads to the intended result

Crimes in the Annex to the Malabo Protocol	Sources
(g) Illicit enrichment	(g) illicit enrichment
(h) The use or concealment of proceeds derived from any of the acts referred to in this Article	(h) the use or concealment of proceeds derived from any of the acts referred to in this Article; and
[…]	(i) participation as a principal, co-principal, agent, instigator, accomplice or accessory after the fact, or on any other manner in the commission or attempted commission of, in any collaboration or conspiracy to commit, any of the acts referred to in this article
	2. This Convention shall also be applicable by mutual agreement between or among two or more State Parties with respect to any other act or practice of corruption and related offences not described in this Convention
Article 28I*bis*	**Article 6 of the African Union Convention on Preventing and Combating Corruption (2003)**
Money Laundering	**Laundering of the Proceeds of Corruption**
1. For the purposes of this Statute, 'Money Laundering' means: any act of—	States Parties shall adopt such legislative and other measures as may be necessary to establish as criminal offences
(i) Conversion, transfer or disposal of property, knowing that such property is the proceeds of corruption or related offences for the purpose of concealing or disguising the illicit origin of the property or of helping any person who is involved in the commission of the offence to evade the legal consequences of his or her action	(a) The conversion, transfer or disposal of property, knowing that such property is the proceeds of corruption or related offences for the purpose of concealing or disguising the illicit origin of the property or of helping any person who is involved in the commission of the offence to evade the legal consequences of his or her action
(ii) Concealment or disguise of the true nature, source, location, disposition, movement or ownership of or rights with respect to property which is the proceeds of corruption or related offences	(b) The concealment or disguise of the true nature, source, location, disposition, movement or ownership of or rights with respect to property which is the proceeds of corruption or related offences
(iii) Acquisition, possession or use of property with the knowledge at the time of receipt, that such property is the proceeds of corruption or related offences	(c) The acquisition, possession or use of property with the knowledge at the time of receipt, that such property is the proceeds of corruption or related offences
(iv) Participation in, association with or conspiracy to commit, attempts to commit and aiding, abetting, facilitating and counselling the commission of any of the offences established in accordance with this article	
2. Nothing in this article shall be interpreted as prejudicing the power of the Court to make a determination as to the seriousness of any act or offence	

Crimes in the Annex to the Malabo Protocol	Sources
Article 28J	**Article 3 of Protocol to Prevent, Suppress and Punish Trafficking in Persons, especially Women and Children, supplementing the United Nations Convention against Transnational Organized Crime (2000)**
Trafficking in persons	
For the purposes of this Statute	
1. "Trafficking in persons" means the recruitment, transportation, transfer, harbouring or receipt of persons, by means of the threat or use of force or other forms of coercion, of abduction, of fraud, of deception, of the abuse of power or of a position of vulnerability or of the giving or receiving of payments or benefits to achieve the consent of a person having control over another person, for the purpose of exploitation 2. Exploitation shall include the exploitation of the prostitution of others or other forms of sexual exploitation, forced labour or services, slavery or practices similar to slavery, servitude or the removal of organs	(a) "Trafficking in persons" shall mean the recruitment, transportation, transfer, harbouring or receipt of persons, by means of the threat or use of force or other forms of coercion, of abduction, of fraud, of deception, of the abuse of power or of a position of vulnerability or of the giving or receiving of payments or benefits to achieve the consent of a person having control over another person, for the purpose of exploitation. Exploitation shall include, at a minimum, the exploitation of the prostitution of others or other forms of sexual exploitation, forced labour or services, slavery or practices similar to slavery, servitude or the removal of organs
3. The consent of a victim of trafficking in persons to the intended exploitation set forth in subpara (1) of this article shall be irrelevant where any of the means set forth in subpara (1) have been used	(b) The consent of a victim of trafficking in persons to the intended exploitation set forth in subpara (a) of this article shall be irrelevant where any of the means set forth in subpara (a) have been used
4. The recruitment, transportation, transfer, harbouring or receipt of a child for the purpose of exploitation shall be considered "trafficking in persons" even if this does not involve any of the means set forth in subpara (1) of this article	(c) The recruitment, transportation, transfer, harbouring or receipt of a child for the purpose of exploitation shall be considered "trafficking in persons" even if this does not involve any of the means set forth in subpara (a) of this article
	(d) "Child" shall mean any person under eighteen years of age
Article 28K	**Article (1)(j)(l) and Article 2 of**
Trafficking in drugs	**The Single Convention on Narcotic Drugs of 1961 as amended by the 1972 Protocol, the Convention on Psychotropic Substances of 1971; and Article 1(e)(i)(j) of the United Nationks Convention against Illicit Traffic in Narcotic Drugs and Psychotropic Substances of 1988, respectively.**

Crimes in the Annex to the Malabo Protocol	Sources
1. For the purposes of this Statute, trafficking in drugs means	Illicit traffic (in drugs) means cultivation or trafficking in drugs (any of the substances in Schedules I and II, whether natural or synthetic) contrary to the provisions of this Convention.'
(a) The production, manufacture, extraction, preparation, offering, offering for sale, distribution, sale, delivery on any terms whatsoever, brokerage, dispatch, dispatch in transit, transport, importation or exportation of drugs	Illicit traffic (in psychotropic substances) means manufacture (all processes by which psychotropic substances (any substance, natural or synthetic, or any natural material in Schedule I, II, III or IV) may be obtained, and includes refining as well as the transformation of psychotropic substances into other psychotropic substances. The term also includes the making of preparations other than those made on prescription in pharmacies) of or trafficking in psychotropic substances contrary to the provisions of this Convention
(b) The cultivation of opium poppy, coca bush or cannabis plant	
(c) The possession or purchase of drugs with a view to conducting one of the activities listed in (a)	
(d) The manufacture, transport or distribution of precursors knowing that they are to be used in or for the illicit production or manufacture of drugs	
2. The conduct described in para 1 shall not be included in the scope of this Statute when it is committed by perpetrators for their own personal consumption as defined by national law	
3. For the purposes of this Article	
(A) "Drugs" shall mean any of the substances covered by the following United Nations Conventions	
(a) The 1961 Single Convention on Narcotic Drugs, as amended by the 1972 Protocol Amending the Single Convention on Narcotic Drugs of 1961	
(b) The 1971 Vienna Convention on Psychotropic Substances	
B. "Precursors" shall mean any substance scheduled pursuant to Article 12 of the United Nations Convention against Illicit Traffic in Narcotic Drugs and Psychotropic Substances of 20 December 1988	

Crimes in the Annex to the Malabo Protocol	Sources
Article 28L	**Article 2 of the Bamako Convention on the Ban of the Import into Africa and the Control of Transboundary Movement and Management of Hazardous Wastes within Africa (1991)**
Trafficking in Hazardous Wastes	
1. For the purposes of this Statute, any import or failure to re-import, transboundary movement, or export of hazardous wastes proscribed by the Bamako Convention on the Ban of the Import into Africa and the Control of Transboundary Movement and Management of Hazardous Wastes within Africa, adopted in Bamako, Mali, in January 1991 shall constitute the offence of trafficking in hazardous waste	
2. The following substances shall be "hazardous wastes" for the purpose of this statute	Scope of Application of the Convention 1. The following substances shall be "hazardous wastes" for the purposes of this convention
(a) Wastes that belong to any category contained in Annex I of the Bamako Convention	(a) Wastes that belong to any category contained in Annex I of this Convention
(b) Wastes that are not covered under para (a) above but are defined as, or are considered to be, hazardous wastes by the domestic legislation of the State of export, import or transit	(b) Wastes that are not covered under para (a) above but are defined as, or are considered to be, hazardous wastes by the domestic legislation of the State of export, import or transit
(c) Wastes which possess any of the characteristics contained in Annex II of the Bamako Convention	(c) Wastes which possess any of the characteristics contained in Annex II of this Convention
(d) Hazardous substances which have been banned, cancelled or refused registration by government regulatory action, or voluntarily withdrawn from registration in the State of manufacture, for human health or environmental reasons	(d) Hazardous substances which have been banned, cancelled or refused registration by government regulatory action, or voluntarily withdrawn from registration in the country of manufacture, for human health or environmental reasons
3. Wastes which, as a result of being radioactive, are subject to any international control systems, including international instruments, applying specifically to radioactive materials are included in the scope of this Convention	2. Wastes which, as a result of being radioactive, are subject to any international control systems, including international instruments, applying specifically to radioactive materials are included in the scope of this Convention
4. Wastes which derive from the normal operations of a ship, the discharge of which is covered by another international instrument, shall not fall within the scope of this Convention	3. Wastes which derive from the normal operations of a ship, the discharge of which is covered by another international instrument, shall not fall within the scope of this Convention
5. For the purposes of this Article, "failure to re-import" shall have the same meaning assigned to it in the Bamako Convention	
6. The export of hazardous waste into a Member State for the purpose of rendering it safe shall not constitute an offence under this Article	

Crimes in the Annex to the Malabo Protocol	**Sources**
Article 28L*bis* **Illicit Exploitation of Natural Resources**	**Article 13 of the African Union Protocol Against the Illegal Exploitation of Natural Resources (2006)**
For the purpose of this Statute, "Illicit exploitation of natural resources" means any of the following acts if they are of a serious nature affecting the stability of a state, region or the Union	Each Member State shall adopt, in accordance with the fundamental principle of its law, legislative measures and other measures that are necessary to establish as criminal offences
(a) Concluding an agreement to exploit resources, in violation of the principle of peoples' sovereignty over their natural resources	(a)The conversion or transfer of property, with knowledge that such property was obtained from the proceeds of natural resources that have been exploited illegally, or concealing or disguising the illegal origin of the property concerned, or helping any person who is involved in the illegal exploitation of natural resources to evade the legal consequences of his or her acts
(b) Concluding with state authorities an agreement to exploit natural resources, in violation of the legal and regulatory procedures of the State concerned	(b) The concealment or conspiracy to conceal or disguise the true nature, source, location, disposition, movement or ownership of the property in question, with knowledge that such property was obtained from, or with, the proceeds gained from the illegal exploitation of natural resources
(c) Concluding an agreement to exploit natural resources through corrupt practices	(c) The acquisition, possession or use of property by a person who knows or knew, at the time of receipt, possession or use of such property, that it was obtained from, or with, the proceeds gained from the illegal exploitation of natural resources
(d) Concluding an agreement to exploit natural resources that is clearly one-sided	
(e) Exploiting natural resources without any agreement with the State concerned	
(f) Exploiting natural resources without complying with norms relating to the protection of the environment and the security of the people and the staff; and	
(g) Violating the norms and standards established by the relevant natural resource certification mechanism	

Crimes in the Annex to the Malabo Protocol	Sources
Article 28M	**Article 8*bis*of the ICC Statute**
Crime of Aggression	
A. For the purpose of this Statute, "Crime of Aggression" means the planning, preparation, initiation or execution, by a person in a position effectively to exercise control over or to direct the political or military action of a state or organization, whether connected to the state or not of an act of aggression which, by its character, gravity and scale, constitutes a manifest violation of the Charter of the United Nations or the Constitutive Act of the African Union and with regard to the territorial integrity and human security of the population of a State Party."	1. For the purpose of this Statute, "crime of aggression" means the planning, preparation, initiation or execution, by a person in a position effectively to exercise control over or to direct the political or military action of a State, of an act of aggression which, by its character, gravity and scale, constitutes a manifest violation of the Charter of the United Nations
B. The following shall constitute acts of aggression, regardless of a declaration of war by a State, group of States, organizations of States, or non-State actor(s) or by any foreign entity	
(a) The use of armed forces against the sovereignty, territorial integrity and political independence of any state, or any other act inconsistent with the provisions of the Constitutive Act of the African Union and the Charter of the United Nations	2. For the purpose of para 1, "act of aggression" means the use of armed force by a State against the sovereignty, territorial integrity or political independence of another State, or in any other manner inconsistent with the Charter of the United Nations. Any of the following acts, regardless of a declaration of war, shall, in accordance with United Nations General Assembly resolution 3314 (XXIX) of 14 December 1974, qualify as an act of aggression
(b) The invasion or attack by armed forces against the territory of a State, or military occupation however temporary, resulting from such an invasion or attack, or any annexation by the use of force of the territory of a State or part thereof	(a) The invasion or attack by the armed forces of a State of the territory of another State, or any military occupation, however temporary, resulting from such invasion or attack, or any annexation by the use of force of the territory of another State or part thereof
(c) The bombardment by the armed forces of a State against the territory of another State or the use of any weapons by a State against the territory of another State	(b) Bombardment by the armed forces of a State against the territory of another State or the use of any weapons by a State against the territory of another State
(d) The blockade of the ports, coasts or airspace of a State by the armed forces of another State	(c) The blockade of the ports or coasts of a State by the armed forces of another State;

Crimes in the Annex to the Malabo Protocol	Sources
(e) The attack by the armed forces of a State on the land, sea or air forces, or marine and fleets of another State	(d) An attack by the armed forces of a State on the land, sea or air forces, or marine and air fleets of another State
(f) The use of the armed forces of one State which are within the territory of another State with the agreement of the receiving State, in contravention of the conditions provided for in the African Union Non-Aggression and Common Defence Pact or any extension of their presence in such territory beyond the termination of the agreement	(e) The use of armed forces of one State which are within the territory of another State with the agreement of the receiving State, in contravention of the conditions provided for in the agreement or any extension of their presence in such territory beyond the termination of the agreement
(g) The action of a State in allowing its territory, which it has placed at the disposal of another State to be used by another State for perpetrating an act of aggression against a third State	(f) The action of a State in allowing its territory, which it has placed at the disposal of another State, to be used by that other State for perpetrating an act of aggression against a third State
(h) The sending or materially supporting by or on behalf of a State of armed bands, groups, irregulars or mercenaries, which carry out acts of armed force against another State of such gravity as to amount to the acts listed above, or its substantial involvement therein	(g) The sending by or on behalf of a State of armed bands, groups, irregulars o mercenaries, which carry out acts of armed force against another State of such gravity as to amount to the acts listed above, or its substantial involvement therein

PROTOCOL ON THE STATUTE OF THE AFRICAN COURT OF JUSTICE AND HUMAN RIGHTS 1 July 2008 (Merger Protocol)

TABLE OF CONTENTS

PROTOCOL

CHAPTER II: TRANSITIONAL PROVISIONS

CHAPTER III: FINAL PROVISIONS

STATUTE OF THE AFRICAN COURT OF JUSTICE AND HUMAN RIGHTS

CHAPTER I: GENERAL PROVISIONS

CHAPTER II: ORGANIZATION OF THE COURT

PROTOCOL ON THE STATUTE OF THE AFRICAN COURT OF JUSTICE AND HUMAN RIGHTS

The Member States of the African Union, Parties to this Protocol,

RECALLING the objectives and principles enunciated in the Constitutive Act of the African Union, adopted on 11 July 2000 in Lomé, Togo, in particular the commitment to settle their disputes through peaceful means;

BEARING IN MIND their commitment to promote peace, security and stability on the Continent and to protect human and peoples' rights in accordance with the African Charter on Human and Peoples' Rights and other relevant instruments relating to human rights;

CONSIDERING that the Constitutive Act of the African Union provides for the establishment of a Court of Justice charged with hearing, among other things, all cases relating to interpretation or application of the said Act or of all other Treaties adopted within the framework of the Union;

FURTHER CONSIDERING Decisions Assembly/AU/Dec.45 (III) and Assembly/AU/Dec.83 (V) of the Assembly of the Union, adopted respectively at its Third (6–8 July 2004, Addis Ababa, Ethiopia) and Fifth (4–5 July 2005, Sirte, Libya), Ordinary Sessions, to merge the African Court on Human and Peoples' Rights and the Court of Justice of the African Union into a single Court,

FIRMLY CONVINCED that the establishment of an African Court of Justice and Human Rights shall assist in the achievement of the goals pursued by the African Union and that the attainment of the objectives of the African Charter on Human and Peoples' Rights requires the establishment of a judicial organ to supplement and strengthen the mission of the African Commission on Human and Peoples' Rights as well as the African Committee of Experts on the Rights and Welfare of the Child;

TAKING DUE ACCOUNT of the Protocol to the African Charter on Human and Peoples' Rights on the Establishment an African Court on Human and Peoples' Rights, adopted by the Assembly of Heads of States and Governments of the Organization of African Unity on 10 June 1998 at Ouagadougou, Burkina Faso, and which entered into force on 25 January 2004;

TAKING DUE ACCOUNT ALSO of the Protocol of the Court of Justice of the African Union, adopted by the Assembly of the Union on 11 July 2003 in Maputo Mozambique;

RECALLING their commitment to take all necessary measures to strengthen their common institutions and to endow them with the necessary powers and resources to carry out their missions effectively;

COGNIZANT of the Protocol to the African Charter on Human and Peoples' Rights on the Rights of Women in Africa, and the commitments contained in the Solemn Declaration on the gender equality in Africa (Assembly/AU/Decl.12 (III) adopted by the Assembly of the Union respectively at its Second and Third ordinary sessions held in July 2003 and 2004, in Maputo, Mozambique and in Addis Ababa, Ethiopia);

Convinced that that the present Protocol shall supplement the mandate and efforts of other continental treaty bodies as well as national institutions in protecting human rights:

HAVE AGREED AS FOLLOWS:

CHAPTER I

MERGER OF THE AFRICAN COURT ON HUMAN AND PEOPLES' RIGHTS AND THE COURT OF JUSTICE OF THE AFRICAN UNION

Article 1
Replacement of the 1998 and 2003 Protocols

The Protocol to the African Charter on Human and Peoples' Rights on the Establishment of an African Court on Human and Peoples' Rights, adopted on 10 June 1998 in Ouagadougou, Burkina Faso and which entered into force on 25 January 2004, and the Protocol of the Court of Justice of the African Union, adopted on 11 July 2003 in Maputo, Mozambique, are hereby replaced by the present Protocol and Statute annexed as its integral part hereto, subject to the provisions of Articles 5, 7 and 9 of this Protocol.

Article 2
Establishment of a single Court

The African Court on Human and Peoples' Rights established by the Protocol to the African Charter on Human and Peoples' Rights on the Establishment of an African Court on Human and Peoples' Rights and the Court of Justice of the African Union established by the Constitutive Act of the African Union, are hereby merged into a single Court and established as "The African Court of Justice and Human Rights."

Article 3
Reference to the single Court in the Constitutive Act

References made to the "Court of Justice" in the Constitutive Act of the African Union shall be read as references to the "African Court of Justice and Human Rights" established under Article 2 of this Protocol.

CHAPTER II
TRANSITIONAL PROVISIONS

Article 4
Term of Office of the Judges of the African Court on Human and Peoples' Rights

The term of office of the Judges of the African Court on Human and Peoples' Rights shall end following the election of the Judges of the African Court of Justice and Human Rights. However, the Judges shall remain in office until the newly elected Judges of the African Court of Justice and Human Rights are sworn in.

Article 5
Cases Pending before the African Court on Human and Peoples' Rights

Cases pending before the African Court on Human and Peoples' Rights, that have not been concluded before the entry into force of the present Protocol, shall be transferred to the Human Rights Section of the African Court of Justice and Human Rights on the understanding that such cases shall be dealt with In accordance with the protocol to the ACHPR on the establishment of the African Court on Human and Peoples' Rights.

Article 6
Registry of the Court

The Registrar of the African Court on Human and Peoples' Rights shall remain in office until the appointment of a new Registrar for the African Court of Justice and Human Rights.

Article 7
Provisional validity of the 1998 Protocol

The Protocol to the African Charter on Human and Peoples' Rights on the Establishment of an African Court on Human and Peoples' Rights shall remain in force for a transitional period not exceeding one (1) year or any other period determined by the Assembly, after entry into force of the present Protocol, to enable the African Court on Human and Peoples' Rights to take the necessary measures for the transfer of its prerogatives, assets, rights and obligations to the African Court of Justice and Human Rights.

CHAPTER III
FINAL PROVISIONS

Article 8
Signature, Ratification and Accession

1. The present Protocol shall be open for signature, ratification or accession by Member States, in accordance with their respective constitutional procedures.

2. The instruments of ratification or accession to the present Protocol shall be deposited with the Chairperson of the Commission of the African Union.
3. Any Member State may, at the time of signature or when depositing its instrument of ratification or accession, or at any time thereafter, make a declaration accepting the competence of the Court to receive cases under Article 30(f) involving a State which has not made such a declaration.

Article 9
Entry into force

1. The present Protocol and the Statute annexed to it shall enter into force thirty (30) days after the deposit of the instruments of ratification by fifteen (15) Member States.
2. For each Member State which shall ratify or accede to it subsequently, the present Protocol shall enter into force on the date on which the instruments of ratification or accession are deposited,
3. The Chairperson of the Commission shall inform all Member States of the entry into force of the present Protocol.

ADOPTED BY THE ELEVENTH ORDINARY SESSION OF THE ASSEMBLY, HELD IN SHARM EL-SHEIKH, EGYPT, 1ST JULY 2008

ANNEX

STATUTE OF THE AFRICAN COURT OF JUSTICE AND HUMAN RIGHTS

CHAPTER I
GENERAL PROVISIONS

Article 1
Definitions

In this Statute, except otherwise indicated, the following shall mean:

"African Charter" means the African Charter on Human and Peoples' Rights;
"African Commission" means the African Commission on Human and Peoples' Rights;
"African Committee of Experts" means the African Committee of Experts on the Rights and Welfare of the Child;
"African Intergovernmental Organisations" means an organisation that has been established with the aim of ensuring socio-economic integration, and to which some Member States have ceded certain competences to act on their behalf, as well as other sub-regional, regional or inter-African Organisations;

"African Non-Governmental Organizations" means Non-Governmental Organizations at the sub-regional, regional or inter-African levels as well as those in the Diaspora as may be defined by the Executive Council;

"Agent" means a person mandated in writing to represent a party in a case before the Court;

"Assembly" means the Assembly of Heads of State and Government of the Union;

"Chamber(s)" means a Chamber established in accordance with Article 19 of the Statute.

"Constitutive Act" means the Constitutive Act of the African Union;

"Commission": means the Commission of the Union;

"Court" means the African Court of Justice and Human Rights as well as its sections and chambers;

"Executive Council" means the Executive Council of Ministers of the Union;

"Full Court" means joint sitting of the General Affairs and Human Rights Sections of the Court;

"Human Rights Section" means the Human and Peoples' Rights Section of the Court;

"Judge" means a judge of the Court;

"Member State" means a Member State of the Union;

"National Human Rights Institutions" means public institutions established by a state to promote and protect human rights;

"President" means the President of the Court elected in accordance with Article 22(1) of the Statute;

"Protocol" means the Protocol to the Statute of the African Court of Justice and Human Rights;

"Registrar" means the person appointed as such in accordance with Article 22(4) of the Statute;

"Rules" means the Rules of the Court;

"Section" means the General Affairs or the Human Rights Section of the Court;

"Senior Judge" means the person defined as such in the Rules of Court;

"States Parties" means Member States, which have ratified or acceded to this Protocol;

"Statute" means the present Statute;

"Union" means the African Union established by the Constitutive Act;

"Vice President" means the Vice President of the Court elected in accordance with Article 22(1) of the Statute.

Article 2
Functions of the Court

1. The African Court of Justice and Human Rights shall be the main judicial organ of the African Union.
2. The Court shall be constituted and function in accordance with the provisions of the present Statute.

CHAPTER II
ORGANIZATION OF THE COURT

Article 3
Composition

1. The Court shall consist of sixteen (16) Judges who are nationals of States Parties. Upon recommendation of the Court, the Assembly, may, review the number of Judges.
2. The Court shall not, at any one time, have more than one judge from a single Member State.
3. Each geographical region of the Continent, as determined by the Decisions of the Assembly shall, where possible, be represented by three (3) Judges except the Western Region which shall have four (4) Judges.

Article 4
Qualifications of Judges

The Court shall be composed of impartial and independent Judges elected from among persons of high moral character, who possess the qualifications required in their respective countries for appointment to the highest judicial offices, or are juris-consults of recognized competence and experience in international law and/or, human rights law.

Article 5
Presentation of Candidates

1. As soon as the Protocol to this Statute enters into force, the Chairperson of the Commission shall invite each State Party to submit, in writing, within a period of ninety (90) days, candidatures to the post of judge of the Court.
2. Each State Party may present up to two (2) candidates and shall take into account equitable gender representation in the nomination process.

Article 6
List of candidates

1. For the purpose of election, the Chairperson of the Commission shall establish two alphabetical lists of candidates presented as follows:

   i) List A containing the names of candidates having recognized competence and experience in International law; and
   ii) List B containing the names of candidates possessing recognized competence and experience in Human Rights law.

2. States Parties that nominate candidates possessing the competences required on the two lists shall choose the list on which their candidates may be placed.

3. At the first election, eight (8) Judges shall be elected from amongst the candidates of list A and eight (8) from among the candidates of list B. The elections shall be organized in a way as to maintain the same proportion of judges elected on the two lists.
4 The Chairperson of the Commission shall communicate the two lists to Member States, at least thirty (30) days before the Ordinary Session of the Assembly or of the Council, during which the elections shall take place.

Article 7
Election of judges

1. The Judges shall be elected by the Executive Council, and appointed by the Assembly.
2. They shall be elected through secret ballot by a two-thirds majority of Member States with voting rights, from among the candidates provided for in Article 6 of this Statute.
3. Candidates who obtain the two-thirds majority and the highest number of votes shall be elected. However, if several rounds of election are required, the candidates with the least number of votes shall withdraw.
4. The Assembly shall ensure that in the Court as a whole there is equitable representation of the regions and the principal legal traditions of the Continent.
5. In the election of the Judges, the Assembly shall ensure that there is equitable gender representation.

Article 8
Term of Office

1. The Judges shall be elected for a period of six (6) years and may be re-elected only once. However, the term of office of eight (8) judges, four (4) from each section, elected during the first election shall end after four (4) years.
2. The Judges, whose term of office shall end after the initial period of four (4) years, shall be determined for each section, by lot drawn by the Chairperson of the Assembly or the Executive Council, immediately after the first election.
3. A Judge, elected to replace another whose term of office has not expired, shall complete the term of office of his predecessor.
4. All the Judges except the President and the Vice-President, shall perform their functions on a part-time basis.

Article 9
Resignation, Suspension and Removal from Office

1. A Judge may resign his/her position in writing addressed to the President for transmission to the Chairperson of the Assembly through the Chairperson of the Commission.

2. A Judge shall not be suspended or removed from office save, where, on the recommendation of two-thirds majority of the other members, he/she no longer meets the requisite conditions to be a Judge.
3. The President shall communicate the recommendation for the suspension or removal of a Judge to the Chairperson of the Assembly through the Chairperson of the Commission.
4. Such a recommendation of the Court shall become final upon its adoption by the Assembly.

Article 10
Vacancies

1. A vacancy shall arise in the Court under the following circumstances:

   a. Death;
   b. Resignation;
   c. Removal from office.

2. In the case of death or resignation of a Judge, the President shall immediately inform the Chairperson of the Assembly through the Chairperson of the Commission in writing, who shall declare the seat vacant.
3. The same procedure and consideration for the election of a Judge shall also be followed in filling the vacancies.

Article 11
Solemn Declaration

1. After the first election, the Judges shall, at the first session of the Court and in the presence of the Chairperson of the Assembly, make a Solemn Declaration as follows:

   " I.............................. Do solemnly swear (or affirm or declare) that I shall faithfully exercise the duties of my office as Judge of the African Court of Justice and Human Rights of the African Union impartially and conscientiously, without fear or favour, affection or ill will and that I will preserve the integrity of the Court.

2. The Chairperson of the Assembly or his/her duly authorized representative shall administer the Solemn Declaration.
3. Subsequently, the Solemn Declaration shall be made before the President of the Court.

Article 12
Independence

1. The independence of the judges shall be fully ensured in accordance with international law.
2. The Court shall act impartially, fairly and justly.

3. In performance of the judicial functions and duties, the Court and its Judges shall not be subject to the direction or control of any person or body.

Article 13
Conflict of Interest

1. Functions of a Judge are incompatible with all other activities, which might infringe on the need for independence or impartiality of the judicial profession. In case of doubt, the Court shall decide.
2. A Judge shall not exercise the function of agent, or counsel, or lawyer in any case before the Court.

Article 14
Conditions Governing the Participation of Members in the Settlement of a Specific Case

1. Where a particular judge feels he/she has a conflicting interest in a particular case, he/she shall so declare. In any event, he/she shall not participate in the settlement of a case for which he/she was previously involved as agent, counsel or lawyer of one of the parties, or as a member of a national or international Court or Tribunal, or a Commission of enquiry or in any other capacity.
2. If the President considers that a Judge should not participate in a particular case, he/she shall notify the judge concerned. Such notification from the President shall, after agreement by the Court, exclude that Judge from participating in that particular case.
3. A Judge of the nationality of a State Party to a case before the full Court or one of its Sections shall not have the right to sit on the case.
4. Where there is doubt on these points, the Court shall decide.

Article 15
Privileges and Immunities

1. The Judges shall enjoy, from the time of their election and throughout their term of office, the full privileges and immunities extended to diplomatic agents in accordance with international law.
2. The Judges shall be immune from legal proceedings for any act or omission committed in the discharge of their judicial functions.
3. The Judges shall continue, after they have ceased to hold office, to enjoy immunity in respect of acts performed by them when engaged in their official capacity.

Article 16
Sections of the Court

The Court shall have two (2) Sections; a General Affairs Section composed of eight (8) Judges and a Human Rights Section composed of eight (8) Judges.

Article 17
Assignment of matters to Sections

1. The General Affairs Section shall be competent to hear all cases submitted under Article 28 of this Statute save those concerning human and/or peoples' rights issues.
2. The Human Rights Section shall be competent to hear all cases relating to human and/or peoples rights.

Article 18
Referral of matters to the Full Court

When a Section of the Court is seized with a case, it may, if it deems it necessary refer that case to the Full Court for consideration.

Article 19
Chambers

1. The General Affairs Section and the Human Rights Section may, at any time, constitute one or several chambers. The quorum required to constitute such chambers shall be determined in the Rules of Court.
2. A judgment given by any Section or Chamber shall be considered as rendered by the Court.

Article 20
Sessions

1. The Court shall hold ordinary and extraordinary sessions.
2. The Court shall decide each year on the periods of its ordinary sessions.
3. Extraordinary sessions shall be convened by the President or at the request of the majority of the Judges.

Article 21
Quorum

1. A quorum of nine (9) Judges shall be required for deliberations of the Full Court.
2. A quorum of five (5) Judges shall be required for the deliberations of the General Affairs Section.

3. A quorum of five (5) Judges shall be required for the deliberations of the Human and Peoples' Rights Section.

Article 22
Presidency, Vice-Presidency and Registry

1. At its first ordinary session after the election of the judges, the full Court shall elect its President as well as the Vice-President from the different lists for a period of three (3) years. The President and the Vice-President may be re-elected once.
2. The President shall preside over all sessions of the full Court and those of the Section to which he/she belongs; in the event of being unable to sit, the President shall be replaced by the Vice president for the full Court and by the most Senior Judge for the sessions of his/her Section.
3. The Vice-President shall preside over all sessions of the section to which he/she belongs. In the event of being unable to sit, the Vice-President shall be replaced by the most Senior Judge of that Section.
4. The Court shall appoint a Registrar and may provide for the appointment of such other officers as may be necessary.
5. The President, the Vice-President and the Registrar shall reside at the seat of the Court.

Article 23
Remuneration of Judges

1. The President and the Vice-President shall receive an annual salary and other benefits.
2. The other Judges shall receive a sitting allowance for each day on which he/she exercises his/her functions.
3. These salaries, allowances and compensation shall be determined by the Assembly, on the proposal of the Executive Council. They may not be decreased during the term of office of the Judges.
4. Regulations adopted by the Assembly on the proposal of the Executive Council shall determine the conditions under which retirement pensions shall be given to the Judges as well as the conditions under which their travel expenses shall be paid.
5. The above-mentioned salaries, allowances and compensation shall be free from all taxation.

Article 24
Conditions of Service of the Registrar and Members of the Registry

The salaries and conditions of service of the Registrar and other Court Officials shall be determined by the Assembly on the proposal of the Court, through the Executive Council.

Article 25
Seat and Seal of the Court

1. The Seat of the Court shall be same as the Seat of the African Court on Human and Peoples' Rights. However, the Court may sit in any other Member State, if circumstances warrant, and with the consent of the Member State concerned. The Assembly may change the seat of the Court after due consultations with the Court.
2. The Court shall have a seal bearing the inscription "The African Court of Justice and Human Rights"

Article 26
Budget

1. The Court shall prepare its draft annual budget and shall submit it to the Assembly through the Executive Council.
2. The budget of the Court shall be borne by the African Union.
3. The Court shall be accountable for the execution of its budget and shall submit report thereon to the Executive Council in conformity with the Financial Rules and Regulations of the African Union.

Article 27
Rules of Court

1. The Court shall adopt rules for carrying out its functions and the implementation of the present Statute. In particular, it shall lay down its own Rules.
2. In elaborating its Rules, the Court shall bear in mind the complementarity it maintains with the African Commission and the African Committee of Experts.

CHAPTER III
COMPETENCE OF THE COURT

Article 28
Jurisdiction of the Court

The Court shall have jurisdiction over all cases and all legal disputes submitted to it in accordance with the present Statute which relate to:

a) the interpretation and application of the Constitutive Act;
b) the interpretation, application or validity of other Union Treaties and all subsidiary legal instruments adopted within the framework of the Union or the Organization of African Unity;

c) the interpretation and the application of the African Charter, the Charter on the Rights and Welfare of the Child, the Protocol to the African Charter on Human and Peoples' Rights on the Rights of Women in Africa, or any other legal instrument relating to human rights, ratified by the States Parties concerned;
d) any question of international law;
e) all acts, decisions, regulations and directives of the organs of the Union;
f) all matters specifically provided for in any other agreements that States Parties may conclude among themselves, or with the Union and which confer jurisdiction on the Court;
g) the existence of any fact which, if established, would constitute a breach of an obligation owed to a State Party or to the Union;
h) the nature or extent of the reparation to be made for the breach of an international obligation.

Article 29
Entities Eligible to Submit Cases to the Court

1. The following entities shall be entitled to submit cases to the Court on any issue or dispute provided for in Article 28:

   a) State Parties to the present Protocol;
   b) The Assembly, the Parliament and other organs of the Union authorized by the Assembly;
   c) A staff member of the African Union on appeal, in a dispute and within the limits and under the terms and conditions laid down in the Staff Rules and Regulations of the Union;

2. The Court shall not be open to States, which are not members of the Union. The Court shall also have no jurisdiction to deal with a dispute involving a Member State that has not ratified the Protocol.

Article 30
Other Entities Eligible to Submit Cases to the Court

The following entities shall also be entitled to submit cases to the Court on any violation of a right guaranteed by the African Charter, by the Charter on the Rights and Welfare of the Child, the Protocol to the African Charter on Human and Peoples' Rights on the Rights of Women in Africa, or any other legal instrument relevant to human rights ratified by the States Parties concerned:

a) State Parties to the present Protocol;
b) the African Commission on Human and Peoples' Rights;
c) the African Committee of Experts on the Rights and Welfare of the Child;
d) African Intergovernmental Organizations accredited to the Union or its organs;

e) African National Human Rights Institutions;
f) Individuals or relevant Non-Governmental Organizations accredited to the African Union or to its organs, subject to the provisions of Article 8 of the Protocol.

Article 31
Applicable Law

1. In carrying out its functions, the Court shall have regard to:
   a) The Constitutive Act;
   b) International treaties, whether general or particular, ratified by the contesting States;
   c) International custom, as evidence of a general practice accepted as law;
   d) The general principles of law recognized universally or by African States;
   e) Subject to the provisions of para 1, of Article 46 of the present Statute, judicial decisions and writings of the most highly qualified publicists of various nations s well as the regulations, directives and decisions of the Union, as subsidiary means for the determination of the rules of law;
   f) Any other law relevant to the determination of the case.
2. This Article shall not prejudice the power of the Court to decide a case *ex aequo et bono*, if the parties agree thereto.

CHAPTER IV
PROCEDURE

Article 32
Official Languages

The official and working languages of the Court shall be those of the Union.

Article 33
Institution of Proceedings before the General Affairs Section

1. Cases brought before the Court by virtue of Article 29 of the present Statute shall be submitted by written application addressed to the Registrar. The subject of the dispute, the applicable law and basis of jurisdiction shall be indicated.
2. The Registrar shall forthwith give notice of the application to the Parties concerned.
3. The Registrar shall also notify, through the Chairperson of the Commission, all Member States and, if necessary, the organs of the Union whose decisions are in dispute.

Article 34
Institution of Proceedings before the Human Rights Section

1. Cases brought before the Court relating to an alleged violation of a human or peoples' right shall be submitted by a written application to the Registrar. The application shall indicate the right (s) alleged to have been violated, and, insofar as it is possible, the provision or provisions of the African Charter on Human and Peoples' Rights, the Charter on the Rights and Welfare of the Child, Protocol to the African Charter on Human and Peoples' Rights on the Rights of Women in Africa or any other relevant human rights instrument, ratified by the State concerned, on which it is based.
2. The Registrar shall forthwith give notice of the application to all parties concerned, as well as the Chairperson of the Commission.

Article 35
Provisional Measures

1. The Court shall have the power, on its own motion or on application by the parties, to indicate, if it considers that circumstances so require any provisional measures which ought to be taken to preserve the respective rights of the parties.
2. Pending the final decision, notice of the provisional measures shall forthwith be given to the parties and the Chairperson of the Commission, who shall inform the Assembly.

Article 36
Representation of Parties

1. The States, parties to a case, shall be represented by agents.
2. They may, if necessary, have the assistance of counsel or advocates before the Court.
3. The organs of the Union entitled to appear before the Court shall be represented by the Chairperson of the Commission or his/her representative.
4. The African Commission, the African Committee of Experts, African Inter-Governmental Organizations accredited to the Union or its organs and African National Human Rights Institutions entitled to appear before the Court shall be represented by any person they choose for that purpose.
5. Individuals and Non-Governmental Organizations accredited to the Union or its organs may be represented or assisted by a person of their choice.
6. The agents and other representatives of parties before the Court, their counsel or advocates, witnesses, and any other persons whose presence is required at the Court shall enjoy the privileges and immunities necessary to the independent exercise of their duties or the smooth functioning of the Court.

Article 37
Communications and Notices

1. Communications and notices addressed to agents or counsel of parties to a case shall be considered as addressed to the parties.
2. For the service of all communications or notices upon persons other than the agents, counsel or advocates of parties concerned, the Court shall direct its request to the government of the State upon whose territory the communication or notice has to be served.
3. The same provision shall apply whenever steps are to be taken to procure evidence on the spot.

Article 38
Procedure Before the Court

The procedures before the Court shall be laid out in the Rules of Court, taking into account the complementarity between the Court and other treaty bodies of the Union.

Article 39
Public Hearing

The hearing shall be public, unless the Court, on its own motion or upon application by the parties, decides that the session shall be closed.

Article 40
Record of Proceedings

1. A record of proceedings shall be made at each hearing and shall be signed by the Registrar and the presiding Judge of the session.
2. This record alone shall be authentic.

Article 41
Default Judgment

1. Whenever one of the parties does not appear before the Court, or fails to defend the case against it, the Court shall proceed to consider the case and to give its judgment.
2. The Court shall before doing so, satisfy itself, not only that it has jurisdiction in accordance with Articles 28, 29 and 30 of the present Statute, but also that the claim is well founded in fact and law, and that the other party had due notice.
3. An objection by the party concerned may be lodged against the judgment within ninety (90) days of it being notified of the default judgment. Unless there is a decision to the contrary by the Court, the objection shall not have effect of staying the enforcement of the default judgment.

Article 42
Majority Required for Decision of the Court

1. Without prejudice to the provisions of Article 50(4) of the present Statute, the decisions of the Court shall be decided by a majority of the Judges present.
2. In the event of an equality of votes, the presiding Judge shall have a casting vote.

Article 43
Judgments and Decisions

1. The Court shall render its judgment within ninety (90) days of having completed its deliberations.
2. All judgments shall state the reasons on which they are based.
3. The judgment shall contain the names of the Judges who have taken part in the decision.
4. The judgment shall be signed by all the Judges and certified by the Presiding Judge and the Registrar. It shall be read in open session, due notice having been given to the agents.
5. The Parties to the case shall be notified of the judgment of the Court and it shall be transmitted to the Member States and the Commission.
6. The Executive Council shall also be notified of the judgment and shall monitor its execution on behalf of the Assembly

Article 44
Dissenting Opinion

If the judgment does not represent in whole or in part the unanimous opinion of the Judges, any Judge shall be entitled to deliver a separate or dissenting opinion.

Article 45
Compensation

Without prejudice to its competence to rule on issues of compensation at the request of a party by virtue of para 1(h), of Article 28 of the present Statute, the Court may, if it considers that there was a violation of a human or peoples' right, order any appropriate measures in order to remedy the situation, including granting fair compensation.

Article 46
Binding Force and Execution of Judgments

1. The decision of the Court shall be binding on the parties.
2. Subject to the provisions of para 3, Article 41 of the present Statute, the judgment of the Court is final.

3. The parties shall comply with the judgment made by the Court in any dispute to which they are parties within the time stipulated by the Court and shall guarantee its execution.
4. Where a party has failed to comply with a judgment, the Court shall refer the matter to the Assembly, which shall decide upon measures to be taken to give effect to that judgment.
5. The Assembly may impose sanctions by virtue of para 2 of Article 23 of the Constitutive Act.

Article 47
Interpretation

In the event of any dispute as to the meaning or scope of a judgment, the Court shall construe it upon the request of any party.

Article 48
Revision

1. An application for revision of a judgment may be made to the Court only when it is based upon discovery of a new fact of such nature as to be a decisive factor, which fact was, when the judgment was given, unknown to the Court and also to the party claiming revision, provided that such ignorance was not due to negligence.
2. The proceedings for revision shall be opened by a ruling of the Court expressly recording the existence of the new fact, recognizing that it has such a character as to lay the case open to revision, and declaring the revision admissible on this ground.
3. The Court may require prior compliance with the terms of the judgment before it admits proceedings in revision.
4. The application for revision shall be made within six (6) months of the discovery of the new fact.
5. No application may be made after the lapse of ten (10) years from the date of the judgment.

Article 49
Intervention

1. Should a Member State or organ of the Union consider that it has an interest of a legal nature which may be affected by the decision in the case, it may submit a request to the Court to be permitted to intervene. It shall be for the Court to decide upon this request.
2. If a Member State or organ of the Union should exercise the option offered under para 1 of the present Article, the interpretation contained in the decision shall be equally binding upon it.

3. In the interest of the effective administration of justice, the Court may invite any Member State that is not a party to the case, any organ of the Union or any person concerned other than the claimant, to present written observations or take part in hearings.

Article 50
Intervention in a Case Concerning the Interpretation of the Constitutive Act

1. Whenever the question of interpretation of the Constitutive Act arises, in a case in which Member States other than the parties to the dispute have expressed an interest, the Registrar shall notify all such States and organs of the Union forthwith.
2. Every State Party and organ of the Union so notified has the right to intervene in the proceedings.
3. The decisions of the Court concerning the interpretation and application of the Constitutive Act shall be binding on Member States and organs of the Union, notwithstanding the provisions of para 1, of Article 46 of this Statute.
4. Any decision made by virtue of this Article shall be made by a qualified majority of at least two (2) votes and in the presence of at least two-thirds of the Judges.

Article 51
Intervention in a Case concerning the Interpretation of Other Treaties

1. Whenever the question is that of interpretation of other treaties ratified by Member States other than the parties to a dispute, the Registrar shall notify all such States and the organs of the Union forthwith.
2. Every State Party and organ of the Union so notified has the right to intervene in the proceedings, and if it exercises this right, the interpretation given by the judgment shall be equally binding upon it.
3. This Article shall not be applicable to cases relating to alleged violations of a human or peoples' right, submitted by virtue of Articles 29 or 30 of the present Statute.

Article 52
Costs

1. Unless otherwise decided by the Court, each party shall bear its own costs.
2. Should it be required in the interest of justice, free legal aid may be provided for the person presenting an individual communication, under conditions to be set out in the Rules of Court.

CHAPTER V
ADVISORY OPINION

Article 53
Request for Advisory Opinion

1. The Court may give an advisory opinion on any legal question at the request of the Assembly, the Parliament, the Executive Council, the Peace and Security Council, the Economic, Social and Cultural Council (ECOSOCC), the Financial Institutions or any other organ of the Union as may be authorized by the Assembly.
2. A request for an advisory opinion shall be in writing and shall contain an exact statement of the question upon which the opinion is required and shall be accompanied by all relevant documents.
3. A request for an advisory opinion must not be related to a pending application before the African Commission or the African Committee of Experts.

Article 54
Service of Notice

1. The Registrar shall forthwith give notice of the request for an advisory opinion to all States or organs entitled to appear before the Court by virtue of Article 30 of the present Statute.
2. The Registrar shall also, by means of a special and direct communication, notify any State entitled to appear before the Court or any Intergovernmental Organization considered by the Court, or should it not be sitting, by the President, as likely to be able to furnish information on the question, that the Court will be prepared to receive, within a time limit to be fixed by the President, written statements, or to hear, at a public sitting to be held for the purpose, oral statements relating to the question.
3. Should any such State entitled to appear before the Court have failed to receive the special communication referred to in para 2 of this Article, such State may express the desire to submit a written statement or to be heard, and the Court shall decide.
4. States and organizations having presented written or oral statements or both shall be permitted to comment on the statements made by other States or organizations in the form, to the extent, and within the time limits which the Court, or should it not be sitting, the President, shall decide in each particular case. Accordingly, the Registrar shall in due course communicate any such written statements to States and organizations having submitted similar statements.

Article 55
Delivery of Advisory Opinion

The Court shall deliver its advisory opinion in open court, notice having been given to the Chairperson of the Commission and Member States, and other International Organizations directly concerned.

Article 56
Application by Analogy of the Provisions of the Statute Applicable to Contentious Cases

In the exercise of its advisory functions, the Court shall further be guided by the provisions of the present Statute which apply in contentious cases to the extent to which it recognizes them to be applicable.

CHAPTER VI
REPORT TO THE ASSEMBLY

Article 57
Annual Activity Report

The Court shall submit to the Assembly, an annual report on its work during the previous year. The report shall specify, in particular, the cases in which a party has not complied with the judgment of the Court.

CHAPTER VII
PROCEDURE FOR AMENDMENTS

Article 58
Proposed Amendments from a State Party

1. The present Statute may be amended if a State Party makes a written request to that effect to the Chairperson of the Commission, who shall transmit same to Member States within thirty (30) days of receipt thereof.
2. The Assembly may adopt by a simple majority, the proposed amendment after the Court has given its opinion on it.

Article 59
Proposed Amendments from the Court

The Court may propose such amendments to the present Statute as it may deem necessary, to the Assembly through written communication to the Chairperson of the Commission, for consideration in conformity with the provisions of Article 58 of the present Statute.

Article 60
Entry into Force of Amendments

The amendment shall enter into force for every State which has accepted it in conformity with its Constitutional laws thirty (30) days after the Chairperson of the Commission is notified of this acceptance.

PROTOCOL OF THE COURT OF JUSTICE OF THE AFRICAN UNION
11 July 2003
(Maputo Protocol)

The Member States of the African Union:

Considering that the Constitutive Act established the Court of Justice of the African Union;

Firmly convinced that the attainment of the objectives of the African Union requires the establishment of the Court of Justice of the African Union;

HAVE AGREED AS FOLLOWS:

CHAPTER I

Article 1
DEFINITIONS

In this Protocol unless otherwise specifically stated: "Act" means the Constitutive Act of the Union;

"**Assembly** " means the Assembly of Heads of State and Government of the Union;

"**Commission**" means the Commission of the Union; "**Court**" means the Court of Justice of the Union;

"**ECOSOCC**" means the Economic, Social and Cultural Council of the Union;

"**Executive Council**" means the Executive Council of Ministers of the Union;

"**Financial Institutions** " means the Financial Institutions established by the Constitutive Act;

"Judge" means a judge of the Court;

"**Member State**" means a Member State of the Union; "**Parliament**" means the Pan-African Parliament of the Union;

"**Peace and Security Council**" means the Peace and Security Council of the Union;

"**President**" means the President of the Court;

"**Protocol**" means this Protocol defining the composition, powers and functions of the Court;

"**Regions**" means the geographical regions into which the continent of Africa, at any time, is divided pursuant to a decision of the Assembly;
"**Rules of Court**" means the Rules of Court under Article 58; "**Registrar**" means the Registrar of the Court;
"**States Parties**" means the Member States that have ratified or acceded to this Protocol;
"**Union**" means the African Union established by the Act; "**Vice President**" means the Vice President of the Court;

Article 2
ESTABLISHMENT OF THE COURT

1. The Court established by the Act shall function in accordance with the provisions of the Act and this Protocol.
2. The Court shall be the principal judicial organ of the Union.

Article 3
COMPOSITION

1. The Court shall consist of eleven (11) Judges who are nationals of States Parties.
2. The Assembly may, when it deems it necessary, review the number of Judges.
3. The Judges shall be assisted by the necessary staff for the smooth functioning of the Court.
4. No two (2) Judges shall be nationals of the same State Party.
5. In the Court as a whole, the representation of the principal legal traditions of Africa shall be assured.
6. Each region shall be represented by no less than two (2) Judges.

CHAPTER II

Article 4
QUALIFICATIONS

The Court shall be composed of impartial and independent Judges elected from among persons of high moral character, who possess the necessary qualifications required in their respective countries for appointment to the highest judicial offices, or are jurists of recognized competence in international law.

Article 5
SUBMISSION OF CANDIDATES

1. Upon entry into force of this Protocol, the Chairperson of the Commission shall request each State Party to submit in writing within ninety (90) days of such a request, its nomination for the office of a Judge of the Court.

2. Each State Party may nominate only one (1) candidate having the qualifications prescribed in Article 4 of this Protocol.
3. Due consideration shall be given to adequate gender representation in the nomination process.

Article 6
LIST OF CANDIDATES

The Chairperson of the Commission shall prepare a list of the candidates nominated, in alphabetical order and transmit it to the Member States at least thirty (30) days prior to the ordinary session of the Assembly at which the Judges are to be elected.

Article 7
ELECTION OF JUDGES OF THE COURT

1. The Assembly shall elect the Judges by secret ballot and by two-thirds majority of the Member States eligible to vote.
2. Where one or more candidates fail to obtain the two-thirds majority required for an election, the balloting shall continue until the required number of Judges has been elected. However, the next ballots shall be restricted to the candidates who obtain the greatest number of votes.
3. In the election of the Judges, the Assembly shall ensure that there is equal gender representation.

Article 8
TENURE OF OFFICE

1. The Judges shall be elected for a period of six (6) years and may be re-elected only once. The term of five (5) Judges elected at the first election shall expire at the end of four (4) years and the other Judges shall serve the full term.
2. The Judges whose terms are to expire at the end of the initial period of four (4) years shall be chosen by lot to be drawn by the Chairperson of the Assembly immediately after the first election has been completed.
3. A Judge elected to replace another Judge whose term of office has not expired shall be from the same region and shall hold office for the remainder of the predecessor's term.

Article 9
OATH OF OFFICE

1. Before taking up his or her duties each Judge shall in open court take the following oath:

"I .... Do solemnly swear (or affirm or declare) that I shall faithfully exercise the duties of my office as Judge of the Court of Justice of the African Union impartially and conscientiously, without fear or favour, affection or illwill and that I will preserve the secrecy of the deliberations of the Court."

2. The oath of office shall be administered by the Chairperson of the Assembly or his or her duly authorized representative.

Article 10
PRESIDENCY OF THE COURT

1. The Court shall elect its President and Vice-President for a period of three (3) years. The President and Vice-President may be re-elected once.
2. The President shall reside at the seat of the Court.
3. The modalities for elections of the President and the Vice-President and their functions shall be set out in the Rules of Court.

Article 11
RESIGNATION, SUSPENSION AND REMOVAL FROM OFFICE

1. A Judge may resign his or her position in writing addressed to the President for transmission to the Chairperson of the Assembly.
2. A Judge shall not be suspended or removed from office save where, on the unanimous recommendation of the other Judges, he or she no longer fulfils the requisite conditions to be a Judge.
3. The President shall communicate the recommendation for the suspension or removal of a judge to the Chairperson of the Assembly and the Chairperson of the Commission.
4. Such a recommendation of the Court shall become final upon its adoption by the Assembly.

Article 12
VACANCIES

1. A vacancy shall arise in the Court under the following circumstances:

(a) death;
(b) resignation;
(c) removal from office.

2. In the case of death or resignation of a Judge, the President shall immediately inform the Chairperson of the Assembly in writing, who shall declare the seat vacant.
3. The same procedure and consideration for the election of a Judge shall also be followed in filling vacancies.

Article 13
INDEPENDENCE

1. The independence of the Judges shall be fully ensured in accordance with international law.
2. No Judge may participate in the decision of any case in which he or she has previously taken part as agent, counsel or advocate for one of the parties, or as a member of a national or international court, or commission of inquiry, or in any other capacity.
3. Any doubt on this point shall be settled by decision of the Court.

Article 14
PRIVILEGES AND IMMUNITIES

1. The Judges shall enjoy, from the time of their election and throughout their term of office, the full privileges and immunities extended to diplomatic agents in accordance with international law.
2. The Judges shall be immune from legal proceedings for any act or omission committed in the discharge of their judicial functions.
3. The Judges shall continue, after they have ceased to hold office, to enjoy immunity in respect of acts performed by them when engaged in their official capacity.

Article 15
INCOMPATIBILITY

1. The position of a Judge shall be incompatible with any activity that might interfere with the independence or impartiality of such a judge or the demands of the office, as determined in the Rules of Court.
2. Any doubt on this point shall be settled by the Court.

Article 16
QUORUM

1. The full Court shall sit except where it is expressly provided otherwise in this Protocol;
2. Except when sitting in Chamber, the Court shall only examine cases brought before it, if it has a quorum of at least seven (7) Judges;
3. The quorum for a Special Chamber shall be set out in the Rules of Court.

Article 17
REMUNERATION OF JUDGES

1. A Judge shall receive an annual allowance and, for each day on which he or she exercises his or her functions, a special allowance, provided that in any

year the total sum payable to any Judge as special allowance shall not exceed the amount of the annual allowance.

2. The President shall receive an additional special annual allowance.
3. The Vice-President shall receive an additional special allowance for each day on which he or she acts as President.
4. The allowances shall be determined from time to time by the Assembly upon the recommendation of the Executive Council, taking into account the workload of the Court. They may not be decreased during the term of office.
5. Regulations adopted by the Assembly upon the recommendation of the Executive Council shall determine the conditions under which retirement pensions shall be given to the Judges and the terms and conditions under which their travel expenses shall be paid or refunded.
6. The allowances shall be free of all taxation.

Article 18
ELIGIBILITY TO SUBMIT CASES

1. The following are entitled to submit cases to the Court:

   (a) States Parties to this Protocol;
   (b) The Assembly, the Parliament and other organs of the Union authorised by the Assembly;
   (c) The Commission or a member of staff of the Commission in a dispute between them within the limits and under the conditions laid down in the Staff Rules and Regulations of the Union;
   (d) Third Parties under conditions to be determined by the Assembly and with the consent of the State Party concerned.

2. The conditions under which the Court shall be open to third parties shall, subject to the special provisions contained in treaties in force, be laid down by the Assembly, but in no case shall such conditions place the parties in a position of inequality before the Court.
3. The States which are not members of the Union shall not be allowed to submit cases to the Court. The Court shall have no jurisdiction to deal with a dispute involving a Member State that has not ratified this Protocol.

Article 19
COMPETENCE/JURISDICTION

1. The Court shall have jurisdiction over all disputes and applications referred to it in accordance with the Act and this Protocol which relate to:

   (a) the interpretation and application of the Act;
   (b) the interpretation, application or validity of Union treaties and all subsidiary legal instruments adopted within the framework of the Union;

(c) any question of international law;
(d) all acts, decisions, regulations and directives of the organs of the Union;
(e) all matters specifically provided for in any other agreements that States Parties may conclude among themselves or with the Union and which confer jurisdiction on the Court;
(f) the existence of any fact which, if established, would constitute a breach of an obligation owed to a State Party or to the Union;
(g) the nature or extent of the reparation to be made for the breach of an obligation.

2. The Assembly may confer on the Court power to assume jurisdiction over any dispute other than those referred to in this Article.

CHAPTER III

Article 20
SOURCES OF LAW

1. The Court, whose function is to decide in accordance with international law such disputes, as are submitted to it, shall have regard to:

   (a) The Act;
   (b) International treaties whether general or particular, establishing rules expressly recognized by the contesting states;
   (c) International custom, as evidence of a general practice accepted as law;
   (d) The general principles of law recognized universally or by African States;
   (e) Subject to Article 37 of this Protocol, judicial decisions and the writings of the most highly qualified publicists of various nations as well as the regulations, directives and decisions of the Union as subsidiary means for the determination of the rules of law.

2. This provision shall not prejudice the power of the Court to decide a case *ex aequo et bono*, if the parties, agree thereto.

CHAPTER IV

Article 21
SUBMISSION OF A DISPUTE

1. Disputes shall be submitted to the Court by a written application to the Registrar. The subject of the dispute, the applicable law and basis of the jurisdiction shall be indicated.
2. The Registrar shall forthwith give notice of the application to all concerned parties.
3. The Registrar shall also notify all Member States, the Chairperson of the Commission and any third parties entitled to appear before the Court.

Article 22
PROVISIONAL MEASURES

1. The Court shall have the power, on its own motion or on application by the parties, to indicate, if it considers that circumstances so require any provisional measures which ought to be taken to preserve the respective rights of the parties.
2. Pending the final decision, notice of the provisional measures shall forthwith be given to the parties and to the Chairperson of the Commission.

Article 23
REPRESENTATION OF PARTIES

1. The parties may be represented before the Court by agents.
2. An agent or party may have the assistance of counsel or advocate before the Court.
3. The organs of the Union, where relevant, shall be represented by the Chairperson of the Commission or his or her representative.
4. The agents, counsel and advocates of the parties before the Court shall enjoy the privileges and immunities necessary to the independent exercise of their duties.

Article 24
PROCEDURE BEFORE THE COURT

1. The procedure before the Court shall consist of two parts: written and oral.
2. The written procedure shall consist of the communications to the Court, the parties and the institutions of the Union whose decisions are in dispute, of applications, statements of the case, defences and observations and of replies if any, as well as all papers and documents in support, or of certified copies thereof.
3. The communications shall be made through the Registrar, in the order and time fixed by the Court either in the Rules or the case.
4. A certified copy of every document produced by one party shall be communicated to the other party.
5. The oral proceedings shall, if necessary, consist of hearing by the Court of witnesses, experts, agents, counsels and advocates.

Article 25
SERVICE OF NOTICE

1. For the service of all notices upon persons other than parties, agents, counsel and advocates, the Court shall apply direct to the government of the State upon whose territory the notice has to be served.

2. The same provision shall apply whenever steps are to be taken to procure evidence locally in the territory of the State concerned.

Article 26
PUBLIC HEARING

The hearing in Court shall be public, unless the Court, on its own motion or upon application by the parties, decides that the public not be admitted.

Article 27
RECORD OF PROCEEDINGS

1. A record of proceedings shall be made at each hearing and shall be signed by the presiding Judge and the Registrar of the session.
2. Such a record shall be kept by the Registrar and shall be the authentic record of the case.

Article 28
REGULATION OF PROCEEDINGS

1. The Court shall have the power to regulate its own proceedings. It shall have the power to make orders for the conduct of the case before it.
2. It shall decide the form and time in which each party must conclude its arguments, and make all arrangements connected with the taking of evidence.

Article 29
PRODUCTION OF DOCUMENTS

The Court may, before the hearing begins, call upon the agents to produce any relevant document or to supply any relevant explanation. Formal note shall be taken of any refusal to produce documents or supply an explanation requested by it.

Article 30
ENQUIRIES

The Court may, at any time, entrust any individual, body, bureau, commission, or other organisation that it may select, and accepted by the parties to the dispute, with the task of carrying out an enquiry or giving an expert opinion.

Article 31
REFUSAL OF EVIDENCE

After the Court has received the proofs and evidence within the time specified for the purpose, it may, unless it decides that the interests of justice so require, refuse to accept any further oral or written evidence that any party may desire to present.

Article 32
DEFAULT JUDGMENTS

1. Whenever one of the parties does not appear before the Court, or fails to defend the case against it, the other party may call upon the Court to give its judgment.
2. The Court must before doing so, satisfy itself, not only that it has jurisdiction in accordance with Article 19, but also that the claim is well founded in fact and in law and that the other party had due notice.
3. An objection by the party concerned may be lodged against the judgment within ninety (90) days of it being notified of the default judgment. The objection shall not have the effect of staying the enforcement of the judgment by default

Article 33
CONSIDERATION OF THE JUDGMENT

1. When, subject to the control of the Court, the agent, counsel and advocates have completed their submissions of the case, the President shall declare the hearing closed.
2. The Court shall adjourn to consider its judgment.
3. The deliberations of the Court shall take place in private and shall remain secret at all times.

Article 34
MAJORITY NECESSARY FOR DECISION

1. All questions shall be decided by a majority of the Judges present.
2. In the event of equality of votes, the presiding Judge shall have a casting vote.

Article 35
JUDGMENT

1. The judgment shall state the reasons on which it is based.
2. The judgment shall state the names of Judges who have taken part in the decision.
3. The judgment shall be signed by all the Judges and certified by the President and the Registrar. It shall be read in open session, due notice having been given to the agents.
4. Subject to Articles 32 and 41 of this Protocol, the judgment shall be final.

Article 36
SEPARATE OR DISSENTING OPINION

If the judgment does not represent in whole or in part the unanimous opinion of the Judges, any Judge shall be entitled to deliver a separate or dissenting opinion.

Article 37
BINDING FORCE OF JUDGMENTS

The judgments of the Court shall be binding on the parties and in respect of that particular case.

Article 38
DECISIONS ON INTERPRETATION AND APPLICATION OF THE ACT

1. Decisions of the Court on the interpretation and application of the Act shall be binding on Member States and organs of the Union notwithstanding the provisions of Article 37 of this Protocol.
2. Whenever questions of interpretation of the Act arise in a case in which States other than those concerned have expressed an interest, the Registrar shall notify all such States and organs of the Union forthwith.
3. Every Member State and organ of the Union so notified has the right to intervene in the proceedings.
4. Any decision taken in application of Articles 38 and 39 of this Protocol shall be by a qualified majority of at least two (2) votes and in the presence of at least nine (9) Judges.

Article 39
INTERPRETATION OF OTHER TREATIES

1. Whenever the question of interpretation of a treaty arises in a case in which States other than those concerned have expressed an interest, the Registrar shall notify all such States and organs of the Union forthwith.
2. Every State Party and organ of the Union so notified has the right to intervene in the proceedings and the interpretation given by the judgment will be equally binding upon it.

Article 40
INTERPRETATION OF A JUDGEMENT

In the event of any dispute as to the meaning or scope of the judgment, the Court shall construe it upon the request of any of the parties.

Article 41
REVISION

1. An application for revision of a judgment may be made only when it is based upon discovery of a new fact of such nature as to be a decisive factor, which fact was, when the judgment was given, unknown to the Court and also to the party claiming revision, provided that such ignorance was not due to negligence.

2. The proceedings for revision shall be opened by a ruling of the Court expressly recording the existence of the new fact, recognizing that it has such a character as to lay the case open to revision, and declaring the revision admissible on this ground.
3. The Court may require prior compliance with the terms of the judgment before it admits proceedings in revision.
4. The application for revision shall be made within six (6) months of the discovery of the new fact.
5. No application may be made after the lapse of ten (10) years from the date of the judgment.

Article 42
INTERVENTION

1. Any Member State that has an interest of a legal nature, which may be affected by the decision in the case, may submit a request to the Court to be permitted to intervene.
2. The Court shall decide upon the request.

Article 43
COSTS

Unless otherwise decided by the Court, each party shall bear its own costs.

Article 44
ADVISORY OPINION

1. The Court may give an advisory opinion on any legal question at the request of the Assembly, the Parliament, the Executive Council, the Peace and Security Council, the ECOSOCC, any of the Financial Institutions, a Regional Economic Community or such other organs of the Union as may be authorized by the Assembly.
2. A request for an advisory opinion under para 1 of this Article shall be in writing and shall contain an exact statement of the question upon which the opinion is required and shall be accompanied by all relevant documents.

CHAPTER V

Article 45
PROCEDURE FOR AMENDMENTS

1. This Protocol may be amended if a State Party makes a written request to that effect to the Chairperson of the Assembly.

2. Proposals for amendment shall be submitted to the Chairperson of the Commission who shall transmit same to Member States within thirty (30) days of receipt thereof.
3. The Assembly may adopt by a simple majority, the draft amendment after the Court has given its opinion on the amendment.

Article 46
POWER OF THE COURT TO PROPOSE AMENDMENTS

The Court shall have the power to propose such amendments to this Protocol as it may deem necessary to the Assembly through written communication to the Chairperson of the Commission for consideration in conformity with Article 45 of this Protocol.

CHAPTER VI

Article 47
SEAT AND SEAL OF THE COURT

1. The seat of the Court shall be determined by the Assembly from among States Parties. However, the Court may sit in any other Member State if circumstances warrant and with the consent of the Member State concerned. The seat of the Court may be changed by the Assembly after due consultations with the Court.
2. The Court shall have a seal bearing the inscription "The Court of Justice of the African Union."

CHAPTER VII

Article 48
APPOINTMENT OF REGISTRAR

1. The Court shall appoint the Registrar and Deputy Registrar(s) from amongst candidates proposed by the Judges of the Court, as it considers necessary, in accordance with the Rules of Court.
2. The Registrar and Deputy Registrar(s) shall be elected for a term of four (4) years. They may be re-appointed once. They shall reside at the seat of the Court.
3. The salary and conditions of service of the Registrar and Deputy Registrar(s) shall be determined by the Assembly upon recommendation of the Court through the Executive Council.

Article 49
APPOINTMENT AND TERMS OF SERVICE OF OTHER STAFF

1. The Court shall employ such staff as may be required to enable the Court to perform its functions and who shall hold office in the service of the Court.

2. The salary and other allowances of the other staff of the Court shall be determined by the Assembly upon the recommendation of the Court through the Executive Council.

Article 50
OFFICIAL LANGUAGES OF THE COURT

The official and working languages of the Court shall be those of the Union.

CHAPTER VIII

Article 51
EXECUTION OF JUDGMENT

The State Parties shall comply with the judgment in any dispute to which they are parties within the time stipulated by the Court and shall guarantee its execution.

Article 52
NON-COMPLIANCE WITH JUDGMENT

1. Where a party has failed to comply with a judgment, the Court may, upon application by either party, refer the matter to the Assembly, which may decide upon measures to be taken to give effect to the judgment.
2. The Assembly may impose sanctions under para 2 of Article 23 of the Act.

Article 53
REPORT TO THE ASSEMBLY

The Court shall submit to each ordinary session of the Assembly, a report on its work during the previous year. The report shall specify, in particular, the cases in which a State has not complied with the Court's judgment.

CHAPTER IX

Article 54
BUDGET

1. The Court shall elaborate its draft annual budget and shall submit it to the Assembly through the Executive Council.
2. The budget of the Court shall be borne by the Member States.

Article 55
SUMMARY PROCEDURE

With a view to the speedy dispatch of business, the Court shall form annually a chamber composed of five (5) Judges, which, at the request of the parties, may hear and determine cases by summary procedure in accordance with the Rules of Court. In addition, two (2) Judges shall be selected from among themselves for the purpose of replacing Judges who find it impossible to sit.

Article 56
SPECIAL CHAMBERS

The Court may from time to time form one or more chambers, composed of three (3) or more Judges as the Court may determine, for dealing with particular categories of cases.

Article 57
JUDGMENT GIVEN BY A CHAMBER

A judgment given by any of the chambers provided for in Articles 55 and 56 of this Protocol shall be considered as rendered by the Court.

CHAPTER X

Article 58
RULES OF COURT

The Court shall frame rules for carrying out its functions and generally for giving effect to this Protocol. In particular, it shall lay down rules of procedure in conformity with this Protocol.

Article 59
SIGNATURE, RATIFICATION AND ACCESSION

1. This Protocol shall be open to signature, ratification and accession by Member States in accordance with their respective constitutional procedures.
2. The instruments of ratification shall be deposited with the Chairperson of the Commission.
3. Any Member State acceding to this Protocol after its entry into force shall deposit the instrument of accession with the Chairperson of the Commission.

Article 60
ENTRY INTO FORCE

This Protocol shall enter into force thirty (30) days after the deposit of the instruments of ratification by fifteen (15) Member States.

Adopted by the 2nd Ordinary Session of the Assembly of the Union

Maputo, 11 July 2003

PROTOCOL TO THE AFRICAN CHARTER ON HUMAN AND PEOPLES' RIGHTS ON THE ESTABLISHMENT OF AN AFRICAN COURT ON HUMAN AND PEOPLES' RIGHTS

9 June 1998

The Member States of the Organization of African Unity hereinafter referred to as the OAU, States Parties to the African Charter on Human and Peoples' Rights:

Considering that the Charter of the Organization of African Unity recognizes that freedom, equality, justice, peace and dignity are essential objectives for the achievement of the legitimate aspirations of the African peoples;

Noting that the African Charter on Human and Peoples' Rights reaffirms adherence to the principles of human and peoples' rights, freedoms and duties contained in the declarations, conventions and other instruments adopted by the Organization of African Unity, and other international organizations;

Recognizing that the twofold objective of the African Charter on Human and Peoples' Rights is to ensure on the one hand promotion and on the other protection of human and peoples' rights, freedoms and duties;

Recognizing further, the efforts of the African Commission on Human and Peoples' Rights in the promotion and protection of human and peoples' rights since its inception in 1987;

Recalling resolution AHG/Res.230 (XXX) adopted by the Assembly of Heads of State and Government in June 1994 in Tunis, Tunisia, requesting the Secretary-General to convene a Government experts' meeting to ponder, in conjunction with the African Commission, over the means to enhance the efficiency of the African Commission and to consider in particular the establishment of an African Court on Human and Peoples' Rights;

Noting the first and second Government legal experts' meetings held respectively in Cape Town, South Africa (September, 1995) and Nouakchott, Mauritania (April, 1997), and the third Government Legal Experts meeting held in Addis Ababa, Ethiopia (December, 1997), which was enlarged to include Diplomats;

Firmly convinced that the attainment of the objectives of the African Charter on Human and Peoples' Rights requires the establishment of an African Court on Human and Peoples' Rights to complement and reinforce the functions of the African Commission on Human and Peoples' Rights.

HAVE AGREED AS FOLLOWS:

Article 1 ESTABLISHMENT OF THE COURT

There shall be established within the Organization of African Unity an African Court on Human and Peoples' Rights (hereinafter referred to as "the Court"), the organization, jurisdiction and functioning of which shall be governed by the present Protocol.

Article 2 RELATIONSHIP BETWEEN THE COURT AND THE COMMISSION

The Court shall, bearing in mind the provisions of this Protocol, complement the protective mandate of the African Commission on Human and Peoples' Rights (hereinafter referred to as "the Commission") conferred upon it by the African Charter on Human and Peoples' Rights (hereinafter referred to as "the Charter").

Article 3 JURISDICTION

1. The jurisdiction of the Court shall extend to all cases and disputes submitted to it concerning the interpretation and application of the Charter, this Protocol and any other relevant Human Rights instrument ratified by the States concerned.
2. In the event of a dispute as to whether the Court has jurisdiction, the Court shall decide.

Article 4 ADVISORY OPINIONS

1. At the request of a Member State of the OAU, the OAU, any of its organs, or any African organization recognized by the OAU, the Court may provide an opinion on any legal matter relating to the Charter or any other relevant human rights instruments, provided that the subject matter of the opinion is not related to a matter being examined by the Commission.
2. The Court shall give reasons for its advisory opinions provided that every judge shall be entitled to deliver a separate or dissenting decision.

Article 5 ACCESS TO THE COURT

1. The following are entitled to submit cases to the Court
    a. The Commission;
    b. The State Party which has lodged a complaint to the Commission;
    c. The State Party against which the complaint has been lodged at the Commission;
    d. The State Party whose citizen is a victim of human rights violation;
    e. African Intergovernmental Organizations.
2. When a State Party has an interest in a case, it may submit a request to the Court to be permitted to join.
3. The Court may entitle relevant Non Governmental Organizations (NGOs) with observer status before the Commission, and individuals to institute cases directly before it, in accordance with Article 34(6) of this Protocol.

Article 6 ADMISSIBILITY OF CASES

1. The Court, when deciding on the admissibility of a case instituted under Article 5(3) of this Protocol, may request the opinion of the Commission which shall give it as soon as possible.
2. The Court shall rule on the admissibility of cases taking into account the provisions of Article 56 of the Charter.
3. The Court may consider cases or transfer them to the Commission.

Article 7 SOURCES OF LAW

The Court shall apply the provisions of the Charter and any other relevant human rights instruments ratified by the States concerned.

Article 8 CONSIDERATION OF CASES

The Rules of Procedure of the Court shall lay down the detailed conditions under which the Court shall consider cases brought before it, bearing in mind the complementarity between the Commission and the Court.

Article 9 AMICABLE SETTLEMENT

The Court may try to reach an amicable settlement in a case pending before it in accordance with the provisions of the Charter.

Article 10 HEARINGS AND REPRESENTATION

1. The Court shall conduct its proceedings in public. The Court may, however, conduct proceedings in camera as may be provided for in the Rules of Procedure.
2. Any party to a case shall be entitled to be represented by a legal representative of the party's choice. Free legal representation may be provided where the interests of justice so require.
3. Any person, witness or representative of the parties, who appears before the Court, shall enjoy protection and all facilities, in accordance with international law, necessary for the discharging of their functions, tasks and duties in relation to the Court.

Article 11 COMPOSITION

1. The Court shall consist of eleven judges, nationals of Member States of the OAU, elected in an individual capacity from among jurists of high moral character and of recognized practical, judicial or academic competence and experience in the field of human and peoples' rights.
2. No two judges shall be nationals of the same State.

Article 12 NOMINATIONS

1. States Parties to the Protocol may each propose up to three candidates, at least two of whom shall be nationals of that State.
2. Due consideration shall be given to adequate gender representation in the nomination process.

Article 13 LIST OF CANDIDATES

1. Upon entry into force of this Protocol, the Secretary-General of the OAU shall request each State Party to the Protocol to present, within ninety (90) days of such a request, its nominees for the office of judge of the Court.
2. The Secretary-General of the OAU shall prepare a list in alphabetical order of the candidates nominated and transmit it to the Member States of the OAU at least thirty days prior to the next session of the Assembly of Heads of State and Government of the OAU hereinafter referred to as "the Assembly."

Article 14 ELECTIONS

1. The judges of the Court shall be elected by secret ballot by the Assembly from the list referred to in Article 13(2) of the present Protocol.
2. The Assembly shall ensure that in the Court as a whole there is representation of the main regions of Africa and of their principal legal traditions.
3. In the election of the judges, the Assembly shall ensure that there is adequate gender representation.

Article 15 TERM OF OFFICE

1. The judges of the Court shall be elected for a period of six years and may be re-elected only once. The terms of four judges elected at the first election shall expire at the end of two years, and the terms of four more judges shall expire at the end of four years.
2. The judges whose terms are to expire at the end of the initial periods of two and four years shall be chosen by lot to be drawn by the Secretary-General of the OAU immediately after the first election has been completed.
3. A judge elected to replace a judge whose term of office has not expired shall hold office for the remainder of the predecessor's term.
4. All judges except the President shall perform their functions on a part-time basis. However, the Assembly may change this arrangement as it deems appropriate.

Article 16 OATH OF OFFICE

After their election, the judges of the Court shall make a solemn declaration to discharge their duties impartially and faithfully.

Article 17 INDEPENDENCE

1. The independence of the judges shall be fully ensured in accordance with international law.
2. No judge may hear any case in which the same judge has previously taken part as agent, counsel or advocate for one of the parties or as a member of a national or international court or a commission of enquiry or in any other capacity. Any doubt on this point shall be settled by decision of the Court.
3. The judges of the Court shall enjoy, from the moment of their election and throughout their term of office, the immunities extended to diplomatic agents in accordance with international law.
4. At no time shall the judges of the Court be held liable for any decision or opinion issued in the exercise of their functions.

Article 18 INCOMPATIBILITY

The position of judge of the Court is incompatible with any activity that might interfere with the independence or impartiality of such a judge or the demands of the office, as determined in the Rules of Procedure of the Court.

Article 19 CESSATION OF OFFICE

1. A judge shall not be suspended or removed from office unless, by the unanimous decision of the other judges of the Court, the judge concerned has been found to be no longer fulfilling the required conditions to be a judge of the Court.

2. Such a decision of the Court shall become final unless it is set aside by the Assembly at its next session.

Article 20 VACANCIES

1. In case of death or resignation of a judge of the Court, the President of the Court shall immediately inform the Secretary General of the Organization of African Unity, who shall declare the seat vacant from the date of death or from the date on which the resignation takes effect.
2. The Assembly shall replace the judge whose office became vacant unless the remaining period of the term is less than one hundred and eighty (180) days.
3. The same procedure and considerations as set out in Articles 12, 13 and 14 shall be followed for the filling of vacancies.

Article 21 PRESIDENCY OF THE COURT

1. The Court shall elect its President and one Vice-President for a period of two years. They may be re-elected only once.
2. The President shall perform judicial functions on a full-time basis and shall reside at the seat of the Court.
3. The functions of the President and the Vice-President shall be set out in the Rules of Procedure of the Court.

Article 22 EXCLUSION

If a judge is a national of any State which is a party to a case submitted to the Court, that judge shall not hear the case.

Article 23 QUORUM

The Court shall examine cases brought before it, if it has a quorum of at least seven judges.

Article 24 REGISTRY OF THE COURT

1. The Court shall appoint its own Registrar and other staff of the registry from among nationals of Member States of the OAU according to the Rules of Procedure.
2. The office and residence of the Registrar shall be at the place where the Court has its seat.

Article 25 SEAT OF THE COURT

1. The Court shall have its seat at the place determined by the Assembly from among States parties to this Protocol. However, it may convene in the territory of any Member State of the OAU when the majority of the Court considers it desirable, and with the prior consent of the State concerned.
2. The seat of the Court may be changed by the Assembly after due consultation with the Court.

Article 26 EVIDENCE

1. The Court shall hear submissions by all parties and if deemed necessary, hold an enquiry. The States concerned shall assist by providing relevant facilities for the efficient handling of the case.

2. The Court may receive written and oral evidence including expert testimony and shall make its decision on the basis of such evidence.

Article 27 FINDINGS

1. If the Court finds that there has been violation of a human or peoples' right, it shall make appropriate orders to remedy the violation, including the payment of fair compensation or reparation.
2. In cases of extreme gravity and urgency, and when necessary to avoid irreparable harm to persons, the Court shall adopt such provisional measures as it deems necessary.

Article 28 JUDGMENT

1. The Court shall render its judgment within ninety (90) days of having completed its deliberations.
2. The judgment of the Court decided by majority shall be final and not subject to appeal.
3. Without prejudice to sub-Article 2 above, the Court may review its decision in the light of new evidence under conditions to be set out in the Rules of Procedure.
4. The Court may interpret its own decision.
5. The judgment of the Court shall be read in open court, due notice having been given to the parties.
6. Reasons shall be given for the judgment of the Court.
7. If the judgment of the Court does not represent, in whole or in part, the unanimous decision of the judges, any judge shall be entitled to deliver a separate or dissenting opinion.

Article 29 NOTIFICATION OF JUDGMENT

1. The parties to the case shall be notified of the judgment of the Court and it shall be transmitted to the Member States of the OAU and the Commission.
2. The Council of Ministers shall also be notified of the judgment and shall monitor its execution on behalf of the Assembly.

Article 30 EXECUTION OF JUDGMENT

The States parties to the present Protocol undertake to comply with the judgment in any case to which they are parties within the time stipulated by the Court and to guarantee its execution.

Article 31 REPORT

The Court shall submit to each regular session of the Assembly, a report on its work during the previous year. The report shall specify, in particular, the cases in which a State has not complied with the Court's judgment.

Article 32 BUDGET

Expenses of the Court, emoluments and allowances for judges and the budget of its registry, shall be determined and borne by the OAU, in accordance with criteria laid down by the OAU in consultation with the Court.

Article 33 RULES OF PROCEDURE

The Court shall draw up its Rules and determine its own procedures. The Court shall consult the Commission as appropriate.

Article 34 RATIFICATION

1. This Protocol shall be open for signature and ratification or accession by any State Party to the Charter.
2. The instrument of ratification or accession to the present Protocol shall be deposited with the Secretary-General of the OAU.
3. The Protocol shall come into force thirty days after fifteen instruments of ratification or accession have been deposited.
4. For any State Party ratifying or acceding subsequently, the present Protocol shall come into force in respect of that State on the date of the deposit of its instrument of ratification or accession.
5. The Secretary-General of the OAU shall inform all Member States of the entry into force of the present Protocol.
6. At the time of the ratification of this Protocol or any time thereafter, the State shall make a declaration accepting the competence of the Court to receive cases under Article 5(3) of this Protocol. The Court shall not receive any petition under Article 5(3) involving a State Party which has not made such a declaration.
7. Declarations made under sub-Article (6) above shall be deposited with the Secretary General, who shall transmit copies thereof to the State parties.

Article 35 AMENDMENTS

1. The present Protocol may be amended if a State Party to the Protocol makes a written request to that effect to the Secretary-General of the OAU. The Assembly may adopt, by simple majority, the draft amendment after all the States Parties to the present Protocol have been duly informed of it and the Court has given its opinion on the amendment.
2. The Court shall also be entitled to propose such amendments to the present Protocol as it may deem necessary, through the Secretary-General of the OAU.
3. The amendment shall come into force for each State Party which has accepted it thirty days after the Secretary-General of the OAU has received notice of the acceptance.

African Union Decisions Regarding the Creation of a Criminal Section in the African Court of Justice and Human and Peoples' Rights

1	Decision on the Single Legal Instrument on the Merger of the African Court on Human and Peoples' Rights and the African Court of Justice (June/July 2008)
2	Decision on the Implementation of the Assembly Decision on the Abuse of the Principle of Universal Jurisdiction (February 2009)
3	Decision on the Meeting of African States Parties to the Rome Statute of the International Criminal Court (ICC) (July 2009)
4	Decision on the Abuse of the Principle of Universal Jurisdiction (July 2010)
5	Decision on the Implementation of the Assembly Decisions on the International Criminal Court (June/July 2011)
6	Decision on the Protocol on Amendments to the Protocol on the Statute of the African Court of Justice and Human Rights (July 2012)
7	Decision on International Jurisdiction, Justice and the International Criminal Court (ICC) (May 2013)
8	Decision on Africa's Relationship with the International Criminal Court (October 2013)
9	Decision on the Progress Report of the Commission on the Implementation of the Decisions on the International Criminal Court (January 2014)
10	Decision on the Draft Legal Instruments (June 2014)
11	Decisions on the Progress Report of the Commission on the Implementation of the Previous Decisions on the International Criminal Court (January 2015)
12	Decision on the International Criminal Court (January 2016)

ASSEMBLY OF THE AFRICAN UNION
Eleventh Ordinary Session
30 June–1 July 2008
Sharm El-Sheikh, Egypt

Doc. Assembly/AU/13 (XI)

DECISION ON THE SINGLE LEGAL INSTRUMENT ON THE MERGER OF THE AFRICAN COURT ON HUMAN AND PEOPLES' RIGHTS AND THE AFRICAN COURT OF JUSTICE

The Assembly:

1. TAKES NOTE of the recommendations of the Executive Council;
2. ADOPTS the Draft Protocol on the Statute of the African Court of Justice and Human Rights;
3. CALLS on Member States to sign and ratify the Protocol on the Statute of the African Court of Justice and Human Rights as expeditiously as possible so as to enable the Protocol enter into force and ensure the speedy operationalization of the merged Curt.

ASSEMBLY OF THE AFRICAN UNION
Twelfth Ordinary Session
1–3 February 2009
Addis Ababa, ETHIOPIA

Assembly/AU/Dec.213(XII)
DECISION ON THE IMPLEMENTATION OF THE ASSEMBLY DECISION ON THE ABUSE OF THE PRINCIPLE OF UNIVERSAL JURISDICTION

The Assembly:

1. TAKES NOTE of the Progress Report of the Commission on the Implementation of the Assembly Decision Assembly/AU/Dec.199(XI) adopted by the Assembly in Sharm El-Sheikh, Egypt, in July 2008 on the Abuse of the Principle of Universal Jurisdiction;
2. ALSO TAKES NOTE of the work of the African Union-European Union (AU-EU) Technical Ad-hoc Expert Group set up by the Eleventh AU-EU Ministerial Troika with the mandate to clarify the respective understanding on the African and EU side on the principle of universal jurisdiction;
3. REITERATES its commitment to fighting impunity in conformity with the provisions of Article 4(h) of the Constitutive Act of the African Union;
4. EXPRESSES its regret that in spite of its previous Summit decision calling for a moratorium and whilst the African Union (AU) and the European Union (EU) were already in discussion to find a durable solution to this issue, a warrant of arrest was executed against Mrs Rose Kabuye, Chief of Protocol to the President of the Republic of Rwanda, thereby creating tension between the AU and the EU;
5. UNDERSCORES that the African Union speaking with one voice, is the appropriate collective response to counter the exercise of power by strong states over weak states;
6. REITERATES its appeal to all United Nations (UN) Member States, in particular the EU States, to suspend the execution of warrants issued by individual European States until all the legal and political issues have been exhaustively discussed between the AU, the EU and the UN;
7. REQUESTS the Chairperson of the African Union to follow up on this matter with a view to ensuring that it is exhaustively discussed at the level of the UN Security Council and the UN General Assembly;
8. URGES the AU and EU Commissions to extend the necessary support to the Joint Technical Ad-hoc Expert Group;
9. REQUESTS the Commission, in consultation with the African Commission on Human and Peoples' Rights, and the African Court on Human and Peoples' Rights, to examine the implications of the Court being empowered to try international crimes such as genocide, crimes against humanity and war crimes, and report thereon to the Assembly in 2010 Assembly/AU/Dec.213(XII)

10. ALSO REQUESTS the Commission to follow up on this matter with a view to ensuring that a definitive solution to this problem is reached and to report to the next ordinary session of the Assembly through the Executive Council in July 2009.

ASSEMBLY OF THE AFRICAN UNION
Thirteenth Ordinary Session
1–3 July 2009
Sirte, Great Socialist People's
Libyan Arab Jamahiriya

Assembly/AU/Dec.245(XIII) Rev.1
DECISION ON THE MEETING OF AFRICAN STATES
PARTIES TO THE ROME
STATUTE OF THE INTERNATIONAL CRIMINAL COURT (ICC)
Doc. Assembly/AU/13(XIII)

The Assembly,

1. TAKES NOTE of the recommendations of the Executive Council on the Meeting of the African States Parties to the Rome Statute of the International Criminal Court (ICC);
2. EXPRESSES ITS DEEP CONCERN at the indictment issued by the Pre-Trial Chamber of the ICC against President Omar Hassan Ahmed El Bashir of the Republic of The Sudan;
3. NOTES WITH GRAVE CONCERN the unfortunate consequences that the indictment has had on the delicate peace processes underway in The Sudan and the fact that it continues to undermine the ongoing efforts aimed at facilitating the early resolution of the conflict in Darfur;
4. REITERATES the unflinching commitment of Member States to combating impunity and promoting democracy, rule of law and good governance throughout the continent, in conformity with the Constitutive Act of the African Union;
5. REQUESTS the Commission to ensure the early implementation of Decision Assembly/Dec.213(XII), adopted in February 2009 mandating the Commission, in consultation with the African Commission on Human and Peoples' Rights and the African Court on Human and Peoples' Rights to examine the implications of the Court being empowered to try serious crimes of international concern such as genocide, crimes against humanity and war crimes, which would be complementary to national jurisdiction and processes for fighting impunity;
6. ENCOURAGES Member States to initiate programmes of cooperation and capacity building to enhance the capacity of legal personnel in their respective countries regarding the drafting and safety of model legislation dealing with serious crimes of international concern, training of members of the police and

the judiciary, and the strengthening of cooperation amongst judicial and investigative agencies;

7. FURTHER TAKES NOTE that any party affected by the indictment has the right of legal recourse to the processes provided for in the Rome Statute regarding the appeal process and the issue of immunity;
8. REQUESTS the Commission to convene a preparatory meeting of African States Parties at expert and ministerial levels (Foreign Affairs and Justice) but open to other Member States at the end of 2009 to prepare fully for the Review Conference of States Parties scheduled for Kampala, Uganda in May 2010, to address among others, the following issues:

   I) Article 13 of the Rome Statute granting power to the UN Security Council to refer cases to the ICC;
   II) Article 16 of the Rome Statute granting power to the UN Security Council to defer cases for one (1) year;
   III) Procedures of the ICC;
   IV) Clarification on the Immunities of officials whose States are not party to the Statute;
   V) Comparative analysis of the implications of the practical application of Articles 27 and 98 of the Rome Statute;
   VI) The possibility of obtaining regional inputs in the process of assessing the evidence collected and in determining whether or not to proceed with prosecution; particularly against senior state officials; and
   VII) Any other areas of concern to African States Parties.

9. DEEPLY REGRETS that the request by the African Union to the UN Security Council to defer the proceedings initiated against President Bashir of The Sudan in accordance with Article 16 of the Rome Statute of the ICC, has neither been heard nor acted upon, and in this regard, REITERATES ITS REQUEST to the UN Security Council;
10. DECIDES that in view of the fact that the request by the African Union has never been acted upon, the AU Member States shall not cooperate pursuant to the provisions of Article 98 of the Rome Statute of the ICC relating to immunities, for the arrest and surrender of President Omar El Bashir of The Sudan;
11. EXPRESSES CONCERN OVER the conduct of the ICC Prosecutor and FURTHER DECIDES that the preparatory meeting of African States Parties to the Rome Statute of the ICC scheduled for late 2009 should prepare, inter alia, guidelines and a code of conduct for exercise of discretionary powers by the ICC Prosecutor relating particularly to the powers of the prosecutor to initiate cases at his own discretion under Article 15 of the Rome Statute;
12. UNDERSCORES that the African Union and its Member States reserve the right to take any further decisions or measures that may be deemed necessary in order to preserve and safeguard the dignity, sovereignty and integrity of the continent;
13. FINALLY REQUESTS the Commission to follow-up on the implementation of this Decision and submit a report to the next Ordinary Session of the

Assembly through the Executive Council in January/February 2010 and in this regard AUTHORIZES expenditure for necessary actions from arrears of contributions.

ASSEMBLY OF THE AFRICAN UNION
Fifteenth Ordinary Session
25–27 July 2010
Kampala, Uganda

DECISION ON THE ABUSE OF THE PRINCIPLE OF UNIVERSAL JURISDICTION
Doc. EX.CL/606(XVII)

The Assembly,

1. TAKES NOTE of the Progress Report of the Commission on the Implementation of Decision Assembly/AU/Dec.271 (XIV) adopted in Addis Ababa, Ethiopia in February 2010;
2. REITERATES its commitment to fight impunity in conformity with the provisions of Article 4(h) of the Constitutive Act of the African Union;
3. ALSO REITERATES its conviction that there has been blatant abuse of the Principle of Universal Jurisdiction, particularly in some non African States and CALLS for immediate termination of all pending indictments;
4. FURTHER REITERATES its conviction on the need for an international regulatory body with competence to review and/or handle complaints or appeals arising out of the abuse of the Principle of Universal Jurisdiction by individual States;
5. REQUESTS the Commission to finalise the study on the implications of empowering the African Court on Human and Peoples' Rights to try international crimes such as genocide, crimes against humanity and war crimes and report to the next Ordinary Session of the Assembly through the Executive Council in January/February 2011;
6. CALLS ON all concerned States to respect International Law and particularly the immunity of state officials when applying the Principle of Universal Jurisdiction;
7. URGES the European Union (EU) and its Member States to extend the necessary cooperation to the African Union (AU) to facilitate the search for a durable solution to the abuse of the Principle of Universal Jurisdiction;
8. ALSO URGES the EU and its Member States to implement the recommendations of the AU-EU Joint ad-hoc Expert group;
9. EXPRESSES APPRECIATION to the Chairperson of the AU and the Chairperson of the AU Commission for efforts made so far towards ensuring that this matter is exhaustively discussed at the level of the United Nations;
10. UNDERSCORES the need for African States Parties to speak with one voice to ensure that the interests of Africa are safeguarded during the forthcoming

negotiations on the Principle of Universal Jurisdiction at the level of the United Nations; Assembly/AU/Dec.292(XV)

11. REQUESTS the African Group in New York to follow-up on the implementation of this Decision in collaboration with the Commission and to ensure that the concerns raised by the AU and its Member States regarding the Abuse of the Principle of Universal Jurisdiction by some non African States are properly addressed at the Level of the United Nations with a view to finding a durable solution and to submit a report thereon to the Assembly through the Executive Council on actions taken;
12. ALSO REQUESTS the Commission to follow-up on the implementation of this Decision and to report to the next Ordinary Session of the Assembly through the Executive Council in January 2011.

ASSEMBLY OF THE AFRICAN UNION
Seventeenth Ordinary Session
30 June–1 July 2011
Malabo, EQUATORIAL GUINEA

Assembly/AU/Dec.366(XVII)

DECISION ON THE IMPLEMENTATION OF THE ASSEMBLY DECISIONS ON THE INTERNATIONAL CRIMINAL COURT

Doc. EX.CL/670(XIX)

The Assembly,

1. TAKES NOTE of the Progress Report of the Commission on the Implementation of Decision Assembly/AU/Dec.296 (XV) adopted by the Fifteenth Ordinary Session of the Assembly in Kampala, Uganda on 31 July 2010;
2. REITERATES its commitment to fight impunity in conformity with the provisions of Article 4(h) of the Constitutive Act of the African Union;
3. STRESSES the need to pursue all efforts and explore ways and means of ensuring that the request by the African Union (AU) to the United Nations (UN) Security Council to defer the proceedings initiated against President Bashir of The Sudan, in accordance with Article 16 of the Rome Statute of International Criminal Court (ICC) on deferral of cases by the UN Security Council, be acted upon, and in this regard, REITERATES its request to the UN Security Council; and REQUESTS the African members of the UN Security Council to place the matter on the agenda of the Council;
4. ALSO STRESSES the need to pursue all efforts in ensuring that the request by the AU to the UN Security Council to defer the investigations and prosecutions in relation to the 2008 post-election violence in Kenya under Article 16 of the Rome Statute be acted upon to allow for a National Mechanism to investigate and prosecute the cases under a reformed Judiciary provided for in the new constitutional dispensation, in line with the principle of complementarity;

5. REAFFIRMS that by receiving President Bashir, the Republic of Chad, Kenya, and Djibouti were discharging their obligations under Article 23 of the Constitutive Act of the African Union and Article 98 of the Rome Statute as well as acting in pursuit of peace and stability in their respective regions;
6. EXPRESSES DEEP CONCERN at the manner in which the ICC Prosecutor handles the situation in Libya which was referred to the ICC by the UN Security Council through Resolution 1970 (2011). The Assembly NOTES that the warrant of arrest issued by the Pre-Trial Chamber concerning Colonel Qadhafi, seriously complicates the efforts aimed at finding a negotiated political solution to the crisis in Libya, which will also address, in a mutually-reinforcing way, issues relating to impunity and reconciliation. In this regard, the Assembly DECIDES that Member States shall not cooperate in the execution of the arrest warrant, and REQUESTS the UN Security Council to activate the provisions of Article 16 of the Rome Statute with a view to deferring the ICC process on Libya, in the interest of Justice as well as peace in the country;
7. REQUESTS the Group of African States Parties in New York and in the Hague as well as the African Members of the UN Security Council to closely follow-up on the implementation of the Assembly's Decisions on ICC;
8. ALSO REQUESTS the Commission in collaboration with the Permanent Representatives "Committee to reflect on how best Africa's interests can be fully defended and protected in the international judicial system, and to actively pursue the implementation of the Assembly's Decisions on the African Court of Justice and Human and Peoples" Rights being empowered to try serious international crimes committed on African soil;
9. REQUESTS the Commission to follow-up on this matter and to report regularly on the implementation of the various Assembly decisions on ICC.

ASSEMBLY OF THE AFRICAN UNION

Nineteenth Ordinary Session

15–16 July 2012

Addis Ababa, Ethiopia

Assembly/AU/Dec.427(XIX)

DECISION ON THE PROTOCOL ON AMENDMENTS TO THE PROTOCOL ON THE STATUTE OF THE AFRICAN COURT OF JUSTICE AND HUMAN RIGHTS

Doc. Assembly/AU/13(XIX)a

The Assembly,

1. TAKES NOTE of the recommendation of the Executive Council on the draft Protocol on Amendments to the Protocol on the Statute of the African Court of Justice and Human Rights;
2. REQUESTS the Commission in collaboration with the African Court on Human and Peoples' Rights to prepare a study on the financial and structural implications resulting from the expansion of the jurisdiction of the African Court on Human and Peoples' Rights and submit the study along with the

Draft Protocol on Amendments to the Protocol to the Statute of the African Court of Justice and Human Rights for consideration by the policy organs at the next summit slated for January 2013;

3. STRESSES the need for the AU to adopt a definition of the crime of unconstitutional change of government and, in this regard, request the Commission in collaboration with the AU Commission on International Law and the African Court on Human and Peoples' Rights to submit this definition for consideration by the policy organs at the next Summit to be held in January 2013.

ASSEMBLY OF THE AFRICAN UNION

Twenty-First Ordinary Session

26–27 May 2013

Addis Ababa, ETHIOPIA

Assembly/AU/Dec.482(XXI)

DECISION ON INTERNATIONAL JURISDICTION, JUSTICE AND THE INTERNATIONAL CRIMINAL COURT (ICC)[1]

Doc. Assembly/AU/13(XXI)

The Assembly,

1. TAKES NOTE of the presentation made by the Republic of Uganda, on behalf of the Eastern African Region, on International Jurisdiction, International Justice and the International Criminal Court, as well as the recommendations made by the Executive Council;
2. REITERATES the African Union's unflinching commitment to combating impunity and promoting democracy, the rule of law and good governance throughout the entire continent, in conformity with its Constitutive Act;
3. DEEPLY REGRETS that the request by the African Union (AU) to the United Nations (UN) Security Council to defer the proceedings initiated against President Omar Al Bashir of The Sudan and Senior State Official of Kenya, in accordance with Article 16 of the Rome Statute of the International Criminal Court (ICC) on deferral of cases by the UN Security Council, has not been acted upon; REAFFIRMS that Member States such as the Republic of Chad that had welcomed President Omar Al Bashir of The Sudan did so in conformity with the decisions of the Assembly and therefore, should not be penalized;
4. FURTHER REAFFIRMS its previous Decisions on the activities of the ICC in Africa, adopted in January and July 2009, January and July 2010, January and July 2011, January and July 2012 respectively, in which it expressed its strong conviction that the search for justice should be pursued in a way that does not impede or jeopardize efforts aimed at promoting lasting peace and reiterated AU's concern with the misuse of indictments against African leaders;

5. STRESSES the need for international justice to be conducted in a transparent and fair manner, in order to avoid any perception of double standard, in conformity with the principles of international law, and EXPRESSES CONCERN at the threat that the indictment of H.E Uhuru Muigai Kenyatta and H.E William Samoei Ruto, the President and Deputy-President of the Republic of Kenya respectively, may pose to the on-going efforts in the promotion of peace, national healing and reconciliation, as well as the rule of law and stability, not only in Kenya, but also in the Region;
6. RECALLS that, pursuant to the principle of complementarity enshrined in the Rome Statute of the ICC, Kenya has primary jurisdiction over the investigations and prosecutions of crimes in relation to the 2007 post-election violence, in this regard, DEEPLY REGRETS the Decisions of the Pre-trial Chamber II and the appeals Chamber of the ICC on the admissibility of the cases dated 30 May and 30 August 2011 respectively, which denied the right of Kenya to prosecute and try alleged perpetrators of crimes committed on its territory in relation to the 2007 post-election violence;
7. SUPPORTS AND ENDORSES the Eastern Africa Region's request for a referral of the ICC investigations and prosecutions in relation to the 2007 post-election violence in Kenya, in line with the principle of complementarity, to allow for a National Mechanism to investigate and prosecute the cases under a reformed Judiciary provided for in the new constitutional dispensation, in support of the on-going peace building and national reconciliation processes, in order to prevent the resumption of conflict and violence in Kenya;
8. REQUESTS the African Union Commission, in collaboration with the African Union Commission on International Law (AUCIL), to organize, with the participation of Member States, all the relevant Organs of the African Union and other relevant Stakeholders, a brainstorming session, as part of the 50th Anniversary discussion on the broad areas of International Criminal Justice System, Peace, Justice and Reconciliation as well as the impact/actions of the ICC in Africa, in order not only to inform the ICC process, but also to seek ways of strengthening African mechanisms to deal with African challenges and problems;
9. ALSO REQUESTS the African Union Commission to follow-up on this matter and to report regularly on the implementation of the various Assembly decisions on the ICC.

ASSEMBLY OF THE AFRICAN UNION

Extraordinary Session of the Assembly of the African Union
12 October 2013
Addis Ababa, Ethiopia

Ext/Assembly/AU/Dec.1(Oct.2013)
DECISION ON AFRICA'S RELATIONSHIP
WITH THE INTERNATIONAL CRIMINAL COURT (ICC)

The Assembly,

1. TAKES NOTE of the Progress Report of the Commission on the Implementation of Decision Assembly/AU/Dec.482(XXI) on the International Jurisdiction, International Justice and the International Criminal Court (ICC) and the Presentation made by the Republic of Kenya as well as the recommendations of the Executive Council thereon;
2. REITERATES, in accordance with the Constitutive Act of the African Union (AU), the AU's unflinching commitment to fight impunity, promote human rights and democracy, and the rule of law and good governance in the continent;
3. REAFFIRMS its previous Decisions on the abuse of the principles of Universal Jurisdiction adopted in Sharm El Sheikh in July 2008 as well as the activities of the ICC in Africa, adopted in January and July 2009, January and July 2010, January and July 2011, January and July 2012, and May 2013 wherein it expressed its strong conviction that the search for justice should be pursued in a way that does not impede or jeopardize efforts aimed at promoting lasting peace;
4. REITERATES AU's concern on the politicization and misuse of indictments against African leaders by ICC as well as at the unprecedented indictments of and proceedings against the sitting President and Deputy President of Kenya in light of the recent developments in that country;
5. UNDERSCORES that this is the first time that a sitting Head of State and his deputy are being tried in an international court and STRESSES the gravity of this situation which could undermine the sovereignty, stability, and peace in that country and in other Member States as well as reconciliation and reconstruction and the normal functioning of constitutional institutions;
6. RECOGNIZES that Kenya is a frontline state in the fight against terrorism at regional, continental and international levels and, in this regard, STRESSES the threat that this menace poses to the region in particular and the continent in general, and the proceedings initiated against the President and the Deputy President of the Republic of Kenya will distract and prevent them from fulfilling their constitutional responsibilities, including national and regional security affairs;
7. RECALLS that following the 2007 Post Election Violence (PEV), the mediation process in Kenya was initiated by AU which led to the enactment of the National Accord and Reconciliation Act and the Agreement establishing the coalition government, and EXPRESSES concern that the ongoing process before the ICC may pose a threat to the full implementation of the National Accord of 2008 and prevent the process of addressing the challenges leading to the post-election violence;
8. EXPRESSES its deep appreciation for the full cooperation that the President and Deputy President of Kenya have demonstrated to the ICC process and CALLS UPON the ICC to show the same level of cooperation in the process;
9. REAFFIRMS the principles deriving from national laws and international customary law by which sitting Heads of State and other senior state officials are granted immunities during their tenure of office;

10. NOW DECIDES:

(i) That to safeguard the constitutional order, stability and, integrity of Member States, no charges shall be commenced or continued before any International Court or Tribunal against any serving AU Head of State or Government or anybody acting or entitled to act in such capacity during their term of office;

(ii) That the trials of President Uhuru Kenyatta and Deputy President William Samoei Ruto, who are the current serving leaders of the Republic of Kenya, should be suspended until they complete their terms of office;

(iii) To set up a Contact Group of the Executive Council to be led by the Chairperson of the Council, composed of five (5) Members (one (1) per region) to undertake consultations with the Members of the United Nations Security Council (UNSC), in particular, its five (5) Permanent Members with a view to engaging with the UNSC on all concerns of the AU on its relationship with the ICC, including the deferral of the Kenyan and the Sudan cases in order to obtain their feedback before the beginning of the trial on 12 November, 2013;

(iv) To fast track the process of expanding the mandate of the African Court on Human and Peoples' Rights (AfCHPR) to try international crimes, such as genocide, crimes against humanity and war crimes;

(v) That the Commission expedites the process of expansion of AfCHPR to deal with international crimes in accordance with the relevant decision of the Policy Organs and INVITES Member States to support this process;

(vi) That African States Parties propose relevant amendments to the Rome Statute, in accordance with Article 121 of the Statute;

(vii) To request African States Parties to the Rome Statute of the ICC, in particular the Members of the Bureau of the Assembly of States Parties to inscribe on the agenda of the forthcoming sessions of the ASP the issue of indictment of African sitting Heads of State and Government by the ICC and its consequences on peace, stability and reconciliation in African Union Member States;

(viii) That any AU Member State that wishes to refer a case to the ICC may inform and seek the advice of the African Union;

(ix) That Kenya should send a letter to the United Nations Security Council requesting for deferral, in conformity with Article 16 of the Rome Statute, of the proceedings against the President and Deputy President of Kenya that would be endorsed by all African States Parties;

(x) Pursuant to this Decision, to request the ICC to postpone the trial of President Uhuru Kenyatta, scheduled for 12 November 2013 and suspend the proceedings against Deputy President William Samoei Ruto until such time as the UN Security Council considers the request by Kenya, supported by the AU, for deferral;

(xi) That President Uhuru Kenyatta will not appear before the ICC until such time as the concerns raised by the AU and its Member States have been adequately addressed by the UN Security Council and the ICC;

(xii) To convene, an Extraordinary Session, towards the end of November 2013, to review the progress made in the implementation of this Decision of the AU Assembly (Ext/Assembly/AU/Dec.1(Oct.2013)).

11. FINALLY REQUESTS the Commission to report on the implementation of this Decision to the next Ordinary Session of the Assembly in January 2014.

ASSEMBLY OF THE AFRICAN UNION
Twenty-Second Ordinary Session
30–31 January 2014
Addis Ababa, Ethiopia

Assembly/AU/Dec.493 (XXII)

DECISION ON THE PROGRESS REPORT OF THE COMMISSION ON THE IMPLEMENTATION OF THE DECISIONS ON THE INTERNATIONAL CRIMINAL COURT

The Assembly:

1. TAKES NOTE of the Progress Report of the Commission on the implementation of the Assembly Decisions on the International Criminal Court (ICC) and ENDORSES the recommendations contained therein;
2. REITERATES the unflinching commitment of the African Union and its Member States to combating impunity and promoting democracy, the rule of law and good governance throughout the entire continent, in conformity with the Constitutive Act of the African Union;
3. COMMENDS Member States which are parties to the Rome Statute of ICC for the unity of action demonstrated at the last Assembly of States Parties in the Hague in November 2013;
4. THANKS the Member State of the United Nations Security Council that supported the request of Kenya and the African Union to defer the proceedings initiated by the ICC against the President and Deputy President of the Republic of Kenya in accordance with Article 16 of the Rome Statute of ICC;
5. ALSO THANKS members of the Contact Group and the African Group in New York for their action in support of the African request;
6. EXPRESSES its deep disappointment that the request by Kenya supported by AU, to the United Nations (UN) Security Council to defer the proceedings initiated against the President and Deputy President of the Republic of Kenya in accordance with Article 16 of the Rome Statute of ICC on deferral of cases by the UN Security Council, has not yield the positive result expected;
7. ALSO EXPRESSES its deep disappointment that the request by the African Union to the UN Security Council to defer the proceedings initiated against the President of the Republic of The Sudan in accordance with Article 16 of

the Rome Statute of ICC on deferral of cases by the UN Security Council, has not been acted upon to date;

8. STRESSES the need for the UN Security Council to reserve a timely and appropriate response to requests made by the AU on deferral in accordance with Article 16 of the Rome Statute under Chapter VII of the UN Charter so as to avoid the sense of lack of consideration of a whole continent;
9. DECIDES that the African Union and its Member States, in particular the African States Parties to the Rome Statute, reserve the right to take any further decisions or measures that may be necessary in order to preserve and Assembly/AU/Dec.493(XXII) safeguard peace, security and stability, as well as the dignity, sovereignty and integrity of the continent;
10. TAKES NOTE of the outcome of the 12th Session of the Assembly of States Parties (ASP) of the Rome Statute to the ICC and WELCOMES the inclusion on its agenda of a Special Segment on "Indictment of Sitting Heads of State and Government and its Consequences on Peace and Stability and Reconciliation" and the amendments to Rule 134 of the Rules of Procedure and Evidence of the ICC;
11. ALSO TAKES NOTE of the Decision of the 12th ASP inviting its Working Group on amendments to continue its consideration of amendments to the Rome Statute submitted prior to the Review Conference and those submitted following the decision by the Extraordinary Summit of the African Union held on 12 October 2013 and CALLS UPON all African States Parties to support the proposed amendment to Articles 16 and 27 of the Rome Statute;
12. DECIDES that:
    (i) African States Parties should comply with African Union Decisions on ICC and continue to speak with one voice to ensure that the African proposals for amendments to Articles 16 and 27 of the Rome Statute of the ICC are considered by the ASP working Group on amendments as well as by the forthcoming sessions of the Assembly of States Parties (ASP) to the Rome Statute;
    (ii) There is an imperative need for all Member States to ensure that they adhere and articulate commonly agreed positions in line with their obligations under the Constitutive Act of the African Union;
    (iii) The Group of African States Parties in New York and the African Members of the Bureau of ASP should follow-up on the implementation of various Decisions of the Assembly on ICC, in collaboration with the commission and ensure that the African proposals and concerns are properly considered/addressed by the ASP and report to the Assembly through the Commission on actions taken regularly;
13. RECALLS its decision aimed at extending the jurisdiction of the African Court of Justice and Human Rights to hear international crimes in the Continent and REQUESTS the Commission in collaboration with all stakeholders to speed up the process with a view to reporting thereon to the Assembly in June 2014;

14. REQUESTS the Commission to present a report on new developments in the issue, which is important to Africa, at its 24th Ordinary Session in January 2015.

EXECUTIVE COUNCIL OF THE AFRICAN UNION

Twenty-Fifth Ordinary Session

20–24 June 2014

Malabo, Equatorial Guinea

DECISION ON THE DRAFT LEGAL INSTRUMENTS

Doc. EX.CL/846(XXV)

The Executive Council,

1. TAKES NOTE of the Report and recommendations of the Meeting of the Specialized Technical Committee (STC) on Justice and Legal Affairs held in Addis Ababa, Ethiopia from 6 to 16 May 2014;
2. ALSO TAKES NOTE of the following Draft Legal Instruments:
   a) Draft Protocol on the Establishment of the African Monetary Fund;
   b) Draft African Convention on Cross-Border Cooperation (Niamey Convention);
   c) Draft African Union Convention on Cyberspace Security and Protection of Personal Data;
   d) Draft African Charter on the Values and Principles of Decentralization, Local Governance and Local Development;
   e) Draft Protocol on Amendments to the Protocol on the Statute of the African Court of Justice and Human Rights;
   f) Draft Protocol to the Constitutive Act of the African Union on the Pan-African Parliament.
3. DECIDES to recommend the Draft Legal Instruments to the Assembly for consideration and adoption, with amendments to the Protocol to the Constitutive Act of the African Union on the Pan African Union in its Article 8(1) as follows:
   a) The Assembly shall determine the subjects/areas on which the Pan-African Parliament may propose draft model laws;
   b) The Pan-African Parliament may on its own make proposals on the subjects/areas on which it may submit or recommend draft Model Laws to the Assembly for its consideration and approval.
4. ENDORSES the recommendation of the 1st Meeting of the STC on Justice and Legal Affairs for strengthening the human and financial resources of the Office of the Legal Counsel of the Commission in order for it to carry out its functions with respect to the operationalization of the STC on Justice and Legal Affairs;

5. REQUESTS:

   a) The Commission to work out the new Structure of the Office of the Legal Counsel and its financial implications for consideration by the Council through the Permanent Representatives Committee (PRC) and its relevant Sub-Committees;
   b) The PRC and the Commission to take all necessary measures to implement this Decision and to report in January 2015.

ASSEMBLY OF THE AFRICAN UNION
Twenty-Fourth Ordinary Session
30–31 January 2015 Addis Ababa
Ethiopia

DECISION ON THE PROGRESS REPORT OF THE COMMISSION ON THE IMPLEMENTATION OF PREVIOUS DECISIONS ON THE INTERNATIONAL CRIMINAL COURT (ICC)

Doc. Assembly/AU/18(XXIV)

The Assembly,

1. TAKES NOTE of the Report of the Commission on the progress made in the implementation of Decisions on the International Criminal Court (ICC);
2. REITERATES, the commitment of the African Union and its Member States to fight impunity in accordance with the Constitutive Act;
3. ALSO REITERATES its previous decisions for the deferral of the proceedings initiated by the ICC against the President of the Sudan and the Deputy President of Kenya in accordance with Article 16 of the Rome Statute which allows the UNSC to defer cases for one year;
4. EXPRESSES

   a) its deep concern following the summoning of President Uhuru Kenyatta through a decision of the Trial Chamber V (b) of the ICC which did not take cognizance whatsoever of the amendments of the Rules of Procedure and Evidence of the ICC adopted by the 12th Ordinary Session of the Assembly of States Parties to the Rome Statute held in the Hague, the Netherlands in November 2013;
   b) its deep concern regarding the conduct of the Office of the Prosecutor and the Court and the wisdom of the continued prosecution against African Leaders.

5. COMMENDS President Uhuru Kenyatta for the leadership demonstrated and the unprecedented act of appointing the Acting President so as to respect the Court Summons and protect the Sovereignty of Kenya;
6. REITERATES the imperative need for all African States Parties (ASP) to ensure that they adhere and articulate commonly agreed positions at the African Union in line with their obligations under the constitutive Act of the Union;

7. REAFFIRMS the principles deriving from national and International Customary Law by which sitting Heads of State and other senior officials are granted immunities during their tenure in office;
8. WELCOMES the decision made by the Prosecutor of the International Criminal Court on 5 December, 2014 to withdraw the charges against President Uhuru Kenyatta while regretting the period it took the Office of the Prosecutor to arrive at the decision and the continued prosecution through disclosure of alleged evidence available to the ICC against him;
9. NOTES WITH CONCERN that the case against the Deputy President William Samoei Ruto is still proceeding before the International Criminal Court and REITERATES to the ICC the imperative need to terminate its prosecution against the Deputy President as per the previous decisions;
10. RECALLS its decision Ext/Assembly/AU/Dec.1 particularly 12(i) that African States Parties should comply with African Union decision on ICC and continue to speak with one voice to ensure that African proposals to the amendments to Articles 16 and 27 of the Rome Statute of the ICC are considered by the ASP Working Group on amendments as well as by the forthcoming sessions of the Assembly of States Parties to the Rome Statute;
11. EXPRESSES its concern on the failure by the ASP to consider the concerns and proposals for amendments by African Union of the Rome Statute of the ICC during the 13th Session of the ASP held in New York from 8 to 17 December, 2014;
12. THANKS Member States, African Group in New York and at the Hague, the Contact Group and other like-minded States Parties to the Rome Statute for their work and continued support in fast-tracking the consideration of African concerns and amendment proposals to the Rome Statute;
13. REGRETS that the AU's endorsement of one person as a sole candidate for the post of judge of the ICC was not respected by some African States Parties;
14. RECALLS its decision Assembly/AU/Dec.529(XXIII) during the 23rd Ordinary Session of the Assembly held in Malabo, Equatorial Guinea in June, 2014 adopting the Protocol on Amendments to the Protocol on the Statute of the African Court of Justice and Human Rights to try international crimes;
15. UNDERSCORES the need to expeditiously operationalize the exercise of the jurisdiction of the African Court of Justice and Human Rights to try international crimes through signing and ratification of both the Protocol on the Statute of the African Court of Justice and Human Rights and the Protocol on the Amendments to the Protocol on the Statute of the African Court of Justice and Human Rights by Member States of the African Union and UNDERLINE the need to ensure predictable and sustainable funding;
16. REITERATES its commitment to fund all AU Organs and Institutions including the African Court of Justice and Human Rights;
17. DECIDES as follows:

    a) to request all concerned to fast track consideration by the ASP Working Group on amendments and by Assembly of States Parties of the African proposals for amendments of the Rome Statute of the ICC;

b) to operationalize the exercise of jurisdiction of the African Court of Justice and Human Rights to try international crimes by signing and ratifying the requisite protocols; and in this respect, to establish a Special Fund and convene a resource mobilization conference to raise funds to initiate and proposed Chambers of the International Criminal Law Section as envisaged in Article 19 *bis* of the Protocol on the Amendments to the Protocol on the Statute of the African Court of Justice and Human Rights;
c) in accordance with its decisions particularly the African States Parties to the Rome Statute reserves the right to take any measures in order to preserve and safeguard peace, security and stability, as well as the dignity, sovereignty and integrity of the continent;
d) pursuant to this decision and its previous decisions, to request the ICC to terminate or suspend the proceedings against Deputy President William Samoei Ruto of Kenya until the African concerns and proposals for amendments of the Rome Statute of the ICC are considered;
e) in the same vein to request the suspension of proceedings against President Omar Al Bashir and to urge the UN Security Council to withdraw the referral case of the Sudan.

18. COMMENDS the Democratic Republic of Congo for complying with AU Decision for non-cooperation for the arrest and surrender of President Omar Al Bashir of the Republic of Sudan;
19. UNDERSCORES the need for all Member States to comply with the position of the Assembly of the Union regarding the warrants of arrest issued by the ICC against President Bashir of The Sudan pursuant to Article 23(2) of the Constitutive Act and Article 98 of the Rome Statute of the ICC;
20. REQUESTS the Commission to present a progress report on the implementation of this decision at its 26th Ordinary Session in January 2016.

ASSEMBLY OF THE AFRICAN UNION
Twenty-Sixth Ordinary Session
30–31 January 2016
Addis Ababa, Ethiopia

DECISION ON THE INTERNATIONAL CRIMINAL COURT
Doc. EX.CL/952(XXVIII)

The Assembly,

1. TAKES NOTE of the recommendations of the Executive Council on the implementation of the Decisions on the International Criminal Court (ICC);
2. REITERATES the following:

   i) The commitment of the African Union and its Member States to the fight against impunity in accordance with the Constitutive Act of the African Union;

ii) Its previous Decision Assembly/AU/Dec.547(XXIV) on the progress Report of the Commission on the Implementation of Previous Decisions on the International Criminal Court (ICC) adopted by the Twenty-Fourth Ordinary Session of the Assembly held in Addis Ababa, Ethiopia, in January 2015, and in particular para 17(d) that requested the ICC to terminate or suspend the proceedings against Deputy President William Samoei Ruto of Kenya until the African concerns and proposals for amendments of the Rome Statutes of the ICC are considered; and
iii) Paragraph 17(e) that requested the suspension of proceedings against President Omar Al Bashir of The Sudan and URGES the United Nations (UN) Security Council to withdraw the referral case in The Sudan.
iv) Its requests to the Peace and Security Council (PSC) to examine the Draft ICC Action Plan on Arrest Strategies that is currently under consideration by the ICC and make appropriate recommendations thereon to the next ordinary session of the Assembly, through the Executive Council, in July 2016 to enable adoption of a Common African Position on same.

3. COMMENDS the Republic of South Africa for complying with the Decisions of the Assembly on non-cooperation with the arrest and surrender of President Omar Al Bashir of The Sudan and DECIDES that by receiving President Bashir, the Republic of South Africa was implementing various AU Assembly Decisions on the warrants of arrest issued by the ICC against President Bashir and that South Africa was consistent with its obligations under international law;
4. REITERATES its decision on the need for all Member States to comply with the Assembly Decisions on the warrants of arrest issued by the ICC against President Al Bashir of The Sudan pursuant to Article 23(2) of the Constitutive Act of the African Union and Article 98 of the Rome Statute of the ICC;
5. EXPRESSES ITS DEEP CONCERN regarding the wisdom of the continued prosecution of the case of Deputy President William Ruto of the Republic of Kenya and CALLS ON the ICC to terminate the case without further delay as any continued prosecution is without foundation given the unambiguous absence of any incriminatory evidence capable of belief;
6. COMMENDS the Members of the Open ended Committee of Foreign Ministers ("Open ended Ministerial Committee") under the chairpersonship of H.E. Dr. Tedros Adhanom Ghebreyesus, Minister of Foreign Affairs of the Federal Democratic Republic of Ethiopia for the work done and REITERATES its previous decision that the Open Ended Ministerial Committee should meet with the United Nations Security Council (UNSC) to engage on all issues that have been consistently raised by the African Union;
7. TAKES NOTE of the conclusions of the 14th Assembly of the States Parties of the ICC (ASP) in which the ASP reaffirmed its understanding on the non-retroactive application of Rule 68 to situations commenced before November 2013 (with regard to the Kenyan agenda) and expressed its "*willingness to consider, within the framework of the appropriate subsidiary body of the*

Assembly, proposals to develop procedures for the implementation of Articles 97, 27 and 98" with regard to the issues raised by South Africa in its statements during the 28th Ordinary Session of the Executive Council and the 26th Ordinary Session of the Assembly respectively in Addis Ababa, Ethiopia in January 2016 and EXPRESSES ITS APPRECIATION to the President of ASP, H.E. Sidiki Kaba from Senegal for ensuring that in spite of perceived resistance by some State Parties, the issues and concerns of the AU and its member states were allowed to be articulated at the 14th ASP;

8. EXPRESSES its deep grieve at the failure of the UNSC to respond to the requests of the AU for deferral of The Sudan and Kenyan cases for the past five (5) years;
9. TAKES NOTE WITH CONCERN of:

   i) The obstinacy of the ICC by the so-called "*Principals of the Court*" comprising the Prosecutor, the Registrar and the President of the ICC, which continues to privilege the views of civil society over clearly held positions of African Member States parties to the Rome Statute;
   ii) The disturbing public dismissive disregard of the decisions of the 14th ASP by the Prosecution in relation to the pending Rule 68 Appeal against Kenya's Deputy President.

10. DECIDES as follows:

   i) The Bureau of the Open-Ended Ministerial Committee be expanded to ensure equitable regional representation AND REQUESTS the Overall Dean and the Regional Deans in Addis Ababa, Ethiopia to urgently undertake consultations with a view to submitting their respective representatives to serve on the Bureau;
   ii) The Permanent Representative' Committee (PRC) be mandated to approve and provide the adequate resources to the Commission, through the Office of the Legal Counsel, to support the work of the Open ended Ministerial Committee in pursuing all political, legal, and strategic avenues in addressing AU's concerns before the United Nations, the ICC and the International Court of Justice (ICJ);
   iii) The Open-ended Ministerial Committee will review the ICC's interpretation of its power pursuant to Article 93 of the Rome Statute that allows the latter to oblige State Parties to forcibly compel unwilling witnesses to testify before the ICC, with a view to rejecting witness compulsion *in toto* and inform the ICC and the next ASP accordingly;
   iv) The Open-ended Ministerial Committee's mandate will include the urgent development of a comprehensive strategy including collective withdrawal from the ICC to inform the next action of AU Member States that are also parties to the Rome Statute, and to submit such strategy to an extraordinary session of the Executive Council which is mandated to take such decision;

v) The Commission will continue to engage with relevant stakeholders within the ICC on issues raised in the various Decisions of the AU Policy Organs on the ICC;
vi) The Commission, through the AU Mission in Brussels, Belgium, will serve as the secretariat to the Open-ended Ministerial Committee and provide institutional support to the African Group in The Hague, Netherlands to ensure effective coordination of its activities;

11. REITERATES:

i) The imperative need for all African States Parties to the Rome Statute of the ICC to continue to ensure that they adhere and articulate common agreed positions in line with their obligations under the Constitutive Act of the African Union;
ii) Its call on all AU Member States to sign and ratify, as soon as possible, the Protocol on Amendments to the Protocol of the African Court of Justice and Human and Peoples' Rights;

12. REQUESTS the Commission in collaboration with all stakeholders to follow-up on this matter to ensure that the African proposals and concerns are addressed and to report to the ordinary session of the Assembly through the Executive Council scheduled for January 2017.

Index

G. Werle and M. Vormbaum (eds.), The African Criminal Court, International Criminal Justice Series 10, DOI 10.1007/978-94-6265-150-0

MIX
Papier aus verantwortungsvollen Quellen
Paper from responsible sources
FSC® C105338

If you have any concerns about our products,
you can contact us on
ProductSafety@springernature.com

In case Publisher is established outside the EU,
the EU authorized representative is:
Springer Nature Customer Service Center GmbH
Europaplatz 3, 69115 Heidelberg, Germany

Printed by Libri Plureos GmbH
in Hamburg, Germany